'The best study we have of globalizati⟨
No other book puts theory together w

'In expanding and updating her excellent book, Flesher Fominaya manages quite a feat: to guide us through theories of social movements but also to tell us about the most important movements in today's fractured world.'

'I strongly recommend this book as a first port of call for the study of social movements… it draws on an impressively diverse range of perspectives to provide fresh insights into recent and contemporary social movements. A "must have" for students around the world.'

SOCIAL MOVEMENTS IN A GLOBALIZED WORLD

SECOND EDITION

CRISTINA FLESHER FOMINAYA

BLOOMSBURY ACADEMIC
LONDON • NEW YORK • OXFORD • NEW DELHI • SYDNEY

BLOOMSBURY ACADEMIC
Bloomsbury Publishing Plc
50 Bedford Square, London, WC1B 3DP, UK
1385 Broadway, New York, NY 10018, USA
29 Earlsfort Terrace, Dublin 2, Ireland

BLOOMSBURY, BLOOMSBURY ACADEMIC and the Diana logo
are trademarks of Bloomsbury Publishing Plc

First published by RED GLOBE PRESS 2020
Reprinted by Bloomsbury Academic

A catalogue record for this book is available from the British Library.

A catalog record for this book is available from the Library of Congress.

ISBN: PB: 978-1-3520-0934-7
ePDF: 978-1-3520-0935-4
eBook: 978-1-3503-1433-7

To find out more about our authors and books visit
www.bloomsbury.com and sign up for our newsletters.

For my father, globe-trotting adventurer, lover of life (1929–2013)

This book is dedicated to my father, Thomas Richard Flesher, one of the most adventurous, determined, principled, irreverent, funny and kind people I have had the privilege of knowing. Thanks to my father and his wanderlust, I had a 'globalized' childhood, growing up in countries all over the world and meeting people from all walks of life. Thanks to his love for my wonderful Spanish mother (which luckily was reciprocated), I was born into a ready-made US/Spanish 'transnational' family. There are many wonderful anecdotes about my father (involving, among other things, Ava Gardner, running from the police on horseback, Acapulco, Orson Welles, Philby's mistress, flamenco and bullfighting) but I think this one is my favourite:

Many years ago my father travelled to Panama for work and got caught up in anti-American riots, forcing him to take shelter on the floor of a student's car as gun shots rang out around the city and then to take refuge in a hotel for a few days until he could be evacuated to the Canal Zone. In the midst of the chaos, he managed to get a postcard to my mother. It had only one line scrawled on it: 'Having a riot, wish you were here.' Here's to keeping a cool head and a sense of humour in the midst of chaos and to living life with passion and compassion.

Thanks Dad

And to my beloved Mamá, María del Sagrado Corazón de Jesús Fominaya Escrivá de Romaní (1932–2019)

SHORT CONTENTS

LONG CONTENTS

LIST OF ILLUSTRATIONS

Figures

Table

Boxes

LIST OF ABBREVIATIONS

AFL–CIO	American Federation of Labor and Congress of Industrial Organizations
ANC	African National Congress
APEC	Asia Pacific Economic Cooperation
ATTAC	Association for a Tobin Tax to Aid the Citizens
BLO	Barbie Liberation Organization
CES	Council for European Studies
CGT	Confederación General del Trabajo
DAN	Direct Action Network
DDoS	Distributed Denial of Service
DIY	Do It Yourself
DRY	Democracia Real Ya!/Real Democracy Now
ECPR	European Consortium for Political Research
ESF	European Social Forum
EU	European Union
GDP	Gross Domestic Product
GJM	Global Justice Movement
HIV	Human Immunodeficiency Virus
ICTs	Information and Communication Technologies
IFI	International Financial Institution
IMC	Independent Media Centre (Indymedia)
IMF	International Monetary Fund
INGO	International Non-Governmental Organization
IRC	Internet Relay Chat
JSF	Juventud sin Futuro (Youth Without Future)
LGBTQ	Lesbian Gay Bi-Sexual Transgender Queer
MAI	Multilateral Agreement on Investment
MENA	Middle East and North Africa
MIT	Massachusetts Institute of Technology
MRG	Movimiento de Resistencia Global
MST	Movimento dos Sem Terra
NGO	Non-Governmental Organization
NSM	New Social Movement
OECD	Organisation for Economic Co-operation and Development
OHCHR	Office of the High Commissioner for Human Rights
OWS	Occupy Wall Street
PAH	Platform for those Affected by Mortgages
PGA	People's Global Action

LIST OF ABBREVIATIONS

PHS	Port Huron Statement
PIPA	Protect IP Act
RTS	Reclaim the Streets
SDS	Students for a Democratic Society
SMO	Social Movement Organization
SOPA	Stop Online Piracy Act
TSMO	Transnational Social Movement Organization
TNC	Transnational Corporation
UGTT	Tunisian General Labour Union
UN	United Nations
UNDP	United Nation Development Programme
UNICEF	United Nations Children's Fund
WEF	World Economic Forum
WHO	World Health Organization
WSF	World Social Forum
WTO	World Trade Organization

PREFACE TO THE SECOND EDITION

The world was exploding in revolt when the first edition of this book came out in 2014, and mobilizations have continued apace since then, although not always in the spirit of democratic renewal that fuelled the global wave of movements of the squares following the global financial crash that were the subject of the last substantive chapter. Since then, much early optimism has turned to despair as extreme right-wing and authoritarian governments have come to power fuelled by right-wing social movements and democracy has come under attack from many quarters. The world watched aghast as parents seeking political asylum in the US were brutally separated from their children, and toddlers and children were placed in cages, recalling the horrors of the past, as officials carried out Donald Trump's inhumane border and immigration policies. And who can forget the devastating photograph of drowned three-year old Syrian refugee Alan Kurdi, an image that reminded us of the ultimate price our fellow humans pay in their desperate attempts to flee war and misery? But not all has been regression: in the same space of time, to name just three examples, the Black Lives Matter movement has raised awareness of the persistent institutionalized racism and violence experienced by blacks in the US, #Metoo rapidly circled the globe as millions of women demanded an end to sexual harassment, and children around the world skipped school to protest climate change – my favourite image of that protest being a single teen standing on a rock by the sea with a protest sign. He was the only student in his school who protested, but he felt connected to and supported by the thousands of other youth protesting around the world. He was a great example of the fact that collective action doesn't always have to mean physical co-presence and that social movements can inspire across space and time.

Throughout these tumultuous few years, social movements have mobilized and continue to call our attention to the central debates and challenges of our era. They do so in a media ecology that is rapidly transforming, as the fourth estate has evolved into a more networked configuration, in which traditional media have lost much control over their gatekeeping function, 'news' and information circulate at a rapid pace from multiple sources of often unknown origin, and the media ecosphere is awash with trolls and 'fake news' as well as new revelations from whistle-blowers on the most troubling activities of politicians and corporations.

The major changes to the second edition have been partly a response to some of these changes and partly a response to constructive criticisms and requests made following the first edition. One was a request for me to include a comprehensive overview of social movement theory so that the book could be assigned as a general social movements text. I have done this in Chapter 1 (Social Movements: Central Concepts and Debates), which has been greatly expanded. Another request was to include more discussion on the Global South, which I have done primarily in Chapter 2 (Globalization and Social Movements) and Chapter 3 (The Global Justice Movement) (the Global South is also discussed at length in Chapters 4 and 7).

In terms of new material, my original intention for the book had always been to include a chapter on right-wing movements, and I have done so here in a dedicated chapter (Chapter 6, Movements on the Right). Initially, I had thought of doing a global overview, an ambition I quickly abandoned. I immediately ran into the reality that most of the English language literature on right-wing social movements focuses on the US and Europe, in part I suspect because the definitions of right and left are themselves very geo-graphically rooted, and meaningful comparisons and discussions are compli-cated even with the differences between right-wing movements in these two contexts. To provide a coherent, comprehensive overview of the most recent literature, I have restricted that chapter's focus to the US and Europe. I have also expanded Chapter 5 (Social Movements, Media, information and com-munication technologies, and Cyberpolitics) not only because research has advanced so much in this short period but also because my own work has included explorations of the impact of the digital revolution on social move-ments and the issues and debates surrounding cyberpolitics.

All the chapters have also updated and revised with some material in the first edition making way for the new additions.

Some new thankyous are also due for this new edition. First to Andrea Teti for carefully reading and commenting on Chapter 6 (Movements on the Right) and for being such a good friend through all life's ups and downs. Second to Kevin Gillan, also for his feedback on that chapter which really improved the final product and for which I am very grateful. Third to Ramón Feenstra for his friendship and support as I balanced three book projects simultaneously. Thanks also to Lloyd Langman for suggesting this second edi-tion and for his support throughout the long process of rewriting. Thanks also to all the lovely reviewers and people who have let me know how much they enjoyed the first edition and made suggestions for this revised and expanded edition. I hope this revised version brings you back for more. Thank you from the bottom of my heart to the Marie Sklodowska-Curie Fellowship for allow-ing me two years to devote to research, public engagement, and academic and activist exchange. I owe many of the insights that have made their way into this book to that opportunity. To those readers coming to this book for the first time, welcome. To those returning, welcome back.

Cristina Flesher Fominaya

INTRODUCTION

The past decade has been a turbulent one. From the relatively small but remarkably successful Saucepan Revolution in Iceland in 2008 to mass mobilizations and strikes in Greece from 2008 to the time of writing, to the wave of mass protests for democracy and socio-economic justice across the Arab world beginning in 2010, the emergence of the Spanish *Indignados* 15-M movement in 2011 and the wave of Occupy encampments in the US following the Occupy Wall Street protests in 2011 – replicated in some 462 local 'Occupy' movements in the US alone. Occupy movements then sprang up in Australia, Belgium, Canada, France, Germany, Ireland, Israel, Slovenia and many more countries. In Hong Kong, China, an Occupy movement for universal suffrage continues to grow, despite arrests and repression. In Turkey, a peaceful protest to protect a central Istanbul Park from demolition turned into a mass protest against President Erdogan's regime, as hundreds of thousands of people responded to police brutality against the original Occupy Gezi Park protesters. Youth participation and leadership have been high in many of these movements and mass student movements also emerged in Canada, Chile, Italy, Mexico, Portugal and the UK. In India, in January 2019, millions of women joined hands to form a 385-mile wall of protest for gender equality and against patriarchal religious discrimination against 'impure' menstruating women. In February 2019, thousands of school children around the world went on strike to protest inaction on climate change that threatens their future and that of the planet. They were following the example of Greta Thunberg, a 15-year-old Swede who skipped class to sit outside government buildings and protest government inaction and failure to comply with the Paris Climate Agreement. These examples point to only a few of the most visible mobilizations.

The global financial crisis has sparked new permutations and alliances between a diverse range of social movements, against a backdrop of declining trust in political elites and institutions in democratic contexts, and a demand *for* democracy across more authoritarian contexts and for 'real' democracy elsewhere. Everywhere, it seems, people are questioning the ability of traditional political actors to represent their interests and are increasingly seeking a more direct and unmediated relation to power and the decisions that affect their lives.

Contemporary social movements provide an ideal lens through which to examine some of the central debates at the heart of contemporary society.

Scholars of social movements in the 1980s coined the rather unfortunate term 'new social movements' (unfortunate because newness is always relative and quickly passes) to describe a perceived rupture of many of the movements of the 1970s and 1980s with previously dominant concerns of class and material struggles and a shift towards issues of culture and identity. The idea was that, in developed nations at least, where most people's material needs were taken care of in a 'post-industrial' society, activists could concern themselves with more 'post-material' issues, such as environmentalism, peace, and movements based around the identity politics of race, ethnicity, gender and sexuality. In reality, many of these movements never lost sight of the issues of the material inequalities that accompanied other forms of discrimination, albeit not always obvious as a central issue. Elsewhere in the world, struggles over people's material needs have never faded from view and have been tied to demands for greater democracy and political participation. More recent movements, including the Global Justice Movement (GJM) and the recent global wave of pro-democracy and anti-austerity mobilizations, have explicitly re-engaged with issues such as disparities in wealth, social inequalities, unemployment and labour precariousness while not losing sight of 'post-material' issues such as the environment, human rights and anti-militarism.

Social movements have been central political actors and have brought about many of the most important social changes since the late eighteenth century. Social movements are a cornerstone of any democracy and, although frequently 'forgotten' by political elites, the right to protest is one of the most fundamental rights of political freedom of expression. Social movements act as an important check on power, emerging in even extremely repressive contexts to not only reform or alter existing institutions but sometimes to transform them altogether. Indeed, many democratic transition processes have been fuelled by social movements, and democracies have also been overturned by them. Given the crucial importance of social movements to democracy, it is curious how little attention is generally paid to social movements in political science and democracy studies, which emphasizes electoral politics and representational forms of political participation. At the same time, while they have been crucial to politics, not all social movements are oriented towards the state or have changes in policies or laws as their central goals. As I will show in this book, social movements also resist on the terrain of culture, emotions and identity, aiming to transform people's hearts, minds and practices.

Contemporary social movements operate in a globalized world. Globalization and social movements are inextricably linked. Allegedly, the origins of the term 'globalization' can be found in an obscure social movement document from a radical left-wing Italian underground periodical (James and Albanese, 2011). The article, written in 1970, was entitled 'The Process of Globalization of Capitalist Society' and discussed the ways in which the corporate giant IBM contained within itself the 'globalization of capitalist imperialism'. Thus, the very term was originally created as a means of critiquing capitalist globalization and its consequences. Social movements have been at the heart of defining and projecting this critique globally – most explicitly, but not exclusively, within the GJM. A critique of neoliberal capitalist globalization is also at the heart of many of the recent mass mobilizations around the world, but a recognition of the costs of the global financial crisis is now deeply connected to a demand for 'real' democracy – whether that means transparency and participation in representative democracies or the overturning of authoritarian regimes and their replacement with democratic systems. Social movements not only have been among the most outspoken critics of neoliberal capitalist globalization but also have been key actors in proposing solutions to global problems caused or exacerbated by globalization, such as climate change, economic crises, poverty and hunger. Within social movement communities and networks, globalization itself is a central mobilizing concept that not only shapes the issues around which mobilization takes place but also influences movements structurally and strategically: as social movements have developed their critique of some of the consequences of neoliberal capitalist globalization, they have also fully embraced the technological opportunities created by it, such as the development of information and communication technologies (ICTs) to develop transnational networks and virtual communities and to reach a global audience. Even movements such as the Taliban, who are radically opposed to 'Western' globalization, have nevertheless embraced the use of ICTs to propagate their messages and mobilize their supporters.

Although the term 'globalization' began as a means of radical critique, it has subsequently been used not only in a critical way but also in a celebratory fashion by proponents of neoliberal capitalist globalization and has simultaneously evolved into a central theoretical concept within the social sciences. Globalization is now an acknowledged empirical reality for most scholars, but what is still debated and analysed is the extent to which globalization has affected and altered our social world and with what effects. Once again, social movements form a central part of these theoretical and scholarly debates. Castells (2004), for example, one of the foremost theorists of globalization and modernity, explicitly links the erosion of national sovereignty as a result of the rise of economic capitalist globalization to the development of social movements. Castells argues that states are active agents of economic globalization rather than agents of the people in the modern world and as a result they suffer a crisis of political representation because many people feel that these global processes have negative effects on citizens and the environment. His theses have certainly been borne out in the mass mobilizations the world has been witnessing since 2008. For many social theorists, social movements do not form an incidental part of their analysis but, rather, lie at the very heart of the possibility for change. Although this aspect of their work is often neglected, major social theorists Giddens, Harvey and Wallerstein, together with others, also see social movements as central to understanding modernity and as a key mechanism for overcoming some of the negative consequences of globalization. Indeed, within globalization studies, theorists such as Kaldor have invoked the GJM as evidence of the very existence of global civil society.

Despite claims that globalization, and particularly the advent of the Internet, has led to a lessening of barriers between activists in different nations, significant barriers remain to transnational activism, and the vast majority of protest and mobilization still takes place within national and local boundaries following national/local logics. A central theme running through this book is the ways the global, national and local intersect in shaping the dynamics of contemporary social movements. In fact, 'globalization' has as frequently provoked movements opposing it as it has enabled the development of new internationalisms or transnational or global social movements. If the GJM pointed to the new ways social movements are becoming global, (see Chapter 3) the recent wave of anti-austerity protests in Europe, pro-democracy and social justice movements in the 'Arab Spring' and the radical democracy experiments of Occupy Wall Street also highlight the reclaiming of the nation-state as the locus and focus of action, despite the strong transnational dimensions of these protests (see Chapter 7).

Responses to globalizing processes are by no means always progressive, despite the tendency among scholars to focus more on progressive movements. For example, the increasing political and economic integration of the European Union (EU) – supranational entity *par excellence* – has provoked strong resistance, not only from progressive movements (who critique what they perceive to be the erosion of social welfare provisions and civil liberties to the advantage of political and economic elites) but also from movements on the right (who feel that national identities are under threat, not only as a result of loss of national sovereignty but also due to EU policies that foster immigration and cultural pluralism and integration). Conservative Christian groups also protest against the secular and pluralistic model promoted by the EU, claiming that it is eroding Europe's Christian identity. At the same time as EU integration is challenged by some social movements, other social movements (and sometimes the *same* social movements) appeal to the supranational authority of the EU to bring pressure to bear on national governments and local authorities when these fail to comply with EU regulations in areas as diverse as environmental or consumer protection or discrimination regarding gender or sexual orientation.

In this book, I provide an exploration of some of the key theoretical debates and empirical examples of contemporary social movements in a globalized world. Although I offer an overview of major scholarly approaches to social movements, I also draw on a wide range of theory and approaches, not only social movement theory *per se* but also insights from social theory, sociology, political science, international relations, media studies, history, cultural and gender studies. Theoretical and analytical insights are illustrated through a rich variety of case studies and examples drawn from movements around the world, drawing on primary and secondary research. I hope that anyone who is curious about contemporary social movements will be able to gain entry into their fascinating worlds, and I have strived to make the book as exciting for scholars as it is accessible for readers with no prior knowledge of the field.

The book is organized as follows. Chapters 1 and 2 provide a conceptual grounding and overview for the substantive chapters that follow. Chapter 1, 'Social Movements: Central Concepts and Debates', provides a comprehensive overview of key definitions and theoretical frameworks of social movements, providing an introduction to social movement theory. In Chapter 2, 'Globalization and Social Movements', I examine some of the theoretical and empirical inter-relationships between social movements and globalization processes, looking closely at some of the specific ways that social movements 'spread' across borders in a globalized world.

In Chapter 3, 'The Global Justice Movement', I take an in-depth look at what many have considered to be the quintessential global movement. I first examine the 1999 anti-World Trade Organization (WTO) protest – the 'Battle for Seattle' – to understand some of the key players, critiques, demands and tactics of the movement. I then situate the Seattle protest in a larger historical context of anti-capitalist mobilizations and examine some of the global networks involved. Next, I look at points of tension between two different approaches to politics and collective action that co-exist in the movement and that continue to represent a key cleavage in many contemporary progressive movements – that between more horizontal autonomous and more vertical Institutional Left actors. Finally, I take up the question of the extent to which the movement was new or different with respect to earlier movements and the extent to which it was truly 'global'.

In Chapter 4, 'Cultural Resistance in a Globalized World', I explore some of the ways social movements engage in cultural resistance, paying special attention to the many forms it takes in a globalized world. First, I highlight some of the ways in which theorists have identified culture as a crucial arena not only of domination but also of struggle in the contemporary world, including discussions of the notions of dominant ideology, hegemony, and counter-hegemonic narratives and strategies. I then discuss some of the challenges facing social movements as they try to change not just policies and laws, but also cultural practices and beliefs, and the strategies and tactics they use to do so. I go on to discuss some of the critiques of the limitations of cultural resistance as a means of effecting social and political transformation. Finally, I provide a series of case studies to illustrate a range of practices and approaches to cultural resistance from around the world, highlighting how these actors link local, national and global concerns, before concluding with a summary of the importance of cultural resistance to social movements. Although the production and use of media and the new forms of social media and ICTs are also crucial forms of cultural resistance, and they are in reality deeply intertwined, their importance to movements (and scholarship) merits a separate, in-depth treatment, which I provide in Chapter 5.

In Chapter 5, 'Social Movements, Media, ICTs, and Cyberpolitics', I focus on the ways social movement actors communicate with their intended audiences and with each other using media. In the first part of the chapter, I discuss some of the challenges social movements face when they engage with mainstream mass media and some of the strategies they develop to minimize or overcome them. I argue that while social movement actors continue to engage with mainstream media – which remain a major source of political information for most people and a continuing major amplifier and shaper of movement messages and audience perception – they also engage in the production of alternative media and are important knowledge-producers in their own right. The second part of the chapter looks at the rise of ICTs as a rapidly developing form of communication of increasing importance to social movements. I provide a critical examination of the ways new technologies facilitate *and* constrain social movements and discuss various forms of cyberpolitical activism and its shifting nature in response to technological innovations and political developments. Cyberpolitical movements, whose political action is motivated by an ideological and practical commitment to harnessing the emancipatory power of ICTs for social and political change and see cyberspace as a primary site of contestation and mobilization (Flesher Fominaya and Gillan, 2017), are discussed through several case studies.

Chapter 6, 'Movements on the Right', addresses right-wing movements in the US and Europe, acknowledging their importance as political actors with particular dynamics that in some respects differ from progressive movements and are similar in others. The chapter highlights the crucial importance of ideational frameworks, ideology and values in fuelling particular movements and their impacts. It also further develops the role of ICTs and media strategies discussed in Chapter 5 in the context of right-wing mobilization. Analysing right-wing movements forces us to question some of the common ideas of social movements (e.g., that they are bottom-up extra-institutional actors), disturbs some of the neat boundaries between progressive and conservative movements, and clarifies and sharpens others. I learned a lot researching and writing this chapter and hope this new addition to the book will be illuminating and stimulating.

In Chapter 7, 'Movements After the Crash: A Global Wave of Protest?', I describe and analyse some of the central mobilizations of the recent and ongoing wave of mobilizations for democracy and against austerity measures, imposed ostensibly to mitigate the effects of the global financial crisis. I offer a series of case studies of Iceland, the Arab Spring in Tunisia and Egypt, 15-M/*Indignados* in Spain and Occupy Wall Street (OWS) in New York and Boston, highlighting some of the key topics of debate and the commonalities and differences across cases. I then raise a series of questions. The first set of questions centres on the extent to which we can understand these protest events as a global wave of protest. In what ways are they connected to each other – that is, what is their *transnational* dimension in terms of ideational and practical diffusion? In what ways are they responding to a common set of concerns and reacting to a common global political economic context? The second question refers back to the discussion of the GJM in Chapter 3: is this a fundamentally new series of protests or is it better seen as a continuation of the central demands, claims and practices of the GJM? Finally, I provide a discussion of some of the challenges and significance of these movements – tentative because these events continue to unfold in a dynamic and changing environment. In the Conclusion, I draw on my research on Spain's 15-M *Indignados* movement to highlight why and how social movements can matter in a time when democracies are under threat, draw out the main themes of the book, and reflect on areas for future research.

1 SOCIAL MOVEMENTS: CONCEPTS AND DEBATES

In this chapter, I will provide an overview of the key definitions, concepts and debates in the literature on social movements that will help make sense of the rest of the book. First, I will look at some definitions of social movements and how and why they are important. Then, I will briefly explore some of the key approaches and critiques of the dominant paradigms in the US and European literature to provide a historical and conceptual background to the discussion that follows.

Social movements: Definitions and conceptual distinctions

Social movements are among the main ways in which people collectively give voice to their grievances and concerns and demand that something be done about them – or take extra-institutional action to change them directly. Social movements have produced some of the most significant social changes of the past few centuries. This simple fact is easy to overlook because the changes that social movements produce often become an aspect of social life that is taken for granted, and the movements that produced them often fade away or grow dormant until new threats to gains already achieved, or new issues of concern, arise. The fact that workers in many countries have collective bargaining rights, that women have the right to vote, or that many governments require companies to conduct environmental impact statements before setting up new businesses are all, in great part, the result of social movements. The 'culture jammed' slogan shown in Figure 1.1 highlights the fact that many workers' right to the weekend off is not a 'natural' or God-given right but, rather, the result of the mass mobilization of workers who faced tremendous opposition, including brutal repression and massacres, to gain rights that are taken for granted today.

Figure 1.1

A 'culture-jammed' slogan

Definitions

But what is a social movement? There is a wide range of definitions in the literature (e.g. Della Porta and Diani, 2009; Tarrow, 2011; Goodwin and Jasper, 2009; Tilly and Wood, 2015), but most definitions of social movements tend to be centred on some or all of the following characteristics:

- *collective* or *joint* action
- some *extra-institutional* or *non-institutional* collective action
- *change*-oriented goals or claims
- a *target* towards which these claims are directed (states, the public, corporations, specific political groups, a cultural practice, etc.)
- some degree of *organization*
- some degree of *temporal continuity*
- some degree of *shared solidarity* and/or *collective identity*.

Some conceptual distinctions

Visible versus latent social movement activity

Goodwin and Jasper (2009: 3) distinguish social movements from social or political *protest*, which they define as 'the act of challenging, resisting, or making demands upon authorities, power holders, and/or cultural beliefs and practices by some individuals or group'. It is important to distinguish between social movements and protest, because protest is only one of the things that social movements do, although most, but not all, protest comes from social movements (see also Della Porta and Diani, 2009). Studying social movements by looking only at protests is to see only the tip of the iceberg.

Social theorist Alberto Melucci's work (1991) was crucial in highlighting the differences between movements' latent and visible phases (see more on Melucci below). During the submerged or latent phases of movement activity, social movements experiment with alternative forms of deliberation and decision-making, generate new lifestyle and cultural practices, develop alternative solutions to social problems and, in some cases, engage in prefigurative politics, all of which I will explore in this book. Furthermore, some movements – such as those focusing on alternative forms of social organization based on cooperation and mutual aid (e.g. community-supported agriculture movements) – might only rarely engage in protest activities.

The activities of social movements in latent phases are largely directed inward towards other social movement participants, crucially in the generation of shared or collective identities, which give a shared collective definition of the social movement that enables it to successfully resist or challenge authorities (Melucci, 1995a, 1995b; Flesher Fominaya, 2007a, 2010a, 2010b). Many movements only become visible to those *outside* the movement when they engage in mobilization and protest. Although some social movement scholars focus primarily on protests, either because they privilege this aspect of social movement activity or because the visibility of mobilization makes it easier to study methodologically, latent social movement activity is a part of the day-to-day activities of movements, whether they are active or in abeyance. The term 'abeyance' refers to periods of reduced visibility and mobilization and depicts the 'process by which movements sustain themselves in non-receptive political environments and provide continuity from one stage of mobilization to another' (Taylor, 1989: 761). Much scholarship on social movements encompasses both their latent and visible aspects.

Prefigurative politics

Eyerman and Jamison (1991) and Cox and Flesher Fominaya (2009) have highlighted the role of social movements as knowledge-producers who provide society with new ideas, ideals and values, theories, practices and even new identities. *Prefigurative politics* refers to the practice of instituting modes of organization, tactics and practices that reflect the vision of society to which the social movements aspire. Prefigurative practices also attempt to transform social movement practice itself as well as that of broader society. So, for example, if a social movement seeks to abolish hierarchical or patriarchal practices in society, then it will often endeavour to engage in social relations (such as decision-making and communication) that are non-hierarchical and not patriarchal (such as consensus decision-making, avoiding sexist language, working to transform consciousness to overcome internalized patriarchy and so on). If they wish to foster deeper democracy and participation in society, for example, they will engage in deliberative and participatory decision-making practices. Breines provides an excellent discussion of prefigurative politics in the US new left student movement in the 1960s, arguing that it represented an essentially anti-organizational philosophy that was 'hostile to bureaucracy, hierarchy and leadership ... its most acute concern was to avoid duplication of the hierarchical and manipulative relationships characteristic of society' (Breines, 1980: 422). These critiques also emerged as a result of hierarchical and instrumental forms of social movement organization in the 'old' left, which reflects how activists engage with social dynamics within and outside the movements in which they are involved.

Social movements versus social movement organizations

It is also useful to distinguish a social movement from a *social movement organization* (SMO), which McCarthy and Zald define as 'a complex, or formal organization which identifies its goals with the preferences of a social movement or a counter-movement and attempts to implement those goals' (1977: 1218) (see also Tilly and Wood, 2012: 6 and Saunders, 2007 for conceptual distinctions between social movements and SMOs). Greenpeace, for example, is not a social movement but an SMO within a much larger environmental movement. This distinction fits with Diani's (1992: 13) understanding of movements as 'networks of informal interactions between a plurality of individuals, groups or associations engaged in a political or cultural conflict on the basis of a shared collective identity'. Diani's definition served in part to 'a) differentiate social movements from related concepts such as interest groups, political parties, protest events and coalitions; and b) to identify a specific area of investigation and theorising for social movement research' (1992: 1).

Debates within movements on the relative advantages or desirability of institutionalization often reflect deep differences in ideological approaches to social movement action, a theme to which I will return in Chapter 3. While institutionalization can mean SMOs are more effective in lobbying governments for specific policy changes, professionalization can mean that SMO elites no longer represent the social movement's grassroots constituents. A significant body of literature also shows that institutionalization leads to de-radicalization of movement demands as SMOs tone down their criticisms in order to receive government funding or to continue to have access to policy-makers (Staggenborg, 1988; Epstein, 2001). Indeed, although much social movement scholarship focuses on SMOs (especially within US Social Movement scholarship in the resource mobilization tradition, which stresses the ability of social movements to acquire resources in order to mobilize effectively around political goals), the question of whether or not SMOs form part of social movements, or can be treated as synonymous with them, is legitimate given the definitions above that stress contentious and non-institutionalized collective action as core elements of social movements. This returns us to the issue of how far scholars highlight *protest* as a central aspect of social movements. Depending on the definition of social movements used, some non-governmental organizations (NGOs) might be better termed 'interest groups' or 'pressure groups' and seen as part of a broader social support for social movements without actually forming part of them. On the other hand, the line between the two is not clear-cut;

organizations such as Greenpeace, for example, are both complex and institutionalized but also engage in contentious politics and direct action.[3]

Progressive, regressive and counter movements

While much of social movement literature focuses on *progressive* movements, it is not the case that all movements are working for progressive social change. *Regressive* movements are those that actively mobilize to return society to the way things were before a change took place or to the way the regressive movements *argue* that society used to be (such as neo-Nazi or xenophobic social movements against immigration) (see Chapter 6); *counter-movements* are usually understood as social movements that emerge in response to a progressive social movement's demands or the changes in policies those movements have brought about (such as anti-abortion movements or movements that seek to deny homosexuals the right to marry or to form civil unions in those states or countries where these rights have been granted). However, these distinctions are not always so neat and linear: at the time of writing, in Europe the rise of extreme right-wing movements with fascistic and racist ideologies has led to the resurgence of anti-fascist (*antifa*) counter-movements. In the European context, fascist/ultra-national and anti-fascist movements wane and rise partly in response to globalization processes, such as the global financial crisis, which creates a context in which anti-immigrant and exclusive national sovereignty arguments can flourish among some sectors of the population.

Some key approaches to the study of social movements

I have already introduced some key definitions of social movements and highlighted the fact that these definitions are contested among scholars. The literature on social movements is vast and diverse but has been fuelled by some central questions: When and why do social movements emerge? How do social movements organize? Who joins social movements and why? What sorts of values fuel social movements and how do these values and ideas become collective action? How do institutions and political opportunities affect social movements? How and why do social movements matter? These are just some of the questions that scholars have asked about social movements, and they are far from agreeing about the answers, although some core understandings have emerged. Different theoretical, analytical and methodological approaches result from scholars asking different questions, being influenced by different theoretical and philosophical traditions, and having different disciplinary starting points. For example, it isn't the same to want to know why individuals join a movement as to want to understand what the relationship between repression and mobilization is.

Although social movements have been around since the eighteenth century (Tilly and Wood, 2012), scholars didn't begin to study them as 'social movements' until the 1970s. In broad terms, prior to the 1970s, scholars in the US primarily understood social movements and protests from a collective behaviour paradigm, whereas the dominant approach in Europe was influenced more by Marxist intellectual traditions. From the 1970s onward, in the US resource mobilization theory and political process theory were the dominant social movement paradigms, whereas in Europe New Social Movement theory was a major theoretical development. In both contexts, scholars were reacting against the theoretical developments that had come before and trying to build on or critique previous approaches. From the 1980s onward, we begin to see greater dialogue between the US and European approaches and a greater attention to culture in both arenas, although again earlier theoretical traditions also influenced the understanding of culture, with 'frame analysis' becoming one of the dominant approaches in the US (see Chapter 5), whereas in Europe, cultural studies drawing on Marxist, Post-Marxist and Gramscian traditions (e.g. in the Birmingham Centre for Contemporary Cultural Studies), feminism, semiotics and the work of theorists such as Raymond Williams and E.P. Thompson influenced the development of cultural approaches to social movement studies (see Chapter 4). Overall, the dominant American tradition has been characterized by a more empirical and scientific approach to social movements, with a strong emphasis on institutions and organizations, whereas the European tradition has been much more influenced by Marxism, European political philosophy and post-Marxism. Each has made significant contributions to our understanding of social movements.

Increasing dialogue between approaches and the welcome integration of non-Western voices and post-colonial theories into dominant English language social movement studies mean that today the field is richer and more diverse than ever. The rise of information and communication technologies (ICTs) and digital media has also led to an emerging and rapidly growing field of social movement research (see Chapter 5). Today, social movement studies is an inherently multidisciplinary and often interdisciplinary field, with important contributions from social psychologists, sociologists, social historians, political scientists, anthropologists, geographers, media scholars and scholars drawing on multiple disciplinary traditions and insights.

In what follows, I will trace out some of the key approaches and concepts in the US and European traditions during primarily the 1960–1990s, before pointing to a brief overview of contemporary social movement studies, highlighting where different areas of study will be more developed in the book. For reasons of space, this is necessarily a very brief synthesis of a very rich field and therefore risks overgeneralizing: not all US scholars or European scholars follow the broad lines of demarcation sketched out here, and each of these areas of inquiry has sparked numerous debates and a wealth of research too vast to be done justice to here. Scholars and students wanting a fuller introduction to the social movement theory can turn to Della Porta and Diani (2009), Edwards (2014), Chesters and Welsh (2011) or Martin (2015) among others.

Collective behaviour theories: Early explanations of why and how protests and social movements emerge

Early social psychological theories, such as that of Gustave Le Bon (1995 [1897]), understood crowd behaviour to be fundamentally irrational, arguing that crowds produce an environment in which individuals lose their free will and agency. Freud (1945 [1921]) too characterized people and crowds as irrational and behaving with a herd-like mentality. But what motivated the crowds to form and act in the first place? In the US, Herbert Blumer, a symbolic interactionist associated with the Chicago School, developed early influential theories of collective behaviour, including political protest and social movements. Blumer (1951, 1971) was interested in how collective behaviour could emerge to create social change – in other words, how group behaviour which is often rule-conforming can sometimes challenge established social norms – and in classifying the different forms of collective behaviour, including unconventional collective behaviour. When groups are engaged in unconventional behaviour in order to challenge social norms, they're engaged in forms of cultural innovation that can sometimes lead to new forms of institutionalized behaviour, which, as it becomes established, develops into the 'new normal' or becomes conventional.

Blumer's (1951) work is important because it questions why people choose to engage in social behaviour that is unconventional and seek change. As a symbolic interactionist, Blumer rejected the idea that social conditions (such as poverty or lack of political freedom) in and of themselves could generate grievances, much less collective action. Instead, human beings need to negotiate shared meanings through repeated interaction and generate a shared understanding of their social conditions as problematic and in need of change. It's the *shared construction* of grievance as a *social problem* that matters.

Blumer (1951) argued that grievances emerged in two key ways: 1) in times of rapid change and disruptions to normal routines which make it difficult for people to continue to follow established norms and conventions (e.g. industrialization, war) and 2) a more gradual change in moral values due to 'cultural drifts' in which people develop new identities and expectations (e.g. women expect to be allowed to vote or to be paid as much as men for the same work). Grievance theory was a popular explanation for collective action and crowd behaviour and remains so (in some forms) to this day. However, people sometimes miss out on the crucial factor Blumer highlighted, which was that structural conditions alone do not cause social movements or protests. Unfortunately, social conditions such as poverty, exclusion, marginalization, exploitation and oppression are widespread yet often (indeed usually) do not produce collective action to protest or resist these conditions. To get around this inconvenient truth, some theorists in the 1970s (e.g. Gurr, 2010 [1970]) developed *relative* deprivation theory, arguing that grievances emerged from the gap between what people believed they were entitled to and what they believed they could actually obtain. The argument ran that as this grievance develops and spreads to a critical mass – when it becomes systemic frustration – it causes outbreaks of dissent. So, for example, in times of economic growth, peoples' aspirations can rise faster than they can be met, which fuels a sense of frustration which can lead to violence.

Unlike Blumer, who thought that protest and social movement collective behaviour could emerge for rational reasons (but see Edwards, 2014: 30 for a discussion of his overall view of collective behaviour in social movements as irrational), relative deprivation maintained a view of protests as abnormal activities that were fundamentally *irrational* and that resulted from people's feelings of frustration and insecurity, which itself was a function of the difference between what their social position was and what they felt it should be. In other words, it wasn't an objective structural condition such as material deprivation (poverty) that caused the grievance, but the subjective understanding of what the individual felt they were entitled to have: the greater the sense of entitlement, the greater the likelihood of discontent and therefore dissent. Relative deprivation theory, which characterized protest as a pathology, met with sharp critiques. First, even if hundreds or even thousands of people share a sense of deprivation and frustration, they still need some mechanism to come together collectively to act towards a common goal. Relative deprivation theory tells us nothing about the organizational forms that social movements adopt. Second, a quick empirical study of different forms of protest reveals that citizens regularly take to the streets to protest different government policies, offering arguments that could hardly be discounted as irrational. A close look at the protesters at a range of protest events would also reveal a wide range of temperaments, with some protest forms being cheerful and upbeat and incorporating song and dance, for example, not just expressions of anger and frustration. As social movement scholar Doug McAdam (in Diani and McAdam, 2003: 282) reflected:

> My first exposure to the academic study of social movements came in 1971, when much to my surprise, the professor of my Abnormal Psychology class devoted several weeks to discussion of the topic. I say "surprise" because, as an active participant in the anti-war movement, it certainly came as news to me that my involvement in the struggle owed to a mix of personal pathology and social disorganization.

In short, relative deprivation theory and other collective behaviour theories that characterized protests and social movements as fundamentally *irrational* simply didn't stand up to empirical scrutiny as a broad explanation for the emergence of social movements and mobilization. But critiques of relative deprivation theory and indeed grievance theory don't mean we need to throw the baby out with the bathwater: many people do have very legitimate grievances and come together to try to express these grievances and demand political, social and economic change. And a shared structural location (class, gender, race), or more precisely the shared experience of exploitation and oppression that stems from these locations, can indeed serve as a powerful factor in bringing people together, as Marxist, feminist and race theory all argue, but that doesn't mean it *will* (see also Tilly, 1978a on shared categorical traits as facilitators of recognition and identity construction). This coming together does not happen *spontaneously* but requires some other mechanisms to make it possible to convert shared grievances or other motivations for mobilization (values, desires for social change) into collective action. For all that critics rightly chastise collective behaviourists for characterizing social movement actors as emotionally driven (and hence 'irrational'), Blumer in particular was valuable for stressing precisely the emotional components of social movement dynamics that the later Resource Mobilization Theory left out (in an attempt to correct the irrationality of the collective behaviourists!). Above all, Blumer was valuable for insisting on the importance of shared meanings that develop through repeated interaction within social movements and for stressing the need for a shared construction of issues as *social problems that require collective action to solve* as a precursor for mobilization.

Another question arises when thinking about motivations to participate: what about *barriers* to participation? After all, why get off the sofa to participate in a social movement when other people are already mobilizing around the issues you care about? This barrier to participation is what is known as (Mancur Olson's) *free rider problem*, whereby individuals who do not exert any effort or incur any cost (i.e. who don't participate in mobilization) will still benefit from the collective action of others. This is because, unlike private individual goods (something for individual use or ownership), collective action pursues collective goods, in other words, benefits or gains that are made available to a wider group of people. So the suffragettes who mobilized for women's right to vote, the environmental campaigners who engage in direct action to protect clean air and water, the union member who strikes for better working conditions, if successful, produce outcomes that benefit everyone to whom that benefit applies and not just the people who fought for those benefits.

Mancur Olson (1965: 2) argues, therefore, that rational agents are *not* likely to cooperate in most settings, even when cooperation would be mutually beneficial for them. He said that, 'unless the number of individuals in a group is quite small, or unless there is coercion or some other special device to make individuals act in their common interest, rational, self-interested individuals will not act to achieve their common or group interests'. As Edwards (2014: 49) argues, 'whilst we may have been unconvinced by collective behavior theorists who cited emotions as the driving force of collective action, it seems now that if we switch back to reason then no collective action should happen at all'. Rational self-interest, therefore, does not account for collective action. So what does? As a rational actor theorist, Olson himself provides some answers in keeping with the rational actor model: for example, people might be coerced into joining (obligatory membership of a union) or they might be sanctioned by others for not joining (peer pressure). But as Olson points out, this only works within an individual's social networks – which in most cases are relatively small numbers of people – because most people won't change their behaviour unless pressure is exerted on a regular basis through interpersonal face-to-face interaction (people are unlikely to care what someone who doesn't know them thinks of them). Much more likely, according to Olson, are inducements or benefits, so-called 'selective incentives', that motivate people to participate because they will gain benefits that they wouldn't gain if they *didn't* participate. These might be material advantages (membership benefits or rewards, such as a discount, a concert or a 'free' calendar) or what Olson recognizes are 'soli-dary' incentives, such as the desire to socialize, gain prestige or status, new friendships and feeling important. There are also moral incentives, such as acting because 'it's the right thing to do'.

Resource Mobilization Theory (RMT): From individuals to organizations

Olson's (1965) rational choice approach focuses very much on individual motivations for protest and mobilization. One approach that maintained a rational actor model but shifted attention away from the individual psycho-logical reasons for protesting or mobilizing to the structural factors that enable mobilization was Resource Mobilization Theory (RMT). RMT emerged in the 1970s in an attempt to correct some of the flaws in collective behaviour paradigms and grievance theories, emphasizing the importance of material and symbolic resources. Resource mobilization theory is not so concerned with *why* social movements emerge but rather *how* movements actually mobilize resources to reach their goals. Deeply rooted in and influ-enced by the US political context and by organizational and economic the-ory, RMT conceives of social movements as being primarily made up of social movement organizations that are formally structured and compete with each other in the political field, seeking to maximize resources and benefits in the pursuit of their interests and on behalf of their members. The influence of economics and organizational theory is evident in the develop-ment of central concepts such as 'social movement industry', which two key proponents of the RMT, McCarthy and Zald (1977: 1219), defined as a concept that 'parallels the concept of industry in economics'. In the lan-guage of classic RMT, people who believe in the movement's goals are known as 'adherents' and those who actually supply the social movement organiza-tion with the resources are described as 'constituents'. Resources can be understood as both material (e.g. funding, facilities, communication infra-structure) and nonmaterial (e.g. expertise, authority, prestige, contacts) and encompass political, economic, social and cultural goods that can be used to reach the movement's goals. Movement success, therefore, depends on strong organizations that can effectively generate resources that can be used to attract and motivate participants and offer incentives for joining and par-ticipating. At the same time that they need to develop their *internal* func-tions to sustain the organization over time (i.e. keep the organization strong with resources, members and efficient organization), social movement organizations must also carry out their *external* functions and try to influence policies and achieve their goals for social and political change.

One important insight from RMT is that movements often emerge from pre-existing organizations, because movements are able to develop quickly if they can draw on the resources of existing structures and associations who can provide not only organizational resources but also networks of activists or potential activists. For example, the US Civil Rights movement of the 1950s and 1960s was strongly sustained by both black churches and organizations such as the National Association for the Advancement of Colored People (NAACP), both of which enabled the development of a mass direct action movement (Morris, 1984). Oberschall (1973) showed that 'bloc-recruitment' of entire organizations into social movement networks was possible, particularly among constituencies possessing strong organizational networks.

Resource mobilization theory offers important insights but has been critiqued for its emphasis on interest-seeking, benefit-maximizing instrumental rationality and for failing to account sufficiently for the role of the emotions, culture, identity, collective identity and expressive action (Jasper, 2010). RMT tells us about how social movement organizations can maximize their resources but it tells us little or nothing about why social movements emerge and who mobilizes and why. Its solution to the free rider problem doesn't break free of the limitations of rational actor theory, and it doesn't place our understanding of social movements in any sort of a wider historical or social context. By focusing so much on resources and organizations, it actually has very little to say about *politics*, which should be central to the study of social movements. In particular, it takes for granted (and therefore largely ignores) the political motivations of the actors involved, including their ideals, goals and even values. Why does this matter? Let's take the example of SMOs, which RMT takes as central units of analysis. Under the RMT schema, the more bureaucratically organized, well-resourced, hierarchically organized and effectively led organizations should be the most successful. That sounds logical, and it is indeed true for many organizations seeking political and social change, not just social movement organizations but also NGOs, political parties and even terrorist organizations. But what the model misses is that many social movement actors are motivated by ideologies and specific goals that might not be compatible with a formal, hierarchical organization or that might even reject engagement with the state or with money. For example, some movements seek to change the way power operates in society and to subvert the status quo rather than getting a better share of the benefits available from the state or market. As we will see with the discussion on autonomous movements in Chapter 3, some movements reject hierarchical forms of organization and seek instead to engage in *prefiguration* by embodying and attempting to put into practice decision-making styles and organizational forms that don't rely on leaders or on investing individual members with more power or authority than others. Feminist movements that reflect on overturning patriarchal relations may also reject hierarchical forms of decision-making and interaction. Lifestyle movements might engage primarily in such activities as communal living, creating solidarity networks or alternative economic organizations such as cooperatives. In other words, it makes little sense to separate organizational forms from organizational goals and from the ideologies and values that motivate social movement actors. And as we already discussed, social movement organizations and social movements are not the same thing. Furthermore, even the most hierarchical formally structured organization that operates in a rational calculating way often fails to reach its goals effectively, because humans are not just rational beings who act strategically but also ideologically, culturally and emotionally (among other motivations). Social movement groups, whether formal organizations, loose affinity groups or temporary coalitions or platforms, organize around a great diversity of issues, values and ideologies, and these will affect their organizational forms and their internal decision-making and strategies. Indeed, how movement groups organize and take decisions, and which tactics or strategies they should adopt, are often a source of great conflict and debate within these groups, often making identifying a single strategic direction difficult even within a single social movement group or SMO. When we expand our gaze from a single organization to the diverse constellation of groups and actors that make up a movement, the picture becomes even more complex.

Political Process Theory (PPT): The importance of political context

One of the earliest and influential critiques of RMT, but which maintained many of its central assumptions, was McAdam's Political Process Model (or Political Process Theory, PPT), which was deeply influenced by his research on the Civil Rights movement in the US (which some would argue led him to unconvincingly overextend the theory's reach beyond his case study, see e.g. Jasper, 2010). In an attempt to improve on RMT, which PPT theorists felt over-emphasized the internal dynamics of social movement organizations, the political process model stressed the dynamic and strategic way that social movements responded to their political environments. This key insight was encapsulated by the term political opportunity structure (POS), which refers to the degree of openness or closure of the political system within which social movements operate and which includes such factors as access to political elites and resources, openings created by crises in the state, a permissive state or a decrease in levels of repression against movements, and so on. POS inhibits or enhances prospects for mobilizations and shapes the sorts of claims and movements that might emerge as well as possibilities for impact and success. As Edwards (2014: 79–80) puts it, 'Their main claim is that activists can be as angry and aggrieved, as well organized, tactically astute, and brilliantly led as they like, but without a favourable political context they will get nowhere ....'

Action Repertoires: What movements do when they mobilize

One of the major figures in the PPT paradigm was Charles Tilly, whose work was very valuable for its contribution to a historical periodization of social movements, which charted the evolution of different protest forms over time and space, and to the 'hows' of social movement organizing. One of his key contributions was his concept of 'action repertoires' which Tilly (2003: 45) defined as 'the set of performances available to any given actor within a regime'. Tilly was interested in how actions become ritualized over time, enabling effective communication between participants on different sides of contentious episodes who could anticipate and coordinate their actions more effectively. As Tarrow (2011: 30) argues, 'the repertoire is at once a structural and cultural concept, involving not only what people do when they are engaged in conflict with others but what they know how to do and what others *expect* them to do'. According to Tilly, groups of actors choose how to act from a repertoire of available actions, but their choices are restricted because their options are limited to those 'performances' with which they are familiar and which they are able to enact given their skills and resources.

The concept of action repertoires addresses an important area of social movements studies, which is how movements learn and change over time. Tilly's historical approach enables him to trace action repertoire developments and make some broader claims about how this change happens. For the most part, he argues change is incremental, as movement actors (and their opponents) learn to adapt to new scenarios. But at movements of great social change – epochal transformations and hinge moments – change can also happen more quickly. Tilly's work also considered movement diffusion processes, which have also shifted dramatically over time. He argued that early modern protest forms were:

- *parochial* because they were usually limited to a single community;

- *segmented* because local issues were addressed directly by the aggrieved party to the offending party, but national issues were mediated by local authorities;

- *and particular* because they were locally rooted and therefore varied greatly from one locale to another.

Tarrow (2011: 40), following Tilly, explains that early modern 'forms of contention would often explode at public celebrations, when people took advantage of the opportunity of numerous people collected in public places, often lubricated by drink, in which high spirits and hot-headedness would combine. But these events were never entirely "spontaneous": they would draw on rich, often irreverent symbolism, religious rituals, and popular culture' (Tilly, 1983: 464). By the 1830s, however, Tilly shows that there was a significant transformation in Western repertoires of contention that were displacing the earlier forms of protest. The most important causal mechanisms of this change were urbanization and industrialization, which brought people together in factories and neighbourhoods, facilitating the creation of associations organized around shared interests (e.g. unions and parties). Urbanization and industrialization also facilitated communication infrastructures (and therefore mobilization) but also meant that many more people were living close to the seats of urban and indeed national power. Instead of conflicts being localized or directed primarily at local authorities or local offenders, aggrieved groups could take their conflicts directly to these power-holders. At the same time, repertoires of contention changed because the authorities (e.g. the police) were also more professionalized and organized. Modern protest forms then became:

- *autonomous* in that interest groups making demands could organize protests on their own initiative and establish direct contact with national elites;

- *cosmopolitan* because the issues that were raised spanned many different localities;

- and *modular* because the protest forms were easily transferable from one setting to another (Tarrow, 2011: 41).

Certain forms of protest became dominant and ritualized, including the demonstration, the strike, boycotts, barricades, rallies and public meetings, and the creation of associations. As Tarrow (1993: 289) argues, Tilly's work highlights how certain repertoires of action shift from unconventional to conventional: 'In each period of history some forms of collective action are sanctioned by habit, expectations, and even legality, while others are unfamiliar, unexpected, and are rejected as illegitimate by elites and the mass public alike. Consider the strike. As late as the 1870s it was barely known, poorly understood, and widely rejected as a legitimate form of collective action. By the 1960s, however, the strike can be considered as an accepted part of collective bargaining practice.'

The routinization and mass dissemination of effective protest forms can have great benefits for social movements because people can learn, adopt and adapt them easily from one scenario to another (as long as they make cultural sense). Routinized mobilization forms can also can bring drawbacks: people can become immune to them and become blasé ('Oh yeah, another demonstration about something or other'), opponents and authorities can anticipate protest actions and effectively counter them or repress them, and they can fail to provide the novelty that media have often searching for (which is one of the reasons disruptive or even violent protest actions get more attention than peaceful forms even when representing a minority of actions at a given protest event; see Chapter 4). Social movement actors, therefore, often seek to innovate but run the risk of having their protest performance be poorly understood or, if they are 'too radical', prompting a repressive reaction from the state (for more on these dilemmas, see Chapter 4).

While critics argue that PPT focuses too heavily on the external structural conditions in which movements operate, McAdam (1982: 44) stressed that it wasn't enough for a powerless group to exist in a favourable context of political opportunities but that social movements must be able to convert political opportunities into an organized campaign of social protest. In *Freedom Summer,* McAdam (1988) explored the values and attitudes that led to recruitment to the US Civil Rights movement. One influential concept coming from the political process approach is that of *cognitive liberation.* Developed by McAdam (1982), it states that people will not usually rebel against the status quo unless they feel that it is unjust or illegitimate (as opposed to natural or inevitable) (note here the similarity to Blumer's insistence that collective action needs to be preceded by the active framing of a social problem as a problem) but also – and this is a crucial insight that fits well with the rational actor model – *that they have the capacity to change it for the better.*

McAdam (2013, n.p.) argues that 'it is the combination of perceived injustice and collective efficacy that is held to be the subjective linchpin of movement activity' and 'the key to movement emergence'. Therefore, while expanding political opportunities, resources and organizational capacity provide 'structural potential' for collective action, they alone do not cause movement emergence. Instead, the transition between opportunity and action relies on 'people and the collective meaning they attach to their action'. McAdam, therefore, defends himself against critics of his 'structural bias', but recognizes that the term cognitive liberation downplays the 'emotional dimensions of collective action'.

It is important to recognize that feelings of injustice and illegitimacy can and often do develop through participation in a movement and don't necessarily have to precede it (Goodwin and Jasper, 2015). It is also worth noting that, contra rational actor model assumptions, many social movement actors recognize that their actions may be futile or have very little chance of success but they do them anyway because *it is the right thing to do* or because they want to bear witness against an injustice. Nevertheless, cognitive liberation is a crucial insight because the belief in the possibility of winning is a motivator that prompts an increase in mobilization that can shift the balance of power between social movements and their opponents.

Overall, however, the political process model is very state-centric: it assumes that what social movements seek is to gain recognition, concessions or gains from the state. But as we will see in this book, social movements have a whole range of objectives, target audiences and motivations, some of which have little or nothing to do with the state (e.g. lifestyle movements). By taking for granted *why* social movement actors mobilized and focusing primarily on *how* they mobilized, the model offers an incomplete picture of social movement dynamics. Because the political process model pays great attention to formal SMOs and perceives social movements primarily as political actors looking at (state) political institutions from the outside in (McAdam, 1982; Tarrow, 2011), it treats the individuals within those movements as largely irrelevant, emphasizing structural factors outside social movement control, with social movement actors responding to political opportunities and depending on internal resources to mobilize (Goodwin and Jasper, 1999). Critics also emphasize PPT's inability to distinguish between short-term strategies and long-term structural contextual shifts (Jasper, 2008), the lack of attention to culture and emotions (Goodwin and

Jasper, 2004), the implicit adoption of rational-choice assumptions carried over from RMT (Opp, 2009) and a tendency to 'read back' favourable contexts for successful movements and unfavourable ones for unsuccessful ones (see Jasper, 2010; Edwards, 2014).

Piven and Cloward (1991) critique the theory for its strong normalizing tendency: RMTs treat protest organizations just like conventional ones, and they blur the distinction between rule-conforming and rule-defying behaviour. In addition, 'protest is often treated by RM analysts as more organized than it is, as if conventional modes of formal organization also typify the organizational forms taken by protest. And some RM analysts normalize the political impact of collective protest, as if the processes of influence set in motion by collective protest are no different than those set in motion by conventional political activities' (Piven and Cloward, 1991: 436). Their words highlight the fact that social movements are challengers of the status quo or of authority holders, often defying rather than reinforcing convention or existing policies, whereas conventional political activities often seek to uphold the existing order (and shore up existing power-holders).

In response to these critiques, McAdam, Tilly and Tarrow each addressed the insufficient attention to culture in their earlier work and later engaged more fully with language, discourse, performances and the symbolic components of movements (e.g. Tarrow, 2013; Tilly, 2008). In a joint book, *Dynamics of Contention* (Charles Tilly *et al.*, 2001: 42), they delineated four central problems with their earlier formulation of PPT '(1) It focuses on static, rather than dynamic relationships. (2) It works best when centred on individual social movements, and less well for broader episodes of contention. (3) Its genesis in the relatively open politics of the American "sixties" led to more emphasis on opportunities than on threats, more confidence in the expansion of organizational resources than on the organizational deficits that many challengers suffer. (4) It focused inordinately on the origins of contention rather than on its later phases'.

Despite this reflexivity and the attempt to correct some of these problems, for advocates of a more cultural approach to social movement studies, they never quite manage to break free of some of the rationalist and structuralist biases of the theory (see Goodwin and Jasper, 1999; Jasper, 2010). Critics also argue that despite the efforts to create a more dynamic model, one of the theory's central problems was that it was missing a (satisfactory) theory of *action* with insufficient attention to the question of who is doing the mobilizing and why (Jasper, 2010). In addition, the theory lacks sufficient recognition of social movement *agency*: social movement activists don't just wait for opportunities and react to them; they create them. They shape the political environment through their actions. They make powerful moral claims and persuasive arguments that shift public perceptions of issues, including political elites.

One of the key ways they do this is through the construction of frames, which are a means of packaging key issues and claims in such a way as to define a problem or grievance and motivate people to take action or support the movement's action around it. Movements often undertake this process strategically and reflexively as a core part of their communication practices.

The study of how movements do this is known as frame analysis, and it is one of the most influential and utilized approaches to the study of social movements. Benford and Snow's (2000) article 'Framing processes and social movements: An overview and assessment' is the second most cited article in social movement studies and is a good place for scholars to get an introduction to this area of analysis.

Why do people join movements?

As we have seen, scholars have proposed grievances, selective incentives, ideology and values as possible reasons for people to join movements. Goodwin and Jasper (2015: 56) offer another important motivator: 'moral shocks' that lead to *self-recruitment:*

> 'Sometimes in the course of daily life something happens to us that distresses, surprises, and outrages us. A loved one may be killed by a drunk driver. Our boss may ask us for sexual favors. Construction on a nuclear power plant may begin down the street. Sometimes we are shocked by information we receive (perhaps from a newspaper or political pamphlet) rather than by personal experience. We learn that cosmetics are tested by being put into the eyes of rabbits, or that NATO is deploying a new type of nuclear missile throughout Europe. These moral shocks are often strong enough to propel us into trying to do something. We may seek out a social movement organization if we know one exists. We may even try to found our own. Although people who join a social movement typically know someone involved in it, moral shocks may still be the trigger that gets them to join. In some cases it can even push us into participation when we do not know anyone at all in the movement. In such cases, we see a process of self-recruitment to a movement: people actively seek out a movement or movement organization in which they can participate, as opposed to being recruited by the movement itself.'

Experiences of moral shocks are often triggers for a lifelong commitment to activism. When Guatemalan human rights lawyer Renata Ávila began to work representing indigenous victims of genocide and other human rights abuses in Guatemala, she experienced such a moral shock:

> 'It was the first time I had to deal with the extreme corruption of the Guatemalan judiciary and the ways in which the law is manipulated in the interests of the powerful. I was shocked to see how my government had constantly lied to me, and to all Guatemalans, I was also shocked by how broken and fraudulent our education system and media were [...] During my childhood and my teenage

years I never heard about the atrocities of the Civil War. I never knew about the 1,500,000 displaced Guatemalan refugees living in misery in the south of Mexico. I didn't know about the killing of children (some of them smashed against trees to save on bullets, others killed while they were still inside the mother's wombs), about the disappearances, torture, and public killing of most of the indigenous leaders. And I hadn't understood how I had been living a lie: how I was going to law school with the sons and daughters of war criminals, and of really corrupt politicians and businessmen. I was simply pretending that everything was okay, whilst I enjoyed the fruits of a rotten system' (Ávila *et al.*, 2017).

Being confronted with horrifying evidence of human rights abuses and their systematic cover-up was the moral shock that sent Renata Ávila on her path to activism, eventually leading her to become a well-known human rights lawyer and digital rights expert who has collaborated on WikiLeaks among other political projects (see more on WikiLeaks in Chapter 5).

The importance of networks

As Goodwin and Jasper (2015) recognize in the quote above, however, one of the main reasons people join social movements is also arguably the most banal: People are much more likely to participate in a movement if they already belong to a social network where people are concerned about the issues that the movement is involved with and are involved in the movement too. Diani and Lodi (1988) showed that 78 per cent of activists had prior connections with activists in the environmental movement in Milan before participating. How people are raised and the socialization process that they are exposed to in their family and through their education and social networks influence how they feel about political activism and about the issues that movements address (although as Klatch, 1999 shows, they can also reject their socialization and join the opposing side). Collective action also requires connections between people: you can't act collectively if you don't have a social connection. Many movements organize in subcultural milieus (e.g. a squatted social centre) that make it difficult or unlikely that people will simply wander in off the street and join in (this is one reason that protest camps in urban areas can increase participation; see Chapter 7). Therefore, many people join movement groups because they know someone else who is already active in those groups, making social networks probably the most important mechanism of recruitment to movements.

In one study, Klandermans and Oegema (1987) sought to discover why people participated in a Dutch peace movement. At the individual level, they conceived of a four-step process: 'Becoming part of the mobilization potential, becoming target of mobilization attempts, becoming motivated to participate, and overcoming barriers to participate' (1987: 519). Their article highlights the importance of networks because, as they argue, 'however successfully a movement mobilizes consensus, however large its mobilization potential, if it does not have access to recruitment networks, its mobilization potential cannot be realized. Networks condition whether people become targets of mobilization attempts. The more a movement's reach-out networks are woven into other organizations, the more people are reached by mobilization attempts' (1987: 520). Their study added to a body of literature that showed the importance of informal networks for reaching potential participants and recruiting people into social movements (e.g. Gerlach and Hine, 1970; McAdam, 1986; Snow *et al.*, 1986). They argued that 'ideological and social incentives appear to be the primary motivations to participate in the peace demonstration…. Knowing other participants turned out to be an important variable in the mobilization process, not only in the case of high-risk activities like McAdam (1986) demonstrated, but in the case of low risk activities as well. Ideological incentives presuppose the presence of ideological and attitudinal support for movement in a society' (1987: 530). Klandermans and Oegema (1987) also showed the importance of motivation in overcoming the many barriers to participation; the higher the motivation to participate, the more barriers people can overcome.

Conceiving of 'social movements as networks of individuals, groups and organizations involved in complex interactions in real and virtual spaces representing and embodying a variety of causes, ideological positions and expressions of identity' (Chesters and Welsh, 2011: 120) is widespread in social movement scholarship. One of the earliest formulations of movements as networks was that of Gerlach and Hine (1970: 55), who were challenging the persistent idea among scholars and activists that centralized bureaucratic movements were the most effective. In their ground-breaking study, they analysed the structure of many different movements and determined that most movements were neither centralized and bureaucratically organized nor amorphous. Instead, they were:

- Segmentary: Composed of many diverse groups, which grow and die, divide and fuse, proliferate and contract.

- Polycentric: Having multiple, often temporary and sometimes competing leaders or centres of influence.

- Networked: Forming a loose, reticulate, integrated network with multiple linkages through travellers, overlapping membership, joint activities, common reading matter, and shared ideals and opponents (Gerlach, 2001: 289–290).

Most simply, networks refer to connections between people and organizations and these connections can be interest-driven (a shared issue of concern between groups) but also shaped by interpersonal relations and ideologies (Diani and McAdam, 2003).

The network concept also enables scholars to get around the tricky issue of empirically identifying the boundaries of a social movement (which can be very hard to pin down empirically since they encompass a wide range of actors and issues and can also extend through time and space) and instead focus on researching actual connections between a set of actors within given social movements (Saunders, 2013).

Social movement scholars have drawn on Granovetter's (1973) discussion of strong and weak ties to show that both have a place in developing social movement networks. Whereas strong reciprocal ties can create strong collective identity and cohesion between actors, they can also form 'closed circuits' and become self-referential, impeding their ability to reach out beyond their closed community. Instead, weak ties, or looser connections, are essential to building up social movement networks, because certain actors can act as bridges between the different organizations and actors and thereby activate multiple networks. Weak ties also have implications for diffusion processes (see Chapter 2) because, as Granovetter (1973: 1366) argues, 'whatever is to be diffused can reach a larger number of people, and traverse a greater social distance… when passed through weak ties rather than strong ties'. The relative strength of ties and their relation to movement recruitment and participation have also been shown to vary across types of movement and forms of protest, with high-risk activism being seen to require more strong ties (you usually need to trust and be strongly committed to and identified with your group to take high risks) than lower-risk activism. Likewise, intense and committed participation requires and creates stronger ties than does occasional participation, whereas more individualistic, conventional forms of participation are less reliant on previous connections (see Stark and Bainbridge, 1980 on faith networks, Diani and Lodi, 1988 on environmental groups).

Saunders (2007: 227) argues that while 'networking is often stressed as an essential ingredient of movement dynamics, few scholars have ever stipulated the type and intensity of networking that must exist in order for social phenomena to qualify as movements'. She argues that 'network links must be more than cursory, and should involve *shared engagement in collective action* in order to have a complete recipe for a social movement'. *Brokers* act as points of connection (2016) between movement actors and can play an important role in movement diffusion and learning processes, within movement communities (in one location) and across them (e.g. transnationally) (see Chapter 2). For example, Romanos (2016: 247) shows how Spanish immigrants in New York City acted as brokers between Spain's 15-M movement and Occupy Wall Street (OWS), bringing the influence of the former to shape OWS self-identity as an 'expansive, inclusive and empathic' movement (for more on these movements, see Chapter 7).

Thinking about networks makes us consider about not only why actors in movements form alliances and connections with each other (across issues, groups and geographical space) (see e.g. Diani, 2015) but also what motivates individuals to join movements in the first place. Motivation also brings us back to the importance of culture and emotions. It is easy to reify networks and see them as a 'thing', whereas what we need to remember is that they are formed of social ties and hence are made up of a web of human social relations. As Goodwin and Jasper (2015: 56) argue: 'social networks are also grounded in the emotional bonds between their members: we pay attention to people in our networks because we are fond of them or trust them. This may be the real power of networks, more influential than the ideas they carry'.

Social movement scholars seeking to overcome the rational actor bias and economistic assumptions that underlie some of the earlier influential paradigms such as RMT have shown that social movement actors do not simply engage in a series of strategic cost-benefit analyses of individual gain or even collective effectiveness when they decide to join a movement. For one thing, people in movements do recognize that movement participation comes at a high cost to them personally: this cost could be giving up a lot of their free time and energy, facing repression or disapprobation from their social milieu or other costs. My own work on global justice activists in Madrid (Flesher Fominaya, 2005, 2010a, 2010b) showed that one of the longest-lasting groups I studied sustained itself over time in large part because of the affective ties between members, despite failing to reach their explicit goals (or even making much progress towards them).

Despite widespread consensus in the field on the importance of networks, not everyone is completely convinced. Passy and Monsch (2014) argue that 'controversial results found in the literature suggest that the influence of networks has been overestimated. By focusing on social interactions, scholars have actually underestimated other processes at work, such as media influences and socio-political events'. Yet Granovetter argued back in 1973 (p. 1374) that 'people rarely act on mass media information unless it is also transmitted through personal ties'. As for socio-political events, on their own they are unlikely to integrate new social movement members without some other mechanisms of integration that facilitate integration, overcome barriers to participation (such as high risks or costs), contribute to identity formation processes and affective and solidarity ties, or shape consensus understandings of social problems and the need to collectively act on them. In short, in the absence of sustained and structured social interaction, socio-political events are unlikely to lead to recruitment.

The reasons people join movements are more complex than the rational actor models implicit or explicit in some of the most influential paradigms suggest. While they certainly may involve some calculations about cost-benefit analysis and subjective perceptions of whether or not the movement will be successful in meeting its goals if they participate, they also include a range of other motivations.

Meanwhile in Europe: Marxist frameworks and New Social Movement Theory

While these important theoretical developments from collective behaviour approaches to RMT to PPT, and the criticism of these (e.g. Piven and Cloward, 1991), were taking place primarily in the US, in Europe, social movement scholarship was tracing a different trajectory and was not as organized into a distinct sub-discipline. While a full treatment lies far outside the scope of this book or chapter, one of the key areas of concern stemming from the powerful influence of Marxism on theory and movements was class analysis. Marxist understanding of social movements is important because it highlights the capacity for workers to self-organize in the face of systematic exploitation. In other words, it is a theoretical framework that takes *agency* and collective action in the pursuit of collective interests as central (in contrast to the emphasis on opportunities becoming available in the environment out of activists' control, as in PPT or RMT). Marxist approaches are also crucial in playing close attention to the importance of class and its relation to mobilization as well as to the ways that the dynamics of capitalism shape all aspects of social movement mobilization. Indeed, traditionally Marxist analysis views working class mobilization as *the* social movement, not *a* social movement, because the central conflict in bourgeois society is over the control of the means of production and therefore this conflict defines and affects all other struggles and is the key to social transformation. In the *Communist Manifesto* (1998 [1848]), Marx and Engels argue that 'of all the classes that stand face-to-face with the bourgeoisie today, the proletariat alone is a really revolutionary class. The other classes decay and finally disappear in the face of modern industry; the proletariat is its special and essential product'. The proletariat, or the working class, then, is a product of the modern industrial era, and as capitalism develops, necessarily the workers that fuel capitalism also develop, increasing in number and strength. As their number and strength grow, so does their consciousness – their awareness of their power and ability to effect social change. While obviously labour movements have yet to triumph over capitalism and the rule of the bourgeoisie, they have indeed achieved fundamental victories in working conditions and workers' rights. Marxist and class analysis is important for the study of social movements because it directs our attention to the way resources are distributed in society and the way that interests are represented and structured within capitalist society. Marxist theory has inspired and influenced a whole range of other theories that have been usefully applied to social movement analysis. Two of the most influential Neo-Marxist traditions are the Frankfurt School, which drew on both Marxism and psychoanalytic theory to explore the possibilities of mobilization for socially marginalized groups, and a Gramscian tradition that analyses the ways that social movements can contest political, ideological and cultural hegemony (see Chapter 4). Neo-Marxist approaches were also important in analysing the relationship between class and race, and in the Marxist feminist tradition, class and gender. In Italy, *autonomism* (not to be confused with autonomous movements as defined in this book, although sharing some elements) produced another important strand of social movement theorizing and activism (e.g. the work of Antonio Negri and Franco 'Bifo' Berardi, see also Osterweil, 2013 and Chapter 3 on the *tute bianchi* and *desobbedienti* in the Global Justice Movement).

New Social Movements (NSMs)

The dominance of the Marxist framework in the European context ran into some serious challenges with the emergence of movements after 1965, in particular that it was difficult to explain them within the logic of a class-centred Marxist analysis. Society was changing, as was the nature of capitalism, and new theories were developing to characterize contemporary society that departed from a classic Marxist analysis, while still building on some of its central insights. One such framework was the concept of post-industrial society, developed by theorists such as Alain Touraine (1988), who argued that modern Western society was shifting from a mass industrial society to what he termed a post-industrial society, or programmed society. In the post-war period, economic and cultural changes transformed the social movement landscape. Rapid growth led to an increase in consumerism and broadened the educational base of Western society, leading to the emergence of a new middle class. Within a short period of time, a whole range of previously marginalized people, including students, women, young people, ethnic minorities, gays and lesbians, and the unemployed, emerged with a wide range of claims that transcended the traditional labour movement demands for the redistribution of material goods or changes to particular policies related to work and capitalism. These so-called 'new social movements' emerged in force in Western Europe in the 1960s and 1970s and included everything from new forms of political parties (left libertarian and new politics parties) to environmental, antinuclear, peace and anti-militarist, civil rights, women's rights, consumer rights, squatters, right to the city and alternative lifestyle, gay rights movements and more. These movements were difficult to explain within a Marxist framework. For one thing, it was difficult to classify their members in terms of a (subaltern) class location; for another, their primary concerns did not revolve around advancing particular economic or political interests (at least not exclusively or directly). What is more, the membership in these new movements and new parties departed from the traditional working class. Instead, they were made up of relatively young, predominantly middle class, highly educated and often professional people. Instead of focusing primarily on material grievances, they were expressing post-materialist values and seeking qualitative changes as much as quantitative ones. Women and minorities were demanding recognition and rights, environmental activists were demanding clean air and water, and anti-militarists and peace activists were demanding an end to wars that were taking place far from their homes. In light of these many salient characteristics, a new social movement (NSM) theoretical paradigm emerged whose key thinkers were Alain Touraine, Jürgen Habermas and Alberto Melucci.

Key components of New Social Movement theory

NSM theory encompasses a range of theorists offering different explanations and analytical concepts to understand the nature and newness of the movements that were flourishing in Western Europe. I won't treat each of these here in depth but will synthesize some of the key claims made across theorists. First, as noted above, the *context* in which these movements were emerging was new: Western European society was more pluralistic and more technologically advanced, and its citizens had greater access to education and welfare services and were experiencing an increasing economic prosperity, all of which, it is argued (Inglehart, 1997), led to a shift from materialist to post-materialist values that in turn shifted the motivations of protesters. This value change led to the emergence and salience of *new claims*. The actors participating in NSMs were seen not only as manifestations of the changes in social conditions but also as agents of change, who were challenging the status quo and contesting the way society was organized.

For Habermas (1981, 1987), for example, actors in NSMs were reacting against the increasing penetration of state and market logics into all arenas of life, in a process that he termed 'the colonization of the life world'. Autonomous actors engaging in participatory and non-hierarchical forms of organization were critiquing and challenging the bureaucratic institutionalized logic that upholds systems of power (economic, political and social). For Habermas, then, society's central struggles had shifted from conflicts over capital and labour (in industrial society) to struggles over the way dominant logics had penetrated into everyday life experiences. These struggles opened the possibility of an expanded and autonomous sphere for public debate, freed from the dominance and constraint of state and economic agendas.

Touraine (1988), agreed that these actors were also engaged in the central social conflict of the times, but he conceived of this somewhat differently from Habermas. For Touraine, this was a struggle over the control of historicity, which encompasses not only a challenge to the way dominant norms shape the social order but also a demand for social movement actors (and indeed people in general) to be able to take part in the decisions that shape their lives. *Historicity* for Touraine refers to the capacity to produce historical experience; actors on both sides of the central conflict were struggling to keep control of the capacity to make history and to shape its direction. At the heart of this struggle was no longer the struggle over material interests as in industrial society, but over cultural values and norms. This is in part because society's economic basis no longer rested primarily on material production but on the flow, use and control of information as the key to wealth accumulation and the maintenance of political dominance. NSM actors were reacting against the technocratic elites who increasingly dominate political decision-making in an information society. As society became more programmed and as information technologies and capitalism advanced, technocratic elites increasingly followed instrumental (e.g. efficiency, profit, econo-centrism) rather than substantive (e.g. 'the good society', the well-being of people and the environment self-determination and autonomy) rationalities.

For NSM theorists, *new ideas or ideologies* were also emerging: no longer were 'progress', increased prosperity or technological advancement seen as unproblematically beneficial. Rather activists in NSMs questioned the environmental and social costs of these advances and put forward alternative visions of the good society. What is more (and in line with arguments of the shift to post-materials values), no longer were social movements seen as made up of clearly defined groups mobilizing in their own interests (e.g. labour or sectorial interests) but rather looser configurations of actors mobilizing in the general interest and to achieve collective public goods. Because of the relationship between ideology, goals and organizational structure (recall the critique above of RMT), *new decentralized and participatory organizational forms* developed alongside but not replacing older more formal, 'vertical' or hierarchical forms. Protest forms also became more diverse and unconventional and strategies became less state-centric. The focus on convincing elites to make concessions gave way in many movement groups to anti-institutional and elite-challenging action, including direct action, expressive action and other important forms of social movement activity that don't involve protest, although they do express resistance, such as consciousness-raising, communal living and alternative lifestyles. In shifting their attention away from an exclusive focus on the state, NSMs became important sites for the symbolic production of meaning and producers of culture. The slogan 'the personal is political' in part highlights *the new centrality of everyday life and experience as sites of political struggle and contestation.* For example, feminists began denouncing domestic violence as a public political issue rather than a private domestic affair.

Beyond simply describing a 'new' empirical phenomena, NSM theories shift attention more broadly to the cultural stakes involved in mobilizing as well as broadening our view of social movements to encompass so much more than formally organized organizations that orient their action towards the state as a result of resources and rational strategic calculations. Instead, the theory directs our attention to culture, complexity, collective identity, historical processes and dynamic social relations, which include emotions and affect and not just rationality and interest. In his focus on historicity, Touraine directs our attention to social movement *agency* or the capacity for social movement actors 'to act upon themselves and to produce their futures and even their memory' (1981: 155). Although all of the NSM theorists were engaged in a critique of Marxist theory, in his search for a single central social struggle, Touraine was clearly still deeply wedded to Marxist categories of analysis. Touraine profoundly influenced his students Melucci and Castells (who developed the theory of the networked information society as a central part of his work).

Melucci (1980, 1994), although influenced by Touraine, did not see contemporary social movements as being characterized by a single central struggle. On the contrary, he stressed the complexity and diversity of movements and rejected the idea that we should conceive of them as unified 'things' or actors who stride across the political stage at given points in history. His work was also important in highlighting the importance of culture and sub-cultural milieus in generating social movement laboratories and in showing that these laboratories are often the sites of social and political innovation that can have impacts far beyond the social movements that develop them. His work was crucial in showing that much of what social movements do is not visible but takes place in 'subterranean' spaces. Much social movement scholarship suffers by not recognizing this fact. As he argues (1994: 107), such approaches suffer from 'a myopia of the visible that concentrates exclusively on the measurable features of collective action – that is, their relationships with political systems and their effects on policies – while it neglects or undervalues all those aspects of the action of movements that consist in the production of cultural codes [...]. In fact, when a movement publicly confronts the political apparatus on specific issues, it does so in the name of new cultural models created at a less noisy and less easily measurable level of hidden action'. What Melucci is pointing to here is that, by the time the public, opponents, media and power holders see visible protest, this is most often the result of long periods of invisible work 'behind the scenes' during which social movement actors are working out their own understandings of the issues and problems they want to change and the challenges and opportunities they face (see the distinction between latent and visible action above). Ethnographic work based on close contact with and participation in social movements has contributed a wealth of research that allows scholars to understand the cultural and subcultural processes that underlie mobilization and offer an inside look at what social movement actors do when they are 'backstage' and out of public view (see e.g. Juris, 2008; Flesher Fominaya, 2010a, 2010b; Maeckelbergh, 2009).

NSM theorists, then, to different degrees, saw new contexts leading to new values (post-materialist), new central struggles (against the dominant social logics, elite-challenging, oriented around culture), new movement actors, new ideas and ideologies, new protest and organizational forms, new mobilized identities, new targets or interlocutors (no longer state-centric), new arenas of mobilization (the personal everyday as well as the public) and new potentialities and outcomes (a revolutionary transformation of society, an expanded and autonomous public sphere).

NSM theory has been subjected to a number of important critiques (Calhoun, 1993; Pichardo, 1997; Tucker, 1991). One major critique is that many of the elements used to characterize the 'newness' of these movements can be found in earlier movements, including the labour movement, which in the NSM framework is taken as the 'old' movement against which the new is contrasted. For example, workers engaged in struggling against the bourgeoisie and overturning capitalism were not just seeking narrow material self-interests but rather mobilizing on behalf of the collective good (from their ideological perspective since for Marx capitalists are also suffering from alienation from their species-being or true essence even if they are not suffering from exploitation). In so doing, labour movement activists were also engaged in knowledge production and cultural and symbolic forms of protest. Critics argue that NSM characterization of the labour movements in these narrow terms is reductionist and fails to capture its full experience. Likewise, the women's movements for suffrage and for women's rights had engaged in many forms of expressive action and direct action as well as constantly challenging the very definition of womanhood through their unconventional protest forms (including chaining themselves to fences, hunger strikes, disrupting Parliament and creating alternative media) long before the advent of 'new' social movements. Critics also argue that identity has been a key feature of movements for centuries. Another valid critique emerged in light of the anti-corporate globalization movement (see Chapter 3) that emerged in the 1990s, which was that struggles over capitalism did not disappear just because other issues were coming to the fore. As Edwards (2004: 114) argues in an evaluation of Habermas on New Social Movements, while 'system-life world conflicts may spark public-sphere generating movements, these movements do not have to be distinct from capital-labour struggles'.

As we will see throughout this book, 'new' expressions of cultural and identity-based movements do not have to be divorced from conflict over capitalism and labour. The Global Justice Movement (Chapter 3), mobilizations around the precariat (Chapter 4) and contemporary anti-austerity movements (Chapter 7) are just three examples. This critique points to a larger issue, which is the danger of restricting theorizing about movements to particular historical periods of time. Such an approach might usefully describe and analyse a particular historical period but might limit the theory's applicability to other (later) historical periods. On the other hand, theorists can theorize only about what they know and can research, not about what may or may not happen in the future.

Despite these valid criticisms, there is no denying that the period in Western Europe and elsewhere from the early 1960s on was characterized by an explosion of unconventional expressive movements that did represent a qualitative and quantitative break with what had come before as well as emerging in a transformed socioeconomic and political context, most notably the shift to a networked information society. Frankly, most of these critiques are missing the much more important contribution of NSM theory, which is to pay attention to elements that may well have been present in previous social movements but were notably absent in social movement *scholarship*. In addition, NSM theory enables us to retain some of the valuable contributions of Marxist theory (the emphasis on agency, consciousness, power and inequality and the way capitalism shapes all of these, for example) while developing our theoretical insights more fully and adapting them to modern society. One of the most important and influential contributions in NSM theory comes from Melucci (1980, 1988, 1989a, 1989b, 1995a, 1995b, 1996) and his understanding of collective identity processes in social movements.

Collective Identity

'What is it that allows actors to identify themselves and each other as members of a social movement? How does a set of individuals become a collective entity we can identify and name as a social movement? How is cohesion and commitment to a movement or movement group sustained over time?' (Flesher Fominaya, 2010a: 393). Much scholarship on the emergence of social movements and their continuity over time has focused on structural, rationalistic and goal-driven explanations, such as resource mobilization theory (Gamson, 1990; McCarthy and Zald, 1973), political process models, (McAdam, 1982; Tarrow, 1989), rational choice models (cost-benefit analysis) and ideologically based explanations. But these approaches leave out important social-psychological, emotional and cultural factors. Instead, a body of work centred on the concept of *collective identity* has yielded a rich trove of insights into social movement cohesion.

What exactly is collective identity? The concept is notoriously 'slippery', and there is no consensual definition (Snow, 2001). Polletta and Jasper (2001) locate collective identity within the individual, defining it as 'an individual's cognitive, moral and emotional connection with a broader community, category, practice, or institution' (p. 285), but it is more often understood as emerging through interaction. In *Feminist Generations*, Whittier (1995: 16) defines collective identity as located 'in action and interaction-observable phenomena rather than in individual self-conceptions, attitudes or beliefs'. Taylor and Whittier (1992: 105) define collective identity as 'the shared definition of a group that derives from members' common interests, experiences and solidarity' (p. 105). All of these definitions draw in part on the work of Melucci (1980, 1988, 1989a, 1989b, 1995a, 1995b, 1996), who developed the most systematic, comprehensive and influential theory of collective identity in social movements.

In a European context of declining class-based movements, Melucci was attempting to understand what was replacing class consciousness as NSMs – whose collective identity could not be explained by shared class position – were emerging. Melucci wanted to understand how it is that a movement becomes a movement in the first place, and he did not believe that collective identities were already formed and available to be mobilized. He therefore sought to understand the relationship between individual beliefs and meanings and collective action by exploring the dynamic process through which actors negotiate, understand and construct their action through shared repeated interaction. He argued that activists develop collective identity through a process that involves developing a shared understanding about what the goals, means and field of action are and should be. Activists do this over time by interacting through particular shared rituals, practices, language and artefacts. In so doing, they develop a shared cognitive framework, but not one that is necessarily unified or coherent, and which can encompass multiple priorities, beliefs and even conflict and contradictions. This means that 'actors do not necessarily have to be in complete agreement on ideologies, beliefs, interests, or goals in order to come together and generate collective action, an assertion that counters more structural understandings of what brings and keeps movement actors together (the concept of class consciousness in the Marxist tradition, for example)' (Flesher Fominaya, 2010a: 395). Collective identity is generated through a network of active relationships in which activists distinguish 'us' from 'them', and the emotional connection between people is a vital part of that. Collective identity can be reinforced through shared experiences of risk, fear, joy and hope and through conflict with opponents.

The concept of collective identity can be fruitfully used to study movements of all kinds, independently of their ideological orientations or organizational forms. Collective identity theory illuminates key processes that sustain or weaken movements over time and contributes to a greater understanding of the cultural and emotional dynamics of mobilization. By showing how important boundary work is (the process through which activists determine the difference between 'us' and 'them'), it helps explain why groups that seem to be natural allies (for example, groups that share a commitment to the same issue or goal) can nevertheless have problems building alliances. At the same time, highly elastic collective identities (collective identities with loose requirements for participation that encompass a very wide range of people) can have the effect of facilitating alliances between groups that might not appear to have much in common, as in the Global Justice Movement (see Chapter 3). For a fuller discussion of the concept and its application in social movement studies, see Flesher Fominaya (2010a, 2019).

Outcomes, success and failure: How and why do social movements matter?

How and why do social movement matter? Starting with the most spectacular consequences of social movements, we can see that revolutionary movements can cause not only the dissolution of states and political regimes but also the emergence of new ones. Mobilizations in Eastern Europe in the 1980s, for example, certainly contributed to bringing down the Berlin Wall in 1989 and the subsequent dissolution of the Soviet Union and its control over satellite countries in the Soviet bloc.

Many scholars studying the outcomes of social movements have focused on the ability of movements to bring about specific *policy changes* within nation-states (Giugni, 2008). These studies have tended to focus on more institutionalized movements and are also driven by a strong emphasis on the determination of movement success or failure. Focusing on policy outcomes is attractive not only because it can be demonstrated or measured (albeit not without important methodological problems) but also because it enables scholars to operate with a clear definition of success: for example, if the movement was advocating for a particular policy (e.g. votes for women) and that policy is implemented, the movement can be said to be successful.

Giugni (2008) argues that the focus on policy outcomes reflects a dominant US social movement research paradigm that emphasizes institutional social movement organizations and political process models that focus on the relationship between social movements and the state. The other reason is that focusing on policy changes is methodologically appealing because they are more easily measurable than other social movement outcomes, such as broad cultural change. However, Giugni points out that in general it is very difficult to measure outcomes because of methodological difficulties. This is partly because it is hard to tell what impact movements have, as opposed to other actors or forces. For example, when we try to draw a link between protest in Eastern Europe in the 1980s and the fall of Eastern European governments, it is hard to disentangle the effects of the protests themselves versus, for example, the importance of internal disputes between political leaders, the pressure of the Soviet Union, the impact of Gorbachev's *perestroika* initiative and so on. Giugni argues that it is also difficult to establish outcomes because movements can have unintended impacts, impacts that persist over time or are felt many years later.

Attribution of success and failure to entire movements is also tricky because it treats a social movement as a coherent unified actor, whereas, in reality, movements are complex dynamic entities made up of multiple groups and actors, some of which may be 'successful' and others which may be less so. Movements can also have impacts on different arenas. One influential formulation is that of William Gamson in 'The Strategy of Social Protest' (Gamson, 1990 [1975]). Here, Gamson delineates the factors most likely to lead to a challenger group's success:

> 'A centralized, bureaucratic group that escapes factional splits is highly likely to be successful; so in fact is a decentralized, bureaucratic group that escapes factionalism, but it is less likely to escape than its centralized counterpart. A decentralized, non-bureaucratic group that experiences factionalism is doomed to failure; but, if it somehow manages to escape factionalism, it still has a modest possibility of success. Its chances of escaping a split are considerably enhanced if it has a centralized power structure' (p. 108).

Gamson's findings indicate then that the three factors most likely to contribute to success are centralized power, bureaucratic organization and ideological convergence (the absence of factionalism). Although Gamson's formulation undoubtedly holds true for many groups engaging in collective action (but see (Goldstone, 1980 for a critique and Edwards, 2014: 80 for a summary of the debate), my own work (e.g. Flesher Fominaya, 1999, 2010a, 2010b) shows that it cannot explain the success of autonomous movements (see Chapter 3) that have neither a centralized power structure, a bureaucratic organization nor ideological unity. Recall too Gerlach and Hine's argument that 'segmentary, polycentric and networked organization was more adapted to the task of challenging and changing society and culture than was centralized organization' (Gerlach, 2001: 290).

Gamson is one of the scholars to look most closely at the political consequences of social movements. Gamson (1990) points to two important political outcomes for social movements: the first is when authorities recognize social movements as *legitimate actors*, and the second is when social movements gain *new advantages* for the movement or group on behalf of which they mobilize.

Changes in policy are only one way that social movements effect social change and, indeed, not all social movements are interested in pursuing particular policy outcomes. Another area of social movement impact is in the *cultural arena*. As I discussed above, prefigurative social movements attempt to embody through practice an alternative vision of society. For these types of movements, it would make little sense to evaluate their success or failure in terms of policy outcomes. In a discussion of the cultural impact of movements and its relation to policy, Meyer (1999: 185–6) uses the example of the US Civil Rights movement to show how formal government policy change was only one parameter of movement impact and mobilization: activists sought to change attitudes about racial integration and brought together symbols from dominant US culture, such as the flag and the

Constitution, and combined them with African-American cultural forms, such as church spirituals, putting them in the service of political goals. Meyer points out that 'the cultural effects of movements, though often neglected by analysts, are often longer lasting and farther reaching than the more narrow short-term policy victories and defeats' (1999: 186).

Social movements have multiple impacts on society, and the attribution of success and failure is problematic when it focuses on only one aspect of movement outcome. Since the definition of success also very much depends on goals and expectations, the evaluation of success is likely to vary from activist to activist and between movement participants and outside observers, including scholars (see Flesher Fominaya, 2010b). For example, second-wave feminist movements mobilized and lobbied for specific changes in the law, such as the right to an abortion or the equal rights amendment to the US Constitution. While they succeeded in the former in at least some states and nations, the US women's movement failed in the latter. Nevertheless, women's movements have done much more than lobby for changes in government policy. Feminist movements have raised awareness of issues such as rape and violence, economic equity issues, drastic inequalities in political representation between men and women, the need for family-friendly policies in the workplace and many more issues. Feminist movements around the world have had an impact on public consciousness and changes in cultural values (Gelb and Hart, 1999). They have also given rise to institutions of their own such as rape crisis centres, women's refuges, women's studies centres, feminist bookshops and more.

The success or failure of the feminist movement (and many movements) can also be seen as temporally contingent because counter-movements emerge to erode or reverse the gains that have been made. For example, in 2012, many of the gains made by the US women's movement were attacked in the Senate by conservative politicians who want to deny women's right to birth control and abortion. This spurred feminist activists to mobilize to preserve the gains made by previous movement waves. In 2016, Donald Trump, an openly misogynistic candidate with numerous allegations of sexual harassment against him and extremely regressive policies on women's sexual freedom and autonomy, was elected president of the United States. In 2017, wearing 'Pussyhats' in reference to Trump's infamous comment about how when he meets beautiful women he feels able to 'grab them by their pussies' (Jacobs *et al.*, 2016), millions of women marched on Washington, DC to 'stand together in solidarity with our partners and children for the protection of our rights, our safety, our health, and our families' (Women's March Manifesto, 2017). The women behind the pussyhat concept, Krista Suh and Jayna Zweiman, saw it as both a denunciation of Trump's sexism and a positive re-appropriation of the word 'pussy' (Reimel and Arneson, 2017). An image of an elderly woman supported by her wheelchair and carrying a sign that read 'I can't believe I still have to protest this shit' sums up well the feeling many women's rights activists have at the two-steps-forward, one-step-back trajectory of the women's movements despite some significant gains.

Movement success and failure can also co-exist in a paradoxical relationship. Rucht (1999: 205) has drawn attention to what he calls the paradox of environmental movements:

> on the one hand, the brief history of the environmental movement can be read as an amazing success story. This success becomes apparent when we consider the movement's growth and consolidation, its role as an agenda setter, its impact on individual attitudes and behavior, and its contribution to the establishment of a new polity and a new industrial sector. On the other hand, however, the movement has been largely unsuccessful in halting environmental deterioration.

This quote highlights the multiple goals and different scope of impact any given movement can have, making single or total attributions of success or failure problematic.

Social movements can affect government policy, public opinion and culture, but they also can have an impact on institutions (such as corporations), although not always in the way that they intended. To continue with the example of the environmental movement, although the movement has had an important positive impact on heightening awareness of issues of corporate environmental destruction, it is also true that many corporations have responded by *greenwashing* or whitewashing rather than actually significantly altering their environmentally damaging corporate practices. Many global corporations spend millions in making their corporate image more palatable to a socially conscious public while pursuing legal actions against the activists who raised public awareness in the first place (Rowell, 1996).

In the McLibel case, the McDonald corporation sued two activists in London for libel after they alleged their food was unhealthy and their packaging environmentally damaging (see Vidal, 1997). Rowell (1996) extensively documents retaliation against environmental activists around the world, including the torture and murder of activists and whistleblowers. However, green backlash does not have to go to such extremes to be effective: counter-movements and their political allies can effectively use media to counter the claims made by social movements. Rowell (1996: ch. 5) highlights a number of tactics, including labelling environmentalists communists, religious fanatics, Nazis, elitists, extremists or 'anti-American', arguing that environmentalists are out to kill jobs, destroy the economy or destroy capitalism or that the counter-movement (or corporation or anti-environmental organization) itself represents the 'true' environmental movement. Sklair (1997: 526) argues that 'There is a good deal of agreement among scholars that... big business often creates "front" organizations to propagate its messages. So, many apparently straightforward "civic associations" which also have many of the characteristics of social movements are largely run by and often largely funded by the corporate elite'. As this discussion shows, it is clear that social movements do not only resist, they also face resistance and repression

(Della Porta and Reiter, 1998; Della Porta *et al.*, 2006; Wood, 2007; Flesher Fominaya and Wood, 2011).

Social movements do not act in a vacuum but in a dynamic interaction with other social actors and their activities can *shift the parameters of public debate*. Della Porta (1999: 94) has shown how in Italy and Germany the relationship between protesters and police has transformed debate about democracy and the rights of demonstrators through a complex process of evolution whereby the first wave of protest polarized public opinion, and large segments of the public viewed protesters in a negative light but, during following waves of protest, symbolic interactions between police and protesters brought about 'a new "basic" consensus on a new definition of protest rights and on how to handle them'. In both countries, whereas 'peaceful' protest was increasingly seen as part of normal politics and the democratic process, 'violent' protest was increasingly criminalized.

As I discussed above, scholars such as Eyerman and Jamison (1991), Cox and Flesher Fominaya (2009), Wainwright (1994) and others have highlighted the importance of social movements as knowledge-producers who *generate important knowledge* about the world and how to change it. Other scholars such as McAdam (1999) have highlighted the *biographical impact* of social movements on the activists who participated in them, and social movement activity can even *transform the urban landscape* in enduring ways, such as when countercultural 'hippies' congregated in the Haight Ashbury neighbourhood of San Francisco in the 1960s and 1970s (an area that continues to be a tourist destination) or when the lesbian, gay, bisexual and transgender movement in San Francisco draws the migration of gays and lesbians to the city to live, transforming the city in important ways.

Finally, as I will discuss more at length in the next chapter, social movements have effects on *other* social movements, both in a specific period of time, as social movements in one place trigger or inspire social protest in other areas, and over time, through the historical transmission of memories, ideas, ideologies, identities and practices from one movement's generation to the next.

Although it is easy to dismiss the outcomes or achievements of social movements once their period of mobilization has waned, the following quote from Hayden (2012) illustrates just how much social movements can achieve in a short period of time:

> The '60s movements stumbled to an end largely because we'd won the major reforms that were demanded: the 1964 and 1965 civil and voting rights laws, the end of the draft and the Vietnam War, passage of the War Powers Resolution and the Freedom of Information Act, Nixon's environmental laws, amnesty for war resisters, two presidents forced from office, the 18-year-old vote, union recognition of public employees and farmworkers, disability rights, the decline of censorship, the emergence of gays and lesbians from a shadow existence ... Perhaps never in US history had so many changes occurred in so short a time, all driven by the vibrancy of participatory democracy.

Today, many of these gains, such as the vote for 18-year-olds or restrictions on censorship, are largely taken for granted and many people do not even associate them with the 1960s movements that achieved them.

Conclusion

Although it provides an orientation to central questions and concepts, this brief discussion only scratches the surface of the vast and rich literature in the field of social movement studies. Jasper (2010: 965) argues that the field of contemporary social movements studies is characterized by an overall trend (which he endorses) consisting of 'a bracketing of big structures in favor of a concern for the micro-foundations of social and political action' in which 'modest theorizing, interpretive and action-oriented' is coming to the fore. This attention to the micro-foundations, however, can and I think should be nourished by social theory more broadly. Social movement scholarship doesn't only have to draw on 'social movement theories'; it can and does draw on a wide range of fruitful social theories that give us purchase on the dynamics of mobilization and social movements. Indeed, there would be no social movement theory without social theory, and theoretical developments such as queer theory, post-colonial studies, and media and communications theory continue to enrich and expand the field. That is the approach I take in this book and it reflects my understanding of the state of contemporary social movement scholarship. Whereas Jasper (2010: 974) laments the fragmentation under way as the field diverges into sub-specialties, I see an increasing dialogue across disciplines and regions, although of course there is still a long way to go. I am wary of synthesis but agree that theoretical debate is fruitful and that much can be learned from tackling research questions by casting our nets wide across the existing literature. Thinking that anything goes, though, would be a mistake. There is much to learn from the concerted effort of scholars who have devoted themselves to understanding how movements work, why people continue to fight for a better world (or hold on to the old one) despite significant barriers and what activists are seeking to change or preserve. Ignoring the existing literature (warts and all) would be as foolish as refusing to continue to critique, improve and refine our understandings.

The world we inhabit today has been profoundly shaped by social movements, from abolitionist movements seeking to put an end to slavery in the eighteenth and nineteenth centuries, to movements that have achieved rights for women around the world, to environmental movements that have changed the way we think and interact with the natural environment, to fundamentalist movements that seek to limit the freedom and autonomy of particular groups of people around the world or to conserve their traditional ways of life in the face of the forces of modernity.

2 GLOBALIZATION AND SOCIAL MOVEMENTS

In this chapter, I first examine the inter-relationships between social movements and globalization processes, illustrating with empirical examples. I then distinguish between transnational and global social movements and discuss transnational-national and local linkages. Finally, I discuss social movement diffusion processes, looking at some of the specific ways that social movements 'spread' across borders and time in a globalized world.

The term 'globalization' encompasses a series of features: an objective 'compression of the world', driven by the expansion of international financial flows, international trade and increased international investment of transnational corporations (TNCs) and banks, made possible by advances in information and transportation technologies; the emergence and acceleration of inter-related systems of economic, political, cultural, technological and social institutions, processes and hierarchies on a global scale; and the increased impact and global reach of these processes and people's increased awareness of them. The subjective experience of these transformations, including the recognition of global interdependence, influences political responses to them, including that of social movements. The transformation of awareness of risk, for example, can also heighten concerns about the consequences of globalization, which can prompt collective action by social movements. Communication, itself facilitated by globalization processes, fosters reflexivity about the risks and negative consequences of globalization or, conversely, the opportunities for global transformation it offers. This communication and reflexivity then stimulate transnational collective action, which can then affect globalization processes, such as the creation of new international non-governmental organizations (INGOs), the adoption of UN resolutions or the creation of new global governance structures such as the International Court of Justice.

Globalization processes fuel the development of social movements, which in turn respond to and shape the development of globalization. Advances in communication and transportation technologies have made cross-border communication and travel easier and cheaper than ever before. This has facilitated the establishment of interconnections between activists in different parts of the world. At the same time, globalization processes have generated a new set of economic, social, political and cultural problems but also an increased awareness of them. This has prompted social movements to mobilize across borders in a coordinated attempt to resist the negative effects of some globalization processes and to develop new transnational alliances to try to create positive global change.

Inter-relationships between globalization processes and social movements

Globalization theorists (Robertson, 1992; Appadurai, 1996; Castells, 2004; Wallerstein, 2011; Giddens, 2011; Beck, 1992) highlight a range of economic, social, cultural, political and technological processes. In this section, I survey and distinguish conceptually between what are in fact inter-related and overlapping processes.

Economic neoliberal globalization

Nelson Mandela (2000) stated in his address on receiving the Freedom Award from the National Civil Rights Museum, 'Where globalization means, as it so often does, that the rich and powerful now have new means to further enrich and empower themselves at the cost of the poorer and weaker, we have a responsibility to protest in the name of universal freedom.' This sentiment captures well the underlying motivation of much social movement activity in the area of economic globalization. I treat economic neoliberal globalization at some length because of its relevance for many of the movements that will be discussed in subsequent chapters.

Not all activists denoted as anti-globalization, or even anti-capitalist, are against capitalism *per se* (although certainly many are), and almost no 'anti-globalization' activists are against globalization *per se*: many embrace an internationalist or cosmopolitan ideal, embrace cultural diversity as a result of migration and cultural exchange and celebrate other globalization processes such as the spread of information and communication technologies (ICTs). What most contest are the negative effects of globalized neoliberal capitalism.

It is no coincidence that so many social movements have emerged and responded to neoliberal globalization. Although global capitalism has been around for centuries, neoliberalism is a relatively recent form of capitalist globalization whose scope and depth are the result of a specific set of ideologies, policies and actions initially put in place by political and economic leaders with a strong belief in neoliberalism. While there are debates on the precise meaning of the term 'neoliberalism', most accounts highlight some central tenets. Harvey (2011: 2) defines neoliberalism as 'a theory of political economic practices that proposes that human well-being can best be advanced by liberating individual entrepreneurial freedoms and skills within an institutional framework characterized by strong private property rights, free markets and free trade'. Mirowski (2009) also highlights (among other central features) the ideas that capital has a natural right to flow across borders (whereas labour does not) and that 'pronounced inequality of economic resources and political rights ... [is] a necessary functional characteristic of their ideal market system'. From the neoliberal perspective, the state's role is primarily to guarantee the free flow of capital, protect private property rights and liberate the powers of finance to ensure the well-being of the largest number of people. Not only should the state use police, military and legal structures to guarantee free markets, but it should also actively open markets in areas where they might not yet exist (e.g. education, health, water, environmental pollution) (Harvey, 2011: 2). 'Freedom' is a central value espoused by neoliberalism (Wainwright, 1994; Mirowski, 2009; Harvey, 2011). Yet, as Mirowski (2009) argues, the neoliberal understanding of freedom is conceived not as the realization of political cultural or human aspirations but, rather, envisions free individuals as 'autonomous self-governed individuals' who are rational and self-interested and seek to improve their own situation through exchange in the market. The neoliberal state is concerned first and foremost with 'freedom' as a means of embodying the interests of private property owners, businesses, multinational corporations and financial capital (Harvey, 2011: 7).

Harvey (2011) shows how neoliberalism went from being a minority view in economic and political circles until the economic crisis of the 1970s. After World War II, and up to that point, many states of diverse forms (e.g. social democratic, liberal, Christian democratic) had as their central goals 'full employment, economic growth and the welfare of its citizens and that state power should be freely deployed, alongside of or, if necessary, intervening in or even substituting for market processes to achieve these ends' (Harvey, 2011: 10).

The historical origins of neoliberal dominance have followed different paths in different countries, yet so great has the expansion of neoliberal thought been over the past decades that Anderson (2000: 3) characterized the 1990s as being defined primarily by 'the virtually uncontested consolidation, and universal diffusion of neo-liberalism'.

The origins of neoliberalism, despite now being seen as a relatively coherent set of fundamental principles, reside in a diverse range of philosophies and ideas that have consolidated over time into a common agenda and vision (Plehwe, 2009). This process was by no means spontaneous but was the result of the efforts of numerous political and economic actors from around the world. Plehwe (2009) shows that the rise of neoliberalism was the result of concerted collective action by a global society of intellectuals and political actors united by the common cause of neoliberalism, originally developed as a means to combat socialism and to provide an alternative to classical liberalism. He argues that neoliberalism must be understood primarily as 'a historical thought collective of increasingly global proportions' (Plehwe, 2009: 4). He points to the work of the influential Mont Pélerin Society, founded over 60 years ago, an organization with some 1000 members connected to a global network of neoliberal think tanks and organized under the umbrella of such foundations as the Atlas Economic Research Foundation. Through conferences and networking, members exchange political and philosophical ideas designed to promote a common neoliberal agenda. They engage in a sort of division of labour whereby intellectuals produce journal articles, survey data, book reviews, interviews, high-profile speeches and so on to influence targeted audiences and select journalists, corporate leaders and politicians work to place neoliberal ideas onto the public and political agenda and to keep them there.

Harvey (2011) argues that although neoliberals had been occupying positions of influence in think tanks and other institutions during the 1970s, the decisive turning point came in 1979, when Margaret Thatcher came to power in the UK, and in 1981, when Ronald Reagan became president of the United States. Under their leadership, their respective states undertook radical economic reforms designed to put neoliberal principles into practice. Deregulation, privatization, dramatically reducing taxes for corporations and the wealthy, reductions in labour union power and a sharp cutting back on social welfare provisions were put into place as the means to cure the financial woes plaguing the US and the UK (Harvey, 2011). Other nations (such as Germany, Italy and France) reversed social democracy policies and pursued a similar agenda (Anderson, 2000). This was accompanied by a staunch and relentless advocacy for the superiority and necessity of neoliberalism as the only viable economic alternative (Mirowski, 2009; Plehwe, 2009; Harvey, 2011).

Despite significant contestation from politicians, organized labour and social movements, neoliberalism became the dominant economic model across the globe and many people began to see it as a natural 'common-sense' political economic framework (for more on dominant ideologies, see Chapter 4). The lifting of controls and regulation on multinational corporations and international financial institutions in the areas of labour rights and environmental protection ushered in a new form of global capitalism with important increases in exploitative labour practices, resource extraction and environmental dumping. It not only increased inequalities and hardship for millions of people around the world (Stiglitz, 2000; Weller et al., 2001) but also benefitted millions of middle-class people in emerging market economies. In countries such as the US and the UK, financial expansion was accompanied by deindustrialization.

This process of neoliberal globalization was accompanied by a global political agenda of (selective) democracy promotion by Western political leaders. Robinson (1996) argues that the promotion of democracy around the world by neoliberal elites can be seen as a sort of strategy whereby states' power is legitimized so as to prevent the development of more radical political alternatives. Proponents of neoliberal capitalist globalization would argue that the spread of democracy prevents the development of authoritarian and dictatorial regimes. Yet, it is also true that many authoritarian regimes have been actively supported by Western democratic governments when it suits their political and economic interests, such as the support for Pinochet in Chile, for the Shah of Iran (Barkawi and Laffey, 1999; Buckley, 2006; Whitehead, 2009), or US and European Union (EU) long-standing support for Tunisian President Ben Ali's brutal regime (see Chapter 7). The relation between neoliberal capitalist globalization and democratization is therefore far from straightforward.

Contrary to criticisms that neoliberalism has failed to deliver on its promise to increase global wealth and decrease economic inequalities between the global North and the global South, some proponents of neoliberal capitalist globalization point to the success stories of the so-called BRIC countries (Brazil, Russia, India and China) as evidence that neoliberal globalization really does work. However, World Bank economist Milanovic (2005) has shown that the apparent convergence between the global South and the global North in terms of economic development is primarily due to the spectacular economic growth of China and India over recent decades. His data and analysis, which span decades and include most countries of the world, throw into question the argument that globalization works to lessen global inequalities. While by no means arguing that neoliberal economic globalization has not benefited anyone, Milanovic's work (2012) shows who has actually benefited globally. Essentially, the primary beneficiaries or 'winners' of the past two decades of globalization have been, first, the very rich, representing the top 1 per cent of global income, who have seen their real income rise by more than 60 per cent over this period (1988–2008); second, the middle classes of the emerging market economies (China, India, Indonesia, Brazil and Egypt), who have seen the *greatest* increases: '80% real increase at the median itself and some 70% around it These two groups – the global top 1% and the middle classes of the emerging market economies – are indeed the main winners of globalization' (Milanovic, 2012: 12).

Other studies have shown a trend in increasing global income inequality over the past decades even among the most prosperous nations. The Organisation for Economic Co-operation and Development (OECD) – whose 34 members encompass, primarily, 'First World' nations in Europe; the US, Canada, Australia, New Zealand, Japan, Korea, Chile and Mexico – regularly report on income inequality among member states.

Their 2019 report stated that 'The gap between the average income of the richest 10% and the poorest 10% of the population was 9.3 to 1 on average across OECD countries in 2016. The gap ranged from 5.2 to 1 in the Czech Republic and Slovenia to almost four times larger in Chile and Mexico (20 to 1). Over the past three decades, the gap between the rich and poor has widened in the large majority of OECD countries. Household wealth is much more unequally distributed than income. On average, households in the top 10% of the wealth distribution own more than half (52%) of all total household wealth, and as much as 79% in the United States'.

Contesting neoliberal capitalist globalization

Neoliberal globalization has produced complex and uneven effects across the globe. Consequently, the response from social movements has been varied and widespread. If proponents of neoliberalism point to the 'winners' of economic globalization, critics, including many social movements, point to the losers. Social movements of many kinds have emerged to resist neoliberal global capitalism, from anti-corporate movements in the US (Starr, 2000), international labour movements to peasant movements. One peasant movement is *Via Campesina*, which emerged in 1993 as a network of small farmers and farm worker organizations from 56 different countries, whose goal was to 'develop solidarity and unity among small farmer organizations in order to promote gender parity and social justice in their economic relations; the preservation of land, water, fees and other natural resources in food sovereignty; [and] sustainable agricultural production based on small and medium-sized producers' (Tilly and Wood, 2015: 107). They organize 'global days of action' every year to 'globalize the struggle against injustice and neoliberalism worldwide' (Tilly and Wood, 2015: 107). This includes issues such as peasant rights, women's rights, and fighting climate change (https://viacampesina.org).

In the US, many of the key anti-neoliberal mobilizations have focused on the exploitative labour practices of multinational corporations. During the 1990s, university students engaged in campus campaigns to shed light on the appalling conditions of sweatshop labour. The term 'sweatshop' refers to manufacturing characterized by poor working conditions, low wages, long hours and often child labour. Student activists targeted corporations such as Nike, GAP, Levi's and other fashionable brands in the United Students Against Sweatshops movement. Activists made links between free trade agreements and the lack of regulation of exploitative labour practices and the connection between labour in the global South that produced items for the global North. This awareness led to consumer boycott campaigns against highly visible corporations as a means of raising awareness and pressuring them to reform their labour practices (Klein, 1999). Workers in the global North also protest against the relocation of factories and attendant job losses.

Another key area of protest has been directed against the policies of International Financial Institutions (IFIs) such as the International Monetary Fund (IMF) which routinely impose austerity measures as a condition of loans to nations facing financial crises. Austerity programmes imposed by organizations such as the IMF on nation-states crippled by debt burdens have been felt most intensely by the most vulnerable in society, who suffer the consequences of cuts in social welfare, health and education. These effects have been felt the deepest in developing countries, where social movements have developed to resist the effects of neoliberal capitalist globalization (Walton and Seddon, 1994). They often perceive global capitalism as a form of 'Western imperialism' that does not bring significant benefits to the people but, rather, increases poverty (Ayres, 2004). When Eastern Europe experienced the collapse of the Communist bloc in the 1990s, they too became subject to IMF structural adjustments programmes.

Social movements in the global South have emerged to respond to and reject the many negative consequences of the shift to neoliberalism their countries have experienced since the 1980s. Movements against neoliberal capitalist globalization in the global South operate on a 'postcolonial terrain' that 'came into being with the advent of decolonization of the global South, in which dominant and subaltern groups are engaged in conflictual encounters over the forms, directions and meanings of development' (Motta and Nilsen, 2011: 3). The transition from developmentalism to neoliberalism intensified with the onset of the international debt crisis in the early 1980s. When interest rates increased in the late 1970s and early 1980s, this had a particularly pronounced adverse effect on the global South. The skyrocketing costs of servicing debts coupled with the decline in the demand for exports from the South meant that many countries could no longer meet their debt interest payment obligations, nor borrow additional money to meet their debt obligations, and some, such as Mexico in 1982, defaulted on their debts. In response to the international debt crisis, the World Bank and the IMF implemented 'Structural Adjustment Programs' in which they allowed states in the global South to have access to debt rescheduling and new loans in exchange for the implementation of a series of neoliberal policies that significantly restructured their economies. These included measures such as cutting public expenditures, deregulating prices and commodity markets through the removal of subsidies and reducing wages as well as privatizing utilities and public sector companies. In light of these deep neoliberal reforms, many social actors protested against the dismantling of rights and entitlements and social guarantees as well as the rising costs of basic food and commodity prices. Many countries that had undergone structural adjustment programs witnessed austerity protests or riots against the IMF. These protests encompassed a wide range of actors, including unionised workers, the unemployed, peasants, shanty town dwellers, students, small business owners and public employees. But as Motta and Nilsen (2011: 13) point out, these movements weren't simply reclaiming past rights and benefits or 'reclaiming the moral economy of developmentalism and state orientated social transformation' but also imagining new forms of socio-economic organization and drawing on a range of mobilizing traditions to do so (which shaped these movements very differently across different national and local contexts). In Latin America, for example, in some contexts, traditional labour movements were brought together with liberation theology and popular education movements. In others, indigenous movements played an important role. These different traditions influenced the political subjectivity (self-conception) and internal organizing forms of movements, encompassing in some cases more decentralized forms of organization and active processes of popular education and collective knowledge production that sought to draw on and empower subjugated and subaltern knowledges (see e.g. Motta's discussion of Venezuela and Sitrin's discussion of Argentina in Motta and Nilsen, 2011). While Latin America witnessed the most visible movements in the 1990s, by the late 1990s and early 2000s strong movements against neoliberal capitalist globalization had emerged in the Southeast Asia, India, South Africa and the Middle East among other regions of the global South (Motta and Nilsen, 2011: 1). International campaigns against neoliberal capitalism have also focused on the human cost of foreign debt on developing countries that divest meagre resources from welfare programmes to pay interest on loans.

As discussed in Chapter 7, anti-austerity protests have also emerged in developed countries, where governments have made cuts to social welfare and rolled back labour protection legislation in response to austerity measures imposed by IFIs as a result of the global financial crisis that started in 2008. While protesters do target their national governments and hold them responsible for such measures, they are also critiquing them for their active participation in the global financial crisis and failure to regulate the financial markets.

Institutional globalization

As the discussion of the IMF above shows, economic globalization is supported by a process of institutional globalization or the existence of transnational organizational infrastructures that support and foster globalization processes. In addition to the IMF, organizations such as the World Bank (WB) and the World Trade Organization (WTO) are key actors in the expansion of economic globalization. Institutional globalization, however, supports numerous processes of globalization. For example, the World Health Organization (WHO) provides an institutional infrastructure that shapes and develops certain health standards, health provision and health research around the world. The United Nations, for its part, is an intergovernmental organization tasked with promoting international cooperation and creating and maintaining international order. NATO, or the North Atlantic Treaty Organization, also called the North Atlantic Alliance, is an intergovernmental military organization dedicated to the collective defence and building solidarity among its members, which include several North American and European countries. The organization is based on the North Atlantic Treaty that was signed on 4 April 1949.

Another key global actor is the Group of 8 or G8 (now the G7 following Russia's suspension in 2014), which is a political forum made up of France, Germany, Italy, Japan, the UK, the US and Canada with representation from the EU as well. Government ministers meet at political summits in which they try to coordinate action around pressing issues such as the economy, terrorism, global energy, food security and other issues. G8 and G7 summits have also been the targets of protest movements, such as the Global Justice Movement (GJM) (see Chapter 3), for the organizations' commitment to neoliberal capitalist globalization and its lack of attention to issues such as human rights, environmental sustainability and social justice. These protests highlight the fact that often it is difficult or impossible to separate economic globalization (or the advance of neoliberal capitalism) from other globalizing processes. Even culture is subject to a global institutional agenda: organizations such as UNESCO (a subsidiary institution of the United Nations) seek to designate, preserve and protect world heritage sites or sites of cultural value for humanity (within a broader mission to encourage international peace and universal respect for human rights by promoting collaboration among nations, eradicating poverty and fostering sustainable development and intercultural dialogue).

The (EU) is the quintessential example of a supranational organization that has progressively increased the political, economic, juridical and even cultural and educational integration of its member states through the establishment of supranational institutions and laws. This integration has not gone uncontested by a range of social movement actors. From very different ideological starting points, actors on the left and right have mobilized against the EU. Campaigns against the proposed EU Constitution provide an excellent insight into the range of issues citizens in member states contest. Protesters on the left contested the neoliberal underpinnings of EU institutions and practices, such as the undermining of labour protection laws and social welfare provisions already present in the Lisbon Treaty that would be strengthened and made more binding and permanent through a constitutional process. In the words of the Spanish 'No to the EU Constitution' Campaign:

> We reject the Project of the European Constitution because it significantly limits civil, national, social and political rights and represents a regression in the legislation ... that governs the member states. It is a neoliberal, militarist and imperialist Constitution that establishes a Europe of States, denying the right to self determination that reinforces the inequality of rights and opportunities between men and women and that maintains a developmental model that destroys the environment. (Nodo50.org, 2004)

For activists mobilizing on the right, key issues of opposition were the EU definition of Europe as a religiously pluralistic entity and socially 'liberal' positions (already enshrined in EU law), such as forbidding discrimination on the grounds of sexual orientation. Many of these activists feel that Europe should be defined primarily or exclusively in terms of its Christian heritage and therefore espouse 'Christian' values (as they interpret them). Another key issue of opposition on the right during the campaigns against the EU Constitution (and to the present) is the belief that Europe's cultural identity is being threatened by the immigration of peoples who do not share European values and heritage. Whereas activists on the left focused their opposition primarily on the issues of rights and protections (of the environment, social welfare and so on) – often with the active participation of trade unions – culture, identity and history frames lay at the centre of protest on the right, with Christian communities mobilizing in favour of 'family values' and Europe's 'Christian heritage' (see more about organizing on the Right in Chapter 6).

EU law requires unanimous ratification of the Constitution by all member states, yet some national constitutions prevent adoption of a constitution without a referendum. For this reason, the EU Constitution was put to referendum vote in France, Holland and Ireland, all of which voted 'No'. The constitutional ratification process was soon abandoned. However, the Lisbon Treaty, which has been ratified by all member states, contains many of the same articles proposed in the constitution, and mobilization against the EU and its institutions continues on the left and the right. Activists across the ideological spectrum argue that the EU has a significant democratic deficit and is not sufficiently subject to democratic oversight. At the same time, the EU has opened up new avenues of contestation for activists in member states: when national governments fail to respond to citizen pressure on issues such as environmental and consumer protection, gender discrimination and even mortgage laws, activists can appeal to the supranational authority of the EU to force compliance with EU law when it is considered to be more in line with social movement goals than national legislation or attempt to pressure the EU to take initiatives and action in areas where national governments are slow or reluctant to act.

More recently, activists across Europe have mobilized against the European Commission, the European Central Bank and the IMF, known as the 'Troika', in the context of the imposition of austerity measures in countries facing the worst effects of the financial crisis, such as Greece, Spain and Ireland (discussed further in Chapter 7).

Geopolitical militarized globalization

While organizations such as NATO (see above) allegedly are committed to the defence of member states, critics argue that they are responsible for the expansion of geopolitical militarized globalization. In the name of humanitarian intervention, NATO has bombed countries at war, such as the former Yugoslavia, leading to anti-NATO protests. At a 2017 protest in Montenegro, which was bombed by NATO in 1999, protesters carried signs reading 'No to War, No to NATO' and 'NATO Killers you have blood on your hands'. Although NATO is a particular target, historically many economic globalization processes, such as colonialism, have been fuelled by military intervention and intervention in states that are hostile to capitalism or neoliberalism or seen as a threat to the expansion of capitalism (e.g. the CIA supported the Chilean military coup against the democratically elected Marxist President of Chile, Salvador Allende, in 1973).

The multibillion-dollar global arms trade (and the nation-states that who benefit from it) also fuels a militarized logic, in which nations ostensibly committed to democracy allow and foster the sale of arms to the most violent, authoritarian violators of human rights in the world. As one of the protesters at the 2017 Defence and Security Equipment International (DSEI) event in London put it, 'DSEI will bring many of the world's most appalling regimes together with the biggest arms companies. Right now UK fighter jets and bombs are playing a central role in the destruction of Yemen; what will be the next atrocity they are used in? War, repression and injustice are fuelled by events like DSEI. It's time to shut it down for good.' Another protester, a Methodist minister who was arrested at the protest after she climbed under a vehicle and attached herself to it, said, 'I know it's against the law, but I think selling weapons is against the law. I just think we shouldn't be selling weapons to Israel … and particularly to Saudi Arabia. It's obscene, it is against God's will' (Gayle and Thalassites, 2017).

Global protests against military interventions and processes of geo political militarization are not new. In the 1960s, for example, the Vietnam War sparked intense anti-war mobilizations around the world. Recently, however, the world witnessed a global wave of protest that was unprecedented in scope and strength of numbers. When the US and the UK decided to invade Iraq, allegedly searching for weapons of mass destruction, they did so without the sanction of the UN.

No weapons of mass destruction were ever found, but the pretext served to launch a war that resulted in the deaths of hundreds of thousands of people, including civilians and soldiers. According to a major study published in a medical journal, the number of estimated direct and indirect deaths attributable to the war in Iraq between 2003 in 2011 was approximately half a million (Hagopian *et al.*, 2013). Prior to the invasion, on 15 February 2003, people around the world said 'NO' to war in their millions in a concerted series of mass protests that took place in over 600 cities (Walgrave and Rucht, 2010). The anti-war demonstrations made explicit links between a rejection of militarism as a means of conflict resolution and the invasion of oil-rich countries as a means to secure access to oil (the slogan 'No more blood for oil' was a common one) and other financial assets. Protesters questioned the legitimacy of the invasion in the absence of a UN Security Council Resolution and highlighted the lack of accountability of democratic governments to the citizens they presumably represented, who had rejected the invasion in most countries, overwhelmingly so in many (for detailed analysis of public opinion in selected European countries, see Verhulst and Walgrave, 2010). The protests were remarkable not only for the high numbers of people who mobilized but also because they spread across a wide geographic area and were coordinated transnationally by social movement networks and transnational organizations.

The military intervention, justified as bringing 'freedom' to the Iraqi people, was closely tied to a neoliberal agenda, as is clear from the four orders issued by the head of the Coalition Provisional Authority, which were to apply to all areas of the economy and establish Iraq as a neoliberal state:

> The full privatization of public enterprises, full ownership rights by foreign firms of Iraqi businesses, full repatriation of foreign profits ... the opening of Iraq's banks to foreign control, national treatment for foreign companies ... and the elimination of nearly all trade barriers. (Cited in Harvey, 2011: 6)

Environmental globalization

Scientists and activists have long recognized that the very nature of our ecosystems means that environmental degradation or disasters in one area can have transnational and global effects. Nuclear disasters such as that of Chernobyl (the former Soviet Union) in 1986, for example, released large quantities of radioactive particles into the atmosphere, covering much of Europe and the Soviet Union. Global environmental movements have emerged to raise awareness of these issues and to hold governments, corporations and the public responsible for their role in fostering, or failing to halt, environmental destruction. Campaigns against global warming are one example that highlights how consumption and production patterns in industrialized societies can lead to consequences that will affect everyone but whose effects will be disproportionately felt by those countries who least contribute to the problems (non-industrialized countries). The global nature of environmental issues cross-cuts numerous forms of inequality, not just between poor and wealthy nations but also within nations, where poor neighbourhoods and marginalized indigenous communities are far more likely to be the repositories of such unwanted industrial by-products as nuclear waste, depleted mines, toxic waste and the siting of nuclear reactors and incinerators. Climate Justice campaigns link awareness of global environmental issues to global injustice frames (Saunders, 2008), such as gender inequality (see Box 2.1). Climate Justice has become one of the most visible arenas of global mobilization in recent years. Non-governmental organizations (NGOs) such as Friends of the Earth and Greenpeace have been joined in the fight by young students who have taken direct action by going on strike from school and marching in Fridays for the Future. With ice caps melting, polar bears starving and heat waves registering the hottest temperatures in recorded history, many people have had enough of waiting for politicians to take meaningful action as opposed to signing declarations and organizing summits that do not result in sufficient action [e.g. Bali Principles of Climate Justice or the UNFCC (COP 15) meeting in Copenhagen and attended by 100 heads of state]. The urgent need to abate global warming by reducing greenhouse gases, finding safe alternative and renewable energy sources and taking other measures is not being addressed by politicians. Although fossil fuel and energy funded climate deniers continue to try to downplay the risks, most people are aware humanity is facing a crisis that poses a threat of extinction. This has prompted the emergence of loosely related groups in different countries calling themselves Extinction Rebellion, which engage in direct action civil disobedience. Hundreds of these activists have been arrested. They have been supported by over 100 UK senior academics who issued a statement saying 'it is unconscionable to us that our children and grandchildren should have to bear the terrifying brunt of an unprecedented disaster of our own making'. Extinction Rebellion has been controversial because of the tactic of property damage some participants have used, alleging it is necessary to grab people's attention. For more on climate justice action, see Smith and Patterson (2019).

Box 2.1 The Gendered Nature of the Impact of Climate Change

Climate Justice Awareness Campaigns – such as that of the United Nations Women Watch on Women, Gender Equality and Climate Change (United Nations Women Watch, 2009) – argue that the threats of climate change are not gender-neutral, highlighting another way in which environmental issues do not affect everyone equally:

> The threat of climate change, manifested in the increase of extreme weather conditions such as, droughts, storms or floods, has been recognized as a global priority issue ... The effects of climate change will vary among regions, and between different generations, income groups and occupations as well as between women and men. Due, in part, to their lower adaptive capacities, developing countries and people living in poverty are likely to experience significant impacts.

Women form a disproportionately large share of the poor in countries all over the world. Women in rural areas in developing countries are highly dependent on local natural resources for their livelihood, because of their responsibility to secure water, food and energy for cooking and heating. The effects of climate change, including drought, uncertain rainfall and deforestation, make it harder to secure these resources. By comparison with men in poor countries, women face historical disadvantages, which include limited access to decision-making and economic assets that compound the challenges of climate change.

It is therefore imperative that a gender analysis be applied to all actions on climate change and that gender experts be consulted in climate change processes at all levels, so that women's and men's specific needs and priorities are identified and addressed.

This example highlights the inter-related nature of globalization processes and their uneven consequences globally.

Cultural/ideological globalization

Cultural/ideological globalization involves the spread of ideas, values and practices around the world through media and entertainment, commercialization and consumerism. The idea of 'democracy' and the process of democratization have been said to be a key feature of globalization and also a key propagator of social movements (Tilly and Wood, 2015). Democracy was a key common theme in the global wave of protests following the global financial crash of 2008 (see Chapter 7).

As I discussed in Chapter 1, some movements aim to transform cultural practices and consciousness. Women's and feminist movements have often focused on this arena because they recognize how deeply rooted patriarchy is in everyday ideas and practices (see, for example, the highly symbolic critique of patriarchal culture in the global 'SlutWalks' in Chapter 4). Another key area of resistance to cultural globalization has come from anti-consumerist movements who work to galvanize the public to resist the internalization of consumption as intrinsically tied to identity, self-worth and status. The *AdBusters* 'Buy Nothing Day' campaign is one example; *Yo Mango*'s ethical shoplifting is another (see Chapter 4).

Lifestyle movements encourage the transformation of lifestyle and consumption patterns as a means of resisting cultural globalization. The Slow Food Movement, for example, emerged in response to the proliferation of mass-produced fast food chains and the globalization of food production. It encourages the promotion, celebration and preservation of local and regional food cultures, culinary traditions, local eco-systems and small local businesses. The movement also educates people on the risks of fast food consumption, defends biodiversity as a means of resisting globalized monoculture agriculture and advocates fair trade. Other slow movements have developed (e.g. slow parenting, slow travel), all of which share a desire to consciously resist the urge to 'speed up' in the modern globalized world.

Cultural globalization can also involve the spread of ideas that facilitate progressive social and political change. The globalization of such concepts as human rights and gender equality, when coupled with the activities of social movements and NGOs that work to develop and extend these concepts and ideas, creates spaces for new social movements and organizations to grow and to successfully challenge the status quo.

However, scholars working in the post-colonial critical tradition point out that cultural and ideological globalization also involves the spreading of the ideologies that underpin Western modernity at the cost of the marginalization of other perspectives. De Sousa Santos (2016: viii), for example, argues that 'Viewed from the perspective of the excluded and discriminated against, the historical record of global capitalism, colonialism, and patriarchy is full of institutionalised, harmful lies. It is a record of social regulation in the name of social emancipation, appropriation in the name of liberation, violence in the name of peace, the destruction of life in the name of the sanctity of life, violation of human rights in the name of human rights, societal fascism in the name of political democracy, illegal plundering in the name of the rule of law, assimilation in the name of diversity, individual vulnerability in the name of individual autonomy…' Social movement scholars such as Janet Conway (2013) and Catherine Eschle (2018) have pointed out how even within progressive movements and organizations such as the GJM and the World Social Forum subjugated knowledges such as post-colonial, anti-racist, feminist and practice-based approaches have a difficult time being recognized and engaged with and are often marginalized or excluded. They argue that the recognition and integration of these subjugated knowledges are crucial task for progressive politics that seek to prefiguratively transform the world towards greater social justice. Even the most progressive social movements, therefore, are also subject to the processes of (colonial, patriarchal and Western-centric) cultural globalization.

Technological globalization

As I will discuss in Chapter 5, the rise and spread of new ICTs have transformed the way that society is organized, which of course includes social movements. Technological globalization has been a crucial facilitator of social movements and of global movement networks. Social movement activists have often been at the heart of technological innovations as well as strategically adapting new technologies to further their goals and the organizational and communication infrastructures and practices.

Undoubtedly, ICTs have offered social movements opportunities to develop new strategies, tactics and forms of alternative media. Indeed, the development of these technologies has been at the heart of social movements such as the free software and free culture movements (see Chapter 5). Many scholars and observers have paid particular attention to the role new media and ICTs play in mobilization. Clearly, the uses social movements make of new technologies vary from movement to movement and from one geographical region to another. As our lives have increasingly integrated digital media, entire areas of activism centred on the consequences of this digital revolution have emerged, including whistle blowing against the increased surveillance of citizens, data activism (e.g. WikiLeaks) and data justice movements. Social movements mobilizing around cyberpolitics have raised awareness about issues such as data mining (the practice of using algorithms to discover patterns in the large data sets so that businesses and other actors such as political parties can develop more effective marketing strategies and target individual consumers/voters more effectively) and state surveillance. Cyberpolitics also involves using technology to facilitate the exposure of political corruption and fraud and to foster political transparency. Technological globalization has fuelled a digital activist imaginary (e.g. hacker ethics and a digitally enabled democracy) in which politics and the digital intertwine: with Anonymous being one well-known example (see Chapter 5). I will return to a discussion of the ways social movements use media and new ICTs, the opportunities and challenges they offer and how they have transformed activist areas of mobilization and imaginaries in Chapter 5 and offer a detailed examination of the role of media and ICTs in the Arab Spring in Chapter 7.

These distinctions between globalization processes serve as useful heuristic devices that simplify complexity to enable greater analytical clarity but, in reality, all of these processes are inter-related. It is also inescapable that the dynamics of global capitalism drive and facilitate the accelerated expansion of each of these dimensions, from Hollywood mega-productions that spread cultural ideals while grossing millions in profits, to global corporations that enable computers and technology to reach the far corners of the Earth, to the military-political-industrial complex that generates global conflicts and military interventions that serve multiple and often conflicting interests (e.g. democratic ideals and control of oil fields). Social movements have been at the forefront of recognizing, highlighting, resisting and protesting the impacts, contradictions and negative consequences of globalizing processes while using the advantages of these processes (e.g. cheaper air travel, new information technologies) to mobilize effectively on a transnational and global scale.

Transnational social movement networks and global social movements

The different globalization processes discussed above shape social movement issues, practices, tactical repertoires, frames and forms of organization. Social movement participants mobilize across borders through the creation of *transnational social movement networks*, which are non-institutionalized links between activists and groups in different countries who share information, strategies, identities and goals and who may collaborate on specific campaigns or mobilizations or through the creation of *transnational social movement organizations* (TSMOs). Tarrow defines *transnational social movements* as 'sustained contentious interaction with opponents – national and non-national – by connected networks of challengers organizing across national boundaries' (1998: 184). Examples of transnational social movements include transnational campaigning against the practices of specific corporations, such as the Global Shell Corporation, which has included environmental action campaigns against drilling in the North Sea, gasflaring in the Niger Delta or the building of a high-pressure raw gas pipeline across land in Rossport, Ireland, to pipe gas from the offshore Corrib Gas Field. Multinational corporations are often targets of transnational social movements because these companies operate all around the world. Other examples include multiple transnational campaigns against global giant Monsanto for practices ranging from the use of lethal pesticides in Third World countries to the planting of unapproved crop trials of genetically modified foods. A wide range of actions against agricultural giant Monsanto by the Organic Consumers Association in the US, for example, can be seen on their webpage (http://www.organicconsumers.org/monsanto/).

Transnational campaigns against the global arms trade, against the use of land mines and against the building of megadams (which displace local communities and have potentially devastating environmental impacts) are other examples that involve close collaboration between networks of activists across borders. In the Northeastern Indian state of Assam, for example, peasants, students and environmental activists from India and around the world are opposing a proposed gargantuan network of dams in one of the world's six most seismically active regions. The transnational movement argues that the project will have devastating environmental, demographic and socioeconomic impacts and is campaigning for the Indian government to stop the project (Sharma, 2012).

Some organizations are interested in promoting international norms, rules and ideas and, crucially, specific *policy* initiatives, in which case they are known as *transnational advocacy networks* and coalitions (Keck and Sikkink, 1998). Many formal INGOs are concerned with single issues, such as gender equality, economic equality, human rights or environmental justice, and seek to influence and intervene in multilateral or intergovernmental policy arenas such as the agencies of the UN, the WHO, United Nations Children's Fund (UNICEF) or the Office of the High Commissioner for Human Rights (OHCHR). However, in keeping with Tarrow's definition, these are not transnational *social movements* because they do not engage in protest or 'contentious politics' but rather prefer lobbying or charitable or voluntary activities as a means of bringing about change. Yet, these advocacy networks do *interact* with social movements. Evans (2000: 233) points out that local organizing efforts interact with transnational advocacy networks in complex ways: 'Acting globally enables local organizing that would otherwise be "outside the envelope"; it doesn't replace local organizing ... Transnational advocacy networks are not a substitute for local action, but a catalyst that enables local efforts to become more efficacious ...'

Scholars have characterized the development of the cross-border activities of social movements in one of two ways: either through the use of the terms *transnational* social movements and networks, as above, or through the term *global* social movement, although they are also often used interchangeably. If the first term still emphasizes the idea that social movements and groups are rooted in national political contexts which they transcend in order to collaborate with other nationally rooted groups and organizations to form transnational networks, the latter refers to a vision of movements that are themselves global in scope and whose self-definitions and interactions are best understood as primarily stemming from and responding to globalization processes.

The distinction between transnational social movements and global social movements is not a very clear one, conceptually. Both involve connections among local, national and transnational levels of collective action and organization. Some scholars seem either to want to reserve the term 'global social movement' for 'good' or progressive social movements in line with the normative definition of global civil society (the versions that explicitly exclude fundamentalist and xenophobic movements, such as Taylor, 2002) or to use the term as a synonym for the GJM (see Chapter 3), which, as a movement of movements that unites a wide and diverse range of groups and organizations around the world, is seen to provide evidence for the global civil society thesis. Taylor (2002: 341) argues that the subjective intention of global civil society activism is to 'confront neoliberal globalization and create a better world through advocating a fairer, freer, and more just global order with regard to economic, political, social issues'. He argues that the transformative dimensions of global social movement activism through prefigurative politics have been overlooked by social scientists.

In this book, I reserve the term *global social movements* for those movements that are heterogeneous, diverse and global in scope; that explicitly link their activism to a recognition of the interconnectedness of issues that are a result of globalization processes and are therefore anti-systemic rather than single-issue; and that self-identify as belonging to a global movement that is committed to collective action and protest ultimately to transform the whole world rather than just parts of it.

Geopolitical and national political agendas and transnational-national-local linkages between social movements

Transnational-national-local linkages between formally constituted organizations are mediated by power and resource disparities between movements and INGOs and by the geopolitical and national political contexts in which social movements operate.

Evans (2000) highlights Keck and Sikkink's case study of rubber tappers in the Amazon in the 1990s (Keck and Sikkink, 1998: chapter 4) to show how they struggled to make their claims heard not only because they were resource-poor, did not have the access to local politicians that the local landowners did and were subject to violent repression but also because transnational environmental groups were seen as 'outsiders' (or even imperialists) interfering with 'national development goals' (Evans, 2000: 232). The accusation of being stooges or tools of Western imperial forces is a common one lobbed at social movement groups in non-Western developing countries and has important implications for social movements and activists. Social move-ment organizations who accept funding from Western organizations, even when they are NGO funding bodies unconnected to any state, run the risk of being tainted by association (as pro-Western); accused of being anti-nationalist, spies or foreign government agents; and/or having their activism delegitimized as being the work of 'foreign hands'. This can happen whether or not social movement groups actually have ties to foreign social movement organizations or NGOs. In Egypt in 2011, the pro-democracy movement that participated in the January Uprisings with the twin demands of *ash-sha'b yurid isqaat an-nizaam* (the people want the downfall of the regime) and *'aish, horreya, adala igtema'eya* (bread, freedom, social justice) was accused by the military junta's authoritarian regime of engaging in plots to destabilize Egypt propagated by foreigners ('foreign hands'), an accusation initially echoed by the old guard leadership of the Muslim Brotherhood, despite the participa-tion of their own (mostly younger) members in the revolutionary uprising (Teti and Gervasio, 2012). The regime also repeatedly attacked NGOs in a widely covered (primarily in state-controlled media) 'foreign funding debate', using ultra-nationalistic language to accuse NGOs of receiving 'unauthorised foreign funding and/or operating without a licence' (Teti and Gervasio, 2012: 107). Teti and Gervasio point out, though, that a genuine foreign funding debate (as opposed to one fomented by the regime to foster hostility to social movement groups and delegitimize them) has been going on within social movement groups for many years. Activists are well aware of the risks or ben-efits associated with accepting foreign or transnational funding.

The issues raised in these internal debates have been well documented by Kapoor (2005) in his work on NGO partnerships with grassroots organiza-tions in rural India. Kapoor argues that critical self-reflection is needed to avoid INGOs and NGOs from imposing their own agendas on grassroots organizations and abusing the unequal power relations between them. Drawing on extensive fieldwork, Kapoor (2005: 211) highlights a number of problems with the ways that INGOs operate in India, which stem primarily from the fact that they tend to work through national NGOs rather than directly with the grassroots organizations:

> When INGOs 'contract' large Indian NGOs to implement projects, these NGOs in turn subcontract the project work through the vil-lage level NGOs and or CBOs [community-based organizations] ... This relationship is often fraught with problems ranging from petty corruption to outright domination, as 'activist' PO's [people's organizations] are disabled, gutted, and tranquilized into a state of apathy and dependence on charity by the lure of temporary goods and services.

National and local NGOs often use funds earmarked for development proj-ects for personal gain and to maintain patronage systems, 'cooking up' proj-ects to secure international funding that do not benefit the grassroots supposed beneficiaries of these projects. These NGOs also use their power and funding to silence and de-radicalize grassroots organizations and to co-opt their leadership. Kapoor (2005: 215) argues that INGOs need to work directly with the grassroots if they actually want to benefit them, but he does so with some trepidation, given that such a move generally brings INGOs into direct contact 'with the vested interests [local power holders] that are often the very cause of problems faced by the marginalized and dispossessed'.

Activists in South Africa's *Abahlali baseMjondolo* shack dweller's movement are also continually being accused of being part of the 'Third Force', a racist accusation that denies agency to poor black people and constructs them as being able to mobilize only if manipulated by covert white elites. In a now classic article that has become one of the most widely reprinted texts in South Africa, activist S'bu. Zikode (2005) responds publicly and compellingly to these accusations:

> There definitely is a Third Force. The question is what is it and who is part of the Third Force? Well, I am Third Force myself. The Third Force is all the pain and the suffering that the poor are subjected to every second in our lives. [...]
>
> Our President Mbeki speaks politics [...] mayors all over the country speak politics. But who will speak about the genuine issues that affect the people every day – water, electricity, education, land, housing? [...]
>
> We discovered that our municipality does not listen to us when we speak to them in Zulu. We tried English ... The only language that they understand is when we put thousands of people on the street. We have seen the results of this and we have been encouraged. It works very well. It is the only tool that we have to emancipate our people. Why should we stop it?

Activists in the global North are also affected by geopolitical considerations when engaging in transnational networking or global protest. For example, some groups are accused of collaborating with 'terrorists' for engaging with or fundraising for 'revolutionary' movements or movements that use armed struggle in other parts of the world. It is important to recognize that the political construction of what constitutes a terrorist group varies greatly depending on the political interests and/or ideological interests of those doing the defining (Jackson, 2009). In many cases, yesterday's 'freedom fighters' are today's 'terrorists', and vice versa. For example, the African National Congress (ANC), whose leader Nelson Mandela was imprisoned in South Africa for 27 years, is widely perceived as a movement of freedom fighters against apartheid in South Africa. Yet, their use of armed struggle is glossed over in retrospective discourse about their activities. Seidman (2001) points out that, throughout the 1980s, Amnesty International refused to take on the cause of Nelson Mandela or any South African prisoner belonging to the ANC because of their use of armed struggle. It should be said that movements also engage in great debates about whether certain groups should be considered a terrorist organization or a revolutionary social movement. Nevertheless, the accusation of supporting terrorism or engaging in it is a very effective means at states' disposal to repress and silence social movements. Flesher Fominaya and Wood (2011) point out that 'The "global war on terror" has fueled anti-terrorism legislation that has been used to quash dissent and to criminalize activists within countries whose states claim a particular affinity with human rights.'

In Denmark, two men were put on trial for supporting Palestinian militants and the Colombian FARC and sentenced to six months in prison (Morris, 2011). In his defence, one of the defendants, Nielsen, the chairman of a committee for former Danish anti-Nazi resistance fighters, said, 'Nelson Mandela was, in spite of the Nobel Peace Prize, first removed from U.S. terror list [sic] in 2008, when he was 90 years old. We have not supported terrorist organizations and we will never do so. But we will always support people who fight for peace, freedom and national independence' (Morris, 2011).

Social movement diffusion processes

Tarrow (1998) argues that some social movements undergo cycles of contention, which he defines as historically specific periods of heightened conflict across the social system where new tactics and frames emerge and are diffused across movements and countries. Creating transnational organizations and networks is just one way that social movements spread across borders. Many forms of social movement *diffusion* across borders happen in the absence of a formal shared organizing structure. Diffusion is the process through which movements import and export ideas, tactics, strategies, organizational forms and cultural practices and can happen either through the direct and active transmission of activists who travel from one social movement context to another or through other indirect mechanisms of diffusion such as media (news, alternative media, important texts). Such diffusion is not new as historical work on transnational social movement diffusion shows (Linebaugh and Rediker, 2001).

Types of diffusion

Organizational forms and practices

The Mexican Zapatista philosophy of the deliberative democratic practice of the *consulta* (public consultation) was taken up by activists in Europe and developed through a series of global 'Encounters' between activists from different parts of the world (see Chapter 3). Deliberative practices often follow institutionalized rituals and methods which are diffused from one context to another, albeit often with some alterations: spokes-councils (where a delegated spokesperson speaks for a network or group) or affinity groups to organize a collective action, consensus decision-making models or the use of hand signals for communications in assemblies are all examples of organizational forms and practices that are diffused through transnational social movement networks.

Narratives, frames and slogans

Framing is a way of selecting and highlighting a particular claim (Entman, 1993: 52) to mobilize supporters, demobilize antagonists and convince observers of the worthiness of their cause (Snow and Benford, 1988). Although some frames are deeply rooted in local or national political and cultural contexts, others are more open to diffusion processes. 'Think Globally, Act Locally' is a political action frame that links global problems with local action and which was used in the 'new social movements' of the 1980s and 1990s and later by the GJM. More recently, the Occupy Wall Street Movement has coined the slogan 'We are the 99%', which is a frame that attempts to bridge differences across the heterogeneous set of actors who make up the movement by highlighting what they have in common (and what most of the public has in common with them); namely, that they are not part of the 1 per cent who control the vast majority of global wealth.

Strategies

Strategies (an overall plan for how change will occur) can be adopted from one context to another. In her study of the diffusion of rape crisis centres, Roggeband (2007) showed that Dutch activists travelled to the UK and the US to study the rape crisis centres there. These activists then decided to establish rape crisis centres in their home country as a means to heighten the visibility of rape as an important political issue as well as to provide an alternative means of support for women who had been raped.

Tactics and repertoires of contention

Tactics are the means through which strategies are put into practice, and repertoires of contention are the set of tactics social movements use to protest. Critical Mass – a form of collective action which consists of a large group of cyclists riding together around the city to reclaim public space that has been given over to the exclusive use of cars (and have fun doing so) – originated in San Francisco in the early 1990s and has since spread to cities around the world. Their slogan is 'We Aren't Blocking Traffic, We Are Traffic'. Tactical innovations are relatively rare but, once proven to be effective (either materially or symbolically), are often widely adopted in other contexts. Cyberactivist tactics such as those practised by Anonymous are deliberately diffused across borders as a means of offering transnational solidarity and support and circumventing national media blackouts during periods of mobilization (see Chapter 5 for more on Anonymous).

Identities

Activists in the GJM felt a shared sense of belonging to the movement and identification with its goals and events, even when they did not have a personal contact with the movement outside their own local or national contexts (Flesher Fominaya, 2005). Pan-Arab identities played a role in the diffusion of the Arab Spring, connecting people across borders (see Chapter 7).

Icons and symbols

The use of the rainbow flag to designate support for the pro-Gay Lesbian Bisexual and Transgender movement is an internationally recognized symbol of 'gay pride'. The 'Nuclear Power No Thanks' logo, which has a smiling sun and was originally made in 1975 in Denmark, was soon adopted by anti-nuclear power activists in dozens of countries, simply changing the language of the slogan. While some icons are made expressly by and for social movements, on other occasions activists 'subvert' or 'culture jam' (see Chapter 4) existing icons or images to give them new meanings. Such was the case of a Greenpeace advertising campaign against the use of palm oil in Nestlé's Kit Kat bars, in which the Kit Kat becomes an orangutan's paw dripping blood.

Forms of communication

The development of alternative social movement-produced media, such as Indymedia, or the use of existing corporate social media, such as Facebook, for protest coordination and the dissemination of injustice frames and demands has been a crucial area of transnational social movement diffusion. These will be addressed fully in Chapter 5.

The importance of cultural translation and resonance in social movement diffusion processes

All of these forms of diffusion have an effect on the development of social movements. However, it is important to point out that diffusion rarely involves a wholesale transmission from one movement to another. Instead, *translation* can be understood as the processes through which social movements adapt ideas, frames and practices that have originated elsewhere to suit their local and/or national cultural contexts. Malets and Zajak (2014) point out that, 'in contrast to a more common usage of the term diffusion, translation emphasizes conscious effort and creativity the social movement actors – individual activists and organizations – employ for changing existing cultural practices'. They highlight the fact that diffusion processes, far from being seamless, are characterized by 'recursive interactions, ruptures, backlash, resistance and feedback effects'. McAdam (1995: 231) argues that spin-off social movements adopt initiator movement influences reflexively; they do not just copy what the initiator movement does.

In his discussion of the social movements in the 1960s in the US, Hayden (2012) illustrates the variety of global and national influences on the radical direct action group 'The Weathermen' and how these were taken up and adapted to their interpretation of the political opportunities available in the US context. It should be noted that Hayden was a rather hostile contemporary of the Weathermen, and this surely influences the tone of this passage, which is nevertheless illustrative:

> Beginning in 1968, the Weathermen (later the Weather Underground) faction surfaced as new 'communist revolutionaries,' inspired by the revolutions in Vietnam and Cuba, and the Black Panthers at home. Instead of the Port Huron concept of a majority progressive coalition, they favored forming clandestine cells behind enemy lines, a formulation that regarded the white American majority as hopelessly racist and privileged. Their ideological heroes included Lin Piao, a leader of the Chinese Revolution, along with Che Guevara and the young French intellectual Regis Debray, with his *foco* theory that small bands of armed guerrillas could set off popular revolutions.

The Weathermen were inspired and hoped to inspire others by drawing on a range of iconic 'heroic' figures from around the world to incite a revolutionary transformation in the US. With greater success, the US Civil Rights movement also drew inspiration from India's struggle against colonialism, through a transnational trans-religious adaptation of Gandhi's passive non-violent resistance or civil disobedience/non-cooperation.

Cultural resonance is crucial for transmission or diffusion processes to take place. Thayer (2000: 336), for example, shows how women in the Brazilian group SOS Corpo (SOS Body) found the gender discourse imported from the transnational networks in which they were involved very inspiring but were unable to use it to full advantage in local organizing until they fused it 'with home-grown concepts of citizenship'. Sometimes, despite the best efforts of social movement actors, diffusion does not take place: Wood (2010), for example, describes how the International Youth Camps developed at the World Social Forum in Porto Alegre, Brazil, between 2001 and 2005 did not diffuse successfully to its new site in Caracas, Venezuela. The *horizontalist* (non-hierarchical and deliberative forms of organization) identities and strategies associated with the youth camps were not translated to the new cultural and political context. Wood argues that the 'new users' of the horizontalist idea were not given time to deliberate on what was, for them, a new form of practice and to see how it might fit with their own local context. In a Western European context, Flesher Fominaya (2014) shows how differences in cultural practices and organizing traditions between social movement actors from different countries can create significant barriers to transnational cooperation. Despite sharing terms such as 'consensus', what this term meant in practice varied greatly between national activist organizing traditions, leading to frustration and misunderstandings. The works of McAdam (1995), Wood (2010), Flesher Fominaya (2014) and Malets and Zajak (2014) highlight the need for social movement actors to engage in active and reflexive translation processes for diffusion processes to take place effectively. Even then, there are no guarantees of success as political aspects of the social movement's local context, such as tensions and polarizations between political parties and unions and social movement groups, can also inhibit successful diffusion processes.

Diffusion across time: Movement continuity

Cross-national diffusion is not simply the spontaneous adoption by receivers of a protest "frame" of an issue or a tactic from one protest site to another. As noted above, it involves specific challenges for activists and the active and creative cultural translation of practices from one political context to another. Although less widely studied than contemporaneous diffusion, cross-national diffusion can also happen across time. Historical distance when combined with geopolitical differences poses additional challenges for social movements engaging across national diffusion. Diffusion and transmission do not just happen in a synchronic way; movements also inherit organizational forms, practices, frames, narratives, identities, tactics and forms of communication from past movements, that is, through a historical process of movement continuity or transmission (see McKay, 1996; Flesher Fominaya, 2013; Romanos, 2013a). This process of transmission is not seamless and is often contested and even unintentional (see Flesher Fominaya, 2014) with meanings changing over time (Douglas, 2008).

The maintenance of collective identity and movement culture (including deliberative practices, master frames etc.) through movement networks in periods of relative latency (or in periods of abeyance) is still a relatively understudied aspect of mobilization that is crucial to explaining the continuity and evolution of movement culture (or conversely its rupture) from one cycle of contention to the next. Despite important work by Taylor (1989) and Polletta (2002) on movement continuity, the same tendency to emphasize ruptures rather than continuity is still present in much scholarship today. Taylor argued that in the case of the American women's movement, a series of abeyance structures provided continuity between different cycles of contention over time. In my work on the Spanish 15-M pro-democracy movement (Flesher Fominaya, 2015a), I showed that their seemingly 'spontaneous' ability to facilitate deliberative consensus-based assemblies of 5000 protesters in the occupied central square of Madrid was the result not of some magical ability but of many years of developing movement practices that had been handed down from one generation to the next. Research on movement learning processes (Doerr, 2009; Polletta, 2002; Romanos, 2013) demonstrates that these abilities cannot be convincingly explained by commitment to principles or by transnational diffusion processes leading to the wholesale 'adoption' of practices (Wood, 2010). In fact, the effective management of large deliberative assemblies has been a key challenge of social movements in Spain over the past two decades, and the adoption of deliberative techniques has been slow and arduous, not least because of resistance from Institutional Left actors and the strong influence of institutional left actors on social movement cultural practices (Flesher Fominaya, 2005, 2007a, 2010b). The development of movement practices over time within autonomous social movement spaces, therefore, is a key factor behind the 'spontaneous' ability of these assemblies to work effectively.

Polletta (2002: 191) suggests a similar evolution for the development of deliberate practices through a range of movements in the US. With respect to GJM activists highly skilled in facilitation, she writes, 'their experience suggests that models for egalitarian forms and deliberative styles are simply available to activists today in a way that they were not for 1960s activists. In some segments of the movement field, participatory democracy has become close being institutionalized'. Polletta (2002: 190) notes that the evolution of deliberative and participatory practices has been accompanied by 'procedural paraphernalia', including 'formal roles' (e.g. timekeeper, facilitator, vibes watcher) and 'sophisticated hand signals'. In the same way, previous experiences in autonomous movements in Spain had nourished the 15-M's movement cultures.

Adopting a genealogical approach to movement learning processes stands in contrast to more structural social movement approaches such as the Political Process Model (PPM, see Chapter 1), which focuses primarily on cycles of visible mobilization. In the ideal typical model of cycles of contention, movements appear in response to political opportunities, consolidate resources that they mobilize on behalf of their constituents, undergo transformations through the process of contention and then disappear after mobilization. Tilly and Tarrow (2006: 132), for example, recognize multiple forms of 'exit' for social movement actors, including institutionalization, interest groups and other pursuits that keep the movement base alive during periods of abatement, but they still conceive of movements as essentially suspended or non-existent between periods of active mobilization. In contrast, a genealogical approach adopts the perspective of social movements from the inside out, paying close attention to their latent activity during periods of abeyance or less visible mobilization and recognizing processes of movement continuity between peaks of visible mobilization. While movements undeniably pass through cycles of highly visible mobilization and sometimes disappear afterward, more often the periods between the cycles of contention are not marked by disappearance but by ongoing social movement activity in a variety of environments.

Although the examples above show there has been historical work on the adoption of previously used tactics within social movements, much less often do we find clear case studies of transnational diffusion across time and geographical regions. The most famous example is arguably the 1960s US Civil Rights movement's adoption of Gandhi's tactics of non-violent resistance, which he and his followers used to resist the British Raj in India in the early 1900s. The effective adoption of his tactics of non-violent resistance across time and space was facilitated by some similarities between these two seemingly very different movements: both movements were demanding equality and rights before the law and for the ability to intervene in politics through voting or self-determination. Both also framed members of the movement as people who were oppressed by a powerful white elite and who were guided by spiritual and religious political leadership. Historical continuity, whether in the same locale or across time *and* space, requires mechanisms of transmission. Diffusion processes link two or more people, groups and organizations by a channel of diffusion which is either directly relational (there is direct contact between the sites) or via an indirect channel, such as the mass media. McAdam and Rucht (1993) argued that the actors and the two sides must share 'both a structure of social relations and a system of values, or culture' (59). They are building on Strang and Myer's (1993) argument that direct relational ties are not necessary but that the adopters must define themselves as similar to the transmitters in some way, and they need to see the idea or item in question as relevant to their situation. As Flesher Fominaya and Montañés (2014) argue, 'social movement actors do not freely adopt tactics from a globally available toolbox; adoption follows paths shaped by political, historical, and cultural trajectories that are not always easily determined'.

Conclusion

The connection between globalization and social movements is not new, although it can be said to have accelerated and changed significantly in recent decades. As long as there have been people who have been aware of issues affecting people and places beyond their local or national context and have mobilized to change them and, conversely, when people in specific local and national contexts are aware of the impact of globalizing processes on their lives, communities and environment and have worked together to try to change or mitigate those impacts, there have been links between globalization and social movements.

Social movements inter-relate with globalization in complex, dynamic and diverse ways. Cross-border collective action can take the form of TSMOs, transnational networks and global social movements. Diffusion processes can be accelerated during cycles of contention but are a constant feature of social movement emergence and development in a globalized world. Transnational diffusion can take place by explicit and direct links between social movement actors and organizations or through less direct mechanisms such as the spread of ideas, values, tactics and issue frames through the media. For diffusion to be effective, local groups and movements must have a certain cultural affinity with new influences or else engage in reflexive acts of cultural translation to adapt them to local contexts. The local configuration of the political context in which social movements act can also limit or foster diffusion processes. Power and resource disparities between INGOs, NGOs and local social movement groups also mediate diffusion processes significantly. While globalization processes are objective and structural, they have powerful subjective effects that affect the collective identities that emerge in response to them.

In Chapter 3, I look at what has been considered the quintessential global social movement, the 'Global Justice Movement'. It provides an excellent case study of the challenges, opportunities and dynamics of social movements in a globalized world.

3 THE GLOBAL JUSTICE MOVEMENT

The great globalization debate

Given how actively globalization is discussed in many fields and institutions, it is not surprising to find many competing claims made for its benefits or costs along the many dimensions (e.g. economic, cultural, identitarian) discussed in Chapter 2. UK-based journal *The Economist*, for example, through detailed coverage of business, finance, economics and politics, offers its readers (an elite group of highly educated people with interests in these same fields) one of the most favourable interpretations of neoliberal capitalist globalization. '*The Economist* is a strong proponent of the neo-liberal view of globalization as a positive and inevitable extension of free trade and market capitalism' (Starr, 2004: 374). Coverage of globalization includes in-depth reporting on the activities of organizations such as the International Monetary Fund (IMF), the World Bank, the World Economic Forum (WEF), the World Trade Organization (WTO) and the summit meetings of the G7 and G8 as well as the activities of multinational corporations and their leadership. In an in-depth analysis of *The Economist's* coverage of globalization, Starr shows how the magazine – despite offering some qualifications about globalization's excesses – consistently offers a picture of globalization as natural, inevitable and, overall, very beneficial: the deepening of capitalist markets across borders represents a major positive financial and economic trend that not only under-lies growth and prosperity but also is the only way to address global issues of inequality and poverty. Any necessary adjustments and excesses along the way (e.g. environmental degradation, industrial decline as industries shift opera-tions across borders, displacement of communities for projects such as dam building and so on) can be managed by expert policies. As such, '*The Economist's* message about globalisation is a standard, neoliberal argument in favour of free trade and lightly regulated capitalism' (Starr, 2004: 378). As a publication with a global circulation of over 900,000 in 2003 and more than 1.5 million in 2012, it is fair to assume that the messages *The Economist* actively shapes about globalization are shared widely, to some degree, by members of the world's political and economic elite (also the target audience of the journal) and by the members of the institutions whose activities *The Economist* covers who, after all, pursue policies consistent with this vision of globalization.

As I will show in Chapter 4, one of the main arenas of social movement activity is to challenge dominant widely accepted narratives that serve to justify and maintain the status quo. And, as I discussed in Chapter 2, social movements not only challenge discourses but also engage in specific actions to attempt to change the policies and actions of political and institutional actors.

In the 1990s, a global movement against neoliberal capitalist globalization emerged, took shape and increased in intensity. This movement offered a very different view of globalization to that offered by *The Economist*, opposing a vision of globalization from above with a view of globalization from below. As I have discussed, globalization processes foster the extension and increased density of transnational networks that encompass both states and civil society. Nation-states are increasingly members of transnational and multilateral organizations; for example, military alliances such as the North Atlantic Treaty Organization (NATO), international financial institutions such as the IMF or supranational political entities such as the European Union (EU) and their sovereignty (autonomy with respect to decision-making processes) over key economic and political issues are transferred to these global arenas. Therefore, in significant ways, important political and economic policy decisions are shifted away from the citizens of any given nation-state. As Touraine (1997) has highlighted, this means that decision-making is increasingly technocratic (made by professional experts who are not elected) rather than democratic (made by politicians elected by and accountable to the citizens). At the same time, civil society, including social movements, is also organizing itself across borders in transnational networks and organizations. The transnational expansion of both state and civil society is facilitated by technological advances that speed up and lower the cost of transportation and communication. This is accompanied by an increasing awareness that individual nations cannot unilaterally address the world's problems, which are global and require global solutions. Social movements around the world realize they need to mobilize collectively to change the global system, not just reform individual parts of it. But, because decision-making in key areas has shifted to transnational and supranational arenas, it becomes harder for citizens to identify and locate those responsible for taking decisions on global issues. Because those issues are themselves global, it becomes easier for states to abdicate responsibility for the protection of citizens in areas such as unemployment, because the sources of the problems are seen to be originating outside the nation-state (in the global capitalist financial system), and the solutions are also mandated often by outside organizations, such as the IMF. Some scholars have argued that it is not just a question of the state retreating and leaving decisions in the hands of non-state institutions but that the states themselves are fully invested in advancing the neoliberal agenda (Castells, 2004; Robinson, 2004; Harvey, 2011). Harvey (2011: 205) highlights the close connection between the shift of decision-making away from democratic oversight and the promotion of the neoliberal capitalist agenda:

> it is the profoundly antidemocratic nature of neoliberalism backed
> by the authoritarianism of the neoconservatives that should

surely be the main focus of political struggle … [In the US] institutions with enormous power, like the Federal Reserve, are outside any democratic control whatsoever. Internationally the situation is even worse since there is no accountability, let alone democratic influence, over institutions such as the IMF, the WTO, and the World Bank.

In the 1980s, many citizens around the world began to become more conscious of this 'democratic deficit', which failed to control the interests of multinational corporations that belonged to no state. At the same time, people became more aware of the role of international institutions, such as the WTO, in actively pushing for the interests of these corporations and for a neoliberal capitalist agenda more broadly. Social movements and citizens' groups also became aware of each other's struggles and made connections between their own local issues and concerns and those of people elsewhere. By the early 1990s, diverse networks and movements around the world had begun to coalesce in what would come initially to be known as the 'anti-globalization movement' and, later, more commonly referred to as the Global Justice Movement (GJM).

The 'anti-globalization' movement burst into the consciousness of the global public with the international media coverage of the mass protests that forced the collapse of the WTO negotiations in Seattle in 1999. Seattle was followed by a long series of international protests against capitalist institutions and countless local and national protests, many of which never made it into the papers (see Collins, 2004). Wherever the representatives of global capitalist institutions chose to meet and whatever the forum (WTO, G8, Davos, World Bank, IMF, EU summits), they were met by a heterogeneous mass of protesters who questioned the neoliberal capitalist economic model and demanded more social justice and more participatory democracy. A central feature of the many mass protests against neoliberal globalization and the institutions that promote and defend it has been the heterogeneity of the protesters. Such is the diversity of actors involved that the movement that was first known as the 'anti-globalization' movement also came to be known as 'the movement of movements'. It was so called because it encompassed such a wide range of movements not only in terms of geographical distribution but also in terms of the issues mobilized, which included corporate environmental degradation, indigenous rights, labour rights, the fight against the trafficking of human beings, anti-militarism, the critique of international financial institutions and the cancellation of debt for developing countries crippled by their debt burdens (see Box 3.1).

Different actors within the movement favoured other names for it: the 'alter-globalization movement' to stress the creation and imagining of alternative worlds (summed up by the movement slogan 'Another World is Possible'); the 'anti-*capitalist* globalization movement' to stress the fact that the critique was aimed at neoliberal global capitalism rather than globalization *per se*; and the 'Global Justice Movement' to emphasize the demand for greater justice and equality for all.

> **Box 3.1 Debt Relief for Developing Countries: The Campaign against Nestlé**
>
> Debt relief for developing countries was one of the many issues activists in the Global Justice Movement mobilized around. In 2003, multinational food giant Nestlé was forced to rescind its demand that Ethiopia pay a US$6 million claim dating from the 1970s when the military regime in Ethiopia seized foreign companies' assets (Denny, 2003). At the time, Ethiopia was in the midst of a famine crisis, and Nestlé had posted sales of US$60 billion the previous year. A campaign led by Oxfam stirred up public outrage, and Nestlé was deluged with letters of protest. The editor of *The Guardian*'s comment that 'corporate greed has buckled in the face of adverse publicity and direct action' situated this campaign within a larger narrative consistent with the critiques being made by the Global Justice Movement, which used direct action and lobbying to raise public awareness of corporate misbehaviour and to pressure them to change their ways.

Whatever the name given to it and whoever the actors involved in a given campaign, the common thread that linked all of them consisted of two central critiques: one, that the, until then, largely unquestioned economic model of neoliberal capitalist globalization was severely flawed and led to extremely negative consequences for people and the environment; two, that representative models of democracy were failing to represent the interest and desires of the citizens and did not allow citizens sufficient input into the decisions that affect not only their lives but also the lives of people around the world. In short, the movement made a *fundamentally anti-systemic critique* that not only called for reforms around specific issues but also questioned the economic and political system as a whole. It saw the issues of economic and social justice, human rights, environmental destruction and the erosion of true democracy as inextricably linked.

Scholars, observers and participants have understood this movement as epitomizing the quintessential interconnection between globalization and social movements and as representing something new and different from the New Social Movements of the 1970s and 1980s. While many have stressed the global and transnational nature of the movement, others have insisted that this 'globality' has been overstated (Tarrow, 2005a; Fillieule and Sommier, 2013); whereas some have stressed the movement's newness, others have highlighted continuity with previous movements (Flesher Fominaya, 2013). The literature on the GJM is voluminous and the movement continues to be a central reference for scholars of social movements and globalization (Hardt and Negri, 2001; Starr, 2000; Tarrow, 2001; Katsiaficas, 2004; Della Porta, 2007).

In this chapter, I will first examine the 'Battle for Seattle' in order to understand some of the main players, critiques, demands and tactics of the movement. Then I will take a step back to situate Seattle in a larger historical context of anti-capitalist mobilizations and examine some of the global net-works involved. Next, I will look at some central debates and cleavages within the movement. Finally, I will take up the question of the extent to which the movement was new or different with respect to earlier movements and the extent to which it was 'global'.

The Battle of Seattle

The explosion of the GJM onto the international scene came about as a result of the extensive international media coverage of the dramatic events of the anti-WTO protests in Seattle, Washington, on 30 November 1999. WTO delegates who had arrived in Seattle were met with the opposition of tens of thousands of protesters, who used blockade tactics to prevent some of the delegates from attending the meeting and who marched through the streets of Seattle. They were met with violent resistance from the police, which is why it is known as the 'battle' of Seattle.

Why did the WTO meeting provoke such a strong response from protesters? The WTO is an intergovernmental organization that regulates tariffs and trade, and as such it represents a key actor in the political integration of the global economy. The WTO promotes a strong neoliberal agenda that seeks the progressive expansion of trade liberalization and to protect global business interests (Harvey, 2011).

For months prior to the WTO meeting in Seattle, labour groups, trade groups, environmental groups, human rights groups and other social movement organizations had been meeting together and mobilizing their membership to organize a massive protest against the WTO. They wanted their protest to denounce the WTO's decision-making practices and policies, which they argued were not only undemocratic but also severely detrimental to the environment and to workers around the world (Murphy and Pfaff, 2005). According to Smith (2001), the WTO held closed-door meetings between core countries (the US, Canada, the EU, Japan) and this core group of states would then force their decisions on members in the global South more vulnerable to the pressures of these much more powerful players.

The protests and the protesters

There were two major protest events on 30 November 1999. The first involved a mass demonstration in downtown Seattle with thousands of protesters engaged in non-violent direct action to occupy the downtown area and to prevent delegates from reaching the WTO meeting. The second event was a protest march and rally organized by representatives of many different labour unions, environmental groups, religious groups and other social movement groups and sponsored by the federation of labour organizations: the American Federation of Labor and Congress of Industrial Organizations (AFL–CIO). The Earth Island Institute had mobilized thousands of activists to highlight the role of the WTO in endangering sea turtles through their tribunal ruling that the US Endangered Species Act was an unfair trade barrier. The act required that shrimp be caught in a way that would not harm sea turtles by using devices that would exclude them from the shrimp nets. Activists prepared 500 sea turtle costumes which became one of the symbols of the 'Battle of Seattle' as they marched alongside the labour union 'Teamsters', chanting 'The people united will never be divided!'

The AFL-CIO and its affiliates represent labour movement organizations with formal dues-paying membership and a clear institutional organizational and decision-making structure. The AFL-CIO sent 30 paid staff members to Seattle to assist local unions and they spent close to $1 million mobilizing opposition to the WTO (Murphy and Pfaff, 2005). They organized the transportation of thousands of their members by bus and rail and engaged in months of active mobilization of their membership to organize the anti-WTO campaign in Seattle. At the other end of the spectrum were grassroots social movement groups organized in affinity groups or merely in friendship networks. These groups provided much of the symbolic protest, street theatre and high-risk direct actions (such as locking their arms together in cement casts to block intersections) that contributed to the media attention the protests received.

Prior to the protest events on 30 November, dozens of different affinity groups met to plan direct actions. The Direct Action Network (DAN), a loose social movement network, coordinated dozens of these affinity groups as well as encouraging and facilitating activists to create puppets, costumes and street theatre. DAN provided intensive training in non-violent direct action tactics and philosophy to activists. DAN worked on a principle of autonomy and decentralization, where people were free to organize their own affinity groups, decide on the type of action they wanted to take and distribute roles within the group. For example, some might be willing to be arrested and go to jail and might take a more active role in the action; others would be assigned the role of legal observer, to contact lawyers and know the legal rights of the protesters. The affinity groups were organized into clusters that, in turn, were coordinated through a 'spokescouncil' where representatives from each cluster would take decisions on behalf of their groups in a consensus decision-making process. There were four basic principles to which all agreed. According to Starhawk (1999), one of the protesters jailed for her participation in Seattle:

> Each participant in the action was asked to agree the nonviolence guidelines: to refrain from violence, physical or verbal; not to carry weapons, not to bring or use illegal drugs or alcohol, and not to destroy property. We were asked to agree only for the purpose of the 11/30 action – not to sign onto any of these as a life philosophy, and the group acknowledged that there is much diversity of opinion around some of these guidelines.

Despite the four guidelines agreed to by the affinity groups, not everyone agreed to them or was organized within DAN. Some protesters organized in anarchist affinity groups within the Black Bloc believed that not only the

WTO but also specific multinational corporations and financial institutions such as the Bank of America, GAP, Nike, McDonald's, Starbucks and Planet Hollywood should be targeted for vandalism. They (and, indeed, most protesters in Seattle) held these corporations directly accountable for labour violations or repression against workers and unions, sweatshop labour to make their products, environmental destruction (such as the destruction of tropical rainforests for grazing land for cows) and the exploitation of workers in developing countries through unfair trade agreements. Yet, unlike most of the Seattle protesters, Black Bloc members vandalized the shop fronts of these organizations during the protests, later justifying their actions in a communiqué that argued that these institutions were guilty of corporate crime (Anarchist N30 Black Bloc, 1999):

> We contend that property destruction is not a violent activity unless it destroys lives or causes pain in the process. By this definition, private property – especially corporate private property – is itself infinitely more violent than any action taken against it [...]
>
> Private property – and capitalism, by extension – is intrinsically violent and repressive and cannot be reformed or mitigated [...] When we smash a window, we aim to destroy the thin veneer of legitimacy that surrounds private property rights. ... Against Capital and State, the ACME COLLECTIVE, Dec. 12, 1999.

Vandalism of corporate targets as a tactic by members of the Black Bloc was to become a topic of hot debate in the movement over the ensuing years reflecting long-standing debates within social movements over tactics: activists disagree over whether this type of action is violent or not; whether it serves the interests of the movement or is counterproductive; whether it is acceptable within the diversity of tactics within the movement or whether other actors in the movement should denounce property destruction and even intervene to prevent it during protest events. Although the Black Bloc formed an important element of the GJM, the tactic of property destruction represents a minority trend within it.

The approach taken by affinity groups loosely coordinated by DAN typically favours autonomy, decentralization, tight coordination *within* groups but loose coordination *between* groups, horizontal decision-making and flexibility, where different groups can adapt to the changing situation on the ground, such as police blockades, and move around the city centre. Each affinity group can decide the content of their banners, costumes, slogans and tactics (i.e. street theatre, direct action) (see also Whitney 2003: 217–27). This approach is very much in keeping with autonomous movement philosophy, which represents one major strand within the GJM (see the section on autonomous movements, p. 83). The direct actions of affinity groups are often carefully prepared and organized but can be contrasted with the more structured and formally organized protest marches organized by Institutional Left groups, such as large trade unions, organizations closely affiliated with political parties and non-governmental organizations. For the latter, slogans and banners are often agreed beforehand (sometimes through protracted contentious internal debates), the exact route of the march and the final destination are clearly and publicly declared, and the march and the rally are carefully coordinated. The differences between these approaches in the GJM will be discussed later, but the 'Battle of Seattle' provides a good example of a mass mobilization against neoliberal globalization that successfully combines participants belonging to these two general approaches to protest. The 'Turtles and Teamsters' together became a symbol of the possibilities of a movement that could collaborate across traditional differences in protest philosophies and repertoires, although not without tensions.

The high level of participation, the colourful nature of some of the protesters and actions, and the property destruction of others made the protests very attractive to news media. But what really made the news outlets of the world take notice was not just the strength of the protests but also the strength of the repression. Over the course of the next days, protesters in Seattle were tear-gassed, shot with rubber bullets in areas of the body that can be lethal and beaten with police clubs (some into unconsciousness), and almost 600 demonstrators were arrested (Cockburn and St. Clair, 2000; Smith, 2001; Murphy and Pfaff, 2005). The mayor of Seattle imposed a 50-block 'No-Protest Zone' and a curfew.

Alliances and exclusions

Despite the remarkable heterogeneity of groups, not everyone is in agreement about the true extent of the alliances between protester groups in Seattle. St. Clair (2004: 69), for example, argues that the police violence in Seattle might have been much less if the labour movement activists had come to support the direct action protesters during the repression they experienced when faced with baton charges, rubber bullets and tear gas:

> As the morning ticked away and the cops got rougher, the street warriors kept asking, 'Where are the labor marchers?' expecting that at any moment thousands of Longshoremen and Teamsters would reinforce them in the desperate fray.

For their part, Mamatas (2004) and Wong (2004) argue that activists and communities of colour were excluded and marginalized by white activists in Seattle. These critiques raise the question of the extent to which Seattle really represented a true alliance between social movement actors across differences or whether it represented a sort of fragmented coalition of groups that were united mainly by the fact that their grievances were directed against a common target (the WTO). The issue of the extent to which the GJM itself truly represented a unified movement was one that was later taken up by a number of scholars with differing conclusions.

Outcomes of Seattle

Activists who were in Seattle, and those around the world watching, felt inspired by the show of strength and solidarity and also by the fact that the WTO talks collapsed and agreement was not reached (although that can be attributed only partly to the protests, given that internal disagreements were strong prior to the meeting). The phrase the 'spirit of Seattle' was invoked over the coming years to refer to the solidarity, courage, creativity and innovation of the protesters.

Seattle was followed by a series of protests around the world. The influence of Seattle could be seen in the diffusion and adoption of slogans, chants and tactics – and, of course, in the development of global protest events targeting the summit meetings of the WTO, the WEF, the IMF and the World Bank, the EU and the G7, G8 and G20, among others. Major mobilizations took place in Washington, DC; Philadelphia; Los Angeles; Ottawa and Quebec City as well as in Barcelona, Cancun, Johannesburg, Davos, Doha, Genoa, Geneva, Gothenburg and Prague, among many others. Perhaps the most significant outcome of Seattle, beyond its inspiration for future mobilizations, was that it put the spotlight on international trade and financial organizations such as the WTO that many ordinary citizens had not been aware of previously, and it also questioned in a public, clear and profound way the neoliberal economic agenda those organizations pursue as well as its detrimental political, social and environmental consequences. The Battle of Seattle, and the GJM protests that followed it, began to question this neoliberal agenda in such a way that governments and international financial organizations were forced to respond. Joseph Stiglitz, chief economist and vice president of the World Bank from 1997 to 2000, was one person who not only heard the protesters' message but also agreed with much of it. Under pressure from World Bank insiders, he resigned his post and became one of the most vocal critics of the global political-economic regime:

> Next week's meeting of the International Monetary Fund will bring to Washington, D.C., many of the same demonstrators who trashed the World Trade Organization in Seattle last fall. They'll say the IMF is arrogant. They'll say the IMF doesn't really listen to the developing countries it is supposed to help. They'll say the IMF is secretive and insulated from democratic accountability. They'll say the IMF's economic 'remedies' often make things worse – turning slowdowns into recessions and recessions into depressions. And they'll have a point ... The IMF likes to go about its business without outsiders asking too many questions. In theory, the fund supports democratic institutions in the nations it assists. In practice, it undermines the democratic process by imposing policies. (Stiglitz, 2000)

The protesters in the GJM not only criticized the global economic order but also linked that to a deep critique of democracy, reflected in the lack of input citizens had in the decision-making processes of international organizations such as the WTO, the lack of accountability of multinational corporations to political oversight and the lack of responsiveness of the political class to the concerns and interests of ordinary citizens, while being heavily funded and lobbied by corporate interests. While clearly activists around the world had been making these critiques prior to Seattle, they had mostly been marginalized, ignored and seen as not central to the political process. In Gamson's (1990) terms, they had not been considered as legitimate political actors whose views needed to be taken into account.

The protest techniques used by the protesters also led to innovations in policing tactics – or, perhaps more accurately, the increase in the use of tried and true methods. Such methods included mass arrests, separating and controlling protesters through the use of barricades (later developing into the kettling tactics used against student and anti-austerity protesters in the UK and elsewhere) and rubber bullets, tear gas and pepper spray, which shifted the terrain of engagement for social movements in the global North after Seattle (Della Porta *et al.*, 2006; Noakes and Gillham, 2007; Wood, 2007).

Seattle was also important as the birthplace of Indymedia, which was to become an important outlet for activist-produced media throughout the GJM. The birth of Indymedia came as a recognition by activists that corporate-controlled mass media could not be relied on to provide unbiased or full coverage of protest events and that activists needed to create their own news outlets. (For more on Indymedia, see Chapter 5.)

Four iconic Global Justice Movement protests and events

Seattle, 30 November–3 December 1999, anti-WTO protests

Tens of thousands of protesters gathered to denounce and block access to the WTO ministerial meeting and were met with severe repression from police. This protest was widely covered in international media and was considered the first major visible manifestation of the GJM.

Prague, 21–28 September 2000, counter-summit protest against the 55th World Bank and IMF General Assembly Meeting

Key claims

World Bank and IMF policies benefit capitalist interests; worsen the living conditions of the majority of the world's population; destroy livelihoods and ecosystems; foment monoculture agriculture, which reduces diversity; force the mass exodus of people from their lands (e.g. through the support of major dam projects, which submerge vast tracts of land), which creates refugee communities which are then criminalized.

Key protest

26 September, fifth day of Global Action, celebrated simultaneously in 40 countries. This call to action was organized through the Initiative Against Economic Globalization and disseminated through activist listserves and Indymedia websites. Thousands of activists travelled to Prague before the summit to prepare actions and engage in assemblies, street theatre and conferences. In Prague, some 20,000 protesters faced some 15,000 police outside the meeting conference centre. The protesters were authorized to march only until 1 p.m. but disobeyed this restriction and formed three major columns that took different routes through the city centre. The *pink column*, led by drag queens, comprised trade unionists, gay and lesbian activists, environmentalists, immigrants, artists, anarchists and trotskyists, primarily from Europe, Latin America and the US. The *blue column* was composed of anarchist and anti-fascist activists from the Czech Republic, Italy, Germany and Greece, who were willing to engage the police in more direct confrontation. The *yellow column* was made up of non-violent active disobedience groups such as *Ya Basta!* from Italy and squatted in social centres around Europe (see Juris, 2008).

The Prague counter-summit represented a development in the form of coordination and organization of the GJM, and the division of activist labour into columns would be repeated at future counter-summit protests.

Porto Alegre, Brazil, World Social Forum, 25–30 January 2001

The World Social Forum (WSF) was an initiative created to bring together social movements and civil society organizations working to resist neoliberal organizations. It represented a desire to move beyond simply protesting at corporate globalization to working toward an alternative globalization. Some of the organizations involved included ATTAC (Association for a Tobin Tax to Aid the Citizens), the Brazilian Worker's Party as well as non-governmental organizations (NGOs) and a multitude of groups inspired by the Zapatista *encuentros* and other anti-capitalist initiatives. Some 12,000 people met to found the Forum, by means of a charter, the first statement of which read:

> The World Social Forum is an open meeting place for reflective thinking, democratic debate of ideas, formulation of proposals, free exchange of experiences and interlinking for effective action, by groups and movements of civil society that are opposed to neo-liberalism and to domination of the world by capital and any form of imperialism, and are committed to building a planetary society directed towards fruitful relationships among Mankind and between it and the Earth.

The WSF process is repeated annually (the tenth anniversary was celebrated in Dakar in 2011 and brought together some 75,000 participants) and influenced the development and spread of European and other regional social forums in the GJM. However, the WSF and the European Social Forum (ESF) were criticized by some participants and observers for their bureaucratic nature, lack of true representativeness, marginalization of the voices of the poor and indigenous communities, and formal bureaucratic organization (see also Hodkinson, 2002; Treanor, 2004; Adamovsky, 2004). Tensions began to emerge by the second WSF between Institutional Left and autonomous actors, or what Petras (2002) described as a division between radicals and reformers. The WSF met in 2016 in Montreal, Canada, and in 2018 in Porto Alegre, Brazil. (The WSF official website can be found at http://www.forumsocialmundial.org.br/.)

Genoa, 19–21 July 2001, protests against the G8 summit

The G8 represents the eight nations with the largest economies in the world (Canada, France, Germany, Italy, Japan, Russia, the UK and the US). The EU is also represented. These eight nations and the EU representative meet as a body periodically to set global political and economic agendas. As such, the G8 wields enormous political power and influences economic globalization. Protesters see the G8 as standing for corporate interests and against the interests of the citizens of the world. Preparatory activities for this counter-summit protest started in the Genoa Social Forum in May of that year. Following the model of the WSF meeting in Porto Alegre, Brazil, activists from all over Europe together with 800 movement groups and organizations gathered under the ESF slogan 'Another World is Possible' to discuss issues such as debt, the fight against poverty, gender inequality, labour issues, the environment and so on. The Genoa Social Forum then, through its webpage and through various listserves, coordinated the preparations for the counter-summit. The Genoa Social Forum organized housing for affinity groups and provided information on the location of the media centre, legal support and maps of the city noting the locations of the various assemblies and activities.

Key protests

On 20 July, approximately 80,000 protesters breached the 'red zone', the area the authorities had marked out as forbidden to the protesters, and the following day some 300,000 protesters mobilized against the G8. The protesters organized in columns and blocs – some but not all of which originated within the Genoa Social Forum. The Yellow Column was actually made up of the Pink and Silver Bloc and the White Overalls (*Tute Bianche*). The Pink and Silver Bloc was organized around the idea of 'tactical frivolity' and incorporated an atmosphere of festival; the White Overalls were dressed in padded outfits after the style of the Michelin Man – not only to protect themselves from the police but also to highlight the need for that protection in the face of police brutality. They engaged in confrontational non-violent direct action. The White Column incorporated activists from the Italian *Rete Lilliput*, advocates of non-violent, non-confrontational civil disobedience; environmentalists; lay Christians; Communist youth groups and social

Figure 3.1

A street theatre contingent forms part of the protests against US President George Bush's visit to the Asia Pacific Economic Cooperation (APEC) Forum in Sydney in 2008.

Copyright: Elizabeth Humphrys

centre activists. The Black Bloc organized their own series of direct actions, which included militant actions, targeted vandalism of property and self-defence. Genoa became infamous within the GJM for the level of police brutality experienced by the protesters, including violent police raids and beatings against unarmed and non-resisting protesters, tear gas and the police shooting and killing of Carlo Giuliani, a 22-year-old activist (for some first-person accounts, see Anonymous, 2001; Federici and Caffentzis, 2004; Juris, 2008) (Figure 3.1).

'Seattle was not the beginning': Precursors to the GJM

Katsiaficas (2004) argues that, while Seattle made a huge impact on the anti-globalization movement and later served as an iconic origin story, it was not the beginning of the GJM. He argues the movement actually originated in Venezuela, South Korea, India, Germany and dozens of other countries outside the US. He writes that, 'In fact, the Seattle protests themselves involved some 1300 civic, social movement and trade union organizations from over 80 countries. And furthermore, on N30, there were major demonstrations in 14 US cities; 20,000 people marched in Paris, 8,000 in Manila, 3,000 in Seoul and thousands more around the world' (Katsiaficas, 2004: 3).

National precursors

In Europe alone, important global justice precursor movements include the anti-roads movement in the UK (Flesher Fominaya, 2013), the anti-nuclear movement (Rivat, 2013), the Confederation Paysanne (Morena, 2013) and organizations such as ATTAC (Fillieule and Sommier, 2013) in France. Anarchist and autonomous movements, the environmental movement, feminist movements, the anti-militarist and conscientious objector movement and the lay Christian movement (*cristianos de base*) were all important precursors to and influences on the GJM in Spain (Flesher Fominaya, 2005, 2007a). Throughout Europe, squatter movements and autonomous movements (Flesher Fominaya, 2005; Owens *et al.*, 2013) were important in providing social spaces where GJM activists could meet and plan movement events (including debates, seminars, workshops, protests, community outreach and education activities, fundraising concerts and parties and so on) and where activists travelling from one city to another could stay during counter-summit protests and other mobilizations. These squatted social centres were also important social movement laboratories (Melucci, 1991) where prefigurative participatory democratic decision-making practices and protest tactics, such as how to resist evictions, had been developed.

In Australia, Humphrys (2007: 2) writes that:

> the most notable precursor to the anti-globalization movement was the 1998 campaign to stop a Rio Tinto uranium mine on Aboriginal land at Jabiluka in the Northern Territory. In the Jabiluka campaign, sections of the environment movement, the indigenous justice movement and the student movement began to draw links between the agenda of multinationals, the culpability of the Australian government and the long-term oppression of the indigenous community.

Many other examples of precursor movements could be traced around the world. In each of these cases, these precursor movements left a legacy of ideas, practices, activists and movement culture that nourished and influenced the GJM. But, most importantly, they had begun to make clear connections between what were previously seen as single issues (i.e. nuclear power) and global capitalism, which was seen as being at the heart of multiple, linked forms of oppression, injustice, and environmental and social degradation. The movements, therefore, began to establish cross-movement alliances nationally and in recognition that the problems were not confined to any one nation but were systemic transnationally.

Zapatistas

Perhaps the best-known and most influential Seattle precursor movement was the *Ejército Zapatista de Liberación Nacional* (the Zapatista Army of National Liberation, also known as the Zapatistas or the EZLN), which originated in Chiapas, Mexico. The issues of land ownership, agriculture and indigenous rights were central to the Zapatista movement. They critiqued the North American Free Trade Agreement (NAFTA) for its neoliberal economic programme that would liberalize trade and investment at the expense of the poor. At issue, crucially, was the lifting of the collective village ownership of land under the *ejido* system to a free market system, which would have severe economic, social and cultural consequences for the indigenous people of Chiapas.

The EZLN first took up arms on 1 January 1994, the day NAFTA came into effect, the implementation of which would threaten indigenous access to collective land, which would worsen their already low conditions of living and destroy the fabric of their communities and way of life (De Angelis, 2000).

In 1996, more than 3000 people from over 40 countries gathered in Chiapas at the invitation of the EZLN for the First Intergalactic Encounter for Humanity and Against Neoliberalism, where people could come together to discuss capitalism, radical democracy and revolutionary activism. The EZLN is an armed guerrilla movement that seeks to protect indigenous rights in Mexico but does not seek to take over state power. Instead, they advocate that civil society organize itself and resist neoliberal encroachments on the rights of citizens. The *encuentro* (encounter) philosophy is based on dialogue that seeks common points of discussion and agreement, with the purpose of motivating people and networks to organize to struggle against neoliberalism but does not propose a specific political programme, a unified ideology or a universal model of action (De Angelis, 2000; Callahan, 2004). The EZLN also engaged in *consultas* (public consultations) and marches, and their slogans 'one world in which many worlds fit' and 'lead by obeying' reflect their commitment to diversity and consultation. The first encounter in 1996 was followed by two more: one in southern Spain in 1997 and another in Brazil in 1999. The Zapatista uprising would inspire many activists in the GJM and led directly, through the 1996 and 1997 *encuentros* sponsored by the Zapatistas, to the formation of the People's Global Action network, which in turn participated in the organization of the 1999 Anti-WTO Seattle protest, widely considered to be the iconic 'birth' of the GJM. They were also an important influence on the creation of Indymedia (see Chapter 5), which was 'born' in Seattle (Callahan, 2004).

Transnational precursors

As can be seen in the example of the Intergalactic transnational encounters, precursors to the GJM can be found not only in specific *national* movements but also in *transnational initiatives* to coordinate global protests against free trade agendas and the institutions that work to further them. Many activists in Seattle, for example, had been active in the Jubilee 2000 campaign (see Chapter 1) or in transnational peace organizations such as the Women's International League for Peace and Freedom (Smith, 2001). Global anti-capitalist campaigns, such as the J18 Carnival Against Capitalism, had been called for by the UK groups Reclaim the Streets and Critical Mass, central actors in the British anti-roads movement. The J18 campaign (18 June 1999) in the City of London formed part of the Global Carnival Against Capital, an international day of protest whose slogan was 'Our resistance is as transnational as capital' and which was timed to coincide with the G8 summit in Cologne, Germany. One important transnational development that predated Seattle was the creation of the People's Global Action against Free Trade and the WTO, later shortened to People's Global Action (PGA), which was to become an important network in the GJM.

People's Global Action

PGA was inspired by the Zapatista encounters, and the idea for the network and its coordination began to take shape at the Zapatista-inspired Second Intergalactic Encounter for Humanity and Against Neoliberalism in Spain in 1997. Its foundational conference took place in Geneva at an encounter that coincided with the second Ministerial Conference of the WTO in June 1998. The purpose of the PGA was to provide a loose network of regional networks that would coordinate and support actions by activists resisting the neoliberal capitalist development paradigm, to project an awareness of these struggles globally and, in keeping with the Zapatista influence, to inspire people to resist corporate domination through civil disobedience and collective action. The PGA was never formally organized, there was no set membership but it was facilitated by a convenors committee that worked mostly through the Internet to coordinate actions and to communicate (Routledge, 2004). The committee was not authorized to speak for the PGA or represent it. The PGA was founded around five guiding principles or 'hallmarks' (see Box 3.2).

At the third encounter in Cochabamba, Bolivia, in 2001, the PGA established four campaigns focused on 'militarism, paramilitarism and state terrorism; territory and sovereignty [e.g. issues of land and water resources and indigenous rights]; privatisation; and construction of grassroots alternatives to the capitalist system and the strengthening of local initiatives and struggles. All of these campaigns relate in particular ways to people's defence of their communities and commons' (Routledge, 2004: 7). In addition to a decentralized multiplicity of local campaigns, the PGA organized a series of caravans, which included 'an Intercontinental caravan in 1999, which brought five hundred Asian farmers to tour Europe; a US caravan that culminated in the WTO protests in Seattle in 1999; and caravans before and after the PGA conferences in Bangalore, India (1999), and Cochabamba, Bolivia (2001). In addition, there have been speaking tours (e.g. which brought Colombian activists from the Process of Black Communities to Europe in 2001), and workshops and seminars, concerning neoliberalism and its alternatives, on several continents' (Routledge, 2004: 9). The PGA was also heavily involved in promoting and coordinating the 'Global Days of Action' against the summit meetings of the WTO, IMF, the G8 and the World Bank. Some of the movements involved in the PGA included the National Alliance of People's Movement (India), the MST landless peasants' movement (Brazil), the Movement for National Land and Agricultural Reform (Sri Lanka), *Ya Basta!* (Italy), the Movement of Global Resistance

---

Box 3.2 The Five People's Global Action Hallmarks

1. A very clear rejection of capitalism, imperialism and feudalism; all trade agreements, institutions and governments that promote destructive globalization.

2. We reject all forms and systems of domination and discrimination including, but not limited to, patriarchy, racism and religious fundamentalism of all creeds. We embrace the full dignity of all human beings.

3. A confrontational attitude, since we do not think that lobbying can have a major impact in such biased and undemocratic organizations, in which transnational capital is the only real policy-maker.

4. A call to direct action and civil disobedience, support for the struggles of social movements, advocating forms of resistance that maximize respect for life and oppressed peoples' rights, as well as the construction of local alternatives to global capitalism.

5. An organizational philosophy based on decentralization and autonomy.

Source: People's Global Action, available at http://www.nadir.org/nadir/initiativ/agp/free/pga/hallm.htm.

(MRG) (Spain), *Comité des Luttes anti-capitalistes* (Canada), the ecological Rainbow Keepers from Russia and Ukraine, groups from the transnational Via Campesina network and many more (Routledge, 2004; Style, 2004; Maiba, 2005).

The challenge of diversity: Central cleavages in the GJM

A global movement encompassing such a wide range of actors necessarily produces internal tension. Indeed, some would argue that the best way to conceive of the GJM is to see it not as a unified empirical entity but rather as a loose-knit heterogeneous network of actors, many of whom may not even have been aware of each other. Indeed, Cumbers *et al.* (2008: 183) argue that although

> GJM networks can be seen as connecting places with each other 'in opposition to neoliberalism' the individual movements that make up the GJM are 'heavily territorialized in their struggles' and very uneven in the extent to which they 'are able to develop extensive translocal connections and associations'.

Local activists who are able to make contact and gain support from international activists with symbolic and cultural capital (including linguistic, media and technical skills that fit into a cosmopolitan international Western framework) are more likely to be able to break into the international 'public sphere' more effectively than other resource-poor groups without these advantages (the Zapatistas, for example, had strong international contacts with media savvy, biographically available, highly mobile, educated and middle-class activists who were connected to important international networks. Other indigenous groups mobilizing in Mexico did not and are much less known). Scholars writing about the GJM as a global movement, it is argued, are imposing a unity on it in a way that simply reproduces activist and intellectual narratives about global civil society and run the risk of ignoring the territorially rooted nature of much mobilization that may go unnoticed even in the same city or nation, let alone come to international attention. While scholars disagree about the extent to which it makes sense to talk about a single global justice movement (I return to this question at the end of this chapter), research has shown the existence of some salient central tensions, cleavages, marginalizations and exclusions that cut across a range of actors working together across geographical space to contest the negative effects and logics of neoliberal capitalist globalization.

Exclusions and marginalizations in the WSF and beyond

The World Social Forum (WSF) was crisscrossed by multiple tensions and cleavages. Janet Conway's work (2011a; 2013) highlights the many forms of marginalization that occur within the supposedly 'open space' of the WSF. Central to her analysis is how the structural relations of power, and particularly the 'coloniality of power', shape interactions within the WSF. By *coloniality of power* she means 'the colonial character of the world system that persists in the present in the global hierarchies of knowledge and power that privilege the modern West' (2011a: 217). She argues that this is especially relevant to consider given how important place-based subaltern movements of the third and fourth worlds are in the WSF. By *subaltern* she means 'populations who are practically excluded from modern politics, despite rhetorics of universal inclusion. These include slum dwellers, tribal and indigenous peoples and *dalits* (those outside the Indian caste system, previously known as 'untouchables'), among other poor peoples' movements' (2011a: 223).

Since the WSF is conceived within the rubric of communication in a 'global civil society', it makes sense to raise questions about the extent to which true deliberation and exchange can take place across class, cultural and colonial differences, which, 'in the context of global coloniality, are constructed hierarchically, including on the putatively egalitarian terrain of the Global Justice Movement' (ibid). In line with other critical post-colonial theorists (e.g. Said, de Souza Santos, Escobar), Conway argues that the global hegemony of discourse constructed around key concepts of Western modernity (that claim to be universal and are based on Enlightenment thinking about truth claims based on 'scientific' knowledge) discredits other forms and traditions of knowledge as *un*scientific and in so doing silences 'the colonial other', including indigenous movements and other subaltern movements across the global South.

These communities are particularly important to integrate, listen to and learn from given not only that they represent the most excluded and oppressed communities under global neoliberal capitalism but also that their cosmologies provide alternative worldviews that can usefully expose the limitations of modern Western thought. Because of the historical process of imperial globality and global coloniality, the different movements represented within the WSF do not come together on an equal playing field but rather one that is shot through with hierarchies and divides: 'North/South, non-indigenous/indigenous, and modern emancipatory/subaltern "other" divides'.

Each of these divides, of course, is composed of many other divides, for example, between different forms of organizing and ideological orientations of activists working *within* the global North and *within* the global South, competition between different indigenous groups (see e.g. Speed *et al.*, 2006), and so on. Conway (2011a: 224) argues that the inclusion of subaltern groups and movements in the WSF transformed its political culture and also

> 'posed deep challenges to the modernization, urbanization and development discourses that continue to underpin the utopias of much of the "anti-globalization" movement. These movements of extremely poor and marginalized people had heretofore been largely invisible on the international stage despite impressive levels of self-organization and forays by individual leaders into UN-sponsored international fora'.

Conway argues (2011a) that the shifting of the geographical location of the WSF events has been crucial to the ability of these movements to integrate and to influence not only the WSF but also the wider GJM, an influence that has grown over time. She highlights the fact that the resources, organizing priorities and capacities practiced by local organizing committees of the WSF also influence which groups are present and have a voice. This reminds us that the WSF doesn't take place in a vacuum but that each WSF encounter is situated in a local political context that is itself shot through with competing interests and hierarchies. Despite the increasing influence of these movements, however, Conway (2011a: 225) argues that important inequalities among movements get reproduced again and again and will continue to do so unless there is

> 'affirmative action to ensure that marginalized and minority populations are present and their voices and perspectives amplified. Feminist commentators on the WSF have been most insistent about this, noting that women regularly make up half the participants but only a tiny fraction of the speakers, and protesting at the historical marginality of feminism as a perspective, despite

the founding presence of feminist networks in the World Social Forum'.

Doerr (2011) and Baker (2013) have also noted the important role of activist translators in challenging hegemonic practices within the social forums and other arenas of deliberation in the GJM. Doerr (2011: 530) explores the work of *Babels* who 'actively encouraged socially disadvantaged groups and speakers of non-Western languages to express themselves in the European level meetings, cooperating with and accompanying them within the social context of the European preparatory assemblies'.

Hegemonic masculinity versus feminist forms of practice and epistemologies are another crucial divide within the WSF and within the GJM more broadly (see Coleman and Bassi, 2011 on militant masculinities in the British anti-globalization movement; Doerr, 2007 on the ESF, and Conway, 2011b).

Eschle (2005) highlights the many critiques by feminists of the marginalization of their concerns in the 2003 WSF. Their laments are all too familiar for women and feminists mobilizing in leftist spaces (indeed these types of criticism spurred the second wave of feminism) and take a particular form in those influenced by orthodox interpretations of Marxism in which 'women's issues' and feminist issues are seen as secondary (less serious and urgent) to the more important struggle against capitalism. Eschle (2005) and Eschle and Maiguashca (2010) trace the way that overtly feminist voices within the anti-globalization movement have been marginalized not only in the sense of 'silencing' in deliberative exchanges but also through exclusion from authoritative movement texts about the GJM (several of them written by women). Eschle (2005) shows that not only are women and women's voices marginalized in these texts but also explicitly feminist contributions are rarely included. Today, feminists have succeeded in showing the ways in which capitalism is itself profoundly gendered and how there can be no progressive social transformation without integrating fully not only women but a feminist perspective into a politics of change, although of course there is still a long way to go. In these analyses (e.g. Eschle, Conway), feminist understandings of the GJM and the WSF are contrasted with the praxis of 'Porto Alegre man', which is a rhetorical representation that refers to the persistence of male domination in the WSF through patterns of hegemonic masculinist practices (see Conway 2013: 22).

Of course, the marginalization and exclusion of subordinate voices, knowledge and cosmologies in deliberative exchanges and decision-making processes that are putatively 'open' and 'horizontal' (but are in fact shot through with hierarchies) are not exclusive to the WSF but cut through the vast array of different groups and movements that make up the GJM. One of the central cleavages and one of the most widely discussed by activists and scholars in the GJM was that between 'horizontals' and 'verticals' and I turn to that now.

Autonomous movements and the Institutional Left

One of the key challenges facing the GJM – or, indeed, any transnational heterogeneous movement – is how movement groups with different ideologies, tactics and agendas can work together across their differences. For example, one point of disagreement in many movements that practice direct action is the legitimacy of using 'violent' tactics or property vandalism. Transnational movements also need to work across cultural and linguistic differences. All of these challenges were faced by activists in the GJM. However, the most fundamental division in the movement – and a tension that continues to be very relevant today for progressive leftist movements – is that between Institutional Left and autonomous approaches to collective action. It is therefore worth taking some time to explore why this tension exists and what some of its implications are for social movements.

The GJM can be seen as having an internal tension between two tendencies that are simultaneously in dialogue with and in opposition to each another. This tension has often been referred to as a conflict between 'verticals' and 'horizontals' (with reference to differences in organizational form), or between 'reformists' and 'radicals' (with reference to differences in proposed mechanisms of change). However, the differences between approaches are more profound and complex than these distinctions imply. On the one hand are the Institutional Left groups that were crucial actors in the development and formation of significant GJM protests and forums. As in the case of Seattle, the labour union federation AFL-CIO was an important player in terms of organization and mobilization. In Europe, especially in France, ATTAC, an organization founded in France in 1998 to promote a tax on foreign exchange transactions with branches in 40 countries, was a key actor in the development of the GJM and a main force behind the establishment of the WSF, along with Brazilian social movements, organizations and the Brazilian Workers Party (Seoane and Taddei, 2002; Fillieule and Sommier, 2013). In the UK, the Socialist Workers Party was one of the organizers of the ESF in 2004. Throughout Europe, organizations closely affiliated with unions and political parties were active in GJM campaigns, forums and mobilizations.

On the other hand, there were the autonomous actors, groups and networks, such as the PGA, who attracted much of the media attention, carried out direct actions and symbolic protests, engaged in confrontations with police and practised prefigurative politics. While both types of groups were involved in the GJM, they did not always work easily together and, in some cases, the differences between them prevented unified collective action. The differences between approaches are summarized in Table 3.1 and discussed in an ideal-typical form to clarify and stress the differences. In reality, within any given local or national context, these differences could be more complex and less neatly separated, and alliances between organizational types are frequent especially in times of 'crisis' (e.g. the invasion of Iraq in 2003). While this discussion makes reference to the GJM, the same tensions have characterized leftist and progressive social movements for many years and continue to do so, not only in Europe but also in the US, Latin America and

Table 3.1 Ideal-typical differences between autonomous and Institutional Left political models

	Institutional Left	Autonomous
Political model	Representative	Participatory
Organizational structure	Vertical with clear division of labour and authority	Horizontal, rarely permanent delegations of responsibility
Decision-making	Votes, negotiations between representatives	Consensus, assembly is sovereign
Subject	Unitary or primary identity (worker/citizen)	Multiple cross-cutting identities, often reject primary identities as basis of collective action
Ideological base	Unitary/explicit	Heterogeneous/often left-implicit
Legitimate political actor	Collective/party/union	Individual acting collectively
Use of acronyms	Important identifier, symbol of political stance and responsibility	Reject acronyms
Political arena	Public/government	Public (streets, public spaces) and private (personal relations, daily life)
Typical repertoire of contention	Manifestos, protest marches, strikes, legal reforms	Protest demonstrations, direct action, civil disobedience, alternative self-managed collective projects (e.g. social centres), counter-cultural lifestyle politics, cyberactivism
Means/ends	Variable	Inseparable, means are ends in themselves if directed at social transformation
Social transformation comes through:	Institutions	Creating alternatives, cultural resistance
Organization is:	Permanent	Contingent, open to continual critical reflection and dissolution

(continued)

Table 3.1 (continued)

	Institutional Left	Autonomous
Stance on anonymity:	Reject	Variable: use of masks, anonymous hacking, sabotage without risking arrest, key tactics of some activists; contested as a legitimate strategy by others
Resources	Varied: access to institutional resources, funding, office space, formal access to mainstream media, legal support	Minimal, limited, contingent, ad hoc and/or rare

elsewhere, albeit with different configurations and extenuating factors. Unlike some characterizations of central cleavages in anti-capitalist movements or leftist movements (e.g. Ibrahim, 2011), I deliberately elect *not* to organize this tension along explicitly ideological lines. Autonomous actors can hold a range of ideologies and many are actively anti-ideological. Likewise, the labels 'socialist', 'communist' and even 'anarchist' (though less often) can characterize the self-identification of actors on *both* sides of this divide.

The central differences reside in the way in which the members of each type of organization understand the legitimate and desirable forms of organizing. For the Institutional Left, the central characteristics are formal structures, representative leadership, formal affiliation, bureaucratic and functional systems of operation, and hierarchical structures of decision-making, all with a clear division of labour between fixed roles. For the autonomous left, the desirable characteristics are non-hierarchical structures, informal groups, without representation for fixed roles, without formal membership and connected between themselves inflexible and informal network. If the organizational model of the Institutional Left has dominated historically, the autonomous forms of organization have become more widespread in recent years, facilitated – according to some – by the development of digital and social media communication.

The Institutional Left

The classic organizational model of the Institutional Left is *representative*, with vertical structures (there are positions with greater and lesser decision-making power), decision-making through a voting system or through negotiations between representatives, and a clear division of labour. The political subject is unitary (the worker, the citizen) and the ideological base is explicit and (in theory, at least) also unitary. The Institutional Left tradition also embraces the notion of an intellectual vanguard and/or party leadership, which is linked to an idea of professionalism. Leadership, and even participation itself, is based on political and ideological credentials and explicit membership (members might have membership cards, pay membership dues and so on).

The legitimate political actor is the collective or organization because that is seen as the source of strength and legitimacy of the organization. Conversely, unaffiliated 'individuals' (political actors who do not form part of an established organization) are disdained because they are seen as less effective in political intervention. This stress on the organization or collective body is linked to the defence of the use of acronyms (which appear on banners, logos, manifestos and so on) that are considered to represent not only a clear declaration of political principles but also a clear declaration of responsibility and accountability towards the members and supporters of the organization. The political sphere of this model is public and within the system of government (through direct membership, affiliation or engagement). The Institutional Left model defends the transformation of society through its institutions, either by controlling them or by influencing them. The typical repertoire of contention consists primarily of marches, manifestos, strikes and threats of strike, and legal reforms.

Autonomous movements

The autonomous model rejects representative democracy and majority rule; instead, it defends a participatory model, based on direct democracy and self-governance, with horizontal (non-hierarchical) structures, decision-making through consensus (if possible and necessary) or common minimum agreements, in the forum of an assembly (usually open), and rarely with permanent delegations of responsibility (with the exception of spokespeople in some cases) (see also Kingsnorth, 2003; Starr, 2004).

The network form of organization and communication allows for the integration and interaction of multiple issues and identities and for a connection among local, national and global levels of action. The networks are 'biodegradable', dissolving and regenerating into new forms of organization and action. Proponents of autonomous movements such as Katsiaficas (1997: 200) would argue that 'The structure of autonomous movements facilitates individual decision making and political development. With initiative coming from many sources, collectives are able to act immediately and decisively without waiting for a central committee to deliberate and approve ideas.' Detractors, including some critics within the autonomous sectors, would argue that consensus and participatory deliberation can slow decision-making and sometimes stop action altogether.

Autonomous activists see collective identity (or the sense of common belonging to the movement) as being based on a recognition of difference and diversity; therefore, the political subject is conceived as having multiple overlapping identities. The ideological base of autonomous politics is hetero-geneous and frequently not explicit. From the autonomous perspective, ide-ologies and orthodoxies are seen as frozen and prescriptive and also tend to divide and exclude, rather than include and increase, diversity (Flesher Fominaya, 2015b).

There is a tendency to reject the use of acronyms or labels, because of the priority given to action and grassroots movements in symbolic representa-tion of all citizens/humans over the interests or representation of particular organizations. Strategically, also, the absence of acronyms is seen as a way to increase diversity and participation because acronyms (as with ideologies and doctrines) create boundaries of exclusion (Flesher Fominaya, 2015b).

The political sphere is public (in the streets and public spaces) but also 'private' in the sense of being personal and part of everyday life. This means that political practice cannot be limited to the public sphere but, rather, needs to reside in all spaces and social relations. The typical repertoire of contention includes protest marches, supporting strikes, direct action and civil disobedience but this 'visible' moment is only part of movement politi-cal practice.

Autonomous movement actors seek to break with the status quo and to provoke reflection and social transformation through prefigurative politics. They attempt to create tools and practices in the present that 'prefigure' the future society that is aspired to and to generate alternatives such as social cooperatives and social centres, self-organized consumer groups and coun-terinformation collectives (Jordan, 1998; Abramsky, 2001; Notes from Nowhere, 2003). Therefore, the way autonomous activists engage in politics (i.e. consensus or deliberative decision-making and direct action) is as impor-tant as the issues and goals they mobilize around (i.e. neoliberal capitalist globalization) (Flesher Fominaya, 2015b).

Autonomous activists' insistence on independence from trade unions, political parties and NGOs forms part of their critique of representative democracy. Instead, they favour the creation of autonomous spaces where decisions can be made and implemented directly through processes of delib-eration and consensus.

The main differences between these approaches in the GJM did not rest on deep differences between analyses of the ills of capitalism. However, they do reflect a long-standing historical confrontation between libertarian/anar-chist autonomous models and Marxist-Leninist communist models which, in Europe, goes back to the nineteenth century. Explicitly 'autonomous' movements in Europe, for example, developed as a rejection of the discipline imposed by Marxist-Leninist parties and organizations. In the GJM, the adoption of the 'anti-capitalist' label represents a shift away from more nar-rowly defined ideological critiques of capitalism to a more global critique that encompasses various ideologies and orientations.

The tensions between these two approaches in the GJM are well docu-mented (e.g. Motta, 2011; Petras, 2002) but rarely systematically analysed as I have done here (see also Flesher Fominaya, 2007a, and see Pleyers, 2010 for an alternative conceptualization). The fundamental differences between these two approaches led to tensions and conflict when proponents of one or the other approach attempted to work together. The greatest problems generated were conflicts not only in attempts to create coordinating platforms at a national or local level but also in transnational attempts at coordination such as the ESF and WSF. The clearest example of this was the creation of *parallel* 'Autonomous European Social Forums' as an alternative to the official ESFs, which are seen by many autonomous actors as dominated and controlled by Institutional Left actors with strong ties to political parties and major unions (Anonymous, 2004).

For their part, Institutional Left actors suffered a sort of crisis in the face of criticisms from autonomous actors and also felt that autonomous approaches were strategically and ideologically flawed. De Angelis (2001) points out how genuinely difficult the autonomous approach is to understand from an Institutional Left perspective. The network form of organization was not only puzzling but also irritating or threatening. Far from expressing a strength, as autonomous actors would argue, it was seen 'as an expression of the low degree of development of the movement, as an early stage in the process of building a political party better suited to "represent" the aspirations of millions' (De Angelis, 2001).

Institutional Left actors saw (and continue to see) themselves as offering an efficient, effective, legitimate and accountable approach, based on the strength of their membership. They pose a legitimate question as to whether social movements can, in fact, effect important political change without engaging political parties and unions directly. Autonomous actors, for their part, often see Institutional Left actors as out of touch, outdated and trying to subvert and control the movement's internal democratic process to gain power for their own organizations (see, for example, Schnews, 2001). In the GJM, autonomous actors provided Institutional Left actors with the benefits of a radical flank effect, where their more spectacular and confrontational forms of mobilization and critique opened up spaces for dialogue within state and transnational institutions between Institutional Left and state and economic actors. As such, the two poles of the movement can be seen as complementing each other despite their real differences. This typology is based primarily on distinctions in the Western European context, although similar tensions and forms of autonomous practice are found around the world. Nevertheless, each local and national experience draws on unique movement traditions as well as transnational ones to shape autonomous practice. Autonomous practice can also be connected to a wide range of issues and goals and mobilized by people with diverse identities and cultures.

Autonomous practice in Argentina

Although the roots of autonomous practice predate the GJM significantly, autonomous principles and practice gained traction during this period. One particularly influential experience happened in Argentina following the economic crisis that prompted the government of Argentina to freeze all personal bank accounts in December 2001 and default on $95 billion of debt.

This crisis (and the freezing of their personal savings accounts) met with massive resistance from the Argentinian people and prompted the rapid development of social movements across the country, which largely adopted horizontal styles of mobilization and self-organization. Hundreds of thousands of people took to the streets to bang on pots and pans and to say '*que se vayan todos!*' (They all must go!) in a mass act of disobedience. The social movements that developed across Argentina following this revolutionary moment were very diverse and encompassed a range of experiences, including factory occupations by working-class people, movements of the unemployed middle-class and autonomous indigenous movements that were fighting to recover stolen land. The commitment to autonomy, horizontality, direct action and pre-figurative politics was a striking characteristic of many of these movements.

As with autonomous movements elsewhere, including other autonomous movements in Latin America, these movements were questioning hierarchical practice, formal representative politics and hierarchical institutions. Instead, they were committed to what is known in Spanish as *auto-gestion*, or collective self-management. Local neighbourhood assemblies broke urban dwellers out of their isolation from each other and brought them together into new forms of social relations, community and solidarity. As Sitrin (2011: 256) describes

'in each neighborhood the assemblies worked, and a number of them still continue to work, on a variety of projects, from helping facilitate barter networks, creating popular kitchens, alternative medicine, planting organic gardens and sometimes taking over buildings, including the highly symbolic creation of community centers in bankrupt and abandoned banks. These occupied spaces house any number of projects, including kitchens, small print shops, daycare areas, afterschool help for kids, libraries, micro-enterprises, free Internet access in computer usage, and even a small movie theater. Events range from the political discussion, to literary and artistic discussions, to salsa and tango classes and improvisational theater'.

Far from being unique to Argentina (despite being a remarkable historical experience), this range of activities is shared by activists practicing autonomous politics around the world (e.g. in many squatted or self-organized social centres; see the example of Bolivian anarco-feminists in Chapter 5). But the Argentinian experience deeply influenced activists outside of Argentina as well, notably in Spain and Italy as well as elsewhere in Latin America.

Another very influential movement that formed part of the same historical moment was the unemployed workers movement known as the *piqueteros*. These workers organized against local governments and corporations and engaged in highly visible and powerful forms of direct action which involved blocking major highways and roads (known as *piquetes*, which is where the name comes from). Just as with the British anti-roads protesters creating temporary autonomous zones (see Chapter 4), these Argentinian unemployed workers were symbolically creating a free space, liberating it from state control and using it as a space within which to resist that control (Zibechi, 2008). As Sitrin (2011: 257) describes, 'not having a location of work, the traditional means of protest for a worker, a strike or job action was unavailable, and thus, the *piquete* was created; blocking the roads to shut down the flow of production at the point of distribution rather than production'.

In addition to these movements, Argentina witnessed hundreds of workplaces being taken over and run by workers, 'without bosses and generally without hierarchy. The majority of these workplaces had been abandoned by the previous owners and after processes of assemblies and discussions were then taken over and put into production by a segment of the employees. Almost every workplace sees itself as an integral part of the community, and the community sees the workplace in the same way' (Sitrin, 2011: 258).

Like the Zapatistas, and the Brazilian MST (Movimiento sem Terra), the Argentinian movements inspired and influenced movements in Europe and continue to do so today. For example, the commitment to autonomy coupled with a close attention to the politics of affect (or how emotional attachments and solidarity form the basis of a respectful and caring model of social relations as the basis of politics) has enriched and influenced autonomous feminist movements in Spain, which have long been engaged in a rich dialogue with movements in Latin America. The similarity between the language and conceptual framework of autonomous activists in Spain and Argentina, despite the many differences between the two contexts, is striking. And yet, as Zibechi (2008) shows, in fact, the Latin American experience during the GJM is radically different from the European one.

Zibechi's Analysis of Latin America's New Social Movements and 'Territories in Resistance'

From the 1990s to about 2005, Latin America witnessed the most important cycle of mobilization in many decades. This broad range of mobilizations can broadly be classed as anti-neoliberal, arguably commencing with the mass resistance in Caracas in 1989 to the Venezuelan government's neoliberal reforms: a conflict that left 500 dead. During this period, Bolivia experienced major social conflicts around gas and water, and there were mass mobilizations in Peru, Paraguay, Ecuador, Brazil, Uruguay and of course Argentina. These many mass mobilizations resulted in a radical shift in the relations of power, bringing down many governments and changing governments across Latin America in a process known as 'the Pink Tide'. What distinguishes this wave of mobilization from, for example, the European wave during the same period, is the territorialized nature of resistance and the centrality of the indigenous political subject. The existence of important indigenous communities in Latin America means that these new resistance movements can trace their genealogy to indigenous histories of resistance to the expropriation of their lands since (at least) the 1960s.

From the 1960s, indigenous communities began a process of recuperation of their lands and they based their demands on the concept of 'territory'. Zibechi (2008) argues that this conception of territory breaks radically from its classically understood connection to the nation-state. Indigenous communities are formed on territories that operate autonomously from the hegemonic power of the state and which claim for themselves the right to autonomy and self-determination without aspiring to control the state (unlike classic Marxist aspirations to claim the state in order to abolish it and private property). He argues that these demands discursively centred on the notion of territory become central to indigenous movements' discourse during the 1990s. These indigenous communities conceive of themselves as 'pueblos' not nations.

The importance of 'territory' is not limited to indigenous communities, however, but also extends to the landless peasantry and the marginalized urban poor. The former can be seen in the Brazilian landless peasant movement MST, which began claiming land in 1979, managing to occupy 25 million hectares in 5000 different settlements since that time. Zibechi gives the example of La Paz, Bolivia, for the latter, in which the popular classes have illegally occupied 70% of the city's urban territory. He argues that during this process of mobilization, new forms of social movements have emerged that can be distinguished from what came before, in particular from classic workers' movements. In a process similar to the NSM theory that I discussed in Chapter 1, but now describing and stemming from the Latin American reality instead of the Western European one that Touraine, Melucci and Habermas were experiencing and writing about, Zibechi distinguishes the key characteristics of these new movements. First, he argues that the indigenous actor is the most important and central figure and offers alternative cosmological visions of the world that are different from hegemonic neoliberal logics. Second, he highlights the fact that women increasingly play a fundamental role as they try to avoid the control, manipulation and oppression- not only of the neoliberal capitalist system- but also of the very patriarchal and sexist aspects of indigenous culture in their communities. The increasing autonomy of youth vis-à-vis the older generation is another important characteristic of these new political subjects.

As discussed above, the new conception of territory as autonomous and separate from the nation-state is a central conceptual category developed within the movements. These movements demand autonomy and self-determination but this is linked to a particular territory (rather than being a claim linked to citizenship within the nation-state as in the European context). Identity is also central but as a permanent re-imagination and reinvention of indigenous culture: for example, some political actors argue that there is no need to reproduce sexist and patriarchal culture as a central component of (indigenous) movement identities.

The tradition of collective empowerment through popular education is another key factor that enables these communities to break free of the dependence on the hegemonic state for education and culture. Indigenous conceptions of community that revolve around families headed by women and that are based on participatory assembly style practices transcend ethnicity and become shared across different groups involved in particular struggles (e.g. among indigenous peoples, peasants and Afro-Colombians in Colombia). The classic division between mental and manual labour is rejected by these new political subjects. Zibechi (2008: 1) points to the possibilities opened up by these new movements but does not romanticize them:

> 'Although the territories of the movements open new possibilities for social change they do not represent any guarantee of emancipatory transformation. In the urban peripheries of many Latin American cities, I have seen territories of complexity and diversity, of the construction of horizontal and emancipatory social relations [...] Next to territories in which domination is cloaked in the vulgar forms of vertical and exclusionary militarization. Moving from one neighborhood to the other, simply crossing the street, can represent an abrupt transition between domination and hope. Like all emancipatory creations, urban territories are subjected to the inescapable depletion of the capitalist market, to the destructive competitiveness of the dominant culture, to violence, sexism, individualism and mass consumerism, among other [forms of subjection]' (Translated from Spanish by the author).

In developing his theory and analysis of the new social movements in Latin America, Zibechi (2008) provides us with an important understanding of the way that neoliberal resistance is also shaped profoundly by the history, culture and politics of specific territories in a globalized world.

What was 'new' about the Global Justice Movement?

Some scholars have argued that the GJM was truly distinctive in comparison with earlier movements in the degree to which it was transnational in terms of networks and communication (Seoane and Taddei, 2002; Maiba, 2005); had an increased capacity to coordinate transnational protests; had a global identity and orientation; had a distinctive division of labour between the organizations that comprised it; had distinctive organizational forms and protest tactics (Smith, 2001; Gillham and Edwards, 2003); and had a novel use of information and communications technologies (ICTs) (Sassen, 2004; Ganesh and Stohl, 2010). I would argue that there was much more continuity between earlier movements than some of these accounts would lead us to believe but that there were some distinctive features, characterized more by degree and scope than novelty.

Autonomy, democracy, and the local/national/global nexus

One important characteristic was the increasing importance of autonomous movement actors in global mobilizations, placing these previously marginalized groups and actors at the centre of political struggles (Humphrys, 2007), and the discussion that follows will focus on the autonomous wing of the GJM. But the focus of autonomous movement actors on putting into practice the principles of self-organization, direct/participatory democracy, autonomy, horizontality, diversity and direct action were not, in themselves, new to social movements. The issue of direct/participatory democracy has been central to the feminist, ecology and peace movements, and other so-called 'New Social Movements' of the 1970s, 1980s and early 1990s (e.g. Freeman, 1973; Polletta, 2002; Della Porta, 2005a). The practice of internal democracy in these movements is linked to a critique of representative democracy and a critique of public institutions which Offe (1997) argues social movements nurture. Giddens (2011) highlights the increase in dissatisfaction with representative democratic processes as a generalized feature of modern mature democracies but points out that, paradoxically, this critique does not extend to the concept of democracy itself, which remains as a central principle of modern societies.

The process of creative experimentation in the search for alternative political models is also not new (Melucci, 1989a). Melucci's understanding of social movements as creative laboratories that self-consciously attempt to engage in practices they hope to see adopted by the entire society; that demand autonomy; that are deeply critical of politics in its institutional and Leninist movement forms; and that emphasize the interdependence of the local and global is as applicable today as it was in 1989.

Autonomous GJMs tried to link the local, the national and the global in new and sometimes contradictory ways. Preservation of the local, the distinct and the autonomous went hand in hand with 'globalizing' resistance to the homogenizing effects of neoliberal globalization itself – through the formation of resistance networks that were (ideally) decentralized and non-hierarchical and had multiple points of contacts. Zapatista leader Subcomandante Marcos's call to 'be a Zapatista wherever you are!' was an appeal to a global identity that can be mobilized from any locality. Autonomous global justice movements not only represent the 'progressive' reaction to globalization (in that they struggle for people's right to determine for themselves what is best for them and reach out to a global identity of resistance) but also actively struggle against a regressive or 'fundamentalist' reaction to globalization (that is, intolerance of difference, preservation of the status quo) by fighting against fascism, racism and anti-migration policies in their respective states. These struggles take place on multiple terrains simultaneously, as they attempt to subvert and transcend the national through the establishment of *'global'* networks of resistance and such practices as 'summit-hopping'; *nationally*, as they resist particular national policies and institutions yet, at times, also appeal to national identities; and *locally* as they hold onto and integrate particular cultural and political traditions into their activities and through the creation of autonomous spaces.

Movement continuity

Many features noted as distinct for the GJM in fact have a long legacy. The concept of movements as polycephalous (meaning 'many-headed') *networks* was developed by Gerlach and Hine in 1970. This concept has been central to what is known as 'New Social Movement' (NSM) theory (e.g. Melucci, 1991; Diani, 1995) (see Chapter 1) and has been a central organizing principle in the GJM.

The self-organization of autonomous spaces to create alternatives was central to the feminist movements of the 1960s and 1970s (in particular, in their more radical forms) and to identity-based movements such as the Black Power movement. Influenced, in part, by these movements (and by a rich anarchist/libertarian tradition), explicitly *autonomous* movements (e.g. Italian Autonomia, Autonomen in Germany, Denmark, Holland and so on) have been very important in Western Europe and clearly influenced the anti-globalization movement, with the Italian Disobeddienti being one obvious example. The Disobeddienti come from the Italian *autonomia* movement and the squatted social centre movement (*centri sociale*) but have also been strongly influenced by the Zapatistas.

Katsiaficas (1997) traces the roots of the European autonomist movements in the 1960 and 1970s. Many of the methodologies and principles embraced by European autonomous groups today emerged from these experiments. In the context of the anti-globalization movement, examples include networks such as Reclaim the Streets (which emerged in the context of the British anti-road protests in the 1990s) and later groups such as the PGA network and *Ya Basta!* in Italy, inspired by the earlier autonomous movements and also by the Zapatista uprising, all with a strong anti-party orientation and a clear rejection of the hierarchical practices and orthodoxies they associate with the Institutional Left.

Distinguishing characteristics between the Global Justice Movement and earlier movements

Della Porta (2005a: 7) argues that studies show that the GJM 'has a more pluralistic identity, weakly connected organizational structure and multi-form action repertoire than those characteristics of previous movements'. I would like to develop these and other features further to highlight some important characteristics that distinguished the GJM from earlier movements.

Democracy and the creation of alternatives

Della Porta argues (2005a) that the concept of democracy and its practice assume a pivotal role for the new global movements. In the autonomous wing of the GJM, the issue of democracy was not one of many issues; rather, it was, in an important sense, the issue with which other issues were inevitably bound. The open assembly, which works on the principles of horizontality, consensus decision-making and a sensitivity to diversity, is the 'hegemonic' model – it is prefigurative politics at work. As I have shown (Flesher Fominaya, 2005; 2007a), those attempting to set up a vertical organizational model were met with fierce criticism and suffered from a lack of legitimacy. As a global justice activist in Madrid told me in 2004:

> Before, if someone was setting up a political project they could choose between different organizational models. Today it would be inconceivable for someone to set up a group or space that wasn't based on the principles of horizontality and openness.

As Della Porta (2005a) points out, issues of internal democracy become more important as the heterogeneity of movements increases. But characterizing democracy as central to the movement, without linking that to notions of autonomy and self-organization, is problematic in that it gives a liberal slant to the movement that can gloss the anarchist/libertarian influence that runs through it and also underplays its fundamentally anti-systemic, anti-capitalist nature. The centrality of democracy to the autonomous GJM resides in both a fundamental critique of representative democracy and a search for practices that replace representation with alternative forms of action and organization. An exclusive focus on democracy also misses the connection between the use of participatory democracy for the creation of alternatives and the belief in the threat to human welfare and survival posed by the current capitalist system.

This idea is apparent in the discussion of Spanish scholar/activist Ramón Fernández Durán (2005), who understood the importance of social movements as resting in their ability to develop new alternative forms of community, necessary to meet 'the inevitable crisis that will be the result of the rapacious abuses of contemporary global capitalism', a crisis he felt 'will threaten survival itself'. From this perspective, the centrality of the issue of democracy moves beyond a mere critique of existing institutions to an active strategy for the creation of necessary alternatives.

From single or total identities to multiple and global identities

This feature has three aspects: first, activists in the GJM felt they formed part of a *global* movement and conceived of their activism in those terms. Activists felt they shared a global collective identity. Second, they allowed for and welcomed multiple identities (even when this created strange tensions such as the simultaneous defence of a nationalist identity and the embracing of a global one). Della Porta (2005b) refers to this as 'multiple belongings and tolerant identities'. The third moment of this feature is the strong anti-identitarian nature of the movement, which is linked to the idea that diversity really works only when no one is pushing their particular identity forward. As shown in the discussion of autonomous political approaches, there is a strong rejection of what is known as 'shopping list politics' (race, gender, class and so on treated separately) and a desire to overcome separate identities to generate a comprehensive critique of capitalism and global injustice. This orientation reflects both a strategic and philosophical component. In their rejection of 'shopping list' politics, autonomous movements force the recognition of the nexus between the myriad critiques and demands underlying any particular issue and deny the reductionism inherent in viewing protests as 'single issue'.

The creation of alternatives as engagement, not separation

The autonomous space is not conceived as a separate, hermetically sealed space but, rather, as an open participatory space. It is not a retreat from society (as with a commune) but, instead, a deliberate incursion into the public sphere to reclaim it for public use (this idea was behind the practice and politics of the influential Reclaim the Streets, which saw reclaiming the streets as reclaiming public inclusive space from the private exclusive space of the car and taking back things which have been enclosed in capitalist circulation and returning them to collective use as a commons). This shift is accompanied by a shift from purist politics to a more practical assessment of needs and strategies (although tensions between more purist/radical postures and more flexible/practical ones exist). One example of this might be a shift from a purist position that all social centres must be (on principle) illegally squatted to the acceptance of social centres that are the result of a 'deal' made with the local council. In short, the idea is not the creation of a parallel 'universe' but, rather, the transformation of the common shared 'universe'. Direct action, together with a focus on practical politics, is a central feature of autonomous politics.

Beyond issues of identity and culture to a direct re-engagement with capitalism

Some scholars have argued that NSMs were distinguished from previous movements by the fact that '[they] are not preoccupied with struggles over the production and distribution of material goods' (Keane and Mier, 1989: 5). While a shift away from material concerns was clear for many movements in the 1970s, 1980s and 1990s, there were actually many feminist and Marxist movements that maintained an emphasis on capitalism and the links between economic and social inequality (see Flesher Fominaya and Cox, 2013). What is true is that issues of culture and identity did become central frames around which many movements organized in that period. The GJM, with its clear anti-neoliberal agenda, by definition took as a central preoccupation the workings of capitalism itself, although this preoccupation extended far beyond a critique of the 'production and distribution of material goods'. But, if it is true that activists in many NSMs were concerned with post-material values and issues (see Chapter 1), by the mid-1990s concerns with the effects of neoliberalism, the erosion of the welfare state in Europe, attacks on labour rights and the rise of 'flexibility' (temporary contracts) had become central issues around which social movements mobilized. In Western Europe, the centre-left political parties that historically constituted a meaningful counterweight to the most negative effects of capitalism and fascism were fully invested in the processes of neoliberal capitalist globalization. Abramsky (2001: 19) linked this changing context to a return to a political engagement with capitalism and the increasing criminalization of protest, arguing that 'as trade unions and political parties are increasingly unable to serve their needs ... people are being forced to look for new alternatives based around self-organization outside of these existing spaces. [...] Increasingly, political activity which is not based in formal established organizations, and the "legitimate channels of dissent", are being equated by the law with terrorism. This is happening simultaneously through national and European Union law'.

The direct re-engagement with capitalism was reflected in discussions around 'precariousness', very prevalent in Spanish, French and Italian movement circles. For activists mobilizing around precariousness, it is not only a state of being but also a subjectivity – one is not simply in a state of precariousness, one is a precarious subject. This goes beyond a specific set of demands relating to labour/worker rights, to an exploration of the underlying construction of a subject who is living with no guarantees due to the flexibility model of contemporary capitalism. The 'precariat' is made up of subjects who may or may not be working and is mobile, flexible and unstable. The Europrecariat call for Mayday 2003 read:

> The precariat rebels! To all the men and women who work temporarily for insulting wages, to all the mediactivists, grassroots unionists, subversive cyclists, flexibility contortionists, to the insurgent precariat, to the millions of migrant workers, to the millions of protestors around the world – we invite you to participate in Mayday 2003! (Anonymous, 2003)

The precarious subject is an actor who pursues strategies to navigate a precarious existence. This includes the attempt to create alternative means of meeting needs that were formerly met by either the state or the market. In this active sense, precariousness provides an impetus (as do all crisis situations) to creative alternatives while developing a critique of the system that creates the precarious subject in the first place. The temporary, transitory nature of work and capital (here one day, there tomorrow) is also mirrored in the very form the anti-capitalist movement takes, and many activists argue that the network form is not coincidental but, rather, reflects the very forms capitalism takes in the contemporary world.

NSM theory is important in emphasizing the symbolic and cultural aspects of protest, the highly self-reflexive nature of contemporary movements and the ways meaning is collectively created. GJM activists were keen to move beyond symbolic protest to a re-appropriation of public spaces through the occupation of squatted social centres (Chatterton, 2010), public street parties, mass protests and refusal to accept the 'red zone' or 'no go' areas or curfews imposed by authorities attempting to control dissent.

Interestingly, many of the claims I have made here and elsewhere (Flesher Fominaya 2005) for the GJM with respect to the re-engagement with capitalism are being made now for the contemporary wave of global protests (see Chapter 7) by scholars such as Della Porta and Goodwin who argue for the need to 'bring capitalism back in' to scholarship addressing recent movements following the global financial crash. I would argue that the lack of scholarly attention to autonomous movements and their relative invisibility with respect to more formally organized social movement organizations (SMOs) has led to a perception that these features are new or related to the increased salience of economic grievances in a post-global crash scenario. I see the anti-austerity and pro-democracy movements following the global financial crash of 2007/2008 (which I discuss in Chapter 7) as being a continuation and evolution of earlier autonomous movements such as those discussed in this chapter who have always been rooted in anti-capitalist analysis, critique and action.

How global was the Global Justice Movement?

As I have shown in this chapter, there are key ways in which the GJM can be understood as being truly global, as it encompassed:

- the integration of activists, movements and organizations from every corner of the world into transnational networks

- the coordination of protest through simultaneous global days of action the transnational diffusion and 'cross-fertilization' of ideas, tactics, slogans, frames and inspiration

- the crucial emphasis on globalization, and specifically capitalist globalization, as a key protest issue, which represented a shift from single-issue to anti-systemic protest

- the targeting of global, multilateral institutions and multinational corporations as the opponent against which the movement mobilized

- the use of the Internet to coordinate and foster mobilization transnationally and in cyberspace

- the creation of a global collective identity with which locally and nationally rooted activists identified

- a transnational shared movement history, with iconic protest and foundational events, which are inscribed into the narratives global justice activists tell about the movement.

Despite these features, as noted earlier in this chapter, some scholars have pointed out that it is important not to overstate the case for 'globality'. For one thing, the national political, cultural and economic contexts shaped not only the different national GJMs in particular ways (for example, the GJM network in Spain might have a greater difference in the precursor movements, actors and organizations, central campaigns and levels of state repression than the GJM in the US or in Brazil) but also the individual protest events, such as the counter-summits. With regard to Seattle, for example, Murphy and Pfaff (2005) argued that, despite the presence of activists from around the world, the vast majority were from the US, and it was *nationally* based interest groups that influenced the predominance of issues and interests represented and *locally* based activist communities who played key roles in the mobilizations. Tarrow (2005b) has argued for the concept of 'rooted cosmopolitans' which highlights the idea that, despite the global orientation of the movement, it is activists 'who grow out of local settings and draw on domestic resources who are the main actors in transnational contention. The special characteristic of these activists is not their cognitive cosmopolitanism, but their relational links to their own societies, to other countries, and to international institutions'. Tarrow (2005a: 43) defines rooted cosmopolitans as 'individuals and groups who mobilize domestic and international resources and opportunities to advance claims on behalf of external actors, against external opponents, or in favour of goals they hold in common with transnational allies'.

Others have also pointed out that most global justice activists never participated in a global justice protest event in another country, so that the image of the global summit-hopper activist represents only a minority of activists in the movement.

Is the Global Justice Movement over?

In this chapter, I have used a 'past tense' narrative in recognition that the specific wave of global justice protests corresponds to an arguably historically bounded cycle of contention. The wave of anti-war protests in the wake of the 9/11 attacks and the subsequent 'war on terror' (see Chapter 2) are seen as different from the GJM, yet also incorporated, and were coordinated by many of the same actors involved in the GJM. The links in those protests between war and corporate profit-seeking (in the control for oil) and a refusal of political elites to heed the wishes of citizens who turned out in their millions to oppose war clearly fitted closely with the GJM's critical agenda. It is difficult to establish a chronological end point to a movement that defies easy definitions and containment. Clearly, global justice protests continued into the late 2000s (i.e. the G8 protest in Gleneagles, Scotland 2005; G8 protest in Heiligendamm, Germany 2007), but the intensity of action did die down and some of the networks dissolved, although others such as the WSF continue to meet annually. Yet, it is also true that the concerns, issues, practices, discourse, tactics and tensions between the Institutional Left and autonomous actors of the GJM are alive and kicking – if anything, in a more intensive form – in the contemporary global wave of pro-democracy, anti-austerity and Occupy mobilizations, as I discuss in Chapter 7. MoveON, for example, put out the following call to protest on 8 May 2012:

> **What**: While Bank of America's CEO and shareholders meet in Charlotte, NC, tomorrow, the 99% is taking to the streets across the nation to protest BofA. As the economy declined, BofA made millions in profits by dodging taxes and foreclosing on homes, which hit communities of color especially hard. Bad publicity is like kryptonite to big corporations—that's why thousands of people are protesting, marching, and raising our voices in solidarity to

draw the media's attention to BofA's shameless practices. Nearly 200 communities are standing up to Bank of America this week, and there's one near you. **Can you join us in Washington tomorrow?**

The message is not very different from that of countless GJM calls to protest, but the context, a global financial crisis that has now affected many people in affluent countries, is. Scholars have explored the connection between the GJM and these contemporary global movements and the impact of its ongoing legacy (Maeckelbergh, 2012; Flesher Fominaya and Cox, 2013; Flesher Fominaya 2017; Daphi, 2019, Giugni and Grasso 2019).

Conclusion

As with all movements, contemporary global movements draw on and share characteristics of earlier movements. In the case of the GJM, there were some significant features that reflected the changing context in which it evolved and which distinguished it from earlier NSMs. Of particular note are the centrality of the notion of autonomy and the creation of autonomous spaces; the centrality of issues of democracy; the emergence of a new 'global' actor who identifies with a 'global' movement; the consolidation of the network as an organizational framework and of the sovereign assembly as a legitimate arena for decision-making; the strong resurgence of anarchist and libertarian influence; a repertoire of action that moved beyond the purely symbolic to a re-engagement with capitalism as the focus of direct action and critique; a shift away from identitarian and ideological politics to an embracing of diversity as a core value; the re-definition the public sphere not only as a commons but also as an arena in which to negotiate conflict and difference; and, in Western Europe in particular, notably in Italy and Spain, the consciousness and theorizing of a precarious subject which is a product of contemporary capitalism itself, a subject that simultaneously suffers from the effects of the capitalist system and uses and subverts the system in order to survive.

4 CULTURAL RESISTANCE IN A GLOBALIZED WORLD

In 2011, Iceland was the best country in the world for gender equality, according to the gender gap index compiled by the World Economic Forum (Hausmann *et al.*, 2011). The gender gap index measures levels of inequality between men and women on four indicators: economic participation, educational attainment, health and survival, and political empowerment. Iceland's score was 85.3 per cent. This means they have managed to close their gender gap up to 85.3 per cent. It also means that, even in the top scoring country in the world, women are less equal to men across these four areas by almost 15 per cent. In the US, 17th on the ranking, the score is 74.1 per cent. Yemen is at the bottom of the scale with 48.7 per cent. The World Economic Forum (2011) notes that, of a sample of 60 countries, 88 per cent have legislation that prohibits gender-based workplace discrimination. Yet, as statistics clearly show, even in countries with the most progressive legislation, on average, women continue to earn less than men for the same work, do a disproportionately greater share of housework and childcare, are underrepresented politically and are much more likely to be abused physically (see UN, 2012; UNDP, 2012). Clearly, political will and legislation alone are not enough to correct the gender gap (or, indeed, other forms of social inequality). Which raises the question: why not?

One answer many scholars have highlighted lies in the concept of dominant ideology or consensual domination, which refers to a system of ingrained beliefs, values and practices widely shared in a society that serve to justify ideologically the domination of the ruling classes and therefore help maintain the status quo. I will develop these theoretical approaches further and their implications for resistance. Continuing with the example of gender inequality, most, if not all, cultures have deeply ingrained notions of women's inferiority, which works to maintain patriarchy and oppression. These ideas and beliefs or 'frames' persist despite the integration of women in the labour market, the existence of political and legal rights and other structural advances (Ridgeway, 2011).

This poses a series of questions for social movements interested in progressive social transformation or a better, more just world. If the *presence* of political will and legislation is not enough to eliminate gender inequality and other social injustices, how then can this be achieved? And in the *absence* of political will and policies to further social justice, in what way can political leaders be convinced that change is necessary? And what can be done if not only political leaders but also the general public do not see progressive change as necessary or even desirable? These challenges are compounded for global or transnational movements or for movements hoping to reach a global audience by the issues of cross-national variations in language, values, norms and the difficulties of cultural translation of movement messages and practices (see Chapter 2). In the struggle to change people's hearts and minds, social movements draw on and create a wealth of cultural resources to engage in cultural resistance.

The nexus between politics and culture is complex. All politics is cultural and culture conveys politics in myriad ways. It could be argued that all politics is transmitted through culture, systems of implicit or explicit meanings that are adopted, complied with, adapted, contested or actively resisted. Political discourse relies on a set of shared meanings to be effective and comprehensible. All social movements engage in cultural politics to a greater or lesser extent and form part of political culture. While scholars and activists hold diverse views on the meaning of the concepts of culture and cultural resistance, for the purposes of this chapter I will define *cultural resistance* as culture consciously created for political resistance and political resistance that actively and consciously draws on culture (see also Duncombe, 2002). Likewise, I will adopt a broad and elastic definition of culture as shared systems of implicit and explicit meaning that can be embodied in a range of artefacts and products, expressed through discourse and symbolic representation or manifested in internalized, routine shared sets of practices and beliefs. In relation to social movements, culture encompasses such things as songs, chants, banners, propaganda, manifestos, speeches, texts, discourses, deliberative practices, political art, graffiti, lifestyle politics, forms of contention, systems of ideas, tactics, creation of free spaces and much more.

In this chapter, I will explore some of the ways social movements engage in cultural resistance, paying special attention to the many forms it takes in a globalized world. I will, first, highlight some of the ways in which theorists have identified culture as a crucial arena not only of domination but also of struggle in the contemporary world. I then discuss some of the challenges facing social movements as they try to change not just policies and laws but also cultural practices and beliefs and the strategies and tactics they use to do so. Then, I discuss some of the critiques of the limitations of cultural resistance as a means of effecting social and political transformation. Finally, I provide a series of case studies to illustrate a range of practices and approaches to cultural resistance from around the world, highlighting how these collective actors link local, national and global concerns, before concluding with a summary of the importance of cultural resistance to social movements.

Dominant ideology, hegemony, culture and resistance

Marx and Engels (1970 [1845]) famously argued that, in any epoch, the dominant ideas in society are those which serve to maintain the dominance of the ruling classes. Those who have control over the means of economic production also have control over the production of ideas, 'the class which is the material force of society is at the same time its ruling intellectual force'. The ruling class 'rule also as thinkers, as producers of ideas, and regulate the production and distribution of the ideas of their age'. Marx argues that, for a new class to take the place of the ruling class, 'it is compelled, merely in order to carry through its aim, to present its interests as the common interest of all the members of society, that is expressed in ideal form: it has to give its ideas the form of universality, and represent them as the only rational, universally valid ones'. Each successive ruling class needs to encompass greater segments of society by making them identify with the ideas that justify ruling-class dominance. Over time, the ideas of the ruling class become detached from the conditions of their production in class struggle, and they seem to exist independently as universal abstract ideas. So, for example, Marx argued that historical accounts will note that, during the time that the aristocracy was dominant, ideas such as honour and loyalty were also dominant, as though these were just the ideas of the times, rather than recognizing the role of these ideas in maintaining the status quo. Ruling ideas become widespread, naturalized and eternalized, seeming to form part of common sense and the natural order of things, as 'just the way things are'.

One of the most influential theorists to highlight culture as a crucial arena for the maintenance of the dominance of the ruling classes is Italian Marxist Antonio Gramsci. Crucially, however, Gramsci did not adopt such a pessimistic view as most of the later Frankfurt scholars who were influenced by his work and saw culture as a terrain not only of dominance but also of resistance. Gramsci's notion of hegemony, or cultural hegemony, highlights the crucial role of culture in maintaining (and potentially resisting) systems of power and domination. Gramsci (1971 [1929–35]) understands that 'common sense' or naturalized, internalized systems of meanings (widely shared beliefs) within societies serve to shape and reproduce inequality. Gramsci, drawing on Marx, but according greater importance to culture and ideology (and, indeed, culture as ideology), developed the concept of hegemony to explain why the proletarian revolution that Marx predicted had not taken place. Why had workers who were labouring under miserable conditions for subsistence wages not become conscious of their oppression and joined together to overthrow the ruling capitalist class? Why, at a time when communism and socialism were available as political alternatives, were so many ordinary working people in Europe opting for fascism and a capitalist state when these systems would not be in their own interest? Gramsci developed a theory to explain how the ruling classes eventually come to dominate the masses more effectively through *consent* than through force (albeit using a combination of the two). Through moral, cultural and ideological leadership, ruling elites attempt to present their interests as the shared interests of all as they compete with each other. However, they do so using a *shared* language that encompasses discourses and normative frameworks that form a system of hegemonic ideologies. Hegemony is organized within both civil society (where political participation is encouraged within certain limits) and the state, which is 'the entire complex of practical and theoretical activities with which the ruling class not only justifies and maintains its dominance, but manages to win the active consent of those over whom it rules' (Gramsci, 1971 [1929–35]: 244).

Crucial to Gramsci is the way cultural domination, rather than coercion, is the means by which ruling-class ideology becomes 'common sense' and the status quo (class inequality) comes to be seen as inevitable, natural and even desirable. Social groups maintain their supremacy through intellectual and moral leadership. Hegemony denotes the way political and cultural resources organize this 'common sense' view (or natural ideology) that presents dominant class interests as universal, through myriad texts, narratives, practices and cultural products. Cultural hegemony is powerful in that the subordinate classes may not only submit to their domination but also actively support and defend the interests of the ruling class, because the relationship between ruling-class interests and culture (as ideology that justifies the continued dominance of the ruling class) is obscured. Gramsci did not believe there was a single dominant class or a single dominant ideology. Instead, various classes enter into shifting and unstable alliances. For Gramsci, hegemony is never static, fixed or complete but needs to be actively maintained in a constant struggle against groups resisting ideological domination. These groups challenge the 'common sense' and produce counter-narratives. The co-optation and marginalization of alternative or radical ideas and practices are among the ways that dominant classes maintain hegemony. Culture therefore is a terrain on which consensual domination is forged but also where resistance to that domination takes place. Following Gramsci, to transform *politics* you would need to challenge the hegemonic ideologies (transmitted through *culture*) that maintain systems of injustice and inequality in place. Many social movements aim to do just that.

Many scholars (from social constructionists, critical theorists, cultural theorists and postmodernists) have drawn on Marx's notion of dominant ideology to explain how people come to accept circumstances that are deeply unfavourable to their own interests. Many widely shared cultural narratives that benefit dominant groups can be easily discerned. For example, the idea that 'If you work hard enough you can succeed' is a cultural narrative that forms part of the 'American Dream' ideology and is widely believed in US society (Hochschild, 1996). Accepting this idea as valid means that, if someone *fails* to succeed, their failure can be attributed to a lack of effort and ambition on their part rather than to disadvantages stemming from factors such as their socio-economic class, ethnicity or gender. The American Dream ideology is spread through a myriad of ways in US culture, from the discourse of presidential speeches to rock songs, and through advertising and popular culture (Hochschild, 1996). So pervasive is American Dream ideology that, in fact, less than 20 per cent of Americans consider race, gender, religion or class as very important factors in getting ahead in life (Hochschild,

1996: 19). Two thirds of poor Americans believe that people such as themselves have a good chance of improving their standard of living (and three times more Americans believe this than Europeans) (Hochschild, 1996: 19). Yet, studies show that not only is income inequality increasing in the US (US Census Bureau, 2010a, 2010b) but also economic immobility is relatively persistent, especially in the lowest and highest quartiles of earnings distribution (Beller and Hout, 2006). There is also substantial intergenerational persistence in family wealth, and again the richest and poorest show the least mobility (Beller and Hout, 2006). All of this means that the likelihood that poor people in the US are going to have a good chance of improving their standard of living is very low. But for those who believe that the current system will allow them and people like them to improve their standard of living (i.e. they believe in the American Dream), there is little reason for them to mobilize to change the structural roots of their poverty. Not only that, they may actively support and promote political projects that disadvantage them socially (Frank, 2004).

Theorists drawing on Marxist, existential and phenomenological traditions have developed a number of insights that provide provocative starting points for reflecting on the problems facing social movements as they attempt to resist or challenge cultural hegemony.

Frankfurt School critical theorists (e.g. Adorno, Horkheimer) highlighted the crucial role of culture in perpetuating injustice and the consent of the masses. Frankfurt School theorists understood mass culture as the key ideological mechanism through which ruling-class dominance is maintained. They argued that the modern culture industry has taken over social institutions such as the Church, education and the family as the primary agent of socialization. Mass culture contributes to the hegemony of the ruling classes by serving to legitimize oppression and inequality. They believed that mass culture dulls the senses and lulls people into a false sense of satisfaction with modern society and their lives, manipulating their emotions and their intellectual reactions. Advertising pushes people to a quest to satisfy new 'needs', such as the latest technological gadget, while repressing their true needs. Mass culture's endless provision of entertainment and cultural products keeps people from recognizing, questioning and resisting their own domination and the status quo. They argued that, while modern mass culture appears to offer people an escape from reality, what it actually does is diminish the chances of people thinking about resisting existing inequalities and questioning the status quo. Critical theorists in this vein have argued that instrumental rationality and the cultural industry (e.g. Hollywood films, television, advertising) produce a one-dimensional society characterized by the creation of false needs, hyper-consumerism, a lack of critical thinking and reflexivity, and false consciousness. All of this creates a rather pessimistic outlook for the prospects for social transformation through collective action.

After all, if the Frankfurt School theorists were right, then ordinary citizens would be incapable of recognizing and critically interpreting mass culture – and domination by elites would be inevitable. However, unless one believes that critical theorists are somehow uniquely able to formulate critical insights, if *they* were capable of doing so, surely some possibility exists for others making the same realization and overcoming modern mass culture's negative effects. In fact, critical media studies have since shown that audiences and consumers are more able to make a critical interpretation of advertising messages than the above discussion argues and vary more in their selection, attention and interpretation of media messages than this model suggests. Stuart Hall (1993 [1973]), for example, showed that while the producers of media texts did, in fact, 'encode' their messages in such a way as to promote or be consistent with dominant ideologies, values and meanings in society, when people 'decoded' or interpreted those messages they did not always simply accept the messages as they were coded. People, then, are not simply 'passive dupes'. Young people today, furthermore, are consuming less mass-produced media and engaging more with social media, which enables more user-produced content. However, media effects, both passive and active, continue to be profoundly influential, a fact advertisers use to great advantage, by means of carefully segmenting target audiences and meticulously researching audience reception of particular messages. The larger question is: if media and mass culture are influential and persuasive, what are the implications of this for resistance and social change? (Figure 4.1)

Figure 4.1

A protester in Barcelona holds up her hand-made sign during the 19 June 2011 protests against the Euro Pact and government implementation of austerity measures. The other side of the sign reads (in Spanish) 'We are not just useful beings; we are also beings who are capable of being happy'

Copyright: Cristina Flesher Fominaya

Despite agreeing with the Frankfurt School characterization of consumer society, Marcuse, a critical theorist who was influential and active in the anti-authoritarian student movements of the 1960s in Europe and the US, offered some hope. As did Gramsci, Marcuse believed in the possibilities of collective action for social transformation. Marcuse was deeply influenced by both existentialism and Marxism and applied insights from both traditions to his reflections on the possibilities for social movement practice. First was the idea that transcendence, or overcoming the limitations of one's current situation, relies on a transformation of the inner psyche, without which shifts in objective circumstances cannot take place or have a radical transformative outcome. In other words, for society to change, people must first become conscious of the need for change and their own capacity to make change happen. Second, that art and sexuality are of crucial importance in the fulfilment and realization of species-being (or our true essence as humans) and therefore that creativity, desire and culture are important for collective action for social transformation. Third, that the critique of dominant 'natural' ideologies (hegemonic ideologies) as perpetuating oppression needs to be of central concern for any group or movement seeking social change; and, finally, that a radical critique of injustice is an important means of encouraging collective protest and personal and social transformation through collective action. In other words, mobilizing critical *ideas* is crucial to mobilizing people and movements.

The importance of culture as a site of conflict in contemporary society

Until the 1990s, with what has been called a 'cultural turn' in social movement studies, many scholars overlooked the cultural aspects of the 'political' activity of social movements. In fact, politics and culture are not opposites but, rather, essential aspects of each other. In marked contrast to the political reductionism of resource mobilization paradigms developed in the US, which, prior to the cultural turn, had traditionally viewed political goals or policy changes as the only serious area of concern for social movement scholars, some European social theorists (and notably those referred to as 'New Social Movement' [NSM] theorists) such as Habermas, Touraine and Melucci have seen conflicts over culture, identity and meanings as central to contemporary social movement struggles and social conflict more broadly. The lack of attention to culture of the resource mobilization and political process paradigms has been extensively critiqued, including by the originators of these approaches. Despite this cultural turn, few social movement scholars in this tradition have seen culture as a central *locus* for struggle in the way that NSM scholars do. NSM scholars have been criticized, in turn, for overstating the importance of culture at the expense of structural explanations of social conflict but, nevertheless, provide important insights into the relation between culture and social movements.

For Habermas (1981, 1987, 1988), a second-generation member of the Frankfurt School, who is influenced by Marxism, phenomenology and

Weber's rationalization thesis, contemporary society is characterized by the colonization of the 'life-world', which encompasses both the private and the public spheres of everyday life (family, education, leisure, work) by the 'system world' (government and market forces). Increasingly, the instrumental rationality of modern bureaucracies and market forces invades even the most private areas of people's lives, and power and decision-making are centralized into fewer hands, resulting in the homogenization of culture and a lack of public discourse about issues that should be of concern to everyone. Habermas argues that the central conflicts in contemporary advanced capitalist society have shifted from capital-labour struggles to conflicts over the colonization of the life-world. (New) social movements are engaged in actively de-colonizing the life-world, by strengthening the autonomy of civil society and developing forms of participatory deliberative communication. Within the relatively autonomous spaces they create within the life-world, they debate and develop critiques of the system-world, its intrusions and effects.

For Touraine (1988: 9), social movements in post-industrial society are 'actors, opposed to each other by relations of domination and conflict [that] have the same cultural orientations and are in contention for the social management of this culture and of the activities it produces'. Conflicts in contemporary society are struggles over these cultural orientations which are linked to a society's historicity. By cultural orientations, he means the instruments of societal self-production; that is, the cultural models that determine a society's economic, social and ethical investments. By historicity, he means society's capacity to act upon itself, to shape the orientation or framework for its organization. Social movements are challenges over which shape these cultural orientations should take. The dominant classes have control over historicity, and social movements contest that control on a shared cultural terrain. So, for example, the struggle over nuclear energy needs to be seen not as a single issue (nuclear power 'yes' or 'no') but, rather, as a broad struggle over what kind of economic, social and ethical investments a society should make to shape itself. Thus, for Touraine, struggles over culture lie at the very heart of contemporary social movements.

For Melucci (1995b: 288), the importance of contemporary movements should not be measured by their immediate political impact but by their ability to transform individuals' internal landscapes, by which he means the 'biological, emotional and cognitive structures on which we base the construction of our experience and our relationships'. According to Melucci (1995b: 288), 'social movements bring to the fore the cultural dimension of human action, its self-reflexive and symbolic qualities' – a task he considers necessary in order to solve the problems and challenges posed by complex societies. Melucci's emphasis on culture has important implications not only for the kinds of activities social movements should engage in and towards whom they should be directed but also for our understanding of social movement 'success' and outcome (see Chapter 1).

Despite being criticized for overstating the extent to which contemporary movements represent a post-materialist politics largely divorced from the concerns of traditional 'old'-social movements (e.g. the distribution of material resources through society), what all of these theorists offer is a vision in which *culture* not only plays a crucial role in *reproducing* consent for the status quo and the social pathologies it produces but *also* is a critical arena for *resisting* exploitation, injustice and hegemony, notably through the collective action of progressive social movements. These insights are as relevant for contemporary social movements as they were for the movements Habermas, Touraine and Melucci were writing about in the 1980s and 1990s.

The challenge of transforming hearts and minds: Strategies and practices of cultural resistance

Fundamentally, all social movements are concerned with the transmission of messages (critiques, demands, alternatives, solutions) to a wider audience, and they transmit those messages in particular cultural contexts. Social movement scholars have shown that, in order to be effective, movement messages need to resonate culturally with the target audience; that is, they need to fit somehow into the receivers' cultural narratives in order to be accepted as valid or comprehensible messages (see the discussion of framing in Chapter 2). Put another way, there have to be implicit or explicit shared meanings between the transmitter and receiver of the messages for communication to be effective.

Convincing target audiences of the validity and credibility of their message is a primary task of social movements, and some social movements devote a great deal of time to framing and packaging their messages effectively. Some professionalized movements or social movement organizations have direct points of contact with their target audience (e.g. they directly lobby policy-makers), but many movements rely on mass media to a certain extent to act as conveyors of their messages to the broader public. Others concentrate their efforts on the production of their own media. Media form a crucial part of cultural resistance and the rise of information and communication technologies (ICTs) has also transformed the production, appropriation, dissemination and reception of social movement media – so much so that social movement media practices will be addressed fully in Chapter 5.

Culture is itself a powerful resource for social movements and scholars have highlighted the many ways activists use culture as a political tool (Duncombe, 2002; Darnovsky *et al.*, 1995; Firat and Kuryel, 2011).

Tactical, symbolic and praxis-based strategies

Piven and Cloward on the power of disruption

Piven and Cloward's seminal book (2012 [1977]), *Poor People's Movements: Why They Succeed, How They Fail*, has shown that for 'poor people's' movements, disruption and direct action (strikes, mass civil disobedience) achieve more gains than organized reform and electoral pressure. They demonstrate for all four of their case studies (the unemployed workers movement, the industrial workers movements, the Civil Rights movement and the welfare rights movement) that independent of ideology (revolutionary or reformist) activists trying to organize the poor have concentrated on developing permanent, formally structured organizations with mass membership. The assumption underlying these attempts is 'the conviction that formal organization is a vehicle of power' (Piven and Cloward, 1977: xx). This organizational model has not succeeded in practice since it fails to realize that elites cannot be compelled to make concessions 'that can be used as resources to sustain oppositional organizations over time' (Piven and Cloward, 1977: xxi). They argue that these attempts at building permanent structures have tamed and demobilized movements instead of pushing for the maximum concessions possible in times of disruption and crisis.

Autonomous activists (see Chapter 3) embrace the lessons Piven and Cloward point to as an organizational philosophy: first, by often refusing to build permanent stable organizations with formal leadership structures that can be co-opted and, second, by seeing direct action and disruption as key mechanisms for effective collective action.

Direct action and civil disobedience

Civil disobedience is a term that is often subject to dispute since those engaging in it use the term to legitimize their action while those contesting that legitimacy (usually state-affiliated actors) will characterize it as something else (criminal activity, trespass and so on). One of the classic definitions comes from John Rawls (1971), who defined it in part as 'a public, non-violent, conscientious yet political act contrary to law usually done with the aim of bringing about a change in the law or policies of the government' and who stresses that the underlying fundamental purpose is to pursue human liberty and equality.

But as Milligan (2013: 14) points out, this definition misses out some crucial elements that activists and theorists (such as Howard Zinn) feel should be included, such as the fact that civil disobedience can be religiously motivated (not just secular), can pursue a different aim from human liberty (such as environmental protection or animal justice or economic justice) and does not necessarily have to be 100 per cent non-violent in practice as long as it aspires towards non-violence – in the face of assault, some self-defence does not disqualify the civil disobedient nature of the action.

Direct action, for its part, has a long and varied history (see Tilly, 1978b; Hill, 1972) and encompasses a wide range of actions and approaches. Examples include strikes and factory occupations, the passive resistance practised by Mahatma Gandhi and his followers to oppose British colonial rule in India, the sit-ins carried out by civil rights activists in the US during the Civil Rights movement (inspired by Gandhian passive resistance), the occupation of abandoned buildings and their conversion into social centres by political squatters in Europe and the US, the non-violent civil disobedience tree-hugging actions of the Chipko movement in India to stop deforestation and reclaim traditional forest rights, the sabotage of bulldozers and road building equipment or chainsaws to preserve the environment, the liberation of animals from animal testing laboratories and much more.

Direct actions can range from explicitly non-violent actions to more con-frontational forms of protest and politically motivated property destruction and sabotage. It can range from a simple but powerful and planned refusal to comply with regulations, laws or customs, as with African-American Civil Rights activist Rosa Park's famous refusal to give up her seat on the bus to make way for a white passenger in Alabama in 1955, to the highly orches-trated confrontations with the police practised by the *Tute Bianche* in Italy (1994–2001). In contrast to the passive resistance practiced by many US Civil Rights activists in the 1960s, Nation of Islam's advocacy for African Americans espoused the idea that people whose rights and lives are threat-ened have the right to defend themselves.

Not all direct actions are spatially and temporally bounded events. The occupation of a building to provide collective housing or to create a social centre for the community is intended to be a long-term affair, and some occupations last for years. Squatting is not just a symbolic act that calls atten-tion to the issues of private property speculation, homelessness and lack of affordable housing but also a physical struggle over the uses of space, reclaim-ing private space for public use. When the authorities come to evict the building, it is usually defended, often through very creative alert and defence systems, and activists then squat another building elsewhere. Even holding a referendum, if that act is illegal, results in a physical struggle over space: plac-ing a table and urn on a public street, which are removed and confiscated by police, is both a symbolic act of resistance and a direct intervention.

For anti-capitalist activists, urban public space is 'colonized' or appropri-ated and organized in such a way as to favour corporate interests and power: formerly free spaces such as commons and parks give way to roads and shop-ping malls, urban landscapes are cluttered with billboard advertising, tradi-tional neighbourhoods undergo 'gentrification' forcing out lower-income residents, and city centres are given over to commercial offices and corporate chains in lieu of family run stores and restaurants.

Direct action and civil disobedience today reflect both an increased awareness of the power of symbolic politics and an awareness of its limita-tions. The *Tute Bianche* (Italy), *Invisibles* (Spain) and *Wombles* (UK), for example, which were active in the global justice movement (GJM), sought to engage in conflict with police and security forces at protest events, not because they were interested in fighting but to make visible the fundamental conflict between authorities and citizens that is invisible when everyone fol-lows the rules. By pushing through police barriers of 'no go' protest zones while protecting their bodies with white padded suits and handmade shields, they wanted to make visible their vulnerability in the face of armed police, their refusal to accept that vulnerability and their willingness to disobey the limits set by the forces of order. They were heightening the impact of sym-bolic protest by deliberately connecting it to a physical struggle.

Direct action sometimes takes forms that are not primarily symbolic and goes beyond denouncing practices to physically undoing them. 'Pixie work', for example, includes such activities as sabotaging road-building and logging equipment during the night, 'liberating' materials destined for road-building for use in reinforcing and supporting anti-roads camps or digging up genetically modified crops. Done under cover of darkness, pixie work is not public and activists do not wait around to be arrested, differentiating this from traditional forms of civil disobedience. In cases like this, activists are likely more motivated by a strategic sense of urgency and impact (e.g. economic losses) than by a desire to symbolically confront hegemony.

The power of direct action and civil disobedience can be seen, in part, by the level of state repression it triggers. Indeed, unmasking the violence of the state, a violence often hidden in the day-to-day lives of citizens, is sometimes what direct actions are designed to do, as with the actions of the *Tute Bianche* or, in a very different way, through violent militant direct action. For most non-violent direct action, however, repression is a frequent but unintended consequence, albeit one that can serve to radicalize and increase support for movements, particularly when it is clear that police or military violence is unprovoked. In the 1960s, civil rights activists in the US were fire-hosed, beaten, and attacked by dogs when they peacefully protested for equal rights for African Americans. In 2011, in an act that led to a viral video, and a photograph that became a meme that circulated around the world, a police officer pepper-sprayed student 'Occupy' protesters at the University of California, Davis Campus, who were sitting on the ground outside and refusing to remove their protest encampment (for more on the Occupy Movement, see Chapter 7). The meme was manipulated to depict the police officer spraying a number of different people and objects. The three dozen students were awarded compensation from the University, but so was the police officer who received worker's compensation for the psychological distress resulting from the hate mail and backlash he received (Garofoli, 2016). In 2011, pro-democracy demonstrators in Egypt's Tahrir Square were shot and killed (see Chapter 7), as were hundreds of pro-democracy Chinese demonstrators in Tiananmen Square in 1989 (BBC Online, 2012), and student protesters massacred in Tlatelolco, Mexico, in 1968 (Doyle, undated). Unfortunately, one could provide countless more examples, with kettling, pepper spray, rubber bullets and water cannons frequently used against non-violent protesters around the world. Of course, not all direct action provokes such a violent response, although it can result in fines, lawsuits, prison and other forms of state repression.

Whereas some activists strongly believe that the power of civil disobedience or direct action lies in the public nature of the act, and the assumption of the consequences of that act within the law, others, such as those who engage in 'pixie work', have no intention of being caught or punished and do not see that as an essential element of their activism. While some activists deeply believe in only non-violent actions, including not destroying property, others are equally committed to sabotage and active resistance as a political practice. Such differences in beliefs about civil disobedience and direct action can lead to tensions and divisions between activists fighting for the same cause. While some observers and participants see multiple approaches and strategies as strength, others adopt a more partial view about the damaging consequences of 'violent', disruptive or more direct actions rather than merely symbolic actions. Once again, the way mass media portray actions also complicates this debate, as mass media often focus on the few who engage in more violent actions rather than more peaceful forms of protest, which some activists (and scholars) claim harms the cause and detracts from the messages social movements are trying to convey.

Radical reflexivity, lifestyle politics and countercultures

In the quest for social change, movements engage in practices designed to change not only the political consciousness of audiences outside the movement but also the political self-consciousness of their own members. *Identity movements* (e.g. the LGBTQ or Black Power movements) have focused on promoting pride as a means of altering outsiders' perceptions of the group in question but also to enable members of the stigmatized or oppressed group to develop a shared sense of pride and solidarity with each other against the negative messages transmitted about them. Just as these negative messages are often transmitted through cultural media such as movies, television, popular jokes and derogatory language, identity movements counter those messages with alternative cultural products and forms of resistance, such as gay pride marches; powerful aesthetic markers such as the afro; and art, songs, poetry, literature, slogans, flags and banners.

Lifestyle politics, such as political vegetarianism or political squatting, with their attendant dress codes and cultural practices, also serve to transmit messages about beliefs and values. The Dongas were a group of people that lived together in protest camps in the UK in the 1990s, following an ecologically sound and communal lifestyle while protesting against the destruction of the countryside and heritage sites by road construction. As one Donga tribe member put it: 'Protesting is not a way of life, but your way of life can be a protest' (quoted in McKay, 1996: 148).

Countercultural movements proclaim beliefs and engage in practices that run counter to the established acceptable cultural and social norms of the day. In the 1960s, in North America and Europe, for example, the idea and practice of 'free love' challenged a multitude of social taboos, from sex outside marriage, to mixed racial relationships, to homosexual partnerships and having children out of wedlock. Today, many of these former taboos are increasingly seen as acceptable and normal in many societies, precisely because of the impact of these social movements over time.

Some countercultural movements are not concerned primarily with reaching mass audiences but prefer to engage in prefigurative politics, creating alternative communities, generating new cultural codes and practices and reappropriating and transforming public spaces. Others, such as the Black Power and Gay Pride movements, actively sought to recruit large numbers of people and find large audiences and engaged in highly public demonstrative acts to do so. Countercultural movements actively create not only alternative culture but also institutional structures that not only sustain movements but also form an essential part of their conception of politics.

The subversive power of humour, satire and irony

Culture is a very effective arena in which to engage in political critique, in part because it is not always immediately recognizable as 'politics'. Humour, satire and irony are important political tools that have long been used by social movements (t'Hart, 2007). Although humour – and especially jokes and the 'whispered jokes' in authoritarian regimes – are commonly considered to be an indicator of 'resistance', recent research has questioned the extent to which one can correlate joke-telling to resistance or to the extent of repression. According to Davies (2007), fewer political jokes were told in the highly repressive Stalinist period in the Soviet Union than in later periods of more routine repression. Nevertheless:

> Jokes under communism had a far greater personal, political, intellectual, and historical importance than is the case with political jokes told in traditional or democratic societies ... The[ir] personal importance [...] can be inferred from the risks that so many individuals took in telling and circulating them when they knew that being reported to the authorities would result in possible imprisonment or deportation and even death. [...]That people took such risks is both an indication of the importance the jokes have for them and the strong and interlocking networks of interpersonal trust and solidarity that they had created, which provided them with some degree of independence from an overwhelmingly powerful state. (Davies, 2007: 292)

It is not only in authoritarian contexts that humour and satire can be used for political purposes. Humour has been used as a political tool by social movements regardless of political opportunity structure. In democratic contexts, it can serve to engage audiences that might otherwise be put off by 'politics'. Activists in the Spanish *Indignados*/15-M movement, for example, decided to disseminate their meeting minutes in a humorous way by embedding them in a funny narrative that would actually be read by others (instead of ignored as 'boring' meeting minutes can be) (Romanos, 2013).

Activists in the GJM often projected a *carnivalesque* atmosphere in their direct actions, including circus, such as clowning elements (through groups like the Rebel Clown Army), and satirizing political and economic leaders through puppets and masks. t'Hart (2007: 18–19) argues that, for the GJM, 'A *carnivalesque* use of humour proved enormously effective in getting the message to the wider public, because of its emphasis on the shared human background of oppressors and oppressed. At the same time, humorous acts often supported the morale of the protesters.'

The use of symbolic protest, humorous signs and clowning also serves to try to overcome the language and cultural barriers of a global audience. Olesen (2007) argues that the Zapatista use of humour transcended cultural barriers and was very successful in transmitting their messages to an educated middle-class audience in the global North. The use of humour when combined with symbolic performance protest is also often attractive to the public and the media and can serve as a powerful communication tool to get issues across. Humour can also serve as an important political tool for the consolidation and *internal* cohesion of movements as well by serving to integrate new members, defuse tension and resolve internal conflicts and through the creation of humorous stories and myths that are told and transmitted through movement networks and form part of their cultural legacy (Flesher Fominaya, 2007b). The role of humour in fostering social movement collective identity has been well documented (Flesher Fominaya, 2007b; t'Hart, 2007).

Culture jamming and guerrilla communication

As the discussion about consensual forms of domination argues, natural ideologies or 'common sense' ideas that reinforce the status quo have widespread acceptance, are often uncritically accepted and are actively reinforced and reproduced by commercial/cultural processes (e.g. television, arts, advertising, everyday discourse). Progressive social movements seek to challenge the uncritical acceptance of dominant ideas. Culture jamming and guerrilla communication are forms of political action that use a mixture of politics, art and humour to attempt to engage audiences emotionally, intellectually and politically in such a way that they rethink established ideas and see them in a new and critical way. Culture jammers understand power as manifest in myriad cultural products, symbols, messages and codes which are all pervasive and diffuse. The idea is to provoke critical reflection and re-evaluation of culturally hegemonic ideas by disrupting or 'jamming' the flow of dominant messages and generating alternative or modified messages or symbolic codes. Culture jammers use pre-existing and accepted aesthetic codes, media forms and corporate images (e.g. logos and slogans) and twist them or turn them, often in a humorous way, to convey an alternative critical message. They seek to make visible the line between dominant and dominated groups and to reclaim meanings and spaces that have been appropriated and colonized.

Culture jamming includes such forms of action as billboard alteration (or 'liberation'), where billboard messages are altered to shift their meaning, the creation of *subvertisements* or counter-advertisements, media hoaxing, activist theatre and place-jamming – the reclaiming of public spaces for the use of communities or citizens as opposed to corporations or privatized uses.

Guerrilla communication is an attempt to provoke subversive effects through the alteration or rupture of all forms of communication media. As German and Italian communication guerrillas Autonome a.f.r.i.k.a-gruppe, Luther Blissett, and Sonja Bruenzels explained in their 1998 listserve message:

> This message is directed to those ... who also refuse to believe that radical politics need to be straight, mostly boring and always very very serious ... It is ... an invitation to participate, criticise, renew and develop a way of doing politics which expresses the

bloody seriousness of reality in a form that doesn't send the more hedonistic parts of ourselves immediately to sleep. Of course, this is a contradiction in itself: How can you be witty in a situation of increasing racism, state-control and decline of the welfare state, to name only a few? ... The starting point for our reflections around guerrilla communication was a trivial insight from our own politics: information and political education are completely useless if nobody is interested. After years of distributing leaflets and brochures about all kinds of disgraces, of organising informative talks and publishing texts, we have come to question the common radical belief in the strength and glory of information ... Guerrilla communication doesn't focus on arguments and facts like most leaflets, brochures, slogans or banners. ... It is direct action in the space of social communication ... Communication guerrillas do not intend to occupy, interrupt or destroy the dominant channels of communication, but to detourn and subvert the messages transported. (Grupo Autónomo, 2000)

Luther Blissett and Sonja Brunzels are multi-use pseudonyms that can be freely used by guerrilla communication activists. The idea is to dissolve the separation between the individual and the collective and also to engage in a guerrilla communication tactic of myth-making, whereby a fake persona takes on a life of its own as multiple actions are linked to this 'person's' name. So, 'Luther Blissett' has been responsible for many media hoaxes and interventions in different countries despite the fact that, as such, he does not exist. The play on the name is compounded by the fact that the original Luther Blissett did exist (he was a footballer) but has nothing to do with any of the actions done under his name. (For more on multiple-use names, see Autonome a.fr.i.k.a gruppe, 1997, or Deseriis, 2011.)

Guerrilla communication activism is highly symbolic and oriented towards media but can also encompass direct action (as with the political shoplifting of YoMango, see below). Guerrilla communication has a long and colourful history, but the rise of new forms of media and technologies has pushed it into new directions and heightened its potential impact. Guerrilla communication takes many forms and is highly creative. Indeed, many artists and others employed in creative professions are practitioners. The creation of fakes or hoaxes is an important part of guerrilla communication theory and practice.[8] Fake newspapers that look almost exactly like the originals and that are distributed for free constitute one example. In Madrid in 2005, free copies of 'Metro' were handed out to commuters as they left the metro station as on any other workday. The issue included special coverage on the proposed bid to bring the Olympic Games to Madrid. The articles seemed genuine in form, but a careful reading of the content revealed Olympic events that included contests such as running down pedestrians along Madrid's congested streets and races between police chasing immigrant street sellers of bootleg CDs and DVDs. The real estate advertisements included such items as the sale of a 1 × 1 metre closet with use of a shared bathroom for 18,000 euros. The newspaper called attention to pressing urban issues – such as extremely high housing prices and pedestrian deaths caused by reckless driving – in a humorous way and poked fun at the politicians who were 'selling' Madrid as an ideal city (and therefore an appropriate host for the Olympics).

In 2008, a similar but much larger-scale action took place in which free copies of 'The New York Times' were handed out to commuters in Los Angeles, New York and some other US cities – only it was not 'all the news that's fit to print' (as the *New York Times'* slogan claims) that they were getting but 'all the news we hope to print': the paper announced the end of the wars in Iraq and Afghanistan and advertisements included Exxon Mobil announcing the adoption of a fair trade policy in which profits would go to producers (Firat and Kuryel, 2011).

Culture jamming can also involve dismantling stereotypes. In 1993, the Barbie Liberation Organization (BLO) (a creation of culture jammers RTmark) undertook an action that involved buying and then switching the voice boxes on talking Barbies and GI Joes, so that Barbie would say things like 'Troops attack!' and 'Vengeance is mine!' and GI Joe would say 'Want to go shopping?' and 'Let's plan our dream wedding!' The toys were then returned to the stores, where unsuspecting buyers purchased them. According to a video issued by the BLO and narrated by Barbie herself, the activists behind the prank were supposedly the Barbie and GI Joe toys themselves, who were rebelling against the companies who 'create them and force them to reproduce negative gender stereotypes'.[9] Actions like these can make it into the mainstream media, and the corporations that are targeted sometimes feel compelled to respond: the *New York Times* issued a statement in the case of the action above (Firat and Kuryel, 2011), as did Mattel, the manufacturer of Barbie.

The logic of guerrilla communication involves reproducing faithfully the codes or symbols of the target in order to provoke confusion and reflection in the recipient or viewer. Often, the targets are global actors such as multinational corporations or businesses providing a global service. In 1999, activists in Germany engaged in a campaign to highlight the fact that Lufthansa, KLM and other airlines were working with the government to deport illegal immigrants and asylum seekers. Instead of denouncing this practice in the way of 'traditional' protest (e.g. calling a press conference, lobbying, marching), the activists instead produced a campaign for Lufthansa advertising 'Deportation Class', with the slogan 'We fly you out' instead of their corporate slogan 'We fly you there'. They distributed glossy flyers and set up a website with the following text:

> See the world through different eyes! Travel in exotic style with Lufthansa's Deportation Class service.
>
> ...
>
> We are constantly expanding and improving our Deportation Class service, which remains the most economical way to travel the globe. With Lufthansa Deportation Class you can now reach dozens of exciting

destinations worldwide – Tunis, Damascus, Jakarta ... And the destinations are only half the attraction! ... In addition to our extraordinarily low fares, you will benefit from the following services:

- After your special cargo area check-in, border police officers will help you through a separate gate into the high security deportee sector.
- While restrained, you will enjoy special privileges such as seating priority ... and even an increased luggage allowance.

    ....

- You will adjust to the delights of your travel destination in an atmosphere relaxed by obligatory sedative usage.
- After being booked in Lufthansa's Deportation Class, you will be driven in a specially protected vehicle from your home to the airport, completely free of charge.

It couldn't be easier ...
Just call our reservation staff today at 800 645 3880 or use our on-line reservation service. Become one of our Deportation Class VIPs!
*Special restrictions may apply. The offer is available only for outbound flights (no round trips available). All flights are strictly nonrefundable and non-transferable[10] (http://www.noborder.org/archive/ www. deportation-class. com/).

Guerrilla communication activists 'Autonome a.f.r.i.k.a gruppe' (2002) understand the campaign in this way:

'The recipient-journalists and their readers, potential customers, everyone confronted with the advertising material of the Deportation Class, are automatically drawn into the contradictions of the capitalist system and its western humanistic ideology: Is Deportation Class really a cynical special offer from Lufthansa for cheap seats on deportation flights? Or is it in fact a particularly successful criticism of their deportation practice? If the recipient decides on the first reading, then they are confronted with the question of whether this entails money-making at the expense of human dignity or a legitimate marketing instrument. If they see through the Deportation Class as a fake, then they cannot simply dismiss it as an absurd slander – it is too close to the logic of the narration of the real Lufthansa ideology. Regardless of which reading the recipient decides to take, once the questions are posed, they stick to Lufthansa. In this way, soiling an image breaks open what is widely accepted and taken for granted in the capitalist system, thus opening up an unmediated view of contradictions between reality and representation.'

Such interventions require significant planning and effort, but culture jammers also can accomplish actions with a simple can of spray paint. Like political graffiti, billboard 'liberations' can be found around most major cities.[12]

Transforming culture through resistance

Cultural resistance can also be thought of as actions that seek to target and transform cultural practices that are oppressive or that activists feel need to be challenged on moral grounds. Sometimes, the challenge is to the society in which the cultural practices or ideologies are rooted; other times, activists try to appeal to international audiences so that pressure will be exerted from the international community. In these cases, even a petition or a call for international solidarity can challenge the practice or cultural system, and activists take care to frame their messages to not only reach the target audiences but also motivate them to take action (perhaps sign a petition or write to their member of parliament or congressional representative), get the message reported on in the media, or even pressure or persuade the international community and leaders to take action. A 'Call for An International Day of Solidarity with Imprisoned Saudi Feminists on June 24' petition from 2018 (available here: https://standwithsaudifeminists.org/) provides a good example of a challenge to a whole series of practices (e.g. restrictions on women's freedom of mobility, expression, and access to public spaces) while calling for the release of political prisoners in Saudi Arabia.

The petition challenges the legitimacy of a government that is trying to improve its image by allowing women to drive (a change widely reported in the media) while jailing those who are trying to transform Saudi Arabia's oppressive patriarchal culture as a whole. The petitioners increase their legitimacy by providing detailed information about each of the cases as well as making foreigners aware of the situation of women and feminist activists in their country.

Critiques and limitations of cultural resistance

So far, this discussion has highlighted the power and importance of cultural resistance for social movements. Yet, social movements engaged in cultural resistance face a series of challenges, limitations and critiques that are well worth considering. The first is that, while the political meaning of a movement message may be clear to the sender, it is by no means necessarily clear to the recipient. Because communication is, by definition, open to interpretation, any message can have multiple meanings. The ambiguity and multiplicity of meaning are precisely what make jokes funny and what culture jammers and guerrilla communication practitioners draw on to twist or turn messages and symbols from their original intended meaning. However, this also means that ambiguous messages may be ignored or missed altogether.

In 2004, autonomous activists in Madrid wore Groucho Marx noses and glasses and marched in a mass protest with a transparent banner, chanting 'The transparent banner unites the people' (*Pancarta trasparente, úne a la gente*). They were poking fun at the political parties and unions who march chanting slogans and waving flags with their acronyms and who, in the experience of these activists, can spend hours debating over the exact wording of the slogans that will appear on their banners. As they marched, they invited passers-by to join them behind the transparent banner, which many did, gladly. Despite their willing participation, however, it is doubtful many passers-by 'got' the critique the activists were making. It was more of an in-joke, and one that infuriated some activists who understood (correctly) that their political practices were being critiqued (Flesher Fominaya, 2007b). Similarly, in Italy in the 1977 movement, the group *Indiani Metropolitani* (Metropolitan Indians) used spectacle and irony to ridicule internal and external opponents and to hamper what they understood as the attempts of the Institutional Left to gain control of the movement. Many journalists and the public either did not get or did not appreciate the message (Cuninghame, 2007).

When activists try to communicate across national boundaries, the problems of cultural translation can further complicate the transmission and reception of their intended messages. While an icon like *St Precarious* or *San Precario* (see below) translates very well across countries with a strong Catholic heritage, its power may be reduced greatly (if not completely) in another cultural context where people might not 'get' the reference to the practice of praying to saints to solve one's problems. Movement repertoires also draw on movement history and represent an evolution of past repertoires which allow participants and observers to make sense of the meanings projected, but sometimes outside (transnational) observers find it difficult to make sense of them.[13]

Some forms of guerrilla communication are so multilayered and theoretically sophisticated that it is difficult even for insiders to understand the meanings and intentions behind them. Luther Blissett and other guerrilla communication groups staged many complex media hoaxes and other 'stunts', later explained by texts whose level of abstraction and ambiguity sometimes makes it difficult to grasp the point of the actions.[14] While open-ended interpretation is part of the philosophy of guerrilla communication, one can question to what extent this ambiguity diminishes political effectiveness. Media hoaxes also leave many people (those who were fooled) feeling duped and foolish. While that might certainly be the point, especially when the targets are mass media and elites, when members of the public are also taken in, and feel 'duped', it may mean the action is doing more harm than good in terms of changing people's minds and hearts about the issues.

Even if the meaning of a message is *clear*, it by no means will be accepted as *valid*. It might be seen as offensive or simply serve to reinforce people's original beliefs. Some people might consider *YoMango* shoplifting (see below) or squatting to be political acts; others might interpret them as criminal acts with no political value or intent (and, indeed, this is the line often taken by political and economic elites and reported in mass media in the attempt to depoliticize these actions). As Sandlin and Milam (2008: 342) argue in relation to anti-consumerist culture jamming, while it 'can facilitate new, creative and spontaneous ways of learning and of seeing the self in relation to others … it also sometimes creates environments that hinder rather than support learning as transgression … some audience members … react with anger not at consumerism but at the culture jammers themselves'. One participant in an online discussion about *Adbusters*, for example, wrote

'I HATE Adbusters. Why? Because they have this preachy holier than thou attitude' (cited in Sandlin and Milam, 2008).

Yet, as Einwohner (2002: 517) points out, for many activists angry responses are preferable to no responses at all: as one animal rights activist put it: 'even if it makes some people mad, at least it gets them thinking about the issue'.

If part of the power of cultural resistance that uses humour, satire or *carnivalesque* elements stems from the fact that it can be more easily accepted because it is not necessarily or immediately recognized as political (it goes in with a spoonful of sugar), this also means that it can be dismissed or trivialized for the same reason. Additionally, some movements and political actors, as well as some members of the public, reject on *principle* the idea that humour or fun has a part to play in politics, which they feel should be about 'serious' issues (Flesher Fominaya, 2007b). Cultural resistance can also have unintended consequences, as when the 1960s counterculture served to create a new breed of right-wing intellectuals (Klatch, 1999) or when the use of celebrities to promote movement campaigns actually makes people focus less on the issues than on the celebrities. Ironic endorsements of political candidates may, in fact, just add to their visibility.

Sometimes, the cultural aspects of certain movements can obscure their potential or intended political meaning. For example, although rave culture can be seen as a political movement, it can also be read as a hedonistic lifestyle choice and therefore not taken seriously as a political statement. Over time, countercultural movements can be absorbed into mainstream culture, losing their critical edge. 'Sex and drugs and rock and roll' started out as a declaration of rebellion but, for many, has lost the countercultural meaning it originally had and has becomes a lifestyle choice like any other. Rebellion can become commodified (Seiler, 2000), and aspects of lifestyle politics (vegetarianism, alternative therapies) can come to form part of the consumer culture they were meant to challenge. Indeed, some critics argue that *all* forms of cultural resistance will eventually become part of dominant culture. As Duncombe (2002: 6) points out, some argue that:

> cultural resistance does not and cannot exist. The dominant system is one of such complete ideological and material hegemony that any cultural expression, even if it appears rebellious, is, or will soon be repackaged and transformed into, a component of the status quo. From this perspective cultural resistance is at best a waste of time and at worst a delusional detour from real political resistance.

Some critics of guerrilla communication or culture jamming reject the underlying premise that people are passive dupes who are unable to reflect critically on the messages transmitted by mass media and consumer culture. After all, this argument goes, if activists can be critical, why can't everyone else? Critics also question the extent to which culture jamming in itself can have any real impact on the intended audience. As Haiven (2007: 107) argues:

> [I don't think] culture jammers should assume the products of their work itself will have any substantial effect on the broader public. There will be extremely few who will walk by a jammed ad or billboard ... and reevaluate global capitalism or their life practices. People are probably less stupid and duped and more helpless and cynical. Being told the enjoyment of their few material pleasures afforded them guarantee their damnation is unlikely to sway many.

Haiven, rather, sees culture jamming as being potentially useful as a means of developing personal and small group 'deep critical solidarity' and as a critical pedagogical practice through which teens and other learners 'take control of the icons and brands and symbols which surround them and shape them as social agents ... I suspect students doing various acts of "culture jamming" and taking them public might be a very important experience in that it not only demands acts of imagination beyond those ascribed by mainstream consumer culture, but invites an imagination of the *public* and forms by which learners can address and change it' (2007: 107).

While his comments are made within the context of a specific critique of *Adbusters*, which represents one particular culture jamming practice, the larger point remains. It may, indeed, be that culture jamming serves as much or more to develop internal social movement cohesion and development as it actually has a measurable effect on 'the public'. But, of course, transformation of critical individual and collective *self*-reflection, and liberation of individual and collective creativity through experimentation and rebellious festivity, has always been an essential part of culture jamming's *raison d'etre*.

Some forms of cultural resistance can become routinized and, therefore, rather than disrupt or intervene in the established order, they can become part of it and reinforce it. For example, some critics argue that when protesters and police confront each other in established patterns, it can become a ritualistic encounter in which everyone is playing their part but the status quo is left unaltered. Innovation then becomes necessary to alter this dynamic.[15] Likewise, *carnivalesque* festivities such as gay pride marches can become depoliticized over time, as the same iconic images of drag queens and the like become familiar and widely accepted cultural referents. Alternatively, gains made by movements through political and cultural resistance can be re-politicized or instrumentalized in ways outside of movements' control and far from their intentions. Mepschen *et al.* (2010: 965), for example, show how the normalization of gay rights in the Netherlands is used as a means of criticizing Islam as being opposed to 'Dutch culture':

> In order to criticize Muslims as backwards and as enemies of European culture, gay rights are now heralded as if they have

been the foundation of European culture for centuries (cf. Wekker, 2009). This instrumentalization of gay rights puts progressives, anti-racists, feminists, and lesbian and gay activists in an impossible position: taking up the defence of lesbian and gay rights and public gayness comes to be associated with Islamophobia, while solidarity with Muslims against Islamophobia is represented, especially by the populist right, as trivializing or even supporting 'Muslim' homophobia.

Finally, measuring the impact of cultural resistance is difficult, precisely because it involves the interplay of resources, tools, strategies and symbols that are wielded by both dominant and dominated actors. The line between mass culture and resistance culture is not always clear, as the two are intertwined in a dynamic and overlapping relationship through space and time, where symbols and meanings are taken up, tweaked, twisted, commodified, re-appropriated and contested. Any impact of specific protest events or campaigns will also depend on the political context, and on the 'political opportunity structures' available to the movements, which can include such factors as levels of repression, an independent public sphere, a sympathetic or a hostile political climate, contacts and receptivity of mass media, and so on. But adopting such an instrumental view of cultural resistance, by focusing exclusively on a narrowly defined and externally imposed understanding of 'impact', overlooks the much broader importance of cultural resistance for social movements, and for the importance it has for activists themselves, as I hope the discussion in this chapter makes clear.

Culture in action: Linking the local, the national and the global

Culture is produced, transmitted and disseminated through globalizing processes, such as capitalism, mass consumerism and flows of technology. But social movements are also important producers and disseminators of culture, and some of the same tools used by actors fomenting 'globalization from above', such as ICTs, are also harnessed by actors involved in grassroots 'globalization from below' to critique and resist what are seen as the negative consequences of globalization and contemporary social problems. Common targets of symbolic and cultural protest are global corporations, global problems and global 'structuring structures' or widely encompassing frameworks that shape most, if not all, facets of human life and relationships such as capitalism and patriarchy. Sometimes, *local* protests are generated as a response to *global* problems and processes (as, for example, when Bolivian collective *Mujeres Creando* link local problems to the global banking system); sometimes, *global* protests emerge as a response to *local* or *national* issues (as when international non-governmental organizations (INGOs) mobilized against the persecution of Ogoni leaders in Nigeria)[16] but do so appealing to universalist ('global') discourses such as human rights and environmental justice.

In this section, I present case studies of some of the myriad ways activists engage in cultural politics in a globalized world. The examples discussed here only begin to scratch the surface of the multiplicity of creative experimentation that social movements engage in but provide an overview of some of the dynamics and challenges of cultural and symbolic protest and the many ways activists draw on cultural resources to link local, national and global issues.

The Mothers of the Plaza de Mayo, Argentina: Mobilizing motherhood in a repressive state

From 1976 to 1982, Argentina's military junta engaged in what is known as the 'dirty war' but was officially known as the Process of National Reorganization, whose purpose was to 'promote economic development, eradicate subversion, and restore the values fundamental to the integral management of the state, emphasizing the sense of morality, fitness and efficiency indispensable for the reconstitution of the nation' (*La Nación*, 26 March 1976, in Navarro, 2001). Unfortunately, the junta's ideas of morality, fitness and efficiency included the use of right-wing death squads that arrested, tortured, imprisoned without trial, executed and 'disappeared' thousands of people. Disappearances of rival political and civic leaders and 'subversive elements' began at least under the Government of Isabel Perón but became a routinized and systematic form of state terror under the military junta that deposed her in a coup d'état in 1976 (Guzman Bouvard, 1994; Navarro, 2001). The death and torture squads operated with complete impunity and were organized under the control of the armed forces. While some people were arrested openly, thousands more were kidnapped, tortured and killed without anyone ever 'officially' knowing what happened to them. Most were young people between 20 and 30 years of age, but people of all ages, including babies and children, formed part of the disappeared. The junta targeted not only working-class people, students and white-collar workers but also a high proportion of lawyers and teachers as well as housewives, journalists, priests and nuns. A 1983 commission was able to document 8,960 'disappeared', but the number was higher, as many were not reported missing for fear of reprisals, and in some cases entire families were made to disappear, leaving no one to report them missing (Navarro, 2001). In the midst of this regime of terror, in 1977, a small group of women who had been desperately going from one government office to the other to try to find news of their missing sons and daughters, and having been denied any information, decided to engage in a simple act of tremendous courage: to gather in the central Plaza de Mayo, flanked by government ministries, to ask a simple question: Where are our children? The mostly working-class, mostly Catholic women drew on their identities as mothers and housewives to defy the military junta's proscription against any form of political protest or activity, to demand relentlessly that someone take accountability for their missing children. They marched every Thursday, despite police harassment, despite one of their leaders herself being 'disappeared', despite having soldiers train their guns on them and threaten to shoot and despite being arrested. They wore white kerchiefs on their heads on which the names of their children were written and carried large posters with the names and photographs of their children. They were initially dismissed as '*locas*' ('crazy women') and not taken seriously by the regime. As Navarro (2001) points out, the fact that 'mothers' were not seen as political subjects allowed them an initial period of relative impunity during which they were able to organize their internal structure. By 1978, their numbers had grown to 1000, and they were forcibly expelled from the plaza in December of that year. Despite repeated police harassment, they continued to march when they could; although repression was so severe in 1980, they were rarely able to do so. Instead, they met in churches, joined with other human rights organizations nationally and internationally, and tried to meet with as many foreign visitors as possible and as many heads of state as would receive them abroad. On Human Rights Day in 1982, they defied the regime and marched for 24 h, circling the plaza. At great personal risk, their relentless courage and persistence drew the world's attention to what was happening in Argentina, and even after the junta fell, they persisted in their marches, seeking justice for their assassinated children and demanding that their murderers be brought to justice and not given amnesty.[17] They made their missing sons, daughters and grandchildren an issue that their nation and the world could not ignore.[18] As Guzman Bouvard (1994) and Navarro (2001) show, they mobilized their political *invisibility* as working-class Catholic mothers and housewives with no political ideology to make *visible* the gross human rights violations of state terror. They drew on their moral authority as mothers, a figure revered in the Catholic and Latin American culture, to mobilize around a deeply personal and deeply political issue, and they served to delegitimize the regime in power as well as become known internationally as human rights activists, which also served their cause.

The British anti-roads movement and the struggle between 'privatized' and 'public' space

In the early 1990s, a vibrant movement developed in the UK to stop the building of new roads that would destroy not only green spaces and heritage sites but also urban communities as householders were forcibly evicted and houses were demolished to make way for bypasses (Flesher Fominaya, 2013). The British anti-roads movement used a range of creative and innovative tactics to draw attention to the links between local concerns and national and global issues.

Claremont Road, London

One protest that lasted for months was the Claremont Road occupation that formed part of the long-running 'no M11 link' campaign. In East London, protesters were joined by local middle- and working-class families who wanted to save their homes from destruction when an extension of the M11 was built in order to shave eight minutes off commuter time into London.

Protesters occupied the condemned houses on Claremont Road and con-verted the street into a vibrant community, with two cafés, an 'art' house, and live music on Sundays. During the time it was occupied, Claremont Road was transformed into an open community space. One entrance to the road was decorated with a sign that read 'Welcome to the State of the Art'. The entire street was filled with sculptures made from the debris of boarded-up houses and rusty old cars and converted to a living space, replete with sofas and chairs. The 30 or so houses were brightly painted; the few windows 'breeze blocked' by demolition contractors were painted with scenes of peo-ple partying and dancing. One 'sculpture' outside represented the daily lives of the now absent tenants, complete with slippers and blow dryer, and sym-bolized the street as a living space, not a space for cars. Number 68 was transformed into the Art House, home to a collection of anti-roads murals, paintings and sculptures. In the kitchen, children and adult artists had painted car monsters and magical penguins. In the bathroom, black stretches of highway snaked along the walls as 'money' flowed down the drains.

Claremont Road was home to about 50 permanent squatter/protesters, about 10 of whom were original inhabitants. All but six vacating households gave spare keys to the protesters so they could barricade the homes against the wrecking crews, whose strategy was to move in quickly and rip out pipes and floors to make the homes uninhabitable for squatters. Even those six houses that were trashed were renovated by protesters skilled at carpentry. The houses were connected to the tree houses outside and to each other by an intricate system of aerial netting and cables, which provided mobility to manoeuvre during an eviction. The aerial systems and the tree houses formed an intrinsic part of the road camp aesthetic developed over time in the move-ment's rural camps but were also crucial tactical devices that delayed eviction and increased the difficulty and costs of physically removing protesters. Lockons, where activists handcuffed hands to each other through concrete blocks on roof tops, was another such tactic,[19] and images of cherry pickers with police on them trying to grab hold of naked greased-up activists skip-ping across rooftops and ropes between buildings made for guaranteed media attention as well.

In the last weeks of the protest, trade union activists, travellers, squatters and hunt saboteurs swelled the ranks. An estimated 500 protesters faced 200 bailiffs, 700 police and 400 security guards in the final 'battle'. Ultimately, Claremont Road was demolished, but the movement kept going.

RTS street parties

One key organization in the movement was Reclaim the Streets (RTS). One of the activities RTS was best known for was street parties. These were adver-tised through posters and on listserves. A telephone number would be listed that people could call to find out the location of the street party. The idea was to reclaim public space, the streets, from cars and give them back to com-munities. Street parties were festive and communal, with music, dancing and other activities, but also deliberately disruptive to traffic. RTS combined the critique of car culture – its individualism (often one person per car in the morning commute, isolated from others, consuming petrol and so on); environmental impact; justification for road-building schemes that themselves deprived communities of homes, greens and collective spaces – with a much broader critique of capitalism and the complicity of the state (politicians) in privileging the interests of car manufacturers, developers and corporations over those of the people. London's permanent rush hour, congested traffic, road-ragers, high asthma rates and other pollution-related illnesses were all issues highlighted by the street parties. The parties also emerged from a countercultural movement of free raves and Do It Yourself (DIY) culture that were an important part of the alternative social movement scene in the UK in the 1990s (McKay, 1998). Ravers had become politicized by the Criminal Justice Bill that criminalized raves and there was a strong overlap between ravers and anti-roads activists. RTS were strong advocates of direct action, which was an important element of DIY culture, as they explain in this excerpt from one of their posters:

> DIRECT ACTION enables people to develop a new sense of self-confidence and an awareness of their individual and collective power ... DIRECT ACTION is founded on the idea that people can develop the ability for self rule only through practice, and proposes that all people directly decide the important issues facing them. DIRECT ACTION is not just a tactic, it is individuals asserting their ability to control their own lives and to participate in social life without the need for mediation or control by bureaucrats or professional politicians. ... DIRECT ACTION is not a last resort when other methods have failed but the preferred way of doing things.

RTS combined local issues, public interventions, festivity and humour, and global politics so successfully that their tactics were 'exported' around the world and became an important cultural influence on the GJM (Flesher Fominaya, 2013), partly through the activism of ex-RTS members in groups such as the Wombles, Peoples' Global Action, London Rising Tide, London Indymedia and London Genetix Engineering Network (Saunders, 2007).

Both Claremont Road and RTS are examples of ways that cultural resistance engages local communities, draws on myriad cultural resources and connects local and global issues, reframing community problems into a wider critique of capitalism and social injustice. The creative innovation of the anti-roads camps, urban occupations and the street parties was later diffused transnationally and influenced movements beyond the UK.

Global SlutWalks: From Toronto to the world

On 24 January 2011, members of the Toronto Police were giving a talk at Osgoode Hall Law School about campus safety and ways to avoid dangerous situations. During the talk, one officer's advice to the women was that if women wanted to stay safe, they should avoid dressing like sluts (BBC

Online, 2011; Topping, 2011). The message this officer was transmitting is that there is a causal relationship between women's clothing and sexual assault, which shifts the responsibility from the male perpetrator onto the woman whose sexuality presumably makes her responsible for being raped or assaulted. The comments outraged many people; in particular, two women who founded SlutWalk to speak out against sexual violence and victim blaming. Along with their team of organizers and volunteers, the group encourage women from all walks of life to come together in solidarity in a 'SlutWalk' march. They were not just protesting against sexual violence, their goal was also to take back the word 'slut'. They issued the following statement:

> We are tired of being oppressed by slut-shaming; of being judged by our sexuality and feeling unsafe as a result. Being in charge of our sexual lives should not mean that we are opening ourselves to an expectation of violence, regardless if we participate in sex for pleasure or work. No one should equate enjoying sex with attracting sexual assault. (SlutWalk, Toronto, 2011)

Through mass media and social media such as Facebook, SlutWalks have spread globally to Latin America, the US, Europe, Asia and Australia. SlutWalks have sparked fierce debates among feminists over whether it is, in fact, empowering to re-appropriate negative or derogatory language and to play up the hyper-sexualized body image that many would argue is itself a product of a patriarchal society. But another interpretation sees SlutWalks as a sort of performative culture jamming, where women are re-appropriating dominant cultural codes that have been used to oppress them and to justify their sexual and physical victimization. Whichever interpretation one adopts, the highly symbolic protests drew global attention to the culture of victim blaming and sexual harassment, rape and abuse.

YoMango: Anti-capitalist shoplifting 'Made in Spain'

YoMango (slang for 'I rob' or 'I shoplift') is the practice of political anti-capitalist shoplifting. *YoMango* draws on the traditions of the European avantgarde, Situationism and autonomism and forms part of the guerrilla communication scene within contemporary anti-capitalist activism. In true guerrilla communication fashion, they subvert the 'codes' of consumer culture and play with them, not only through the production of stickers, banners, graffiti and pins but also through 'direct interventions' in the form of political shoplifting, which they then write about and publicize on the Internet and in other activist arenas. Like the Situationists in the 1950s and 1960s, they seek to break through the 'false' desires produced by consumer culture and the individualism fostered in capitalism, to reclaim the values of collectivism and cooperation. They do so through constructing creative public interventions that make people stop and rethink everyday practices and beliefs.

Like much guerrilla communication, *YoMango* actions work on a number of different levels: collective shoplifting expeditions are designed to bring down superstores' security systems, not only to facilitate the removal of goods from the store but also to highlight and critique the surveillance to which citizens are subjected as they pursue their daily lives. One form of action involves activists going through the store sticking security tags onto shoppers and dropping them into their carts so that all the alarms will go off as they try to checkout. Once the security systems have been effectively subverted (through either overloading the system or occupying the full attention of all the security guards), they run out with shopping carts loaded with goods which are then taken to a social centre and shared or distributed in the community. Not all *YoMango* actions are collective, but the idea is that if you rob from a store individually you need to make the book, CD, or whatever you shoplift, available to the greater collective by passing it on to a popular library, social centre or someone else who can use it. The struggle to maintain the political edge is not always easy, but *YoMango* is not simply shoplifting. One activist told me:

> My life has changed since I discovered **YoMango**. It is amazing what happens when you enter a store to shoplift instead of buying. Price becomes irrelevant, and objects recover their use-value. I no longer think 'this one is cheaper, or that one is more expensive so it must be better', I only think in terms of what I actually need. That is really the subversive part, not stealing from a mega store. It's the refusal to accept the consumer mentality that is relentlessly fostered on us.[20]

YoMango offers workshops where people can learn techniques of political shoplifting and tries to make the practice as autonomous as possible by making kits which anyone or any group can take and use to offer their own workshop and to pass on the resources that have been collectively generated. *YoMango* is not an organization but a practice that is extended throughout movement networks. There are *YoMango* collectives in Spain, where it originated, as well as Latin America. In Italy, it goes by the name of IoFrego and in the UK Just Nick It. *YoMango* actions have taken place at European Social Forums in Italy and other transnational forums.

YoMango focuses not only on the act of shoplifting but also on creating their own lifestyle brand in a parody of the branding of consumer items. The *YoMango* website encourages people to 'Live the *YoMango* lifestyle, because you're worth it', and one of their slogans is '*YoMango* [I shoplift] because you're worth it', a clear twist on the L'Oréal slogan 'Because you're worth it'. *YoMango* activists in Barcelona altered a massive advertisement[21] for L'Oréal with the words '*YoMango*, the other side of desire' (*YoMango, la otra cara del deseo*) (see *Yo Mango*, 2011). *YoMango* produces stickers which are distributed and stuck on store windows with slogans like 'Super 100% discount!',

'Happy Shoplifter', 'Alone you can't, with friends you can'. In a column called '*YoMango*, because you're worth it' (2012), they write:

> Don't worry, we have good news for you: *YoMango* can give you back your enjoyment, desire and happiness. It can even make you feel younger, or haven't you heard that shoplifting is a teen thing? And so it is, but it is also for all those who don't want to grow old to the beat imposed by capitalism, the rhythm of consumption, tick-tock, ticktock.[22]

Chainworkers Crew, Italy: The construction of the precarious subject and the art of media hoaxes

The issue of precarious labour has become an important axis of mobilization in Europe. The EuroMayDay parades, which highlight the issues of labour precariousness for millions of European flexible workers, began in Milan in 2001 (Chainworkers, 2001) and have spread to over 20 cities. While the exact nature of which types of contract and employment conditions constitute precarious labour is a question of debate; in broad terms, 'labour precariousness' refers to short-term, unstable and poorly remunerated labour. As a political issue, it is linked to a wider critique of hyper-flexibility of labour contracts in contemporary capitalism and the resulting economic vulnerability of many workers, a disproportionate number of whom are young workers (under 35). In Spain, for example, in the final trimester of 2011, the percentage of workers with temporary (as opposed to permanent) contracts was almost 25 per cent of the labour force (Instituto Nacional de Estadística, 2012). Many teachers and researchers are hired each fall, terminated each summer and rehired each fall (if they are lucky), leaving them with no income or benefits over the summer. Shop assistants, flight attendants, construction workers and many other types of worker can be hired, terminated and rehired each week in an endless series of short-term contracts, some lasting only hours. Precarious labour creates uncertainty, financial vulnerability and high levels of stress. It is also linked to increased rates of workplace accidents and health risks. According to the labour union Union General De Trabajadores (2012), precarious workers are often overqualified for their jobs, work very long hours, have limited or no opportunities for advancement, have fewer rights as employees and are rarely unionized. Workers with these types of contracts and conditions often also suffer from low morale, which can negatively affect productivity (Arribas, 2012; Union General De Trabajadores, 2012).

As discussed in Chapter 3, in the late 1990s, activists in Europe, and especially in Italy, Spain and France, began to theorize and develop the concept of a precarious subject and the notion of 'precarity'[23] or precariousness around which to mobilize (Flesher Fominaya, 2005). The conceptual identity was new and therefore not immediately recognizable or understandable to those coming to it for the first time. Before mobilizing around the issue of precariousness, activists first had to produce a collective identity of the precarious subject and their life experience. This developed into a theoretical body of work, consisting of movement writings (reflective texts, manifestos, web-posts, laboratories) themselves the product of diverse activists in discussion groups organized within autonomous social centres and other movement milieus. Although many different groups are involved, the Italian group Chainworkers Crew has been an important influence and has made strong use of icons to transmit its political messages (Mattoni and Doerr, 2007). One humorous and powerful icon that draws on strong Catholic traditions in Italy, France and Spain, and therefore translates effectively between them, is that of a new saint, 'Saint Precarious' (*San Precario*), patron saint of the precarious workers. Chainworkers Crew created the icon and reproduced it on posters, flyers and stickers.

Chainworkers Crew also perpetrated an elaborate media hoax and collective action that involved the invention of a hip young Anglo-Japanese fashion designer named Serpica Naro (which is an anagram of *San Precario*).[24] After generating media hype around the non-existent designer, they organized a fashion show during the Milan Fashion Week in 2005. In a typical guerrilla communication twist, part of the hype involved a group of activists (also invented by them) who protested against Serpica Naro for her exploitation of precarious workers. Through the design of the clothes themselves, those involved in the fashion show/collective action highlighted issues precarious women face in the workplace (and out of it) as a result of their precarious condition, such as sexual harassment, economic dependence on men and high levels of stress (Mattoni and Doerr, 2007). Once the fashion show was over, Serpica Naro's publicist, 'Nadja Fortuna' revealed the hoax.

The Chainworkers Crew mobilized multiple cultural resources and developed a network of precarious fashion workers and other supporters who harnessed their creativity and talent to devise and produce all the elements involved, including the clothes, models and catwalk; engagement with mass media; production of their own media; and all the imagination, iconography and visual and textual basis for the action (Mattoni, 2012). As Mattoni (2012) explains, access to specialized knowledge and resources necessary for the action – such as knowing the official requirements for inclusion in the show – was possible through its connection to the precarious workers involved in the Milan Fashion Week, who used the information, knowledge and resources gained through their labour to construct an action of resistance that highlighted their situation. Many of these workers were not previously politically active but were politicized through this action. Chainworkers Crew also drew on the skills of their own activists employed precariously in the communication sector to develop the web presence of the fake designer. Apart from the short-term effect and critique of the action itself, it developed a social movement network by bringing together activists and people not previously politically active (Mattoni, 2012).

Once the action was over, Chainworkers posted this on their website:

> Serpica Naro doesn't exist. Everyone who identifies with Serpica can take part in it. Serpica Naro is a place where imaginary and

self-production, creativity, radicalism and style meet ... Serpica Naro will be a web site to invent a precarious style lab, to put self-productions together and to share work-knowledges and information ... Serpica Naro as Metabrand for self-production is the answer through which we declare the fashion week is over and the season of precarious conspiracy has started! (Chainworkers Crew, undated)

The action worked on number of levels. First, it critiqued and ridiculed the mass media and the fashion industry, the former for its lack of rigour in determining true versus fake news, the latter for its insistence on establishing elite criteria for 'designer' clothes and charging a fortune for them, when in reality they themselves could not distinguish Serpica Naro knock-offs (which were made by drawing on elements of 'real' designer clothes) from the 'real' thing. The action also called attention to the precarious nature of labour used to produce high-end fashion and connected this to a wider critique of precarious labour conditions in contemporary global capitalist production regimes. It also projected an *alternative* model for cultural production, one based on pooling collective resources and DIY creativity, and recognizing the collective nature of production, rather than exalting individual 'genius' or talent. By explaining and disseminating the action through mass and alternative media, they also offered the action as a cultural resource to other groups, as it became part of the cultural stock of guerrilla communication.

Mujeres Creando: Performative culture jamming and alternative institution building in Bolivia

Mujeres Creando (Women Creating) is an anarcha-feminist group based in Bolivia who engage in performative culture jamming and direct action. They also run a social centre and a radio station, host art installations and workshops, edit a monthly magazine, publish books and engage in other forms of activism. The name of their social centre is the Virgin of Desires, and on their website they have a prayer to Our Lady of Desires in which they ask her to free them from racists, homophobes, sexists and classists. The centre has spaces dedicated to art, education, study groups, political outreach, shopping, eating, counselling, exercise, daycare and a domestic violence refuge. They recently started serving two sandwiches in their café named after terms used in Bolivia to describe women in a derogatory way. By doing so, they are reclaiming the words and giving them a positive connotation. In a context of highly chauvinistic laws and a repressive state, *Mujeres Creando* call themselves a politically neutral group not in search of a rebellion or a revolt, but in a quest of women's rights, equality and a chance to be visible. Of course, their activism is deeply political and all the more powerful precisely because these women take sacred cultural images, such as Christ on the cross and the Madonna, and link them directly to their daily experience of oppression, violence and poverty as women and mothers. They are also fierce critics of the Bolivian president Evo Morales for his repression of social movements and his continuation of male chauvinist privilege. They use street theatre, graffiti and other public interventions as a means of practising politics and engaging the emotions of their audience:

> We believe that how we relate to people in the street is funda-
> mental ... For us, the street is the principal site for our struggle ...
> It is very important that what we do in the street interacts with
> people, that we speak to people, that they see the graffiti, that it
> provokes something in them, laughter, annoyance, rage ...
> Creativity is human – it belongs to all women and men. But many
> want to dispossess us of this creativity ... They want to turn cre-
> ativity into something elitist, saying the artists are the creative
> ones, the inspired ones ... We do not allow ourselves to be dispos-
> sessed of an instrument of struggle and in everything we do, in
> the books we make, in the street actions, in the graffiti ... Then
> some people say to us: 'You're artists'. But we are not artists, we
> are street activists. (Notes from Nowhere, 2003: 258–9)

Like the rest of the groups discussed here, *Mujeres Creando* mix a careful attention to local concerns with global issues. Their activism has targeted the banking system, which they have critiqued for charging high interest rates to poor people and exploiting ignorance by convincing people with little edu-cation to take on loans without understanding the implications of the con-tracts they are signing. In this way, they make connections between global financial systems and local users of financial services in Bolivia. In their magazine, they have also targeted the McDonald's and Coca-Cola corpora-tions and have published information about the Multilateral Agreement on Investment (MAI), an issue many GJM activists have mobilized around, as well as spreading information about the anti-globalization protests in Seattle, Prague and elsewhere. By drawing on national and religious symbols, they frame their messages using cultural tools and narratives which are already available to them in the dominant national culture and give them a 'twist' in the spirit of guerrilla communication, making them resources with which to speak about their oppression. You can see images and more on their website www.mujerescreando.org.

Conclusion

Cultural resistance is a powerful and essential part of collective action, be it primarily local, national or global in scope. In a globalized world, activists reflect on the opportunities and challenges posed by myriad globalization processes from global environmental destruction to new information tech-nologies, commonly targeting global corporations, highlighting global issues and problems, and raising consciousness about globalized frameworks that shape the daily lives of billions of people around the world, such as capital-ism and patriarchy. For activists themselves, cultural resistance can be an important means of developing political self-consciousness (e.g. as with pride movements or the construction of new political subjects such as the precarious issue), building solidarity, trust and networks, for attracting new members, for engaging in activity which they find politically meaningful, for innovating tactically and for expressing creativity. Cultural resistance produces new cultural products, ideas and forms and, through it, social movements also inscribe new meanings on existing objects or representations to stimulate reflection and critique. Cultural resistance opens up free spaces – figuratively, in the sense of creating new ideas, discourse and ideals, and physically, as when new spaces for cultural and political activity are opened up by squatting social centres or establishing alternative institutions (schools, cafés, shops, credit unions and so on). Cultural resistance is also a political intervention in the public arena that can directly engage audiences as spectators or participants. It transmits messages that try to engage others' emotions, values, ideas or beliefs by drawing on cultural symbols and narratives and re-appropriating them or giving them new meanings. Cultural resistance can make visible social, political and economic conflicts by forcing a confrontation between authorities and citizens through direct actions. Movements pass on traditions of cultural resistance (e.g. tactical repertoires, myths, forms of democratic practice) as a legacy that is adopted and adapted by future movements (McKay, 1996; Cuninghame, 2007; Flesher Fominaya, 2013; Romanos, 2013). Contemporary activists use the tools and resources developed in capitalism – technology, knowledge, information – to present creative critiques on the more negative effects of globalization. While cultural resistance is a powerful tool, it is also open to misinterpretation, unintended consequences, co-optation and commodification, routinization, trivialization, depoliticization and backlash. For all these reasons, creativity, innovation and reflexivity are important elements of social movements that engage in cultural resistance. Activists draw on influences from around the world and strategically connect to a range of audiences (local, national and global), trying to overcome barriers and challenges posed by variations in language and culture across nations. If cultural resistance has limitations, there is no question that it is also a powerful and transformative form of collective action, often with a global reach, thanks to the power of media and ICTs, the focus of Chapter 5.

5 SOCIAL MOVEMENTS, MEDIA, ICTS AND CYBERPOLITICS

In Chapter 4, I discussed cultural resistance and argued that one of the key ways social movements engage in cultural resistance is by means of the production and dissemination of multiple forms of media. In this chapter, I focus on some of the ways social movement actors communicate with their intended audiences and with each other using media. First, I discuss some of the 'dilemmas of mass media': challenges social movements face when they engage with mainstream mass media and some of the strategies they develop to minimize or overcome them.

The second part of the chapter looks at the rise of information and communications technologies (ICTs) as a relatively new form of communication of increasing importance to social movements in a globalized world. The advent of new media and ICTs, in particular social media, has transformed what used to be mainstream-dominated media systems into multifaceted media environments. Media today are more diverse and offer more options for access to political information. Social movement actors also communicate through a wide range of interconnected outlets, and the advent of ICTs has not only broadened but also changed some of the forms, impact and reach of their political messaging. Engaging in effective political communication in an evolving media environment is a key challenge for social movement actors and one that presents specific constraints as well as emerging opportunities created and facilitated by the development of new ICTs. In addition to the integration of new media and ICTs into social movement activity more broadly, struggles over the use, ownership and control of cyberspace have given rise to cyberpolitics and forms of 'hacktivism' that form an important and influential arena of social movement activism. This is addressed in the third part of the chapter.

Dilemmas posed by mass media

As Malcolm X once famously said, 'If you're not careful the newspapers will have you hating the people who are being oppressed and loving the people who are doing the oppressing.' His words summarize a key problem facing many social movements as they try to navigate the many dilemmas posed by mass media.

The globalization of mass media has radically transformed the nature of contemporary politics, including social movements. Some scholars argue that mass media coverage is crucial to social movements' ability to convey their messages to a wider audience. Gamson and Wolfsfeld (1993) argue that social movements are dependent on mainstream media for three key reasons: to mobilize support, to reach out for supporters beyond those already in agreement with movement claims and to increase the legitimacy of their claims and demands. Yet, social movements also face enormous constraints in this endeavour. Numerous studies have shown that social movements are under-represented in mass media (McCarthy *et al.*, 1996; Oliver and Maney, 2000; Rucht, 2005), that media coverage is biased by the reliance on 'expert' opinions versus grassroots movement spokespeople (Ryan *et al.*, 2001) and that protest coverage is biased in favour of power holders and elites (Ryan *et al.*, 2001; Gitlin, 2003 [1980]). Newsgathering routines (journalistic practices) have a great influence on what gets reported and how (Ryan, 1991; McCarthy *et al.*, 1996; Gitlin, 2003 [1980]). Journalists are looking for news that is notorious, consequential, extraordinary and culturally resonant (Ryan, 1991). Description bias is another problem: studies show that even when protest events are covered, the news is framed in ways that can undermine social movement messages and agendas (Smith *et al.*, 2001). Ryan *et al.* (2001) show that social movements and community organizations operate at a considerable disadvantage when trying to influence news portrayals of issues than do their better-funded opposing groups and organizations.

Corporate ownership of global media and the concentration of media in very few hands, coupled with the fact that often 'public' media such as state TV are subject to government control and oversight, mean that despite the ideal of an independent press, in reality the decks are firmly stacked against social movement messages that are critical of political and economic elites. Chomsky and Herman (2010: xi) argue compellingly that, in the US, media serve to propagandize and serve the interests of the 'powerful societal interests that control and finance them'. They use a propaganda model to show how media function to represent the agendas of dominant social, economic and political groups that exercise power nationally and globally. Other media scholars disagree and argue that media have a liberal bias that is overzealous in its watchdog function and, for example, disproportionately report on bad economic news and the effects of this on workers and the public (Harrington, 1989; Blood and Phillips, 1995). While one might suppose that a diversity of possible media sources could help avoid this bias, scholars such as Bagdikian (2000) have shown that, increasingly, fewer corporations monopolize an ever greater share of media: whereas, after World War II, 80 per cent of US daily newspapers were independently owned, by 1989 the reverse was true, with 80 per cent owned by corporations. In 2000, despite the existence of over 25,000 media outlets, 23 corporations controlled most of them (Bagdikian, 2000: 4). Media monopolies, of course, are not limited to single nations. Media conglomerates such as News Corporation, owned by Rupert Murdoch, stretch across the world, exerting global power. Murdoch was listed as the 24th most powerful person in the world by *Forbes* in 2012 (*Forbes*, 2012). Yet, mass media configurations do vary greatly around the world. In Europe, for example, the mass media landscape is often highly differentiated ideologically, with newspapers and television channels ranging from social democratic, liberal, Catholic, far-right, multiple shades of nationalism and minority language newspapers with particular audiences. European social movement actors engage with a range of mass media outlets rather than necessarily framing or pitching their messages to a hypothetically central mainstream media sphere. As I will discuss, social movements also produce their own media, sometimes with a wide audience. Bagdikian's discussion, while pointing to a disquieting and documented phenomenon, is somewhat problematic in that it assumes that people are not critical consumers of media. As I discussed in Chapter 4, British media studies scholars, such as Stuart Hall (1993 [1973]), have shown that people are capable of critically interpreting news messages and disagreeing with them.

Not all scholars are so pessimistic about mass media's coverage of protest and social movements, arguing that mainstream media are sometimes supportive of certain movements and protests (Cottle, 2008; Cammaerts and Carpentier, 2009).

If it is hard enough for social movements to obtain sufficient attention and space in print media, this is complicated further with television news coverage because the very form of television news, with extremely short sound bites, means that social movements rarely have the opportunity to present nuanced or detailed accounts of their critiques or activities. However, as a visual medium, television is a potentially powerful transmitter of symbolic and iconographic movement messages.

Despite these constraints, social movements have many motivations for engaging with mass media. In his book *The Whole World is Watching*, originally written in 1980, former president of Students for a Democratic Society (SDS) and media critic Todd Gitlin (2003 [1980]: 242) argues that opposition movements engage mass media for many rational/strategic purposes, including recruiting supporters, challenging the authority of dominant institutions, placing issues on the public agenda, presenting a countercultural alternative or redressing grievances.

Gitlin shows that whereas initially it is difficult for social movements to have their messages included in news coverage, once they do receive media attention their troubles are far from over. With reference to the case of the US anti-war movement and the New Left, specifically the role and coverage of SDS in the 1960s and 1970s, Gitlin shows that the routines of 'objectivity' structured into the production of news serve to reproduce hegemony. According to the rules of objectivity, news media cannot simply ignore social movements completely: they therefore apply a whole 'apparatus of techniques' that tame and constrain the opposition that 'they dare not ignore' (Gitlin, 2003 [1980]: 259). Gitlin's discussion assumes a democratic context or at least one in which governments and media feel a need to respond to mass protest (see Chapter 7 for a discussion of media blackouts in periods of protest).

In the case of the New Left, the media turned certain movement leaders into celebrities, which not only distanced them from the base of the movement but also gave the false impression that the leaders *were* the movement.

According to Gitlin, media inflated the importance of revolutionary rhetoric beyond what it actually represented within the movement itself. Once public opinion had shifted against the Vietnam War, the media put forward 'clean cut' moderate spokespeople against the war as the acceptable face of opposition, contrasting them with unacceptable, scruffy, draft-card-burning radicals and allowing them to speak on behalf of anti-war activity. He argues mass media pursued a deliberate frame of 'moderation-as-alternative-to militancy', in line with a broader media strategy of imposing news frames from above. One common recurring aspect of this to this day is the juxtaposition of 'violent' and 'peaceful' protesters with an overemphasis on 'violent' protest. This juxtaposition can make the public less receptive to movement messages and also helps justify state repression of opposition movements.

Gitlin (2003 [1980]: 292) concludes that news coverage of social movements serves as a form of social management that manages and contains cultural resistance, a pessimistic conclusion for social movements, only moderately mitigated by his recognition that media sometimes magnify and hasten manageable forms of political change and by his provision of some suggestions for media engagement by opposition movements. His discussion also downplays to some extent the ways in which movement actors themselves play off good protester/bad protester discourses by presenting *themselves* as the preferred peaceful legitimate option as against more militant protesters (or vice versa).

Despite Gitlin's pessimistic assessment, and as he himself shows, the power of the media is not lost on activists, as the iconic chant 'The whole world is watching' demonstrates. In 1968, anti-war and countercultural demonstrators who were in Chicago to disrupt the Democratic National Convention chanted this as they were dragged off and beaten by police. Their message was that, despite the police violence, the world would be aware of both their protest and the repression. Confrontations between protesters and the police lasted eight days, and colourful events highly attractive to media, such as the Yippies' nomination of Pigasus the Pig for president, drew extensive media attention. (The Yippies were members of the Youth International Party who practiced street theatre and political pranks and who wanted to bring young people to the city 'to smoke pot and groove on rock bands'.)

Gitlin's (2003 [1980]) work highlights the problem with media framing of protest and protesters: mainstream media tend to trivialize, marginalize, polarize,[3] emphasize internal dissension and violence and delegitimize movements by undercounting their numbers or disparaging their effectiveness or tactics. These biases operate transnationally as well (Mac Sheoin, 2013). Yet, selection and description bias is not the only obstacle social movements face; another key disparity lies between the resources that political and economic elites and state actors have to influence media coverage and content and those available to social movements. One key mechanism used by elites to influence media coverage is the establishment of official media centres to cover key events such as G8 summits or World Trade Organization (WTO) meetings. In these cases, millions are spent providing journalists with every facility (catering, high-tech equipment, prepared press statements even before the events begin, perks and souvenirs) often physically separating them from contact with 'real people' or protesters and restricting their access. Police also have a particular relationship with mainstream media. As Mac Sheoin (2013) discusses in an extensive overview of studies on media coverage of the global justice movement (GJM) (Chapter 3), the relation between police and journalists at protest events is designed to favour the police's preferred narrative in a number of ways: through 'embedding', which involves allowing journalists to accompany the police on the job, literally providing them with the police's point of view, and by the provision of pre-emptive statements about such things as the likelihood of violence, which justifies police repression even before protest has begun. Both tactics are designed to facilitate press access while limiting or controlling coverage. Journalists wanting to cover protest itself or documenting police brutality are often met with police brutality, arrests, smashing or confiscation of equipment, and surveillance (Mac Sheoin, 2013).

Social movement media strategies

Cultural hegemony, mass consumerism, corporate dominance of mass media, problems with bias and coverage, and the resource and power differences between social movements and their opponents mean that social movements face considerable challenges in their attempts to transmit their claims and to traverse the gap between their intended messages and their target audiences. In a globalized world, competition for media coverage amidst information overload and media bias combines with cultural and linguistic barriers to create serious constraints for social movements. Different movements develop multiple strategies to address these challenges. Well-funded professionalized social movement organizations can afford to engage media professionals and lobbyists to convey their messages through mainstream media to target audiences. Movements with little money have to draw on a wealth of other resources (creativity, networks, contacts) and use a diverse range of strategies to engage with mass media.

Mass media strategies

Rucht (2005: 36) developed a typology of the strategies activists use to deal with the problems with mass media coverage of social movement activity that he calls 'quadruple A': abstention, attack, adaptation and alternatives.

Abstention is when negative experiences with mass media motivate social movement actors to disengage from attempts to influence mass media. *Attack* consists of active, and sometimes even violent, critique and action against mass media outlets that grossly misrepresent social movements or the issues they defend. *Adaptation* involves accepting the logic and reality of mass media dominance and developing strategies to influence coverage of social movement activities and issues positively. *Alternatives* 'is the attempt by social movements to create their own and independent media (or public forums of communication) in order to compensate for a lack of interest, or bias, by the established media'. As Mattoni (2012) argues, the problem with this model is that mainstream media remain at the centre of all of these options. However, it is clear that social movements have always produced alternative forms of media and political communication as a central part of their activity (Downing 2008, Mattoni 2012). Engagement with mainstream media can be a source of conflict within activist communities as to which strategies should be adopted, with some favouring abstention from collaboration with mainstream media or corporate platforms such as social media websites on ideological grounds, but most engaging in multiple media strategies, including having spokespeople, calling press conferences, issuing press releases, giving interviews and trying actively to produce counter-spin, or developing alternative narratives to official or dominant accounts. Nevertheless, most social movement actors do orient some of their actions toward mass media and use some particular strategies to do so.

Mobilizing icons

Szasz (1995) has argued that the production of *iconic* political communication – as opposed to rhetorical or even symbolic forms – can be a very effective means of connecting the movement to the intended audience despite constraints in political context[4] (such as a conservative period). Mass media lend itself to image-oriented political messages that can be transmitted in encapsulated high-impact ways. He uses the example of the issue of 'toxic waste' which he shows was very effectively mobilized in the US but only, he argues, because viewers or recipients of the message of the risk of toxic waste could connect that with their own experiences and communities (and imagine that a facility could be built in their neighbourhood). Otherwise, viewers are only momentarily upset by news stories that then fade 'when the kaleidoscopic flux of news moves on to other things' (Szasz, 1995: 214). The movement was able to make hazardous industrial waste sites a key concern in mass perception in the 1980s, and this mass concern fuelled the growth of the movement (which went on to connect toxic waste sites to issues of racism and poverty and became the environmental justice movement).

Another example of the mobilization of icons for political purposes was the 'Dying for Diamonds' campaign carried out by one of the UK's largest development charities, ActionAid (Gaber and Willson, 2005). 'Marilyn Monroe' dressed in pink satin singing 'Diamonds are a Girl's Best Friend' waited to greet diamond industry representatives as they arrived at a meeting in London in 2002. She was accompanied by men clad in top hat and tails carrying placards with statistics highlighting the issue of 'conflict diamonds' which fund human rights abuses and wars in Africa. ActionAid estimates these diamonds cost 2.5 million lives in the Democratic Republic of the Congo, 1.5 million homeless in Liberia, the abduction of 10,000 children in Sierra Leone and 90,000 amputees in Angola. The charity wanted the diamond industry to adopt a strong self-regulation scheme and to raise awareness among UK retailers and the public about the issue of conflict diamonds so people would pressure retailers and suppliers for diamonds to be conflict-free (Gaber and Willson, 2005). The mobilization of the iconic image of Marilyn and her diamonds juxtaposed with very unglamorous statistics created a strong visual message that was widely disseminated by mass media. It linked a global problem to national and local business practices and consumption, bringing responsibility for the issue of conflict diamonds in Africa to the UK.

Public agenda setting

Chomsky and Herman (2010) argue that, despite the propaganda model under which mass media operate, the public will not necessarily believe or accept the messages media are conveying. Where public opinion or interest diverges strongly from elite interests, and where people have access to alternative information that deviates from the 'official story', they will be able to form their own opinions. Some social movement groups therefore devote time trying to influence the 'public agenda', or the environment in which people will interpret media messages, through intensive community outreach, in schools, churches and other civil society institutions and through the production of alternative grassroots media (Gamson, 1992; McCarthy *et al.*, 1996).

Unconventional protest

Unconventional protests may be more likely to attract press attention. Direct action and civil disobedience, discussed in Chapter 4, often lend themselves to powerful media images. Direct actions which have a performative or symbolic element (songs, chants, rituals, slogans, icons) in addition to a strategic one are often attractive to media looking for a good image to sell a story, whether or not that is the primary intention of the activists. Disruptive tactics may also help draw coverage (although not necessarily favourable to social movement agendas). A study on newspaper coverage of Indigenous protests in Canada concluded that 'increasing the size and the length of an event does not improve coverage. The latter is determined exclusively by the form of the event, and it is disruptive tactics alone that increase front-page coverage. The inclusion of pictures, however, is largely determined by media news routines rather than by activists tactics' (Wilkes *et al.*, 2010: 1).

Yet, unconventional protest poses dilemmas as well: coverage might not be favourable toward the protest and, especially in cases of performative violence (such as smashing or burning automated bank tellers), media coverage can focus on the protest *tactic* and ignore the protest issues, or can focus on the minority of activists engaging in damage to property, rather than the majority of 'peaceful' protesters. Activists recognize this dilemma and often call for peaceful protests, trying to discipline or dissuade more radical actors. Yet, it is also clear that, in the absence of spectacular numbers of protesters (and, sometimes, even when numbers are very high), mainstream media outlets are likely to ignore mobilizations that do not involve some aspect of unconventional protest. While this does not have to be violent by any means, standard protests are likely to receive less media attention (Dalton, 1996).

As seen in Chapter 4, the use of celebrities is another way some movements try to attract mainstream media attention. While this can raise awareness of issues, it can also shift attention away from the issue onto the celebrities themselves.

Movements as producers and disseminators of counter-narratives

Social movements can use protests to bear witness against injustice (Della Porta and Diani, 2009), corruption or wrongdoing by political elites and, in this way, attempt to counter dominant elite narratives. One example, in which mainstream media played an important role, was the case of the Spanish political flash mob of 13 March 2004. Just two days after the train bombings that killed 192 people in Madrid and one day before the general election, activists outside the Popular Party headquarters chanted a refrain again and again: 'The whole world already knows' (*El mundo entero ya lo sabe*). They were referring to the fact that the Popular Party government had been insisting that the Basque nationalist terrorist group ETA had been responsible for the bombings and that for the first two days most national mass media had been supporting this version of events. However, foreign media and, crucially, social movement alternative media and listserves had been disseminating news that, in fact, Al-Qaeda-linked groups had claimed responsibility for the bombings. The chant, therefore, was conveying the message not only that the Popular Party was deliberately lying to try to win the elections but that 'the game was up' because the whole world already knew the truth. Their words echoed a feature of contemporary society that globalization theorists have highlighted: today, world citizens become aware of events almost as quickly as political elites do, and sometimes before, making political cover-ups and disinformation campaigns more difficult. Social movement activists in 2004 had some tools not available to the activists in Chicago in 1968 who chanted 'The whole world is watching!': they had called the protest using SMS messages and the Internet. Social movement alternative media were also important in countering the official story within an extremely short time frame (Flesher Fominaya, 2011). In this case, foreign mainstream media picked up the protests before national media did. When the Popular Party presidential candidate made a public announcement criticizing the protesters that was aired on national news, many Madrid residents became aware of the protest and took to the streets, swelling the original crowd to about 5,000 people and then spreading the protests throughout the downtown area. This case demonstrates the complex interplay between mainstream and alternative media as well as the opportunities offered by new ICTs in facilitating mobilization and producing a strong counter-narrative to the 'official story'. It also highlights the importance of the *global* reach of media in shaping a *local* protest action that had a *national* impact. Communication flowed from foreign mainstream media to activist alternative media, which was then disseminated via listserves and telephones as people called each other to talk about what had happened and to question the official version of events. As the shock of the bombings turned to anger at the government, activists mobilized their networks to the flash mob protest using SMS messaging. These messages, in turn, spread quickly beyond the original activist recipients to broader social networks, and people incensed by the government's statements channelled their anger into the flash mob (Flesher Fominaya, 2011).

Figure 5.1

A sign at the 19J 2011 anti-austerity protest in Barcelona, Spain, reads 'Enough Manipulation'

Copyright: Cristina Flesher Fominaya

Moving beyond the mass media model

As the example of the 13-M flash mob shows, while there is no question that mass media continue to exert a powerful influence around the world, it is also true that social movements are less dependent on mass media than models that place mass media at the centre of social media strategies would suggest. Social movements have long been engaged in *alternative* media practices, which encompass many of the forms of cultural resistance discussed in Chapter 4, such as culture jamming and graffiti, the productions of broadsheets, manifestos, free radio programmes, books, zines, cartoons, radical theatre, music, pamphlets, magazines, flyers, film, TV programmes, video and more. In so doing, social movement actors create an alternative public sphere (Downing, 2001) or what Fraser (1993) calls counter-public spheres, highlighting the plurality of voices engaged in contesting dominant or hegemonic narratives or frameworks. Downing (2001: 19) points out that these alternative spheres are never hermetically sealed off from the rest of social and political life but are also shaped by the contexts of state power and hegemony, and radical media activists face and have experienced state repression, including execution, intimidation, jailing, surveillance and torture. Downing points to the crucial role social movements have not only in producing and disseminating counter-narratives but also in maintaining critical discourses and information during periods of 'political quiescence', or what social movement scholars refer to as 'latency' or 'abeyance'.

Social movement produced media can extend to wide audiences. From the proliferation of the socialist and communist press in 1920s Germany to the practice of *Samizdat* in the Soviet bloc countries – which was the practice of producing, reproducing and disseminating documents and manuscripts from person to person as a means of circumventing state censorship – or the creation of free radio projects, such as Radio Alice in Italy that reached mass audiences, social movements have created their own extensive media and communication networks (see Downing, 2001). Community media, which refers to the practice of enabling people to produce their own media, geared towards its usefulness to the user group and its accountability to the community (rather than to a state or corporate board of directors) is another rich area of social movement media production with a long history (Howley, 2005).

If these examples show the long history of the creation of alternative media, it is also true that the media environment has radically changed with the development of new media technologies. Today, social media platforms such as Facebook and Twitter have made it easy for 'ordinary citizens' (or non-activists or political communication specialists) to engage in the production and dissemination of political messages. This means that, in a globalized world in which political communication is often facilitated and transmitted through ICTs, it becomes more difficult to distinguish clearly between the recipients and producers of political messages and challenges our ideas about the clear distinction between cultural producers and cultural consumers (see Burgess and Green, 2009). In much the same way as many actions of cultural resistance have no known authors or originators (recall the practices of billboard liberation or graffiti from Chapter 4 or the difficulty of finding the origin of memes), the production and dissemination of political communication in cyberspace often cannot be traced or attributed to particular groups or authors. This can have benefits and limitations for social movements. As I noted in Chapter 4, the downplaying of authorial ownership in social movements has both ideological and strategic rationales. Activists questioning a neoliberal ideology that focuses on the individual as opposed to the collective production of art and knowledge, and that stresses individual rights to intellectual property, may reject the idea of attributing authorship to political messages. In a repressive context where criminal charges may be brought against individuals for circulating political images or messages, anonymity is also a strategic option facilitated by the Internet. Hacktivist collectives such as Anonymous (see below) encompass both of these rationales.

The dissemination of political messages also has an element of serendipity in that certain messages that resonate culturally or provoke an emotional response are likely to be shared and transmitted through activist and friendship networks. The Internet, in particular, makes this process of sharing easier, faster and with a potentially larger audience than ever before. Individuals can alter or modify the messages or images along the way, producing a range of variations on the original messages through such means as memes (a concept or image that passes from one user to another on the Internet, often with variations on a similar theme) and mash-ups (a combination of multiple sources of video into a new product). Messages can originate in 'alternative' media environments and make their way into mainstream mass media and vice versa. This dynamic media environment should not lead to the conclusion that the production of alternative grassroots or social movement produced political communication is simply the product of random spontaneous action (although sometimes it is!). Social movement actors devote significant time, energy, resources and organization in the production of alternative grassroots political communication.

As Rucht (2005) and others have shown, more established and resource-rich social movement groups are best placed to adopt strategies that involve influencing elites by such practices as hiring professional journalists or public relations specialists to lobby and 'spin' movement demands. Groups with insider contacts in political and media elites will be better placed to exert influence and control over the political messages, although such influence is likely to be limited in inverse relation to the degree to which the political message critiques the status quo. As Gitlin (2003 [1980]) and others have shown, mass or mainstream media representations are rarely sympathetic to anti-systemic messages or those highly critical of the status quo. As I have argued, however, and as Mattoni (2012) shows, social movement actors are not dependent on integration into elites but, rather, produce and develop their own networks and resources to engage in effective political communication.

Although I will be focusing below on the ways in which ICTs have transformed the ways social movements communicate with their target audiences and with each other, it is clear that social movements engage in a range of media practices, offline and online, low-tech and high-tech, and hybrid forms of media.

ICTs and social movements

'Social movements do not emerge out of technology.' – Geert Lovink

While social movements have benefited from the introduction of new forms of technology for many years, few technological advances have altered social movement communication processes as rapidly and profoundly as ICTs. ICTs have fundamentally transformed the global economy, and they have reshaped human interaction in both work and leisure. It comes as no surprise, therefore, that they would also have a tremendous impact on social movements and political communication. A key area of scholarship on social movements and mobilization has centred on the role of the new ICTs and social media in fostering protest, communication and diffusion processes. Given the importance of ICTs for social movements, an abundance of research on ICTs and social movements has focused on aspects such as national and transnational networking (Keck and Sikkink, 1998; Olesen,

2005); the relation between political commitment and type of ICT use (Mosca and Della Porta, 2009); collective identity formation in virtual communities (Ayers, 2003; Mosca, 2007); cyberactivism (Ayers, 1999; Myers, 2001; Coleman, 2012a, 2012b); the creation of alternative media online (Downing, 2001); the relation between mainstream media and movement -produced media, activist use of ICTs (Gillan *et al.*, 2008); and the relation among ICTs, social movement media and their publics (Castells, 2009; Atkinson, 2010).

The term 'new media' has been adopted by many scholars to refer to a collection of technological innovations, defined by the following characteristics: their hybrid or recombinant formations, which enable users to bring together pre-existing technologies in a range of innovative ways; their contribution to the development of communication systems as 'reorganizing, unfolding [...] networks of networks' structured centrally on hyperlinks; and their enabling of on-demand access to information (Lievrouw, 2011: 8–16). 'Newness' doesn't refer so much to a clear break between old and new media but rather to the way that the possibility for innovation is built into a system defined by hybrid and recombinant technological formations. This has transformed the way social movements communicate internally and externally and has implications for changes in communication, self-expression, collective identity formation, personal network building and activist communications strategies. This is partly due to the increasingly digitally mediated nature of the everyday lives of increasing numbers of people but also to the emergence of techno or cyberpolitics as a distinct sphere of political activity (more on this below).

As new forms of technology emerge, they are developed, adopted and adapted strategically by social movement actors, who develop cultural competencies, practices, preferences and repertoires alongside these technological developments, and these are not uniform across contexts. For example, activists in the same broad movement network or wave of action such as the pro-democracy and anti-austerity movements that filled the squares of Europe following the global financial crash of 2007/2008 (see Chapter 7) had very different technological and media repertoires. Spain's pro-democracy 15-M movement used a system of collaborative documents (Titan Pads) as a core internal organizing structure, whereas activists in Ireland's similar Occupy movement didn't. Although initially such differences in use between activist communities were attributed to the 'digital divide' – a term that refers to the unequal access to particular technologies and to the Internet across *inter alia* nations, segments of the population and age groups – studies show that even when differences in technological access and ability are overcome, significant differences between technological use (adoption and adaptation) remain (see Sádaba, 2019). This highlights the socio-cultural nature of technological uptake in social movements (and more generally), meaning that the underlying attitudes and political ethos of activists as well as their cultural milieus shape ICT use. In this regard, the influence of hacker ethics in many technopolitical or cyberpolitical movements is particularly important as an ideational framework that shapes not only ICT use but also political practice more broadly.

Advantages of ICTs for social movements

Until recently, the positive consequences of ICTs for social movements have often been taken as a given (Garrett, 2006), leading to a dominance of what has been termed cyberoptimistic approaches. Cyberoptimists believe strongly in the democratizing and mobilizing potential of ICTs for social movements, pointing to the use of ICTs to engage in cyberprotest, hacktivism, and subversive direct action and to develop multiple forms of alternative media. ICTs offer fast, cheap ways to disseminate information, are useful for coordination, and can strengthen the hand of resource-poor groups by increasing their political leverage, presumably resulting in more egalitarian and empowering flows of many-to-many communication. ICTs have been particularly useful in connecting people across geographical distance and have facilitated the development of transnational networks (Myers, 1994; Froehling, 1997; Carty, 2002; McCaughey and Ayers, 2003; Van de Donk *et al.*, 2004; De Jong *et al.*, 2005). Mobile technologies and SMS messaging have enabled activists to coordinate mass protests in record time (Hermanns, 2008), giving rise to the 'flash mob' phenomenon.

From a cyberoptimist point of view, ICTs can decrease the moral distance between world citizens through the development of a collective consciousness and foster the development of transnational protest communities and counter publics (see e.g. Drache, 2008; Fenton, 2008).

Techno-utopianism was a feature of rising initial excitement as new ICTs became widespread, with Rheingold (1993: 14) defining the political significance of ICTs as lying in their 'capacity to challenge the existing political hierarchies' monopoly on powerful communications media'. Rheingold also stressed their potential to revitalize citizen-based democracy (see also Shirky, 2009; Benkler, 2006).

A central debate is the extent to which ICTs can foster deliberation and democratic participation, within social movement networks and groups and also between social movement actors and their audiences (see Dahlberg, 2001: 158).

ICTs are unquestionably central to activists' repertoires of communication, mobilization and deliberation processes and have been harnessed in many creative and strategic ways to increase the power and reach of social movement communication and actions. ICTs have radically transformed the ability for movements to connect with each other and reach global audiences and have generated new forms of cyberactivism. Social movement actors use ICTs in a number of key ways, and patterns and forms of use are constantly evolving (see Box 5.1).

ICTs play a crucial role in many mobilizing processes (see also Chapter 7). During the Ukrainian 'Orange Revolution' in 2004, for example, ICTs were used in a number of ways. The Ukrainian run-off election results were disputed and activists set up a tent city in the central plaza of the capital demanding free and fair elections and the annulment of results widely reported to have been the result of massive corruption and fraud (Kuzio, 2006). University students used their cell phones to record professors telling them how to vote and then posted these recordings on the Internet. The recordings were later used as evidence in court proceedings over election fraud. The Orange Revolution has been called the first Internet revolution: in a highly repressive context, people set up private chat rooms, blogs and email lists to discuss strategies and tactics, and hosted non-governmental organization (NGO) websites. Media technology was used to produce reports for independent Internet news channels such as ERA news (http://eratv.com.ua) (Kuzio, 2006).

ICTs have also facilitated various forms of *tactical media*. 'Tactical media' is a term given to 'expressions of dissent that rely on artistic practices and "do it yourself" (DIY) media created from readily available, relatively cheap technology and means of communication (e.g., radio, video and Internet)' (Renzi, 2008). Central to the concept is its temporary and constantly shifting nature. One powerful and widely disseminated form of tactical media is the video mash-up. Mash-ups enable people creatively to combine images and sound to create their own political statements but can also transform the original message or images from their original form, decontextualizing them or omitting key information. One example was the 2003 video 'Bushwhacked' in which UK satirist Chris Morris cut and reassembled numerous speeches of George W. Bush to create a new video with a radically altered text that read in part:

Box 5.1 Some Key Ways Social Movements use ICTs

- To communicate with each other via email listserves, Internet Relay Chats, SMS messages and so on

- To develop collectively various products, such as flyers, news, magazines, manifestos, free software, databases or wikipages

- To create and disseminate tactical media (see p. 128)

- To network between chapters of the same organization or with different organizations

- To create alternative grassroots media portals, such as the global Indymedia network portal (see p. 137) or host servers for social movement web media (e.g. Nodo50.org)

- To create counter-knowledge or counter-narratives, such as conducting their own polls or surveys that contradict official polls or posting video evidence of police brutality at protest events

- To intervene directly in institutional politics, such as creating online petitions or campaigns intended to influence electoral politics (e.g. MoveOn.org)

- To generate resources through such actions as crowdfunding to support actions

- To engage in hacktivism or cyberactivism, which encompasses a wide range of actions that cover everything from exposing names and profiles of the accounts of child pornographers to bringing down

---

the webpages of corporate or political targets through Distributed Denial of Service (DDoS) attacks (where a flood of messages is sent to a target website, forcing it to shut down and denying service to its intended users) or preserving the digital commons (see p. 135)

- To disseminate news, information and calls for mobilization and action via various platforms, including SMS, social media, email lists, blogs, websites, and so on. To build collective identities, create alliances and overcome isolation

- To take advantage of digital swarming, which refers to wireless-enabled pervasive and interconnected networks that are mobilized for a collective purpose, allowing for rapid intelligent collective action

- To get around media blackouts, both to communicate with a 'global audience' and to share information about police brutality, road closures and so on during periods of mobilization.

- To develop code and platforms specifically to advance political objectives such as avoiding surveillance, resisting data extraction, making data/knowledge open or hacking political targets (people, institutions)

Mr. Speaker, Vice President Cheney, members of Congress, distinguished citizens and fellow citizens. Every year, by law and by custom, we meet here to threaten the world. The American flag stands for corporate scandals, recession, stock market declines, blackmail, terror, burning with hot irons, dripping acid on the skin, mutilation with electric drills, cutting out tongues, and rape. Our first goal is to show utter contempt for the environment ... And this year, for the first time, we must offer every child in America three nuclear missiles ... Secretary of State Powell will plant information to incite fear about Iraq's links to terrorist groups. And tonight I have a message for the people of Iraq – go home and die. Trusting in the sanity and restraint of the United States is not a strategy and it is not an option. (Cited in Meikle, 2008: 367)

The Bushwhacked video was widely disseminated but by no means unique: YouTube was full of Bush mash-ups in 2004 (Meikle, 2008).

Satire and humour are not the only uses Internet videos are put to by social movements. Another important use involves posting of images of police behaviour during protests, which has enabled activists to counter false police narratives of provocation; to contrast media and police characterizations of protesters as dangerous and violent; to document police brutality to influence public opinion, and to bring criminal charges in some cases. This has become a form of political activism in its own right and can have the effect of radicalization and the raising of consciousness. In this way, activists can use ICTs to question the legitimacy of state authorities and to increase their own legitimacy.

Some images of the victims of police violence become global icons, such as the image of Carlo Giuliani, a young activist shot dead by police in Genoa while protesting at the anti-G8 summit in 2001, or Khaled Said, a young Egyptian brutally beaten to death by Egyptian police, whose image was widely circulated on social media and the Internet, acting as a trigger image for the Egyptian revolution in 2010–11 (see also Chapter 7). Both Giuliani and Said have become the subject of a diverse range of images (videos, mash-ups, graffiti, posters) that mythologize and iconize them, turning them into powerful symbols of resistance (sometimes in ways that may have little to do with their actual biographies in protest or activism *per se*) (Olesen, 2013). Yet, as Olesen (2013) argues in relation to the case of Khaled Said, although the cell phone image of Said's horribly disfigured morgue photograph was emotionally charged, this alone is not what transformed it into a globally iconic image. After all, unfortunately, many people are tortured to death every day around the world. The transition from local incident (from the city of Alexandria, where his murder took place) to national and global symbol of injustice required the agency of specific actors whose strategic and creative interventions *universalized* his case and made it representative of police corruption and brutality in Egypt and then a global symbol of resistance against corruption and brutality and for democracy. Olesen shows that, first, the family posted the image from the morgue, juxtaposing it with an image of Said before his death (handsome, young), itself a shocking visual contrast. Then, a journalist decided to write a critical piece alleging he was murdered in the Egyptian newspaper Youm7; third, Google executive Wael Ghonim and Mohamed Ibrahim created a Facebook page called 'We are all Khaled Said' (Olesen, 2013). In each stage, the image acquired new meanings and reached a wider audience. Olesen (2013) stresses the crucial role of political activists, and therefore agency, in the promotion and dissemination of iconic global mobilizing images. Clearly, ICTs provide powerful tools for activism, but these need to be creatively and strategically harnessed to be effective.

The idea that the architecture of Internet communication carries *inherent* democratic potential or even that it constitutes a neutral autonomous sphere is naive but still widely assumed. Opposing this with a 'techno-pessimism' or 'cyber-scepticism' would be similarly over-simplistic. Instead, social movement actors have to negotiate the opportunities and challenges posed by new media and ICTs and their potential to advance or limit their political effectiveness.

Challenges and limitations of ICTs for social movements

Cyber-sceptics have called into question the glowing claims for ICTs as a means of fostering mobilization and participation. As Askanius and Gustafsson (2010: 36) argue, 'social networking has often, in the techno-optimistic accounts, been inextricably linked to the dynamics and practices of new social movements and seen to be emblematic of democratic and empowering practice ... however ... there is nothing inherently democratic in networked technologies'. The use of ICTs is by no means unproblematic for social movements; it also presents some specific challenges. Rather than view the relationship between ICTs and mobilization as either mostly positive or negative, it is more useful to examine the ways in which it facilitates social movement communication and mobilization processes and how it poses new challenges or limitations.

One key problem is that of information overload. For example, one claim made for the benefit of the Internet for social movements is the ease with which even small resource-poor groups can set up a website if they have the access and technical savvy to do so. But just having a website does not mean anyone will actually visit it. The world wide web is awash with information and options: amidst all that 'noise', why or how will a potential sympathizer reach that particular webpage (Wright, 2004; Dahlberg, 2005, 2007)? Activists recognize these limitations and develop strategies to overcome them. Cammaerts (2007) discusses a counter-campaign against a fascist party in Antwerp: while the campaign activists made sure they had a 'nice' website, they also printed 40,000 posters to place around the city, reaching the attention of the mainstream media and reaching audiences who would not come across their webpage. Cammaerts also argues that, important as the Internet is, other forms of media are equally, or more, important in disseminating movement messages beyond 'the likeminded'.

Another set of issues relates to unreliability of sources and misinformation (Mosca, 2007): how can potential audiences verify the reliability of information coming from groups they do not know very much about? Often, Internet sites with political content do not identify the authors of the sites' content (for ideological and strategic reasons), which can potentially lead audiences to dismiss the veracity of the claims made. The issue of fake news has emerged as a serious challenge for democracy since access to credible and reliable information is understood to be one of the foundations upon which democratic participation is based. For social movements, the issue of fake news is particularly challenging since activists are rarely considered credible or authoritative voices and need to work hard to establish themselves as such. As members of the public become increasingly cynical or relativize the veracity of information according to ideological preferences in the face of a perception of widespread fake news, activists face difficulties in establishing the credibility of their claims. At the same time, some right-wing activists (and other political actors, including presidents!) have effectively adopted a tactic of deliberately spreading false information which progressive activists then need to attempt to counter (see Chapter 6).

The use of the Internet and cell phones to disseminate images, videos and mash-ups also presents something of a double-edged sword. The examples given already attest to the powerful nature of these images and their effectiveness in providing 'moral shocks' that trigger shifts in consciousness and a desire to act. Yet, because videos are also easily subject to manipulation through photoshop, testimonial recordings or images, for example, are vulnerable to dismissal from sceptics who question their authenticity. In some ways, it is precisely the adaptability and ease of creative manipulation of ICTs that provide their strength, power and usefulness but also a constantly evolving set of challenges for social movements and opportunities for social movement opponents.

Another challenge is the ease with which false identities can be assumed online. One implication of this is the co-optation of Internet sites by non-movement actors in order to produce 'fake' grassroots media, which is difficult for users to distinguish from real grassroots media. While activists can 'clone' or create websites that look almost exactly like official political and corporate sites to subvert their content or redirect their web search (e.g. fake presidential campaign pages such as °TMark's gwbush.com website, so that someone Google-searching George W. Bush, for example, would end up on a page critiquing Bush), the same can happen in reverse. Additional problems include the commodification of alternative media for profit; state and counter-movement construction of media that looks very similar to that of grassroots opponents; and the gradual mainstreaming of formerly radical media.

Cammaerts (2007) shows how political culture jamming is not limited to progressive, radical or grassroots social movement actors but can be used as a tactic by political parties, reactionary groups and corporate actors. One example is the UK Labour Party production of fake movie posters on huge billboards and on TV adverts for the 2001 general election campaign. One image had the slogan 'The Tories Present: Economic Disaster II' and in smaller print 'coming to a home, hospital, school or business near you'. Starring in the 'film' were two prominent Conservative Party politicians. The use of the culture jam or political jam technique by a range of actors blurs the line between radical and non-radical media and makes distinguishing between them more difficult. The ease of setting up a convincing-looking website also raises the issue of assessing the real levels of support behind specific movement campaigns and projects: just as anyone can write a manifesto in the name of an organization that may in fact have one member, even the most impressive-looking website can be the work of a few highly skilled activists with little real support behind them.

Social movement websites hoping to open up democratic deliberative platforms that allow users to post comments or contribute news items face an additional problem: trolling or spamming by users hostile to the website's ideology or demands. This has led site administrators to attempt to moderate the content, opening them up to accusations of censorship or partiality, and restricting access to some users (a problem faced by Indymedia). Striking a balance between openness and vulnerability to attack and repression from actors hostile to social movements is an additional challenge.

Repression, censorship and digital divides

Morozov's (2012) work on the 'net delusion' acts as an important indicator of how the Internet can be used to oppress and control people. He shows how authoritarian regimes in China, Iran, Russia and elsewhere use the Internet in highly sophisticated ways to repress social movements by such tactics as identifying, tracking and arresting dissidents; carrying out cyber-attacks on websites and blogs of independent media, NGOs and social movements; filtering and censorship; and paying bloggers to spread pro-government messages. He argues compellingly that, while much attention has been paid to how progressive activists have used the Internet to foster democracy, not enough attention has been paid to how states have been using it as a tool of repression. Morozov does feel the Internet can have a democratic function, and actually worked to train pro-democracy activists throughout the former Soviet Union (with the NGO 'Transitions Online'), but he argues that a cyber-realist approach is needed to fulfil the Internet's democratic potential. He points out that much of the cutting-edge research used to develop such tools as face recognition software, sophisticated user content analysis, and social media analysis (mostly developed in Western universities) has been harnessed by governments to repress and censor dissidents and control citizen access to online content. He argues that cyber-utopians naively believe that simply having access to political content on the Internet will play a role in fostering democratic transitions. Instead, he argues that, even if people in authoritarian regimes are online, it does not mean they are necessarily accessing political content and that, even if they are, this will necessarily translate into political action in the 'real' world. His work highlights the dark side of the Internet as a force for social change. Since the publication of Morozov's book, China has advanced in its use of facial recognition software, combining it with over 200 million surveillance cameras, the interception of citizen communications and a system of 'social credits' (Mozur, 2018) (there are no official documents to explain how this works), whereby citizens are awarded points for good behaviour which makes them eligible for discounts or, on the contrary, lose points or get blacklisted for committing crimes or being reported to the authorities (Kobie, 2019), all of this underpinned by a comprehensive cybersecurity law to create a veritable dystopia.

Stoycheff and Nisbet (2016) discuss the ways in which authoritarian governments not only restrict Internet freedoms, particularly to political content, but also establish '"psychological firewalls" that paint the internet as a scary world full of political threats. This rationale increases threat perceptions among the public. This, in turn, increases the public's support for online political censorship' (n.p.). The authors highlight the limitations of techno-deterministic narratives that assume technological affordances will shape use: as they argue, we need to dispense once and for all with 'the "if we build it, they will come" philosophy underlying a great deal of internet freedom promotion [that] doesn't take into account basic human psychology in which entertainment choices are preferred over news and attitudes toward the internet determine its use, not the technology itself' (ibid).

Social media censorship, legal restrictions to protest online and the criminalization of Tweets and even calls to action are additional concerns for activists using Internet platforms for communication (Hintz, 2015, Leistert, 2015, Manion and Goodrum, 2000).

Restricted access on a more fundamental level comes from the *digital divide*, which refers to the unequal access of segments of the population to the production and consumption of new technologies (Norris, 2001). This inequality stems from unequal skills, resources and capital and follows particular patterns: within nations, urban residents tend to have greater access than do rural ones; generationally, youth have greater technical skills and access overall than do older users; there are gender divides between technological skills; and, globally, there are still great differences in resources, penetration of Internet infrastructures and degrees of government restriction to its access and use for political communication. The digital divide not only affects the possibilities for social movements reaching a global audience but also affects dynamics *within* social movements. Pickerill (2004), in a study of environmental activists in Britain and Australia, found that some hierarchical cliques formed around technological expertise, with more power in the group belonging to those with more expertise. Despite this, her overall assessment of the impact of ICT use is positive for the groups she studied.

Pickerill's work highlights how technology and media use can be at the centre of diverse forms of divisions within social movement communities, and later studies did not result in such a positive assessment. Control of technology and differing levels expertise can have profound effects on social movement groups. Technological expertise can (and does) influence access to and control of technology and media, which can (and does) create important hierarchies within social movement communities as well as affecting the closed or open nature of internal movement organizational dynamics (Juris et al., 2013; Pickerill, 2004; Costanza-Chock, 2012; Flesher Fominaya, 2016). This digital divide can intersect with other divides such as *age* (e.g. where older activists who may be less digitally connected or savvy feel left out when groups rely exclusively or unreflexively on technologically mediated forms of communication), *gender* (e.g. in hacker or radical geek spaces in which women are still minorities and face significant sexism) or *economic inequality* (e.g. where some members do not have constant access to the Internet or mobile phones). Gender also shapes patterns of mediated interaction which can marginalize, silence, delegitimize or exclude women's voices (and privilege male authority). Digitally mediated interactions in cyberspace are often extremely hostile for women (and people of colour), further decreasing participation and affecting their possibilities for leadership, representation, and expression. Dahlberg (2001: 623), for example, highlights the problems stemming from a lack of reflexivity in cyber-deliberations, including the failure to achieve respectful listening or commitment to difference, the dominance of discussion by few individuals and groups and exclusions because of social inequalities. Despite these important impacts, there is a tendency to neglect the emotional and subjective aspects of ICT use in favour of their technological aspects (i.e. costs, affordances, and leveraging) (Flesher Fominaya, 2016).

Commercial platforms and clicktivism

The idea that social movement groups will gain increased political leverage from the advent of the Internet due to its relative cheapness and ease of accessibility is also questioned by Margolis and Resnick (2000), who argue that political players with power in the real world can also gain the upper hand in cyberspace. The advent of social media sites such as Facebook has allowed social movement actors to access pre-existing social networks and to disseminate their messages there. Yet, commercial social media platforms pose another set of dilemmas: activists producing radical media are increasingly using commercial platforms to do so, rather than independent radical media platforms, which has the potential to damage their credibility and dilute the impact of political messages designed to critique the companies that own these social media platforms themselves: 'When an ad for a quick money loan by SMS is right next to a debate stream on the causes and consequences of the global financial crisis on Attac's Facebook group, the inherent paradoxes in current media practice seem evident' (Askanius and Gustafsson, 2010: 35). Askanius and Gustafsson (2010: 36) point out that, increasingly, online interaction is being concentrated into fewer corporate controlled spaces, which raises critical questions for those movements that are working against neoliberal global capitalism or that exist to question political and economic elites: 'What are the dangers of public discussions and networks being controlled by corporate enterprises? What interests do owners and managers have in gathering information on potentially subversive issues and individuals? And how do commercial platforms change the nature of alternative media practices within a social movement context?'

Tufekci (2015) further alerts us to the ways that corporate-owned social media pose significant risks to democracy, including electoral processes, through their ability to modify their algorithms to manipulate and bias information that users see. The extent to which these corporate 'psycho technologies' can be used to manipulate not only users' impressions but also their emotions, allied to the opacity of data mining practices and its uses by corporate platform owners, has negative implications for social movement actors (see e.g. Leistert, 2015).

Another claim made for the benefit of the Internet for political communication and activism is the ease with which 'actions' can be set up online. One example is the easy creation of online petitions or letters of protest that can be signed and sent at the click of a mouse or trackpad. Yet, this raises the issue of whether such 'clicktivism' or 'slacktivism' really makes a difference in the 'real' world. It takes little effort to sign a petition and even less to 'like' or share something on Facebook. Does this form of 'action' translate into action offline? Do people who engage in clicktivism also engage in non-virtual forms of protest and activism? To what extent do these online actions bring about significant social transformation? At the very least, Cammaerts (2012: 128) argues that these forms of online participation 'do contribute to the building of collective identities and global awareness'.

Another crucial arena that poses a constantly evolving and contested context for the use of ICTs by social movements is the legislative context that regulates ICT use.

This is a tremendously important aspect that, in itself, has been the basis of significant social movement activity, such as the mobilizations against SOPA ('Stop Online Piracy Act') and PIPA ('Protect IP Act') legislation in the US.[8]

This area includes movements for open-access, free software movements and the many battles against 'economic, political and legislative trends that threaten to convert the Internet into yet another commercial medium, stripped of its unique potential for facilitating progressive political debate and transformation' (Villarreal and Gil, 2001: 201),

Cyberpolitics

The development of new media and the Internet has created new fields of contention over the governance of communication networks, the production of software, access to information and indeed the fundamentals of technological design (Jordan, 2002, 2015; Kirkpatrick, 2011). The creation of these new tools has inspired, and been inspired by, new forms of activism (Stalder, 2010). I use the term *cyberpolitical movements* to refer to movements that take the virtual arena as the central focus and purpose of their mobilization. That is, movements not only that use ICTs strategically (almost all movements do this independently of political orientation, even the Taliban) but whose political action is motivated by an ideological and practical commitment to harnessing the emancipatory power of ICTs for social and political change and who see cyberspace as a primary site of contestation and mobilization (Flesher Fominaya and Gillan, 2017).

Cyberpolitics can take many forms, including the creation of alternative citizen media of all kinds; digital guerilla communications; digitally enabled culture jamming (Baker and Blaagaard, 2016; Castells et al., 2006: 202–6; Carty, 2002; Coleman, 2015); various forms of 'hacktivism' to target or expose political opponents; digitally enabled whistle-blowing; struggles over the use, control and ownership of the Internet; creation of and commitment to the 'digital commons'; free access to software, culture, knowledge and information; and the right to privacy, anonymity and control of personal data.

The transfer of so many forms of communication, consumerism, bureaucracy and political participation (including voting) to the online realm has huge implications for data use, abuse, commodification and user privacy, and *data activism* works to highlight and contest the problematic aspects of these changes. *Data justice activists* also work on addressing the digital divides that deny or give very unequal access to the Internet and other forms of digital/ ICTs. For example, data activism works to highlight and resist the commodification of personal data – data extraction being one of the core ways 'free' social media platforms like Facebook make money – and the social and political implications of data use/control. Algorithms are often secret and can be dangerous: after all, they are written by humans on the basis of assumptions about human conditions and behaviour that can fail to take into account the individual circumstances of different people, leading to very problematic outcomes and forms of discrimination, especially against marginalized communities and groups like poor people, people of colour and women (see Eubanks, 2018 and O'Neil, 2017). An MIT experiment in 2002 sent 5000 CVs for job advertisements to large companies using automated screeners to filter the applications. Half had invented names that were typically US 'white' and half had names typically 'African American'. The white-sounding names got 50 per cent more call-backs (Pascual, 2019). The recognition that algorithms and machine learning and the automated systems based on them can propagate bias at an intense rate has led to the establishment of social movement organizations (SMOs) such as the *Algorithmic Justice League* founded by Joy Buolamwini, which highlights algorithmic bias, provides a forum for people to express concerns and experiences of coded bias, and works to develop practices and commitments towards accountability in the design, development and deployment of coded systems (see www.ajlunited.org for videos and more information). Another organization, *Algorithm Watch* (https://algorithmwatch.org/en/), analyses and raises awareness about ethical and social problems related to algorithm use. Data Justice Activism is a good example of cyberpolitics that brings together (h)activists, coders, artists, academics, journalists, citizens, legislators, regulators and companies.

In what follows I delve more deeply into cyberpolitics. First, through a key movement family with a strong technopolitical component: the movements for free culture, free software and open access. Second, I discuss a case study of a globally influential activist self-publishing model that predated 'social media', the influential Indymedia network, and show how technological advances facilitated first its growth and then its decline. Third, I discuss hacktivism and 'hacker ethics' to show how ideational principles (that is, normative ideas about cyberspace, technology and their relation to politics) shape social movements beyond the use of ICTs, using 'Anonymous' as a test case for whether collective action online can meet the definitional criteria for social movements laid out in Chapter 1. Finally, I discuss another very influential form of cyberpolitics: digitally enabled whistle-blowing, known as 'leaktivism', which is also based on particular technopolitical frameworks that motivate collective action and reveal the nature of contemporary cyberpolitical struggles today.

The ICT/social movement nexus: Free culture, free software and access to knowledge movements

Often missing from accounts of the use of ICTs by social movements is the degree to which activists themselves have been key actors in producing and developing the very technology that social movements use. While a full discussion of the relation between the development of ICTs and social movements is outside the scope of this chapter,[9] three key inter-related movements should be highlighted: the Free Software, Free Culture and Access to Knowledge (a2k) movements (Stalder, 2010). In all of these movements, 'radical techie' activists combine with other activist groups to create and preserve the *digital commons*, which 'comprises informational resources created and shared within voluntary communities, [which are] typically held de facto as communal, rather than private or public (i.e. state) property' (Stalder, 2010). The Free Software movement came out of the very culture of original software development where producers and users were one and the same and only artificially separated when software became standardized for mass markets by companies such as Microsoft. The Free Software Movement was founded as an alternative to software commercialization and was based on 'four essential freedoms in relation to software: the freedom to run software for any purpose, the freedom to change the program without restrictions, the freedom to distribute copies of the program to help others and the freedom to distribute changes of the program so that others might benefit from your work' (Stalder, 2010). Stalder writes that 'The Free Software Movement has become a powerful political force, supported by a growing segment of the information technology industry.' The Free Culture Movement was inspired by the Free Software movement and by the dynamic sharing and use of cultural products through the Internet (new digital mass culture) which, in many cases, was done by violating existing copyright law. International and national copyright laws were strengthened and copyright infringement cases multiplied while digital culture users and producers began to organize to protect the sharing of culture. Leading Free Culture proponent Lawrence Lessig wrote a series of books in which he argued for the need to protect a cultural commons against a culture dictated and controlled by copyright permissions (e.g. *Code and Other Laws of Cyberspace*, 1999). Alternative copyright models were developed and are widely used today, such as creative commons licences which allow producers to share their work freely, with certain conditions. Wikipedia is another example of the Free Culture movement's success (Stalder, 2010).

Finally, the Access to Knowledge movement, which also encompasses the Open Access Movement, is centred on the fundamental notion that knowledge that benefits the public should be freely available. It began around the fight over access to anti-retroviral drugs in South Africa, where pharmaceutical companies sued the South African government for buying generic models of patented drugs in order to provide medical treatment to their HIV-positive citizens. A high-profile international campaign was launched by groups such as Doctors without Borders to allow South Africa to provide the drugs; that succeeded in having a non-corporate or non-personal intellectual property knowledge regime recognized by the UN sub-organization the World Intellectual Property Organization. A development agenda was formulated which stated that concerns for intellectual property rights 'need to be balanced with concern for social development' (Stalder, 2010).

This fight was consistent with a major goal of the a2k/Open Access Movement – to allow scientific knowledge to be shared freely so it may benefit everyone. Activists in this movement make use of the Internet to develop alternative publishing models to enable everyone anywhere to access scientific knowledge either immediately, as with open-access journal publishing, or within a reasonable time with some other models. An increasing number of academics are arguing for the adoption of open-access models and form part of this movement (Böhm, 2013). Media interest in legal cases such as that brought against activist Aaron Swartz have heightened the profile of open access as an issue of concern for wider society and, as the case of the South African government's right to acquire generic rather than name-brand drugs shows, at the heart of the open-access movement are profoundly ethical issues of social justice and social equality – both between the global North and South and across the digital divide. The 2008 Guerilla Open Access Manifesto, penned by Aaron Swartz and others, sums up some of these issues:

> Information is power. But like all power, there are those who want to keep it for themselves. The world's entire scientific and cultural heritage, published over centuries in books and journals, is increasingly being digitized and locked up by a handful of private corporations. ... Providing scientific articles to those at elite universities in the First World, but not to children in the Global South? It's outrageous and unacceptable. ... We can fight back. Those with access to these resources – students, librarians, scientists – you have been given a privilege. You get to feed at this banquet of knowledge while the rest of the world is locked out. But you need not – indeed, morally, you cannot – keep this privilege for yourselves. You have a duty to share it with the world. (Cited in MacFarquhar, 2013)

The Free Software Movement/Open Source Movement is not without internal conflicts and critics, and should not be romanticized, yet has been enormously influential in shaping the technologies and practices of contemporary social movements and forms part of the history of hacktivism, which I will discuss further below.

Indymedia: Using ICTs for the radical transformation of the global reach of grassroots alternative media

The Independent Media Centres, more commonly known as Indymedia, originated in Seattle in 1999 in the context of the GJM anti-WTO protests (discussed in Chapter 3). Indymedia's founders began with a clear recognition of the problems of selective and descriptive bias in mainstream media and of the pressures corporate ownership places on editorial decisions and content when covering protest – in particular, anti-corporate protest, such as that in Seattle. They wanted to harness the possibilities of the Internet to establish a new form of news coverage with a global reach that would allow *users* to also be *producers* of content. During the Seattle WTO protests, their website had almost 1.5 million hits.[10] With the slogan 'Don't Hate the Media – Be the Media', they used the principle of open publishing on websites built with open source code to allow copyleft publication of news. They made available their open publishing software freely for download so others could reproduce their alternative media model. From the original Seattle Indymedia of 1999, the network grew to over 160 autonomous Indymedia collectives around the world by 2010 (Sullivan *et al.*, 2010). While each collective has its own mission statement, they are united by a common 'brand' name (Indymedia or IMC); they are all hyperlinked together and to a global Indymedia portal (www.Indymedia.org) and by their commitment to open publishing and the citizen journalism model to upload content, their use of open source codes and a commitment to non-corporate, grassroots, independent and alternative media covering social and political issues. Each Indymedia is also committed to creating and maintaining links between social movements in local, national and global contexts. New media groups wanting to become part of the Global Indymedia Network need to adhere to a set of 'principles of unity' and meet certain membership criteria (Indymedia Documentation Project, 2007).

The combination of commitment to consensual and participatory practices, transparency and an autonomous network form, coupled with deep commitment to fighting against corporate enclosure or control of the Internet through controlling commercial software packages and state enforcement of copyright laws, means that Indymedia crosses between anti-corporate/free software/open-access social movement and radical alternative media project.

Because not everyone has access to webnews, they also use the Internet as an audio streaming device, broadcasting live protest coverage from the streets to global audiences. Some Indymedia collectives also published print newsletters (Platon and Deuze, 2003). But who is Indymedia? In the broadest sense, one could argue that it is a global community of user/producers who write articles, contribute videos and images, and provide commentary and testimony about issues of concern to progressive social movements. But websites do not run themselves, and behind each autonomous Indymedia site lies a collective of two main groups of activists: those involved in the technical maintenance of the websites and those involved in editorial decision-making (with a crossover between the two) (Platon and Deuze, 2003). Although there is an open publishing model, content selection still takes place, as does the placing of news items on the websites: racist, fascist, homophobic and sexist posts are not allowed; posts inciting violence generate debate within the editorial collectives, and irrelevant posts are also filtered out (Platon and Deuze, 2003). In short, there is an editorial collective operating behind every Indymedia site, each located within specific political milieus and responding to the proclivities and realities of the collective and the networks in which they are embedded. The decisions taken by the IMC collective can cause conflict with other social movement actors within the local and national networks who have different views and who complain about censorship and biased moderation.[11] Although all IMCs are aligned with the general principles, each operates with autonomy, making global collective decision-making difficult. This can sometimes cause problems within the network, as when the Argentinian IMC collective refused Ford Foundation funding on ideological grounds, vetoing the other IMCs from taking the funding (Pickard, 2006; Sullivan et al., 2010). The tension between unity and autonomy is a constant one in networks that simultaneously seek participatory methods on a 'global' scale yet maintain regional or group-level autonomy.

Indymedia has had a tremendous impact on the way social movement actors produce and consume news and has provided coverage that mainstream media have ignored or presented in ways that are unsupportive of progressive social movements. It is no surprise, therefore, that IMCs have also faced serious problems with repression and surveillance. IMC servers (and many other alternative media servers) have been seized on numerous occasions in different locations around the world, including in the US and the UK (Sullivan et al., 2010; Milan, 2012), and IMC activists and IMCs have been subject to various forms of repression (for a comprehensive list from 2001 to 2005, see Salter, 2006).

While Indymedia is one of the most well known, it is by no means the only Internet-based alternative news service. There are many such media projects all over the world. Global audio streaming offering live broadcasts of protest events is also a technique commonly practised by social movement actors (see e.g. Mattoni and Doerr, 2014).

Indymedia marked a global turning point for ICT-facilitated alternative media and was an extremely successful experiment in virtual democratic, participatory, collective self-organized news production – not only online but also in the physical offline media centres it established. Yet, in a dynamic and changing media environment, the IMC model has entered a decline. While there are still many IMCs around the world that continue to carry out their mission statements and serve important functions for the communities they serve, the way users and producers engage with ICTs has changed dramatically in the past few years. Now, blogging and the use of social media have largely replaced posting to news sites like Indymedia and, crucially, the development of 3G portable devices has placed the technological means of production in the hands of anyone who can afford it and can use it. Even some mainstream media such as the British Broadcasting Corporation (BBC) now have a web upload feature for people to send eyewitness reports and images.

In their farewell statement, Indymedia London (IMC, 2012) recall its importance and the reasons for its decline, arguing that when Indymedia started, at a time when blogging had yet to become prevalent, it was one of the only ways that people could publish their own news stories from protests and campaigns using an open publishing and direct media model. This ability to use Indymedia as a tool for the collaborative creation of news was an important means of challenging the dominance of mainstream news journalism. In so doing, Indymedia 'broke new ground, technically, socially and politically'. Far from limiting itself to being a virtual platform for digital communication, Indymedia collectives set up numerous tools on the ground to facilitate coverage of protests, including setting up physical media centres and providing spaces for alternative media groups and activists to plan coverage and coordinate their efforts. They also set up systems to 'gather and distribute news from participants on the frontline with staffed "dispatch" phone lines, using Internet chat and wiki's to coordinate volunteers and translations, streaming and broadcasting FM radio, mixing video streams, broadcasting SMS messages', creating a true media revolution. The original Indymedia 'vision' has been realized, yet as they explain, this success has also led to their decline:

> No longer is it necessary to set up 'Public Access Terminals' in the street to provide power and connectivity, most people have this in their hands with their 3G mobile phones, collectively documenting minute by minute as events unfold. Self-publishing is the norm. But be careful what you wish for ... we won, but we also lost. Corporate commodification of the self through social media platforms and the corresponding loss of privacy create considerable pitfalls alongside the huge opportunities ...

Importantly Indymedia has remained one of the few online places that allows users to publish anonymously and without a logon ...

Indymedia London raises similar issues to those raised by Askanius and Gustafsson (2010). While commercial products and social media platforms have placed the means of self-publishing in the hands of users, this has come at a price. Sites such as Facebook and 'sharing' interfaces such as Microsoft Windows Live are 'free' but only if you agree to share personal details – not only your own but those of your 'friends' and the content of your newsfeed, all of which can be traced back to the person creating the post. Quite apart from the ideological implications of using commercial social media as an outlet for 'alternative' and critical media, the loss of the anonymity provided by Indymedia is also a high price to pay, given the reality of surveillance and repression of social movements today in both authoritarian and democratic contexts (Della Porta, 2013).

However, if the rise of social media for social movement communication is inexorable, then analysing the implications of their use for mobilizing processes becomes an important task. I will look at the debate over the role of social media in the 'Arab Spring' in Chapter 7.

Hacktivism and Hacker Ethics

Hacktivism, a term reportedly coined by Cult of the Dead Cow member Omega in 1994, refers to the use of computer hacking for political purposes, sometimes clandestinely. It brings the skills of computer hackers together with the commitment of political activists and forms part of a rich and influential tradition of social movement activism. It is different from electronic activism which simply uses technology in legitimate ways to advance political goals (e.g. coordinating, disseminating or publishing information about political activities).

While not all hackers are hacktivists, hacktivism developed from early hacker activities. Initially, most hackers were motivated by a commitment to exploration of cyberspace, just to see what was out there and how far they could go as an intellectual challenge and test of their skills (which confers status in hacker communities). Early hackers would penetrate security systems of government agencies just for the challenge rather than for any political purpose (Jordan, 2015). Over time, as they interacted with other hackers and became immersed in the hacker lifeworld, not only through daily online interactions but also at hacker conventions, some hackers began to develop an awareness of and commitment to certain political principles such as guaranteeing user anonymity and privacy online by circumventing surveillance systems, sharing code, information and knowledge openly and cooperatively, as part of their critique of intellectual property law (as in the free/open source software and access to knowledge movements above), and exposing and pressing for government transparency. As with other social movement communities, hacktivist collective identities and communities develop through shared experiences of activism and mobilization, including participation in networks like Indymedia and mobilizations in the anti-globalization movement (see Chapter 4) and the free/open software movements.

Hacktivist history encompasses groups such as the Electronic Hippies, who, in 2000, organized a 'WTO virtual sit-in' to overload the official WTO webpages; the Critical Art Ensemble, who engage in tactical media activism and have been active since 1987; or the Chaos Computer Club, who use and promote hacktivism as a means of guaranteeing freedom of information and transparency in government and organize an annual hacker conference in Berlin (http://ccc.de/en/updates/2011/staatstrojaner). One of the most influential early groups is the Cult of the Dead Cow (cDc), established in Texas in 1984 and originally organized through affiliated Bulletin Board Services (BBSs) across the US and Canada. Initially, they distributed music and created a usenet news group (a precursor to the Internet forums used today) and were interested in experimenting with media and humour to grab public attention. Over time, several other off-shoot collectives and projects developed from the cDc, which were committed to issues such as anti-censorship technology in order to further human rights on the Internet, streaming radio with hackercon presentations and educational programming, and the development of several 'hacker tools', including censorship resistant network proxies, encrypted instant messaging clients and computer programs to carry out distributed denials of service (DDoSs) as well as 'Back Orifice', a computer program designed to demonstrate the lack of security in Microsoft's operating system Windows 98. The cDc describes themselves (among other descriptions) as 'a leading developer of Internet privacy and security tools, which are all free to the public'. (Despite their underground credentials, they too have a Facebook page and sell their own merchandise.) In 2019, a former cDc member, Texan Beto O'Rourke, put himself forward as a 2020 presidential candidate for the US elections. (For more on the cDc, see Joseph Menn's 2019 book *Cult of the Dead Cow*.) As the names of the groups mentioned above indicate, humour and having fun are also core part of hacker culture.

Hacktivism includes electronic civil disobedience, or the 'peaceful breaking of unjust laws' (Manion and Goodrum, 2000). Hacktivism has been used for myriad political purposes such as to help advance the Zapatista rebellion in Mexico (see Chapter 3), to protest and circumvent human rights violations and Internet censorship of authoritarian regimes. One example is the Hong Kong Blondes in China, who disrupt computer networks within the People's Republic of China (PRC) in order to allow PRC citizens to access censored content online to carry out DDoS attacks on political targets such as government or corporate websites (see section on Anonymous below). Another example is the SciHub project founded by Alexandra Elbakyan, which obtains paywalled scientific papers using illicitly obtained usernames and passwords (often freely provided by academics who believe in open access) to authenticate university proxy servers, and makes them freely available to all. Electronic disobedience takes civil disobedience (see Chapter 4) and transfers the practices of trespass and blockade to the Internet and combines symbolic and direct forms of action (Manion and Goodrum, 2000).

The term hacker has various definitions and connotations in popular culture. For many hacktivists, one important distinction is that between political hackers (or hacktivists) who use their skills for political purposes and not for personal gain versus 'crackers' who use their skills for personal gain or criminal activity or who commit vandalism and destruction of websites. While the law may view hacking as a criminal activity regardless of intent, hacktivists do not see it that way, and hacktivism is distinguished from computer-based activity linked to organized crime, state surveillance, cyberwarfare or cyberterrorism (which uses hacking to cause loss of life, mass economic disruption or the destruction of critical infrastructures) (Manion and Goodrum, 2000).

Although hacktivism can take many forms, much hacktivist activity is motivated by an ideational framework known as 'hacker ethics', a term first used by Levy (1984) and which has expanded and developed since then. Levy's book *Hackers: Heroes of the Computer Revolution* tells the story of early hackers who developed a vision, a dream and an ethic of how computers could change the world. These early hackers' core principles were:

- Access to computers and anything which might teach you something about the way the world works should be unlimited and total. Always yield to the Hands-On Imperative!

- All information should be free.

- Mistrust Authority Promote Decentralization.

- Hackers should be judged by their hacking, not bogus criteria such as degrees, age, race or position.

- You can create art and beauty on a computer.

- Computers can change your life for the better.

Hackers are motivated by a desire to fix problems and solve puzzles, hence the widespread use of the term "hack" to describe a shortcut, workaround or clever solution to a problem. There is also an element of subversion to established ways of doing things, not just technologically but also in media, institutions and government. Although most people think of hacking as something related to the Internet, the hackers Levy (1984) was describing and their ethics were pre-Internet (and form part of the radical geek commitment to free/open software). Over time, these early hacker ethics have developed and expanded as hacker movements and communities have grown. Although specific hacker ethics are themselves subject to debate and discussion (e.g. over whether it is defacements, denial of service or individual direct actions are unethical as a denial of free speech) and take somewhat different forms in different activist communities, I will delineate some core principles that are drawn from my research on Spain's 15-M movement and its technopolitical frameworks (Flesher Fominaya 2020) but are more widely shared across hacktivist communities:

Knowledge and code are developed in a networked community of people.

This community is based on the free exchange of information that benefits the community and which is also the basis of the community, the code and the technology.

Resources should be shared and not wasted.

This philosophy is developed within an explicit and clear rejection of intellectual property laws, especially those that govern the proprietary rights of software but also within a broader rejection of the commodification of knowledge, which belongs to the community and should be freely accessible to all.

Information (including code) should be valued on its merits and not by who produced it.

The collaborative nature of the development of knowledge implies a rejection of the atomised liberal individual as producer of knowledge and a total commitment to freedom of expression but also a commitment to the right to privacy and the freedom from surveillance by the state or other authorities. (The Computer Chaos Club understands this as 'Make public data available, protect private data'.)

Therefore:

A defence of the digital commons and of the commons more broadly is an ethical and political priority.

Politics in general should also follow these principles through the production of codes, models, tactics and practices that are easily replicated, open to modification and adaptable to the needs and priorities of the users.

Transparency of information, logics and motives and the exchange of information are political priorities and the development of digital technologies can and should facilitate them. Not only should information be exchanged, but how that information and knowledge was produced should also be shared. This principle reflects an understanding of knowledge as a practice rather than a product: one learns by doing.

The ideal political model is a horizontal network in which information, power and the capacity for change flow between local, national and global nodes. In this way, any actor/node in the network can be put at the service of any other actor no matter where they are, facilitated by the global digital network.

These principles not only are influential in activist communities that engage specifically in cyberpolitics but have become influential beyond these communities through interaction between groups drawing on different movement traditions in specific mobilization experiences. In Spain's 15-M movement, for example, a commitment to hacker ethics became widespread even among activists with little or no IT expertise. At the same time, hacker ethics have also evolved to integrate feminist principles in addition to the autonomous principles they already share much of their 'DNA' with (see Flesher Fominaya, 2020 and the discussion of autonomy in Chapter 3). The hacker idea of breaking down complex problems into do-able tasks, for example, shares much with the autonomous practicality principle of starting from where you are and what you have at hand. Other synergies between autonomous and hacker ethics include a commitment to openness, transparency, horizontal, decentralization, networked politics and the efficient use of communal resources to benefit the community. Hacker ethics are open to debate and critique, one criticism, for example, being that a naive commitment to openness does not guarantee democratic access to information: other conditions such as being able to find relevant information easily and being able to understand it (a concept known as *open intelligence* or *open source intelligence*) also need to be met. Nevertheless, a digitally enabled democratic imaginary lies at the heart of technopolitical frameworks that draw on hacker ethics (for more on hacker ethics, see Manion and Goodrum, 2000, Coleman, 2013, Jordan, 2015).

Anonymous: Cyberactivism on a global scale

> Anonymous – a name taken by different individuals and groups to organize collective action – ... is a cluster of ideas and ideals adopted by various, at times unconnected hackers, technologists, activists, geeks, and human rights activists, and is grounded in the concept of anonymity. It is a banner for online political campaigns and street demonstrations, actions ranging from fearsome pranks to hacking for sensitive information to human rights technological support for revolutionaries in Tunisia, Egypt, and Libya. (Coleman, 2012a)

At first glance, Anonymous seems to be difficult to characterize as a social movement because anonymity means it is difficult to see how the different actors involved relate to each other and coordinate action. Yet, if the autonomous groups discussed in Chapter 3 often refuse to name themselves and are difficult to 'see' or identify as distinct groups or organizations within protest campaigns because of this, Anonymous becomes highly visible and identifiable through the use of the name 'Anonymous' and the use of the Guy Fawkes mask as an iconic symbol of that anonymity. The use of masks to become 'visible' was also used by the Zapatistas (see Chapter 3), but if the Zapatistas grounded their struggle clearly in the Lacandon forest of Chiapas and in the indigenous people who live there, for Anonymous the mask represents an unknown (and presumably unknowable) group of actors who, through the Internet, can act anywhere in the world at any time. The Zapatista 'mask' is a balaclava, with militaristic connotations of armed struggle. In contrast, the Anonymous mask is a Guy Fawkes mask, popularized by the 2005 film *V for Vendetta*, and represents a cunning, subversive trickster who fights back against the (not) all powerful state. The slogan 'We are Anonymous. We are legion. We do not forgive. We do not forget. Expect us' conjures up a massive faceless group of radical techie activists who can strike at any time.

While Anonymous is now arguably the best-known hacktivist or cyberactivist group, they are by no means the only or the first, as is clear from the discussion above.

In fact, Anonymous evolved from a group of users on 4chan around 2005 who used the name Anonymous to troll (prank, harass) just for 'the

Figure 5.2

An activist wears an 'Anonymous' Guy Fawkes mask at the Global Day of Action in support of #Occupy Everywhere, 15 October 2011, Boston.

Copyright: Jeffrey S. Juris

lulz' (or the laughs, from 'lol', acronym for 'laugh out loud') and only really began to coordinate political actions when they decided to protest against the Church of Scientology (Coleman, 2011, 2012b). In that case, they posted a 'secret' Scientology video on YouTube, which was then pulled after the Church of Scientology claimed it was copyrighted material.

In response, Anonymous attacked a number of Scientology sites with DDoS and fax-spammed local offices. They explained their action (Project Chanology) in their own YouTube video (http://www.youtube.com/watch?v=JCbKv9yiLiQ) (their preferred method of explaining their political actions) whose text read, in part:

> Over the years, we have been watching you, your campaigns of misinformation, your suppression of dissent, your litigious nature. All of these things have caught our eye … With the leakage of your latest propaganda video into mainstream circulation, the extent of your malign influence over those who have come to trust you as leaders has been made clear to us. Anonymous has therefore decided that your organization should be destroyed, for the good of your followers, for the good of mankind, and for our own enjoyment …

> We shall proceed to expel you from the Internet and system-
> atically dismantle the Church of Scientology in its present form.
> (Anonymous, 2008)

> Knowledge is free
> We are Anonymous
> We are legion
> We do not forgive
> We do not forget
> Expect us.

Coleman (2011) points out that this video itself was in part tongue-in-cheek, done also 'for the lulz'. However, some Anonymous members began to debate taking a more serious approach to protesting against the Church of Scientology and to make the transition from online to offline activism, eventually organizing a coordinated set of protests on 10 February 2008 around the world in front of Scientology churches, with most protesters wearing the Guy Fawkes mask and using humour and satire to denounce Scientology (Coleman, 2011). Over time, Anonymous began to foray into other more 'serious' political actions centred on government efforts to stop music and film file sharing (Operation Payback) and, most notably, the DDoS attacks in the context of WikiLeaks, which was the public release of classified diplomatic cables (in 2010) and subsequent publication of classified government documents and emails (see WikiLeaks.org). Once WikiLeaks released the first batch of diplomatic cables, Amazon, Paypal, Visa, Bank of America and Mastercard disabled donation support and services for WikiLeaks, and Anonymous struck back. Over the course of a few days, Anonymous disabled the websites of some of the most powerful corporations in the world (Coleman, 2011). As Coleman (2011, 2012a, 2012b) highlights, what is remarkable is not just what they did but how they did it, in that they used Internet Relay Chat Networks (IRC channels) to decide collectively on strategies and tactics and to coordinate up to 7000 activists at a time. IRCs are central to Anonymous' means of operation; they are the primary virtual 'place' in which they congregate and plan their actions. Coleman (2012a, 2012b) explains that, once an IRC is installed and configured, it still requires a system or net administrator and a team of individuals to help maintain it and fend off attacks. In keeping with the spirit of autonomy, users are usually free to initiate their own channels but, as with the case of Indymedia, control of the technical resources does confer increased power within the community. Once again, the logic of autonomy (Flesher Fominaya, 2005) means that those unhappy with the direction a particular operation is taking, or the ad hoc leadership that develops therein, are free to develop their own. In keeping with this fluid nature, different sets of activists were involved in the Scientology and Operation Payback actions (Coleman, 2011). Nevertheless, it also appears that some of the operations were carried out by a small group of hackers known as LulzSec, some of whom have since been arrested (Penny, 2011; Norton, 2012; Ronson, 2013).

While some states and observers have attempted to characterize Anonymous and other cyberactivist groups as cyberterrorists and threats to national and global security, Penny (2011) argues that:

> Most security experts agree that sophisticated cyberattacks by nation-states, like the Stuxnet attack on an Iranian nuclear facility last year, are a far greater threat to global security than autonomous hacking collectives knocking out company websites.
>
> The former is the digital equivalent of state espionage; the latter, the equivalent of a road blockade or banner drop.

While I would argue Anonymous and other cyberactivist groups have a much greater political impact than a banner drop, the larger point Penny makes is to highlight the degree to which organizations such as the FBI and other nations' homologous groups concentrate their efforts on launching 'a global manhunt for members of Anonymous, LulzSec and other groups' (2011: 20). However, since cyberactivism is a global mass movement, it is unlikely that the arrests of suspected hackers will stop it – as indeed the arrests of alleged members of LulzSec have not. Nevertheless, the actions of the FBI do affect the individual cyberactivists who are arrested, as the punishment for their 'crimes' can be out of all proportion to the offence, and this trend is increasing. One of the most tragic and mediatized cases involved one of the young inventors of Reddit (an open-source social media site), Internet freedom activist and techie entrepreneur Aaron Swartz. For reasons that are not totally clear, although copyright and freedom of information issues were important to him, as the open-access manifesto shows (pp. 136–7), Swartz downloaded several million academic journal articles at MIT (MacFarquhar, 2013). At issue was not his right to download (MIT has an open-access network) but, rather, the number of articles he downloaded in violation of his fair use agreement. Soon after he was arrested, he returned all the data. Despite this, and the fact that Jstor considered the matter closed, MIT cooperated with federal prosecutors who charged him under the Computer Fraud and Abuse Act with numerous counts of felony and asked for a 35-year prison sentence. In despair, and having suffered from depression for some years, Swartz took his life at the age of 26 (Ronson, 2013).

Is Anonymous a social movement?

Does Anonymous force us to rethink our definitions of social movements? As a community of loosely connected individuals who most likely have never met in person, operate primarily in the virtual sphere and encompass a wide-ranging set of sometimes contradictory ideals, ideologies and actions, it is possible to question whether they can be considered a social movement. Indeed, this is the tack a 4chan chatroom moderator's lawyer is taking in defending her for being a member of Anonymous and participating in an 'attempt' on Paypal: 'Anonymous doesn't exist' (Ronson, 2013). Yet, if we go back to the components of the characteristics of social movements outlined in Chapter 1, Anonymous fits the definition very well:

- They engage in collective or joint *actions*.

- They operate in order to advance *change*-oriented goals or claims – in this case, to preserve the freedom to share information on the Internet, increase transparency and expose the actions of targets (such as governments, corporations or the Church of Scientology), to defend the freedom to hack software and hardware and make them freely available, and to protect individuals against surveillance, among other goals.

- They engage in *extra-institutional* or *non-institutional* collective action – often legally but, sometimes, illegally (and some have been arrested and prosecuted; see Penny, 2011).

- They have some degree of *organization*, coordinated most often through their IRCs which, in the case of the WikiLeaks support operation, involved an extraordinary level of coordination among an extremely high number of people.

- They have some degree of *temporal continuity*, with a clear origin in 4chan and a subsequent evolution to the present time.

- They establish clear *targets* towards which their claims are directed (e.g. states, official and corporate websites).

- And they clearly have a degree of *shared solidarity* or *collective identity*, built up through shared interactions over time, which is manifested in the consistency of the use of the name Anonymous, the use of the Guy Fawkes masks, a shared ethos and set of informal rules that guide their behaviour (e.g. participatory culture, collective development and planning, shared ownership, self-organization) and particular repertoire of tactics and images that form their 'signature' (e.g. the replacement of corporate logos with a headless man in a suit, the face replaced by a question mark, once they have hacked a website, and the subsequent video explanations of their actions narrated by a 'disembodied' automated voice) (see also Firer Blaess, 2016).

The link between online and offline activism is also becoming clearer in Anonymous' trajectory, as is their global reach in terms of interventions, as their assistance to activists in the Arab Spring in Tunisia and Egypt (2010) and their involvement in Occupy Wall Street (2011) (discussed in Chapter 7) show. A group of Anons first launched #OpTunisia on an IRC in January 2011 in support of the protesters against President Ben Ali in Tunisia and, in particular, his censorship of WikiLeaks sites (which released information relevant to the Tunisian government) and other Internet sites, including Facebook. Anons engaged in DDoS attacks and the hacking and defacement of Tunisian government websites and worked to help the transfer of news in and out of Tunisia. They also distributed a care package to help Tunisian activists get around the restrictions, including a Greasemonkey script to avoid proxy interception by the Tunisian government of Facebook users … Within that digital care package was a message to the people of Tunisia from Anonymous:

This is *your* revolution. It will neither be Twittered nor televised or [sic] IRC'ed. You *must* hit the streets or you *will* loose [sic] the fight. Always stay safe, once you got [sic] arrested you cannot do anything for yourself or your people. Your government *is* watching you.' (Anon, cited in Norton, 2012).

Norton (2012) writes that:

OpTunisia was the first of what became known as the Freedom Ops, Anonymous operations that mostly started in Middle Eastern countries in support of the Arab Spring, but spread much further ... At any time on IRC there were ops for any number of countries, not just Middle Eastern ones. There were channels for Britain, Italy, Ireland, the USA, Venezuela, Brazil, and many more, as well as Syria, Bahrain, Yemen, Libya, and most of the rest of the Middle East.

- With its trickster ethos, Anonymous fits clearly within the traditions of carnivalesque and satirical forms of cultural resistance discussed in Chapter 4, drawing people into activism and participation using a combination of fun and moral outrage yet harnessing ICTs in all their forms to maximize their global reach and impact. Anonymous also fits well with the definition of autonomous groups developed in Chapter 3: they reject hierarchies (although, as with all autonomous groups, informal hierarchies and ad hoc leaderships do emerge), they refuse representation or delegation of responsibilities, they engage in participatory decision-making processes and, crucially, they embody the logic of the collective as a means of rejecting the neoliberal logic of the individual. They do this in many ways, through placing the collective development of knowledge at the centre of their action (e.g. free software, open source codes), through their collective guardianship of the Internet and defence of the free exchange of information and media (as against the corporate commercialization of same), and through the exaltation of anonymity against the neoliberal logic of celebrity culture and the cult of individual achievement. In many ways, Anonymous is the antithesis of corporate social media forums such as Facebook – where the emphasis of the timeline, for example, is on self-publication of highly personal expressions of individuality and milestone events. As I will discuss in Chapter 7, corporate social media can be harnessed effectively in mobilizing processes. Yet, Anonymous maintains its commitment to a cyberactivist ethos shared by a vast community of 'radical geeks' around the world (Milan, 2012). Full of tensions, conflicts and contradictions, at its core it rejects the intrusion of the state and the market into the private lives of citizens and the individualization, atomization and commercialization of all aspects of human life. Instead, it works autonomously, yet collectively, to generate a counter-public sphere that revels in its own chaotic, dynamic and unpredictable nature.

Leaktivism: Whistle-blowing, journalism and cyberpolitics

One form of cyberpolitical activism that has caught the attention of nation-states and the public is 'leaktivism'. Leaktivism is a form of whistle-blowing and investigative journalism that uses the Internet to obtain and make available confidential information for the purpose of exposing wrongdoing (such as corruption, state surveillance, unethical or illegal practices) with the aim of furthering democratic accountability or exposing undemocratic behaviour. The close emphasis on transparency, accountability and democracy makes leaktivism a feature of monitory democracy (Keane, 2009) in which power is constrained by citizens' oversight and control.

Although the collaboration of whistle-blowing and news journalism pre-dates the Internet, leaktivism blends a commitment to technopolitical democratic imaginaries with a set of practices facilitated by the use of ICTs. *Leaktivists* are a modern form of 'watchdogs' who work undercover and often anonymously to engage in three distinct but related arenas: resistance to censorship and surveillance; exposure of corruption, injustice and illegal and/or authoritarian state or corporate activity; or making the public aware of secret or hidden information regarding issues of global public concern such as climate change or nuclear accidents. Some of the most well-known cases internationally are WikiLeaks and the Edward Snowden leaks on the US National Security Agency's (NSA) mass spying on citizens, but leaktivism encompasses a wide range of cases and practices.

WikiLeaks

WikiLeaks is an organization made up of a very small group of activists who obtain and make public classified documents, videos, cables and other materials from anonymous whistle-blowers around the world, the most famous (or infamous depending on your view) of which is hacktivist WikiLeaks founder Julian Assange. They have published many different leaks, including those relating to political scandals around the world (e.g. oil scandals in Peru, nuclear incidents in Iran, and internal banking documents relating to Iceland's banking collapse). They have collaborated closely with traditional news journalists at the *New York Times, The Guardian, El País, Le Monde and Der Spiegel*, first to ensure amplification of their message and later to ensure veracity and the redaction of personal information not relevant to the public interest (Benkler, 2011). Although WikiLeaks was initially widely hailed as champions of free press and democracy, the media narrative began to change with the publication of leaks on US intelligence and military operations. One key leak was a video sourced from whistle-blower Chelsea Manning, titled 'Collateral Murder', which shows US attack helicopters enthusiastically firing on and killing individuals in Iraq, some of whom appear to be unarmed civilians, including two Reuters news correspondents (Benkler, 2011, https://collateralmurder.wikileaks.org/). Manning is a former US intelligence analyst who leaked military and diplomatic documents to WikiLeaks, which made them public in 2010. She served seven years of a 35-year military sentence and was freed after former president Barack Obama commuted her sentence. At time of writing (2019), she is again in jail after refusing to testify in a grand jury investigation into WikiLeaks.

WikiLeaks has published many further releases of documents embarrassing to the US government, including Afghanistan and Iraqi war logs and US State Department diplomatic embassy cables, for which they have been accused of putting the lives of Americans at risk and threatening US national security. However, as Benkler (2011) notes (see also Laura Poitras' 2016 film 'Risk'), WikiLeaks sought advice on redaction from the US State Department (they refused) and worked closely with traditional news media to manage the release. Despite this, WikiLeaks were widely reported to have 'dumped' the leak in an irresponsible manner and they were harshly denounced by US and other government authorities as a threat to US democracy. As a non-profit organization, WikiLeaks is funded by crowdfunding donations, which were subsequently blocked by PayPal, Mastercard, a Swiss Bank and Bank of America in protest over their political activity, a troubling example of 'the ability of private infrastructure companies to restrict speech without being bound by the constraints of legality, and the possibility that government actors will take advantage of this affordance in an extra legal public-private partnership for censorship' (Benkler, 2011: 396–7).

Despite the turn toward vilification even from some of the news media that had collaborated with them, WikiLeaks maintained its widespread credibility within many pro-democracy activist communities. An important turning point for some came with the timing of the release of emails stolen from the Democratic Party, including Hillary Clinton's campaign manager by Russian intelligence officers (WikiLeaks claims this was not the source of the leak) just a few days before the 2016 US general election, prompting the reopening of an FBI investigation into the Clinton campaign, which is widely believed to have affected the election outcome. Subsequent information such as leaked correspondence between Julian Assange and Donald Trump Jr.; revelations by *The Guardian* that Trump's campaign manager Manafort had met with Assange, which Manafort denies (Pilkington, 2017, Harding and Collyns, 2018); and Poitras' (2016) revealing and critical film 'Risk' shifted the perception of some supporters of WikiLeaks as a pro-democracy/freedom of press/leaktivist organization to an organization controlled by one person – Assange – to pursue his own personal political agenda (including a hatred of Hillary Clinton; see Lee and Currier, 2018). WikiLeaks subsequently became an important part of US special counsel Robert Mueller's investigation into possible Russian interference into the 2016 presidential election and whether Trump's campaign knew Russian hackers were going to give WikiLeaks the stolen emails from Clinton's campaign. At the time of writing, Assange is facing possible extradition from the UK to the US on charges of violating the US Espionage Act.

While many continue to support Assange and WikiLeaks for what they see as truthfully reporting on corruption in the Democratic Party, others are angry at what they perceive as actively manipulating democratic elections and alleged collusion with Russia (Ball, 2018). Because Assange is the founder and highly visible spokesperson of a very small organization, his personal image is closely tied with that of WikiLeaks (rightly or wrongly) and revelations and allegations that damage his credibility and reputation by extension also affect WikiLeaks. Whatever their view on the leak of the Clinton campaign emails, the allegations of collusion with Russia or Assange's sexism, most pro-democracy activists support responsible leaktivism, including WikiLeaks, as an important means of exposing corruption and wrongdoing and checking state power as part of the fourth estate and reject the idea that such activity should be criminalized. The intensification of the persecution and criminalization of whistleblowers who expose government wrongdoing at great personal risk, including imprisonment and torture, is an extremely worrying trend for democracy and human rights.

15MpaRato

Like data activism, leaktivism involves networked collaboration among several types of actors, including hackers, lawyers, journalists and the citizens and activists who support their work. Organizations like WikiLeaks and 15MpaRato, which I will turn to now, manage to have a tremendous impact despite involving a very small number of active people. In this regard, leaktivist projects like WikiLeaks and 15MpaRato highlight the fact that social movement activity takes many forms, of which mass mobilizations is only one, and that often times these smaller more focused "catalyst" groups can have a greater and more targetted impact than street protests or mass online actions. Indeed, as Benkler (2011) points out, the need to protect anonymous sources and confidential personal information in leaked documents precludes using an open networked model of collaboration as it is crucial to limit carefully the number of people with access to this information. Therefore, leaktivism combines a commitment to openness and the exposure of unethical behaviour with a practice of secrecy and anonymity. This is why collaboration between professionals with legal protections, knowledge and ethical codes (e.g. journalists and lawyers) is an important part of responsible leaktivism. In Spain, a group emerging from the 15-M movement (see Chapter 7) called 15MpaRato managed to harness the power of the Internet and digital tools in a very effective way. The name 15MpaRato is a clever wordplay on former International Monetary Fund (IMF) director and Bankia director Rodrigo Rato's last name, which in Spanish means 'a while'. 15MpaRato means '15M going after Rato' but also means '15-M is going for a while'. This group of until recently mostly anonymous activists coordinated an initiative that has exposed some of the most significant political and economic corruption scandals in Spain in the past several years. In the wake of the financial crisis, the Spanish government bailed out the banks with public money. It later transpired that these same banks had engaged in massive fraud, but no one was bringing charges against those responsible. In the absence of action from the state, a small group of people decided they would do it on behalf of, and with the help of, the people.

Deeply influenced by hacker ethics, they harness the power of the Internet to get the most out of collective intelligence, networked resources and a detailed plan with a committed activist core to make it happen. Like WikiLeaks, they coordinate online using a variety of tools and they draw on the wealth of resources of the movement community, including expertise and financial support. But at their core is a small group of people, who, like WikiLeaks, rely on strong relations of trust and solidarity (and if these relations break down, the projects are compromised).

As I describe in my book on the 15-M movement (Flesher Fominaya 2020: 170),

"When 15MpaRato first set their goal to gather the evidence they needed to bring Rato to trial, they thought it would take them a year. They launched a campaign on 23 May 2012, asking citizens to provide any evidence that would serve to put Rato in jail, using their secure Xmailbox (known in English as Xleaks but in Spanish as *BuzónX*). BuzónX is a secure way for anyone with information about corruption to make it available to journalists, lawyers, activists and auditors. They use a TOR network to conceal whistle-blowers' IP addresses (TOR is a portable browser that does not leave traces). Only accredited journalists can read the emails in the Xbox because, under Spanish law, journalists have the right to withhold informers' identities in court.

After the journalists filter the messages, they draw up a fully anonymized report containing the information considered worthy of follow-up, which is then sent to a second mailbox that other Xnet members can access (Sainz, 2014). Leaked documents submitted through BuzónX enabled them to gather the necessary evidence on Rato's activities within 2 weeks.

Their initiative was widely reported in the media, and with this another key motivation of 15mpaRato was also achieved: the spreading of the idea that ordinary citizens could take action against those responsible for defrauding the public and use existing institutions to bring them to account, even if those institutions were failing to regulate or carry out their duty to citizens. By 4 June 2012, thanks to citizen input, the draft lawsuit against Rodrigo Rato was almost complete. On 5 June 2012, they launched their first crowdfunding initiative (using goteo.org) to raise legal fees, reaching 130 per cent of their target in 24 hours".

This small band of hactivists managed to bring charges against Rato but , more importantly, to transform public perception about the causes and consequences of the crisis and austerity politics. They uncovered corruption that went far beyond Rato and the fraud at Bankia Bank. The lawsuit's intent was to demonstrate that Bankia was engaged in a scam, including forgery and manipulation of documents and misleading advertising with the intention to defraud. By 2014, the media narrative had radically shifted in many news outlets, with one major national newspaper headline reading: 'The Bankia case was a massive fraud, Rato knew it, and hid it.'

15MpaRato's work did not stop with the Bankia/Rato lawsuit. An even greater scandal was yet to be revealed. An anonymous email provided some 8,000 emails revealing the existence of 'black' or opaque Visa Cards with which luxury goods and vacations were charged against the accounts of the savings banks without declaring it to the Treasury, thereby evading 15.5 million Euros in taxes. The emails also revealed that 58 members from all the major political parties and trade unions also had these black credit cards, revealing complicity of corruption between the banks and politicians and collusion to 'loot Bankia in exchange for credits to parties and trade unions' (https://xnet-x.net/docs/15MpaRato-dossier-english.pdf).

With just a few active people at their core, 15MpaRato managed to maintain an important media presence that was fuelled by the cleverness of their campaigns and the strength of their evidence, supported by a network of critical newspapers (such as *infolibre, Público and eldiario.es*) that made sure the news was simply too big to ignore. They built up trust and legitimacy within activist networks through their responsible behaviour as whistleblowers and their effectiveness against powerful vested interests, with no private funding or formal organizational structure. But they could not have succeeded without being able to draw on the resources and networks created through the mass mobilization that was the 15-M movement. In this way, 15MpaRato was a major contributor to that movement's ability to shift the public narrative on austerity, democracy and political corruption as a social problem that required citizen action, but also was enabled by the 15-M movement's work in transforming that narrative and creating active movement communication and action networks.

Conclusion

The globalization of mass media and the advent of the world wide web and the development of new ICTs have had a radical impact on social movements, facilitating movements' transnational connection to each other and their ability to reach global audiences. Social movements engage with a vast range of media forms to reach target audiences, both internal and external. Although mainstream media models have dominated much work on social movements and media, highlighting their importance for social movements, social movements are also producers of their own media. Indeed, social movements have been at the forefront of developments in the production of new forms of ICT-facilitated activism or *cyberactivism*. The increasing importance of ICTs in social and political life has also had a deep influence on the dynamics of social movement communication, throwing up important opportunities and challenges. The advent of ICTs has led to an explosion of research on ICTs and social movements, some of which overstate their importance for social movements and can sometimes fall into a sort of technological determinism that neglects the importance of collective human agency. The best approaches recognize the complexity of new media ecologies, in which online and offline media forms interact and in which social movement actors engage in crucial face-to-face interactions with one another as well as virtually. The discussion of the relation between ICTs and social movements demonstrates the need to recognize the relationship between ideational frameworks and activist repertoires in social movements: in other words, the importance of *praxis*. This enables us to make important distinctions between, for example, hacktivism as a form of political practice and hacking for individual non-political purposes or between the use of ICTs by social movement actors in general and their use by hacktivists committed to cyberpolitical ideals. Too often, ideational frameworks that underlie social movement practices are ignored or seen as incidental, greatly reducing our understanding of why and how social movements emerge and develop, their internal debates and dynamics and why they choose to engage in particular forms of actions (and not others). This is why ethnographic work on cyber-activism that gets 'behind the scenes' and doesn't just rely on online publicly content is so valuable. Activists' choices of organizational and action forms are made not just made for practical or strategic reasons but also for ideological and cultural ones, even when these might not be the most effective or efficient.

I will further explore the relation between activism and the online realm in right-wing movements in Chapter 6 and the role of media and ICTs in the mobilizations following the global financial crisis of 2007/2008 in Chapter 7.

Hacktivism and cyberpolitics raise questions about whether it is possible for digital tools and networked politics to strengthen democracy by fostering more horizontal and inclusive participation, expose wrongdoing and counter the power of political and economic elites, or whether instead 'the Internet is quickly becoming subordinated to the pecuniary interests of the technoelite, which merely pays lip service to the growth of electronic communities and participatory democracy' (Manion and Goodrum, 2000: 18). My impression is that initial optimism is rapidly giving way to a more pessimistic view. But as many critics, activists and scholars note, unless we protect the right to access the Internet, share information and protest online, we will never find out.

6 MOVEMENTS ON THE RIGHT

Right-wing groups are complex and internally differentiated and span a wide range of issues. Like all movements, they are shaped by the national and local cultural contexts in which they are embedded yet increasingly organize across borders and cultures. Although right-wing movements are present in many places around the world, in this chapter I limit the discussion to movements in Europe and the US, drawing on the rich body of work that is emerging in this area. Caiani (2017: 5) notes that in Europe and the US 'right-wing mobilization is a significant – and increasing – phenomena in the past 10–15 years' with more than a quarter of mobilizations identified as violent.

Consider these two recent news accounts of right-wing protests:

'The region of Saxony, where Chemnitz is located, is a stronghold for the anti-Islam far-right party, the Alternative for Deutschland, and has long struggled with neo-Nazi aggression. Last Sunday, right-wing extremists and hooligans took the streets, harassing those who looked foreign and shouting xenophobic slurs. The next day, violence reached a pinnacle as 6,000 right-wing protestors mobilized in the streets, facing off against 1,500 counter-demonstrators and overpowering ill-staffed police forces' (Hucal, 2018).

'...A column of about 250 mostly young white males, many wearing khaki pants and white polo shirts, began to stretch across the shadowy Nameless Field[...] at the University of Virginia. Their torches, filled with kerosene by workers at a nearby table, were still dark. 'Stay in formation!' barked an organizer carrying a bullhorn. 'Two by two! Two by two!' Within minutes, marchers lit their torches. Additional organizers, wearing earpieces and carrying radios, ran up and down the line shouting directions. 'Now! Now! Go!' The marchers took off at a brisk pace and immediately began yelling slogans: 'Blood and soil!' 'You will not replace us!' 'Jews will not replace us!' (Heim, 2017).

Are these activists simply part of a 'lunatic fringe' – a small minority of extremists who bear little relation to mainstream politics? Such an interpretation would greatly underestimate the political importance and reality of right-wing movements. In both cases above, these groups are organized by committed activists. Like most movements, they have an organizational infrastructure and a collective identity, they are embedded in social movement communities, and they effectively mobilize discursive frames and engage in performative protests that draw on cultural and historical symbols to transmit their ideologies, claims and demands.

The first example, from Germany, is a grassroots movement that is also institutionalized as a far-right party (Alternative for Germany). The second example was the precursor to the ill-fated 'Unite the Right Rally', a protest organized by neo-Nazis waving confederate flags (the Confederates were against the abolition of slavery in the US Civil War) in which a woman was killed and many more people were injured in clashes between protesters, counter-protesters and police. President Trump's response (CNN, 2017) was to denounce the 'egregious display of hatred, bigotry and violence on many sides', reminding people that the protesters 'had a permit' and claiming the counter-protesters 'did not have a permit'. By focusing on permits, rather than the content of the protesters' messages, and attributing hatred, bigotry and violence on 'many sides', Trump was drawing a moral equivalence between on the one hand white supremacy, which calls for the extermination of Jews, and the expulsion of immigrants and on the other, the defense of democracy based on pluralism and rights for all citizens. Trump's words were sympathetic to his supporters in the rally, some of whom were wearing the red 'Make America Great Again' hats that were an aesthetic marker of the Trump campaign, others wearing hard hats with US flag stickers. After his response drew outrage and strong declarations from other Republicans, he issued another statement declaring that groups like the Ku Klux Klan (KKK) and neo-Nazis were opposed to 'everything Americans hold dear', but the next day he went back to blaming 'both sides' for the events in Charlottesville.

The Charlottesville episode highlights a number of themes that broadly distinguish right-wing movements from progressive or left-wing ones: mobilization on behalf of a restrictively defined 'in-group' group (as opposed to universal interests); mobilization to maintain privilege (as opposed to fighting inequality); a higher propensity to violence as a political method; and an ambivalent position between grassroots and elite-driven mobilization (as opposed to mobilization from below against elite targets).

These examples also raise other questions. One set of questions relates to grievances and beliefs: To what extent are the claims made by these 'extreme' groups shared by the general population? Do these right-wing groups simply reflect what many other people are thinking but are afraid to express publicly? Or does the mobilization of right-wing groups in fact *generate* commitment to right-wing ideologies through their movement narratives and practices? In other words, do they *create* grievances through their social movements or simply channel and reflect pre-existing grievances?

Another set of question relates to the relationship between different movements on the right. Is the difference between extreme or far right-wing groups and conservatives a *categorical* difference, as might be suggested by the strong repudiation of some Republican politicians against the hate and

violence expressed by the Unite the Right protesters? Or is it simply a question of degree, as suggested by US President Trump's reluctance to condemn
them outright? Of course, a single case does not enable us to answer that
question, and distinguishing clearly between conservative, right-wing and
'extreme', 'radical' or 'far' right-wing groups has been the subject of scholarly
analysis in the field as we shall see.

In this chapter, I will first provide some definitional clarity to help us
understand the distinct characteristics of movements on the right. Following
this introductory overview, I discuss four key social movement processes
through the lens of right-wing movements using illustrative empirical examples: 1) key discursive frames and the importance of media communication
strategies, 2) collective identity formation online, 3) action repertoires and
4) the intensifying effects of movement participation and the role of movement culture. I then analyse the argument that right-wing movements are
motivated by a defence of privilege (*In Defence of Privilege: power devaluation
theory and the role of grievances),* before tackling the ambivalent location of
right-wing movements (*Elite-driven or Grassroots Movements? The Case of the
Tea Party).* I end with a reflection on the challenges faced by those contesting
right-wing movements and why it matters.

Defining right-wing movements

In this section, I first discuss the relative scarcity of literature on right-wing
movements before providing some key definitions that highlight the importance of core ideas and values. I then present and critique an influential argument that explains these movements as 'movements of losers' in globalization
processes. In light of the difficulties in neatly defining right-wing movements, I close this section with a debate on the relation between movements
at two different ends of the right-wing spectrum: *Conservatives and the Far
Right: difference in degree or difference in kind?*

An emerging literature

Despite their significant presence and political importance, right-wing
movements have received relatively little attention in the literature (Caiani,
2017; Parkin *et al.,* 2015). There are several reasons for this. One is that
scholars interested in the radical right have focused almost exclusively on
political parties and elections (and indeed radical right parties are among the
most studied in European political science), neglecting the relationship
between these parties and the social movements that support them and the
broader social movement milieu in which the ideas that are mobilized discursively in the electoral sphere are nurtured and disseminated (Caiani,
2017). Second, although the recent literature on right-wing social movements is growing, it tends to focus on the political violence and terrorism
associated with more extreme groups (Della Porta, 2013; Caiani *et al.,* 2012;
Caiani, 2017). Another reason is that social movement scholars are often
attracted to social movement scholarship because they identify with the

movements' goals and objectives, and most often they hold progressive, not conservative, values.

Access and risk are also factors affecting those scholars who engage in qualitative and ethnographic methods and who would have difficulty being accepted into right-wing subcultures, where activists often are sceptical of researchers' intentions (Blee and Creasap, 2010). Some scholars find immersion difficult for personal and political reasons (Westermeyer, 2016; Hardisty, 2000), finding the experience draining and depressing. Despite this, scholars such as Hardisty (2000) advocate for the need to study these important movements and to recognize the threat they pose to democracy. At the same time, she argues that research into right-wing movements should not demonize, trivialize or stereotype their participants (Hardisty, 2000). For Hardisty (2000: 10), there is a political imperative to pay attention to these movements which do not simply represent an 'alternative' viewpoint but 'combine reactionary social policies with ideological fervor grounded in fundamentalist religious beliefs and long-standing racial bigotry'. She notes that the negative effects of economic restructuring have left many working-class and middle-class people feeling insecure and resentful and *mobilizing* that resentment, she argues, is at the heart of contemporary right-wing movements.

Another reason for the scarce attention to right-wing movements is suggested by Mudde (2010), who argues that much work on the far, radical or extreme right has characterized these movements as a sort of pathology, lying outside the realms of normal democratic behaviour and therefore scholarship, meaning that instead of studying these groups as part of political life in democracy they have been seen as anomalous and therefore requiring special categories of analysis. Mudde argues that this is problematic because in fact the values and views members of right-wing groups hold are much more widespread than liberal scholars assume (although they differ in intensity or degree) and because these groups can be fruitfully studied using established concepts in political science.

Definitional criteria: The importance of core ideas and values

The first and most important distinction between progressive and right-wing movements rests on the ideological or ideational frameworks and associated values that underlie the motivations, goals and discourses of right-wing movements. Characterizing this distinctiveness is itself a complex endeavour, not only because of the great variety of right-wing movements that exist and their different manifestations in different contexts but because scholars disagree about the best way to define them and on the best terms to describe them. Nevertheless, some core elements can be distinguished, even if they might not all be present or present in the same degree or configuration from movement to movement. Some scholars, such as Blee and Creasap (2010: 270–271), writing from a predominantly US perspective, distinguish between conservative and right-wing movements: *conservative movements* are those that 'support patriotism, free enterprise capitalism, and/or a traditional moral order and for which violence is not a frequent tactic or goal', whereas *right-wing movements* are those that 'focus specifically on race/ethnicity and/or that promote violence as a primary tactic or goal'. They note that in practice a single movement is likely to have characteristics of both, making the classification of rightist movements a difficult task. Later (2010: 273), they write that 'Right-wing movements in the United States openly and virulently embrace racism, anti-Semitism and/or xenophobia and promote violence'. However, most scholars writing in the European context would reserve such a definition for extreme, far or radical right-wing movements.

Carter (2005), writing about Western European political parties, distinguishes the extreme right from the right by the presence of two characteristics: anti-constitutionalism and anti-democratic values, and a rejection of fundamental human equality. Caiani *et al.* (2012: 5) characterize extreme right-wing movements (a term they prefer to radical right-wing movements) as being multifaceted but with a common ideological core centred on 'hierarchy and order; a state-centered economy; and the importance of authority'. Following Heitmeyer (2003: 401), they stress the importance of ideologies of inequality that center on 'exaggerated nationalism, racist denigration, and totalitarian views of the law'. Furthermore, 'ideological characteristics of the extreme right also include xenophobia, ethno-nationalism (rooted in the myth of an ancient past), socio-cultural authoritarianism (law and order, [anti-abortion]), as well as, more recently, anti-system populism. Within a conception of economic protectionism and welfare chauvinism, migrants are stigmatized as cultural threats, often criminal, and as consumers of scarce resources (housing, employment, and so on)'.

In contrast to earlier incarnations of extreme right movements and ultra-nationalist movements, some modern extreme right movements downplay or even reject racial superiority arguments, instead sanitizing their racist ideologies by framing them in terms of non-hierarchical differences between races (i.e. separate but equal) that lead them to advocate for apartheid systems in which each race lives in their own communities and spaces (Simpson, 2016; Caiani *et al.*, 2012; Caren *et al.*, 2012).

Right-wing ideology also has a logical affinity with 'a preference for disruptive or violent action' (Caiani *et al.*, 2012: 6), which is another defining characteristic of extreme right-wing movements. As Caiani *et al.* (2012: 5) note: 'because they dehumanize opponents, ideologies of inequality are more prone to justification of violence'.

Mudde (2007; 2010) defines the ideological core of what he terms the populist radical right as being a combination of nativism, authoritarianism and populism, values he argues are shared by more than the 'tiny minority' of the European population than is usually claimed and also have strong roots and history in the US. Nativism is an ideology that claims that 'states should be inhabited exclusively by members of the native group ("the nation") and that non-native elements (persons and ideas) are fundamentally threatening to the nation-state's homogeneity' (Mudde, 2010: 1173). Authoritarianism is 'the belief in a strictly ordered society in which infringements of authority are to be punished severely', a core tenet of conservativism (2010: 1174). He defines populism as having the central idea that society should be 'ultimately separated into two homogeneous and antagonistic groups, "the pure people" versus "the corrupt elite"' (2010: 1175).

Conservatives and the far right: Difference in degree or difference in kind?

By distinguishing conservative or right-wing from *extreme* or radical right movements, some of the definitions above suggest a categorical difference between them. Other scholars, however, see a spectrum moving from conservative to far/radical/extreme right wing that would imply some overlap in core values from one to the other. When US President Trump met refugee families hoping to apply for asylum after trekking from Honduras to the US border with armed guards who fired tear gas on them instead of border personnel to process their applications in accordance with international human rights legislation, he was clearly engaging in violent actions motivated and justified by a far-right ideology (e.g. nativism, xenophobia). Yet cognitive linguist and philosopher George Lakoff explained staunch Republican support for Trump's actions by referring not to far-right ideology but by showing its connection to what he calls *the conservative moral hierarchy*:

> 'Why are staunch Republicans fine with tear gassing refugee children? It's the conservative moral hierarchy. All conservative policy flows from this hierarchical view of the world. Any time you find yourself asking "why" they do as they do, consult this chart and you will find the answer.'

This moral hierarchy (see Figure 6.1) underlies what Lakoff (2014) terms the 'strict father worldview' that forms the backbone of US Republican ideology and legislation and that is shared by US conservatives more broadly. Lakoff argues that it is a mistake to see these positions as irrational or stupid, showing that in fact they stem from a moral position. Strict father morality is not the view of 'a bunch of crazies or mean and greedy – or stupid – people, as many liberals believe. [...] People who have strict father morality and who apply it to politics are going to believe that this is the right way to govern' (Lakoff, 2014: 8). The conservative view of the moral hierarchy stems from a belief that those who are moral should rule. In a well-ordered world (ordered by God), the moral have come out on top. Essentially according to Lakoff, from the perspective of a conservative worldview's moral hierarchy, if people are on top it is because they *deserve* to be there (recall the American Dream idea in Chapter 4). This belief enables the distinction between 'good' and 'bad' social programs, where the good programs (e.g. homeland security, tax cuts, loopholes and corporate subsidies and a Conservative Supreme Court) benefit the deserving (those on top) and the bad programs (e.g. Medicaid for the poor, raising minimum wage, early childhood education) benefit the undeserving (those on the bottom).

Lakoff argues that many conservative beliefs are deeply embedded in Enlightenment thinking, such as the belief that it is irrational to go against

The Conservative Moral Hierarchy:

- God above Man
- Man above Nature
- The Disciplined (Strong) above the Undisciplined (Weak)
- The Rich above the Poor
- Employers above Employees
- Adults above Children
- Western culture above other cultures
- America above other countries
- Men above Women
- Whites above Nonwhites
- Christians above non-Christians
- Straights above Gays

Sound familiar?

Figure 6.1

George Lakoff Tweet 26 November 2018 available: https://twitter.com/georgelakoff/status/1067157764319862784?lang=en

your self-interest, and indeed most modern economic theory and foreign policy are based on that assumption. He argues that this belief in the rational actor model is so widespread that it also leads to Democrats, progressives and liberals to ask again and again how it is that poor people can vote for conservative political parties whose policies clearly represent the interests of the most elite segments of society. What Lakoff points out (2014: 17) is that people do not vote based on their self-interest or even on their hoped-for future self-interest (in the case of those who believe that someday they will also sit in the top percentage). People vote their identity and their values and for people they can identify with. Indeed, people in social movements mobilize around these things too, which is why paying attention to the role of cultural politics is so important when analysing right-wing movements.

For some, the lines between conservative or right-wing views and extreme right-wing views are blurred in their effects on certain segments of the population (usually foreigners, black/brown people, or poor people) if not explicitly in their rhetoric. Let's take an example from the UK. As Home Secretary for the Conservative government, Theresa May introduced a 'hostile environment' policy for illegal immigration, an approach that was reinvigorated under Amber Rudd's tenure. While ostensibly designed to dampen illegal immigration, the policies led to several scandals, including that of the 'Windrush Generation', in which long-term legal UK residents originally from the Caribbean were served with deportation notices. A review of these policies by the Home Office in 2013 showed that policies such as immigration rental checks had not resulted in any measurable impact with regard to decreasing illegal immigration but 'may provoke discrimination against those perceived to be a higher risk based on an unfounded belief that the person may be a foreign national'. An evaluation of a pilot scheme two years later found reports of discrimination and exploitation by rogue landlords and that black and minority ethnic people were being disproportionately asked for documentation (Cowburn, 2018). Hostile environment policies led to immigration checks across public services and increased information sharing across agencies, banks and police with immigration services. A former head of the civil service said that the 'hostile environment' legislation was deeply contested in the UK, with some ministers seeing it as reminiscent of Nazi Germany (Cowburn, 2018).

Right-wing movement messages, therefore, get support and legitimacy from political elites whose policies and rhetoric create a 'hostile environment' for target groups (and vice versa). Following the 2019 attacks on two mosques in New Zealand by right-wing extremists that left 40 people dead and several dozen more critically injured, Tore Bekkedal, a survivor of the right-wing terrorist massacre in Utoya, Norway, in 2011, tweeted:

'One of the worst parts of surviving Utøya is waiting for the next far-right attack. Waiting for the same stupid platitudes from the enablers of the far right. Our PM is in coalition with the far right and funds their hate blogs over the state budget. She shares responsibility'.

With respect to Europe more broadly, increasingly restrictive immigration and asylum policies and the diffusion of multiple forms of border controls have created an environment in which the problematization of immigration (and therefore the construction of 'the immigrant' as inherently problematic) becomes widespread, and more extreme right-wing discourses find resonance with broader narratives, even within some progressive pro-immigrant/solidarity movements where there is an ambivalence between 'deserving' and 'undeserving' migrants (Monforte, 2019).

The widespread xenophobia in many right-wing groups goes hand in hand with a strong nationalist orientation. Like European right-wing nationalist movements, US conservative movements defend a staunch patriotism that also sees the US as superior to other countries, and some find supranational organizations, such as the World Bank, deeply suspicious (Blee and Craesap, 2010). However, while many right-wing nationalist movements in Europe defend a strong authoritarian state, with strong support for Russian President Putin being a feature of German Identitarians, for example (Simpson, 2016), US conservative movements have a more ambivalent relation to the state. On the one hand, they resent the government and argue for strong limits on government interference, control, taxation and regulation (of the environment, of corporations), defending certain individual liberties (such as gun ownership) but not others (abortion), and freedom of choice in schools (Blee and Creasap, 2010; Durham 2000; Van Dyke and Soule, 2002). At the same time, they look to the state to enforce their own views of morality, believing that government regulations should be used to uphold 'traditional family values' (Skocpol and Williamson, 2016: 58). Some Conservative US movements seek to ban the teaching of evolution and sex education as being anti-Biblical; others contest state laws on gender equality on the same grounds, and as being against the 'natural order' (Blee and Creasap, 2010; Irvine, 2000; Van Dyke and Soule, 2002), seeking bans on 'immoral' behaviours such as prostitution, pornography and abortion and supporting harsh penalties, including the death penalty for those caught engaging in them (De Witte, 2006; Blee and Creasap, 2010). Strong moralism has been a long-standing feature of US Conservative movements, such as Evangelical Christian movements and the KKK (McVeigh, 2001). These widespread differences between families of movements in the US and Europe highlight the importance of culture and history in shaping the ideological framing of social movements, even as they also share certain characteristics (e.g. exclusionary conceptions of the nation based on deep patriotism and feelings of superiority).

While the above definitions of extreme and radical right ideologies and values have focused more on xenophobia and authoritarianism, other scholars have explained and defined right-wing movements in terms of their commitment to preserving privileges. Kincaid (2016: 529) writes of the US that 'successful right-wing movements deploy frames that ennoble the defence of privilege as a fight for the cause of liberty, and in opposition to tyranny'. What Kincaid is pointing to is the importance for social movements, of whatever ideology, to tap into and resonate with widely held cultural narratives and tropes. Right-wing movements effectively deploy cultural tropes to sanitize and normalize discourses that, if stated more explicitly or bluntly, would meet with greater rejection. So, instead of arguing directly for white supremacy (although some movements do), activists in racist movements in Europe appeal to the purity of the native population and an idealized and mythologized historical past to justify their calls for a society based on the exclusion and expulsion of contaminating foreign elements. It isn't that they are arguing for the superiority of their in-group, so the argument goes, it just *happens* to be that 'pure' Germans/Poles/Austrians/Hungarians/French, and so on, are white Christians. The argument here is framed around a right to diversity, by which they mean the right to create separate communities organized within the 'parameters of the claimed ethno-cultural identity' or, in other words, apartheid (Virchow, 2015: 180 quoted in Simpson, 2016: 39). Another version of this narrative is framed as cultural incompatibility and a desire to avoid culture clashes, as the narrative of Italy's fascist group *Casa Pound* shows (Campani, 2016: 42):

> Casa Pound loves difference, Casa Pound wants to preserve difference, Casa Pound advocates a different world that is the opposite of rejection or hatred of other cultures or races, or of other ethnic groups ... on the contrary, we believe it is a form of violence that is preached by the left, that is, forced inclusion, integration. Integration is violence, if you look at it from a certain point of view. (Interview with Casa Pound militant, Florence)

The benign tone of this activist's words is belied by the fact that *Casa Pound* activists were behind the violent attacks on immigrants and refugees in Rome in 2014 that included rioting; attacking buildings – where mostly unaccompanied minors, refugees and asylum seekers were housed – by throwing stones at immigrants and windows, blocking the streets and burning garbage containers (Selmini, 2016). In this way, ideologies that are radically divergent from democratic ideals such as equality still sound palatable as they are wrapped in the language of 'diversity'. For others, such as the youth organization of the Germany's National Democratic Party, the threat to native culture is interpreted explicitly and literally as the imminent extinction of 'our people' as a result of a democratic system that allows immigrants into Germany (Simpson, 2016: 40). In a similar vein, far-right groups organizing under the PEGIDA banner (*Patriotic Europeans against the Islamization of the West*) in Germany 'ostensibly repudiate any connection with neo-Nazi ideology and practice' (not least because that would open them up to persecution under German law), yet their web presence is full of stories of German victims of migrant and refugee violence (Simpson, 2016: 41). Lakoff (2018) notes that President Trump too has invoked the migrant threat in terms of violence in a highly gendered way that ties into 'strict father ideology', combining a masculine saviour trope with the threat of foreign criminal elements: i.e. ('our') women need to be protected from foreigners who will come into the country to rape and murder them.

Blee and Creasap (2010) state that scholars are divided about the extent to which coded racism (i.e. not explicitly racist but with messages that point to racial groups as problematic) is a feature of 'New Right' groups. Some, such as Ansell (2001), feel mobilizing white Evangelicals is dependent on the racially coded discourse that excludes from the in-group anyone who does not subscribe to the 'traditional values' that are held by the desirable members of a revived nation (e.g. immigrants, welfare recipients, people who benefit from affirmative action). But other scholars argue that ethnic minorities, such as Native Americans and blacks, have been part of Evangelical movements, such as the Promise Keepers, who support 'traditional family values' and that the Promise Keepers have declared racism to be a sin and advocated racial reconciliation as part of movement practice (Blee and Creasap, 2010; Heath, 2003).

These European and US far-right messages are supported by self-credentializing 'intellectuals' who actively propagate them through the media, often using fake news and pseudo-science to sound credible while rewriting history to appeal to sentiments of national pride and superiority and a (delusional) belief in a return to a (non-existent) glorious past that will solve the many real problems in the present (Simpson, 2016; Caiani *et al.*, 2012). While rational thinking can immediately destroy many of these narratives (e.g. the idea of a pure race defies scientific understanding of human evolution), the continual repetition of false claims is an effective persuasive rhetorical device, and when these narratives are propagated by political leaders and self-proclaimed experts, they become all the more effective. According to the *Washington Post* (Kessler *et al.*, October 18, 2018) US President Trump, for example, lied 6,420 times in 649 days. The White House also has issued at least one doctored video (Rupar, 2018), which 'appears to have originated with far-right conspiracy website Infowars'. This, it seems, is the new normal, and it makes competing politically using the 'old' values of verifiable facts and figures a difficult game. Lying may be immoral but it is effective: Immigration leads in Trump's 'misleading' claims, with taxes coming a close second, both hot-button issues for US Republicans, showing that he is not lying randomly, but as an effort to keep his supporters onside, as part of an effective political strategy that appeals to his base (see also Kennedy, 2018).

Movements of losers?

Although some approaches to right-wing groups have focused on social psychological traits and social background, such as exposure to traditional, nationalist or authoritarian values or stigmatization (Caiaini, 2017; Ignazi, 1992), social movement approaches take us away from the individual characteristics of right-wing movement participants to show that group dynamics are crucial to understanding why and how social movements emerge, are sustained and are organized and what consequences they have. Adopting this approach shows that, as in progressive and left-wing movements, right-wing movements mobilize around a broad range of issues, have varied repertoires of collective action, develop rich subcultures and communities of practice that serve to recruit new members, strengthen collective identity, develop political organizing skills and intensify ideological commitments. They use the Internet to nurture collective identity in online movement communities, to frame issues and engage in propaganda. They organize visible protest actions, strengthen adherents' beliefs and sense of belonging through the production of alternative media and cultural products (e.g. zines, music, videos). They are also diverse and internally differentiated with regard to issue priorities and particular ideological frameworks. What then differentiates right-wing movements from progressive or left-wing movements?

Some argue that right-wing movements are motivated by particular grievances, characterizing right-wing movement as the 'movements of the losers of modernization', and that radical right movements have been built on successfully mobilizing people who have lost out in periods of rapid mass social change to processes of economic and cultural globalization (Kriesi et al., 2008 in Caiaini, 2017). This is undoubtedly the case and there is evidence of similar processes in the USA. But we need to be careful not to oversimplify this as being a natural or inevitable outcome of globalization processes, for at least three reasons.

The first is that scholarship has shown that, in general, grievances alone do not cause social movements (Buechler, 2000): some collective set of actors and organizations need to mediate between grievances to convert them into issues people are willing to mobilize around. As Hardisty (2000: 13) writes of contemporary US right-wing movements:

> The contemporary right is a well-financed and well-run movement that combines shrewd strategic planning for political success with a rigid set of ideological principles [...] It has an exceptionally

strong movement infrastructure, made up of membership organizations, networks, think tanks, media outlets, campus publica-
tions, coalitions, interest groups, PACs, and funders.'

The second critique is that the same events and processes produce very different responses from people who are similarly situated. *Globalization* has produced anti-globalization movements of both right-wing and left-wing
characteristics. *Immigration* produces pro-immigrant open border movements
advocating for solidarity, multiculturalism and diversity as well as anti-immigrant nationalist movements advocating for closed borders. The '*refugee crisis*' in
Europe produced a pro-refugee mobilization that demanded humane responses
to the refugees' plight and also movements that call for their internment in
camps or for their precarious boats to be intercepted at sea so they cannot reach
safe harbour. *Austerity politics* produce demands for universal social welfare for
all and protection for society's most vulnerable (e.g. Spain's *Indignados* movement, see Chapter 7) but also movements calling for a restriction of rights and
benefits to an exclusive 'in-group' (e.g. 'native' non-immigrants). Della Porta
(2015) shows how grievances are developed by losers of globalization in both
progressive and right-wing movements against austerity.

The third argument against right-wing movements as 'losers' of globalization is that many right-wing movements are populated by privileged people
(and led and driven in part by privileged actors) who are defending that
privilege. Approaches that focus exclusively on grievances overlook the creative collective action and agency of political actors that mobilize on the
right, that exploit political opportunities and create the frames, organizations, media and leadership to galvanize right-wing mobilization. Grievances
are not irrelevant, and we will look at some compelling arguments for the
particular importance of grievances in motivating right-wing movements
below. Yet many movements (indeed most of them) are motivated by, and
mobilize, grievances, and this alone obviously cannot help us distinguish
right-wing movements from progressive ones.

Understanding core processes through the lens of right-wing movements

Key discursive frames: Movements, media and elites

According to a study on five European democratic countries (Koopmans
et al., 2005), levels of right-wing mobilization are strongly affected by national
social and cultural factors, such as the construction of citizenship, as well as
by discursive framings of migrants and ethnic diversity, which affected levels
more than any other variable in the study. Through discursive and symbolic
acts movement actors attempt to contest dominant values and narratives and
substitute them with others. When successful, they 'normalize' what were
previously considered unthinkable, radical or unacceptable values and ideas.
The success of right-wing movements, therefore, represents an increasingly
effective challenge to democratic values such as equal rights, commitment to

pluralism and human rights as well as to the democratic system itself. Caiani (2017: 6), drawing on Prowe (2004), writes that '...waves of right-wing violence have been linked to the spreading of values such as radical nationalism, intolerance, xenophobia, authoritarianism, opposition to the Left and anti-parliamentarianism'.

Discourse plays a key role in the shift from politics centred on *issues* to cultural politics focused on specific *social groups* and *values*. Instead of focusing on social processes and problems that affect society as a whole (even if unequally) such as economic downturns, the problem is framed as being caused by a constructed 'other' (e.g. immigrants, Muslims) who is seen as the cause of misfortune. These discourses are often beneficial for political elites, if they can follow a logic of internal divide and conquer, by convincing voters that their 'enemy' or the cause of their problems is another social group rather than their own government policies (e.g. austerity politics, insufficient social welfare and public services, widespread political corruption and fraud of public money, bank bailouts with public money). Right-wing movements, even when they are actively hostile to government elites (and they often are, especially in the US), can therefore nevertheless benefit them by spreading discourses that deflect blame directed at elites to marginalized social groups. In the regional Spanish elections in Andalusia, Spain, in November 2018, many were shocked at the entry for the first time in democracy of an extreme right-wing party, Vox, which gained an astonishing 12 seats out of 109 (almost 11 per cent, representing almost half of the share of the vote of the historically dominant socialist party, the PSOE). Fact-checking organization *Maldito Bulo* showed that ten fake 'news' items, including doctored images and videos related to 'immigrants', were widely circulated in the run-up to the election, including claims that Muslims were demanding free apartments and social welfare, beating up health workers, demanding Christmas decorations be taken down, denying non-Muslim children ham sandwiches in school and so on (Desalambre, 2018). All of these were completely false but contributed to the construction and demonization of a 'foreign' other who was threatening the culture and economic well-being of local Spaniards (never mind that Andalusía was ruled by the Moors for 800 years and that Moorish culture forms a deep part of Spain's cultural heritage that draws in much of the tourism revenue).

These narratives feed into Vox's extreme right ultranationalist messages from a party whose highest level of support (19.4 per cent) came from Malaga's richest municipality (Benahavis), (Cenizo, 2018). Although other European far-right parties like the FPÖ (Freedom Party of Austria) in Austria and the FN (National Front) in France have been disproportionately supported by the working class (Mudde and Rovira, 2013), this is not the case in Spain. Vox uses lies to deliberately obfuscate key issues and to promote hatred against their targets, women and foreigners, as well as inflate the perception of support in sectors that don't support them, and to 'grow on the basis of lying'. In a news program on 7 December 2018, journalist Javier Ruiz of Channel 4 analysed three lies from that day's Vox's Twitter and press statements that are revealing of discursive strategies common in far right-wing parties and movements more broadly. The first lie was to say they had been the most voted party in the poorest neighbourhood of Seville (they got a bit over 5 per cent of the vote and were in fact the last party in share of the vote), an attempt to shore up credibility with working-class voters. The second lie was to denounce a 'huge problem' with false allegations of gender violence by women, citing a figure of 0.02 per cent. Ruiz pointed out that not only is the figure insignificant, the percentage quoted was incorrect. In fact, according to official court records in the period between 2006 and 2016, there have been over 1 million official reports of gender violence (1,055,912) of which 76, which is 0.00007 per cent, were found to be false. So, Vox shifts the focus away from male perpetrators of violence against women to women who falsely accuse men. The third lie uses the same issue for a racist agenda: Vox leader Santiago Abascal stated that 'we need to look carefully at how many of the 44 women who were killed by gender violence in Spain... – how many were in fact killed by foreigners?' Ruiz responded, 'Vox doesn't need to investigate because the Council of the Judiciary states that two out of three perpetrators of gender violence in Spain were Spanish men ... There is no innate violence among immigrants and no innate pacifism amongst Spaniards. Vox is lying, their discourse is false, and it is intentionally incendiary.'

Although some scholars have noted an inverse relation between strong radical right parties and radical right movements (where parties are strong, movements are less likely to be and vice versa) when looking at general trends cross nationally (Caiani, 2017), recent research shows that there is significant influence between them, and the close relationship between many radical right-wing movements and parties has led to emerging scholarship on radical right-wing movement-parties (Caiani and Cisar, 2019). In Europe and the US, the emergence of some radical right parties and/or candidates has been fuelled by grassroots movements. The circulation of incendiary lies as a political strategy has been widely used by right-wing movements (e.g. the fake videos and news stories about immigrants noted above) but has also been effective for (radical) right-wing parties and politicians in both Europe and the US. Therefore, paying attention to what these politicians say and do matters, as they provide a powerful platform for their political agenda as well as affect the media agenda (Benkler et al., 2018). The widespread circulation of news through social media and the fact that people get their information from a wide range of sources mean that even if journalists like Ruiz in the case of Vox in Spain, or the Washington Post in the case of Trump, can with a quick 'fact check' dismantle lies and show them to be false, there is no guarantee or even likelihood that the people who received the false information will then receive the correct information or that they will believe it. As Livni and Timmons (2018) point out, journalists are faced with a catch-22: coverage of Trump's or other far right-wing politicians' false statements is problematic because by reporting them, even when they might clarify they are false, they are still repeating them. They suggest that linguist and propaganda scholar George Lakoff might offer an antidote through his 'recipe' for a truth sandwich:

'The recipe is simple. Reality is the bread and propaganda is the filler – when reporting on the president, Lakoff says, journalists should start with reality, then explain the president's statement, and then finish with more facts – voilà, a truth sandwich.'

Truth sandwiches may be one way forward when faced with politicians who systematically lie as a political strategy, but what is clear is that the old rules of journalism are losing ground in a world where the media ecology has been transformed, the traditional authorities for determining news content have lost power, algorithms generate news visibility (independently of its veracity) and anyone can circulate 'news' which has been generated anywhere, facilitating the production and circulation of deliberately false news by government agencies or entrepreneurs looking to profit from its production (Aro, 2016; Pew Research Center, 2017). While trolling and propaganda are not new (and by no means exclusive to the right), digital technology has vastly and rapidly shifted their scale and level of organization (including automated propagation via social bots), which poses new challenges for journalists and new opportunities and challenges for social movements and politicians (Pew Research Center, 2017).

However, right-wing messages are not just elite-driven or propagated via mass media. Right-wing and radical right-wing groups also disseminate their messages to the wider public using similar mechanisms to other social movement groups, using public symbolic protests, leafleting, web campaigns and other communication strategies. The radical or far right has been particularly savvy in their use of the Internet, 'weaponising the internet to spread hate' (Dearden, 2017). Researchers at the Institute for Strategic Dialogue (ISD) show that extremists have been ahead of the curve in exploiting social media mechanisms and algorithms to radicalise new audiences and to target young and easily manipulated members of society. They carefully frame their narratives publicly to avoid falling foul of legislation against hate speech and terrorism and also to make their views more mainstream and publicly acceptable. The researchers at ISD suggest that governments have underestimated the sophistication of far-right messages. For example, although publicly the Identitarian movement rejects accusations of anti-Semitism and racism, *inside* their movement channels online their rhetoric is very different, and members and supporters include neo-Nazis, 'former Holocaust deniers' and former KKK leader David Duke. Jacob Davey of ISD warns that extreme right activists represent a threat by 'mainstreaming fringe ideas so as to appeal to a broader constituency', manipulating issues such as migration, sexual offences, the refugee crisis in Europe and terrorism, but using sophisticated messaging to stay 'just within the law' (Dearden, 2017).

The movements work transnationally as well, with Identitarians, far-right extremists in the US and other extremist right-wing groups and Europe boosting each other's social media presence through Twitter and Facebook posts and far-right websites such as the Daily Stormer. Other key forums include 4chan, Gab and Discord, where far-right extremists use memes and references from popular culture to promote far-right ideals, often cast in narratives about white victimhood and even 'white genocide', highlighting 'perceived threats to ethnic and religious identity and mass immigration' through which they have 'drawn in a huge spectrum of right-wing support by appealing to a populist base' (Dearden, 2017).

Organization Hope not Hate argues that while some far-right movements appear to be separate from each other, there is a great deal of ideological crossover and increasing levels of cooperation between the so-called 'alt-right' (extreme right-wing neo-Nazis) and 'Identitarianism' (the movement that started in France and spread internationally through the launch of Generation Identity, the youth wing of the movement). The Identitarians not only pay close attention to Trump's media tactics and that of US right-wing groups but also borrow tactics from progressive groups like Greenpeace, planning colourful protests and political stunts, such as climbing on top of Berlin's Brandenburg Gate and unfurling massive Identitarian banners reading 'Secure Borders, Secure Future' in 2015 (DW, 2017), that they then share by posting videos online (Bell, 2016). They also have carefully studied the rhetoric and narratives of left-wing identity movements to put forward their defence of cultural identity (The Economist, 2018), and many Identitarians adopt a hipster aesthetic also more commonly associated with progressive alternatives and deliberately distance themselves from neo-Nazi aesthetic, despite many members originally coming from this background (DW, 2017).

Identitarianism, like many far-right movement ideologies, embraces a deeply misogynistic world view, with Markus Willinger, a key activist arguing that 'women *want* to be conquered' and calling for a return to 'traditional gender roles' (Mulhall, 2017a). 'Preserving' European culture not only involves a return to traditional gender roles but also propagating a deeply racist vision of European culture whose 'ethno-cultural identity' needs to be 'defended' against people of colour, Muslims or other minority groups, and their appeals to an 'ancient European heritage' are framed in biological and historical terms that rewrite European history to eliminate the reality of centuries of migration and cross-cultural diffusion (including intermarriage). The 'European New Right' claims to be a 'laboratory of ideas' that creates 'a space of resistance against the system', a system they feel has been dominated by social democratic and conservative liberalist ideologies, and argue that the New Right 'transcends left-right political paradigms', a claim that can readily be dismissed given the direct ideological parallels with fascism (Mulhall, 2017a). Matthias Quent, Director of the Institute for Democracy and Civil Society (Jena, Germany), warns that sophisticated messaging makes it difficult for police, media, stakeholders and state authorities to really understand the threat that the anti-democratic core at the heart of the [identitarian] movement poses (DW, 2017). Successful mainstreaming of extreme right-wing messages has been a deliberate and effective tactic of some right-wing movements, which have carefully 'whitewashed' their public image and discourse by distancing themselves from overtly Nazi and Fascist symbology, shunned street violence and in some cases adopted the same recruitment techniques used by Jihadis (ironically, given their claim to being anti-Islamist activists). The online realm is key to their success. Both types of group share a narrative that their motivations lie in fears about threats posed to their respective cultures and way of life (Dearden, 2018).

While online hate speech is widespread, the role of right-wing groups in specifically targeting youth and vulnerable people in a transnationally coordinated way reflects social movement organizing which is skilled, sophisticated and strategic and which seeks to build support for radical right political projects often by portraying the groups as legitimate mainstream movements to protect European culture (Dearden, 2018). Ironically, the rejection of overt violence *increases* the potential for radicalization. Others such as Combat 18 and the Nordic Resistance Movement are able to 'recruit for overtly violent aims' (Dearden, 2018). In this, the UK has been shown by ISD researchers to be an important bridge between the US and Europe and presents a fertile terrain for far-right organizing (Dearden, 2017). Even proscribed organizations are hard to really stamp out as they reorganize online under a different name. A case in point was Scottish Dawn, which was exposed as an alias of National Action, which had links to the Identitarians. Former British Home Secretary Amber Rudd banned National Action to prevent the growth of the organization and the radicalization of new members, but their Scottish Dawn website was still in operation afterward. Identitarian Projects like *Defend Europe* have managed to crowdfund 'hundreds of thousands of pounds from dozens of countries', using the web effectively to generate resources to support their movement (Dearden, 2017). As Caiani *et al.* (2012: 75) note, mobilizing online has certain added value for radical right-wing groups: extreme right groups may find offline organizing to be restricted by legal regulation and turn to the Internet as a safer space for organizing, remaining visible but avoiding prosecution.

Collective identity online

The web also provides an important arena for the development of collective identity in online social movement communities. Collective identity is important for all social movements, and it is established, developed and maintained in social movement communities through discourse, practice and shared experiences. For identity-based movements, such as white nationalist movements, activists' individual or personal identities are being mobilized politically. Identity-based movements potentially can develop very resilient identities because of the strong overlap between movement identities that are mobilized (e.g. white nationalism) and participants' personal identities. For white nationalists, this overlap is particularly important because their fantasy of an imagined all-white community becomes real in the subcultural spaces of white nationalist movements. Yet, as with subscribing to particular ideologies, which can and often do intensify over time through movement engagement, the deepening of personal identity (e.g. identifying strongly as a white member of a white nation) comes through active participation in the movement community, creating a resilient collective identity, as Caren *et al.* (2012) show for the case of the online social movement community *Stormfront*. They argue not only that do online social movements communities create free spaces for movements but that these free spaces become all the more important as shelters for participants who 'may be reticent to express their views and ideologies in other settings [...] Both online and offline, these free spaces provide opportunities for movements [to] develop counter hegemonic frames outside of the purview of the dominant group' (2012: 168–169). Collective identity doesn't develop primarily through online activities that seek to broadcast propaganda and frames to a wider public audience but rather through the deliberative online forums in which members work through and develop their views within the community (Caren *et al.*, 2012; Flesher Fominaya, 2019). This is not unique to white nationalist identity-based movements, of course, but the safe havens provided by online communities (and indeed the anonymity possible online) become particularly important for movements who face stigma or legal restrictions on voicing their opinions publicly.

Action repertoires

Radical right-wing groups motivated by racial or ethnic hatred don't limit their activity to spreading hate messages or organizing rallies such as the Unite the Right Rally attended by American white supremacists, neo-Nazis, neo-Confederates and militias in Charlottesville, Virginia, USA, that cost the life of counter-protester Heather Heyer, killed by a neo-Nazi driver who drove into the crowd, killing her and injuring 35 people. Some also engage in activities such as desecrating cemeteries (e.g. neo-Nazis against Jewish cemeteries), burning crosses (e.g. KKK against Jews, black people), graffiti with racial slurs (including homes and offices of members of targeted groups) or violence (e.g. physically attacking, beating and killing members of the target groups, destruction of churches, synagogues and mosques). The Identitarians (discussed above) carry out activities as diverse as blocking roads and occupying mosques and, in their most notorious *Defend Europe* action, the young anti-immigrant and anti-Muslim activists used their crowdfunded 67,000 pounds (75,000 euros) to hire a boat to impede search- and-rescue, vessels from saving migrant and refugee lives in the Mediterranean. The vessel was festooned with bright red and white banners reading 'NO WAY! You will not make Europe Home'. Each year, thousands of refugees – often fleeing war-torn countries – and other migrants risk their lives in the treacherous crossing of the Mediterranean to try to reach Europe. They are often exploited by traffickers who sell them passage on dodgy inflatable and precarious boats with fake safety vests, and these crafts often sink. In 2018 alone, 2,262 people, including babies and children, have drowned attempting the crossing, according to the United Nations Refugee Agency (UNHCR). By attempting to impede the work of search-and-rescue vessels that have rescued tens of thousands of refugees and migrants from drowning, these activists are literally trying to kill people. Support for the initiative came from the *Daily Stormer*, a leading Nazi website (cited in Mulhall, 2017b):

> 'This is a great initiative... These parasites need to be inculcated with a deep fear of making the trip across the Mediterranean Sea. Right now, the Negroes believe that Europeans will come and pick them up to bring them to our countries... Godspeed, men. Your ancestors are proud.'

Although the *Defend Europe* vessel was thwarted by various means (refusing to allow them to dock in some cases, for example), it was still allowed to sail. Other activities that promote or engage directly in violence are considered criminal in some countries. Because this type of organized behaviour is high-risk and carries legal penalties in most contexts, groups engaging in these activities need to overcome a higher barrier to recruitment than other groups with less risky/costly tactics. Meadowcroft and Morrow (2017) showed how the far-right group English Defence League (EDL) overcame the collective action problem (see Chapter 1) by offering the selective incentives of access to violence, increased self-worth and group solidarity.

Here, we can see that the importance of collective identity formation through group solidarity sustains groups on both the left and the right, but high-risk activity on the left (or in progressive movements) is generally undertaken on behalf of everyone/the public good (e.g. direct action against nuclear energy because it is unsafe and contaminates everyone) or others (e.g. direct action against migrant deportation or whaling), where the activity itself is non-violent but exposes activists to potential violence in the form of police repression and/or high cost (prison, fines). Right-wing high-risk activity, in contrast, is generally on behalf of members of the in-group and against some other group, and the violence is perpetrated by the activists, which then exposes them to potential violence from police and/or legal repression. This distinction is in keeping with the general distinction between right and left in terms of the exclusivity or inclusivity of the in-group or group on whose behalf you organize, for example universal human rights (inclusive) vs. rights for a specific group (e.g. only whites, only citizens, only men, only straight people) (exclusive). Extreme left-wing groups, of course, have also used violence to pursue their political goals, but the propensity to violence of right-wing groups is more widespread according to the literature and the evidence (Caiani *et al.*, 2012) and, as noted above, is tied to the values that are espoused (dehumanization/devaluation of others increases propensity to violence).

Although violence is an important part of some radical right-wing movement subcultures, the radical right has a diverse action repertoire beyond violence which includes many cultural activities, including music, social events, publishing, producing media and even environmental activism. Such is the case of the German neo-Nazi group Balaclava Kitchen (*Balaklava Küche*), who present vegan cooking videos on their YouTube lifestyle cooking show. During the presentation of their show, they mix in racist commentary and Holocaust denial as well as making digs at political opponents and reporters critical of the far right, all while presenting and preparing the food. For example, when presenting tofu, making a comment that 'white is always good'; playing with the idea of natural selection by commenting 'the puny and weak are taken out' as they choose the vegetables; or repeatedly making Holocaust denial jokes with the number 6 million, which is the approximate number of Jews who were killed in the Holocaust (Forchtner and Tominc, 2017). Numerous scholars have noted that the present-day extreme right opposes cultural, political and economic globalization (Caiani *et al.*, 2012; Sommer, 2008; Forchtner and Tominc, 2017; Kriesi *et al.*, 2008; Mudde, 2007), and the members of Balaclava Kitchen are no exception. Their critique of multinational food companies rests on their view that they form part of an unjust food system, but in line with a concern running through numerous extreme right groups, the rejection also comes from the desire to establish a sovereign nation that is free from foreign influence and able to sustain itself without foreign exchange (an economic model known as *autarky* that was adopted by fascists such as General Franco in Spain). They encourage their viewers to eat quality food and to avoid food produced by US or Israeli multinational companies, to avoid wasting food, to decrease the environmental impact of their shopping by avoiding the use of containers and to avoid products that are linked to animal testing. In this way, they mix ideas and lifestyle elements that are more commonly associated with the progressive left to promote a young German neo-Nazi lifestyle through an entertaining cooking show (Forchtner and Tominc, 2017). This is another example of how the same macro-process – 'globalization' – and the dominance of food production by exploitative resource destroying multinationals can produce a 'foodie' culture that rests on a shared opposition and some shared solutions (a rejection of globalization that leads to veganism and an environmentally aware food consumption culture) but motivated by a very different set of values on the left and the right.

For conservative movements that seek to preserve and uphold traditional values, lifestyle politics are also important and are woven into the everyday lives of activists. Christian conservative housewives in the US, for example, developed a form of kitchen table activism whereby they got together to write letters to politicians as part of their anti-feminist mobilization (Blee and Creasap, 2010; Hardisty, 2001).

The intensifying effects of movement participation

As with other kinds of movements, research shows that participants in right-wing movements construct and intensify their beliefs, feelings of grievance and ideologies as a result of participation in movement communities (Bjørgo, 1997; Blee, 2013; Caiani, 2017; Westermeyer, 2016). This shows that while holding some values and grievances is important for potential recruits, people do not necessarily join these movements because they feel they can defend their self-interests through them, but may be drawn by other factors, such as a sense of belonging, cultural activities or some selective incentives. Bjørgo's (1997) research on far-right groups in Denmark, Sweden and Norway shows, for example, that in many cases young people do not join these groups because they are racist; they become ideologically and politically committed to racism as a result of their participation in these groups. Initially, they are drawn for a number of reasons, including a feeling of being protected by group membership. In addition to the incentives for access to violence noted above (Meadowcroft and Morrow, 2017), access to alcohol and right-wing hate music is also more important than political ideology (Caiani, 2017; Wagemann, 2005).

Therefore, while ideology is a core distinguishing factor of right-wing movements, it is not necessarily 'given'; vague predispositions held by individuals can become strong ideological commitments through the process of participation. Blee (2013), for example, based on her study of US racist groups, argues that some women join racist hate groups out of a desire to conform to patriarchal gender norms rather than out of a motivation of racist political ideology. However, as Lakoff notes in his conservative moral hierarchy (see Figure 6.1 above), male superiority is deeply entwined with racist ideologies and is in line with what he terms a 'strict father' ideology. The relation between racism and anti-feminism in right-wing groups is nevertheless not straightforward, with some far-right/fascist groups in Europe advocating for abortion and gay rights, while others are strongly opposed (Lazaridis *et al.*, 2016). A pro-abortion or pro-Gay rights stance, however, is not necessarily aligned with feminism or a belief in women's equality.

In defence of privilege: Power devaluation theory and the role of grievances

Conservatives are people who make 700 $ an hour convincing people who make 25$ an hour that people who make 12$ an hour are the problem – Meme

Power devaluation theory

Power devaluation theory, or PDT, was developed by McVeigh (1999; 2001) to explain support for right-wing movements. PDT argues that 'right-wing movements mobilize when their power in political, cultural, and status-based markets are devalued' (Parkin *et al.*, 2015: 330). The theory was developed to complement *political mediation theory*, which highlights the motives of institutionalized political actors in seeking to facilitate the growth of a social movement, and *status politics theory*, which focuses attention on the role of cultural values and beliefs in motivating social movement mobilization. Power devaluation 'draws attention to economic and political factors that provide incentives for individuals to support conservative movements', such as the KKK, which was the empirical basis for McVeigh's (2001: 4) research. Many scholars who have studied the KKK have focused on the appeal of racism, religious bigotry and moralism for its followers, and status political theorists have understood it as a middle-class reaction to cultural challenges posed by immigrants from South and Central Europe who were seen as culturally inferior to the white 'Nordic' supremacists (McVeigh, 2001). KKK members in the 1920s were attracted by the strong moralistic position of the Klan against 'vice', and they were avid supporters of Prohibition. The Klan's recruiting appeals mixed 'Racism, nativism, anti-Communism, antiliquor, and pro law and order rhetoric' (2001: 10). As in the Fascist movements in Europe in the 1930s, women were seen as the natural guardians of the 'nation's morality through their duties as homemakers and mothers and were encouraged to be politically active' (ibid). Political mediation theory argues that under favourable political circumstances organizationally strong movements can gain concessions from policy-makers, arguably in an attempt to slow their momentum (Amenta *et al.*, 1994;

McVeigh, 2001). Power devaluation refers to a loss in 'purchasing power' in the economic and political arena. In economics, this can be caused by structural changes or the emergence of new competitors due to demographic changes (such as immigrants). Political power devaluation can be caused by changes in electoral laws, the expansion of suffrage to include previously disenfranchised groups, the emergence of new political contenders and demographic changes (McVeigh, 2001: 11). Power devaluation leads to new grievances that can potentially be effectively mobilized by right-wing organizations, and McVeigh (2001: 12) suggests that support for right-extremism will likely be highest when a group's economic and cultural power are devaluing simultaneously, since when one or the other form of power remains intact these groups can shore up their power through institutional means. McVeigh stresses that grievances do not cause support for right-wing movements but provide incentives for support. As Parkin *et al.* (2015) highlight, power devaluation alone is not sufficient to act as a catalyst for mobilization since movements must communicate to their potential supporters what it is that devalues their power and what the movement is going to do to reverse or end this power devaluation. In this endeavour, media and movement leaders play a key role in shaping the perceived reality of movement participants. Potential supporters need to interpret their grievances as being able to be addressed through collective action, and here social movement organizations' ability to effectively frame the problem and its solutions in line with potential recruits' interpretative orientations and their life experience is key (although how that life experience is interpreted can itself be shaped by movement framings) (Snow *et al.*, 1986; Gamson, 1992).

Note too that having a grievance as a result of power devaluation does not imply that the 'losers' are necessarily disadvantaged economically (e.g. poor or deprived) or politically, only that they are experiencing a power devaluation *relative to what they previously experienced.* This could in fact mean mobilizing to keep hold of a privileged position vis-à-vis other social groups whom that they do not want to share power with. Parkin *et al.*'s (2015) research does partially support power devaluation theory as a factor explaining Tea Party mobilization.

For his part, Kincaid (2016) argues that right-wing movements are unique in terms of the role that grievances play in motivating them. He notes that right-wing movements are not easily explained invoking the common characteristics attributed to left-wing movements that dominate scholarship on social movements more broadly. Right-wing social movements often act 'on behalf of relatively advantaged groups with the goal of preserving, restoring and expanding the rights and privileges of its members' (McVeigh, 2009: 32) as opposed to 'social movements on the left, which often seek to expand the rights, benefits, and privileges for members of relatively disadvantaged or oppressed groups' (Kincaid, 2016: 528). Because grievances are a constant for marginalized and oppressed groups, they are generally considered less important in explaining social movement mobilization by or on behalf of these groups. Since inequality and oppression are widespread throughout the world and ever-present, they can't explain why movements to challenge them emerge in some places and at some times and not in others. Yet Kincaid (2016) and McVeigh (1999) argue that for right-wing movements grievances do play an important role.

Defending privilege in practice

What does invoking cultural narratives in defence of privilege look like in practice? Kincaid (2016) uses the case of mobilization against a Texan school funding scheme that would redistribute funding from wealthier school districts to poor school districts to explore how this issue was effectively mobilized to push the Republican Party to the right in a sustained way over time. In Texas, the disparity between rich, mostly white, school districts and poor districts that mainly serve Latino and other minority communities has historically been great. A 1984 court case claiming state school finance violation of the state's constitution resulted in a Texas Supreme Court order for the state to create a new finance system by 1990. A ballot initiative that would grant the state authority to redistribute school finance funds more equitably failed to pass when 63 per cent of Texans voted no, spurred on by intense lobbying by the Republican National Committee. This left the state legislature in need of an alternative in order to satisfy the Supreme Court ruling and to find a way to redistribute or recapture funds from wealthier property-rich school districts to poorer districts (in the US, school funding is often linked to property taxes which means wealthy neighbourhoods will have much better-funded schools in the absence of some system to redistribute funds). Whereas early Republican rejection of the so-called Robin Hood program was framed as a tax issue, it wasn't until the Christian Right became involved and mobilized frames around the defence of 'traditional culture' and 'family values' in education that the issue really took off (the irony of defending white European culture as traditional in a state that used to be part of Mexico should not be lost on readers). Since in Texas wealth and racial stratification are closely aligned, the distance between the defence of wealth privilege and racial privilege is negligible, especially with regard to this issue.

By framing the narrative as an issue about the right to parental control over education, it enabled movement participants to present themselves 'not as wealthy suburbanites defending their privileged schools, but as victims of government overreach and political correctness run amok' since their narrative about the program tapped into their framing of conservativism as 'an ideological defence for embattled middle-class whites, victimized at the hands of an out-of-control liberal elite bent on spreading multiculturalism' (Kincaid, 2016: 530). In this way, the Christian Right 'created a moral language that highlighted the racial and political dimensions of the controversy without resorting to outright racism' (ibid). This is a good example of the way that economic justice issues (e.g. a stark disparity in school funding and therefore academic achievement, life chances) are shifted into political cultural terrain.

Kincaid argues that the data in his study show that a threatened loss of economic resources fuelled the mobilization against the so-called Robin Hood program. The Christian Right, however, was crucial in providing a narrative that combined material and symbolic threats posed by the Robin Hood scheme, which subsequent Republican candidates have effectively been able to draw on in their election campaigns. Ironically, when these Republican politicians entered the state legislature, they found they had little power to change the Robin Hood scheme without embarking on a campaign of tax reform precluded by their own party ideology which opposed such reforms. Because the rhetoric had 'linked material grievances to cultural defence, future political challengers would be able to make the claim that the material grievances had not been addressed because current politicians were not fervent enough in their defence of traditional cultural values' (Kincaid, 2016: 545). These Republicans' inability to satisfactorily address education policy continued to push the Republican Party to the Right, as new even more conservative right-wing candidates successfully presented themselves as being able to address the issue.

Elite-driven or grassroots movements? The case of the Tea Party

The defence of privilege as a core aspect of right-wing movements raises the question of the degree to which these can truly be grassroots as opposed to elite-driven movements. The US Tea Party movement, for example, is a radicalised conservative movement associated with the radical base of the Republican Party and widely credited with that party's increasing shift to the Right. One of their key slogans is to 'Take Back America' (whom they want to take it back from is not explicitly specified on their signs). Tea Party Movement supporters are against 'excessive' taxation, immigration and government control or interference in private enterprise (corporations and businesses) and one of their core founding organizations – the free market advocacy organization Americans for Prosperity – is funded by the billionaire Koch brothers, who also own a share in Time Inc., the global media company. As Jane Mayer, author of *Dark Money, The Hidden History of Billionaires behind the Rise of the Radical Right* (2017a), writes in the *New Yorker*, 'For decades, Charles and David Koch have spent a staggering amount of money from their family's private oil, gas, and chemical fortune to attack government regulations – particularly concerning the environment, where their company has a history of record-breaking violations' (2017b). It makes sense, therefore, that they would actively support the Tea Party Movement. Tea Partiers lobby hard against Affordable Health Care for society's most vulnerable (who in the US have little or no access to free health-care as there is no universal public health-care provision); regulation to slow climate change or protect the environment; or to raise the minimum wage. In terms of their policy orientation, they are a movement that seeks to protect the interests of the wealthy and ensure that people experiencing poverty or other social and economic disadvantages are not helped by any form of state assistance or support. Constitutional fundamentalism also is a widespread element, with the US Constitution seen as a sacred foundational document in the same way Christian fundamentalists view the Bible (i.e. as unchangeable and the basis for practice and policy) (Westermeyer, 2016; Skocpol and Williamson, 2016). But the support for the movement includes many conservatives with a complex set of fears and angers that find hope and expression in Tea Party rhetoric and are also fuelled by it. Strong supporters represent about a fifth of voting age adults, some 46 million US Americans according to Skocpol and Williamson (2016). They tend to be white, older than 45, male, married, and have higher education and income than average. Despite their relatively prosperous demographic, most grassroots supporters are not wealthy but are comfortably well off (Skocpol and Williamson, 2016: 23). They overwhelmingly vote Republican, but some declare as 'independent', and many are critical of all politicians, including Republicans. Ideologically, they make up the most conservative wing of the Republican voter universe. According to one poll, almost 40 per cent are Evangelical Christians (Skocpol and Williamson, 2016: 35). Yet the Tea Party is not ideologically homogeneous, being made up of libertarians and social conservatives who can have opposing views on issues such as abortion, gay marriage and drug laws (ibid). Anti-intellectualism and a scorn for 'experts' are other widespread sentiments among supporters and this includes politicians, especially those who fail to interpret the Constitution 'correctly' (such as President Obama, who was a prime target of Tea Party opposition and whose credentials as a Professor of Law at the University of Chicago were deemed irrelevant in his failure to 'properly' interpret the US founding documents) (Skocpol and Williamson, 2016: 53). Despite a certain amount of hype about newly mobilized activists, Skocpol and Williamson note the widespread presence of skilled and experienced Tea Party activists in key organizing roles throughout the movement (Skocpol and Williamson, 2016: 41). They note that although men outweigh women in support for the Tea party, their observations suggest that women play the central role in organizing the movement (ibid 43).

Scholars of the Tea Party Movement see it as being made up of three interconnected components: well-funded large organizations such as Americans for Prosperity, Tea Party Patriots and FreedomWorks; conservative mass media outlets such as Fox News and nationally syndicated conservative radio talk shows; and local chapters of the Tea Party (Westermeyer, 2016; Skocpol and Williamson, 2016). But whereas Skocpol and Williamson (2016) contend that Fox News and other conservative media are not just transmitters of Tea Party media messages but actually 'orchestrators' in that they actively frame and propagate those messages, Westermeyer (2016) challenges the idea that local Tea Party activists are simply passive receptors of elite political actors' orchestrations. Instead, drawing on his ethnographic study of local Tea Party chapters in North Carolina, he argues that local chapters were receptive to these messages but also actively produced new meanings in their 'communities of practice' in which they also learned new skills and became strongly identified with 'remarkably consistent political identities across space and time' (2016: 122). It was the local chapters that provided citizens with spaces in which to 'create, materialize, and perform practices and activities' that were in line with the political vision of the movement and they created vibrant grassroots communities that brought 'newly energized conservative discourse into local, state and national political arenas as well as circulating new themes and issues back into the wider Tea Party and conservative universe' (2016: 122). In this way, the local chapters were key to the Tea Party's remarkable success. Therefore, despite being initially elite-driven, despite elite funding and support, and despite ultimately serving elite interests, the Tea Party Movement is also influenced and sustained from the grassroots. Skocpol and Williamson (2016) also argue that despite elites wanting to attribute their own views to Tea Party grassroots activists, the reality on the ground is much more complex and heterogeneous than any such claims will allow. While they do 'decry big government, out-of-control public spending and ballooning deficits', they are 'not opposed to all forms of regulation or big-tax supported spending'; instead they favour 'generous' social benefits for Americans who 'earn' them; yet in an era of federal deficits, they are very concerned about being stuck with the tax tab to pay for 'unearned' entitlements handed out to unworthy categories of people' (Skocpol and Williamson, 2016: 55–56). Many older Tea Party supporters will soon be cashing their Social Security cheques and will benefit from Medicare, both supported by taxes. In other words, Tea Party supporters believe they should benefit from federally funded health-care but not poor people, as they opposed and strongly lobbied against the Patient Protection and Affordable Care Act (PPACA). The PPACA does not provide universal health-care or state-funded health-care but requires everyone to pay for health insurance or pay a tax penalty and its goal is to limit insurance costs to no more than 9.53 per cent of income. Government subsidies are available for low-income people under the plan. But Tea Party activists feel they, and people like them, deserve their benefits after a life of hard work, whereas extending benefits to others who are unworthy would be wrong. In this way, we can see the same exclusionary in-group defence of certain benefits and privileges that right-wing groups support for members of their groups but not for others (e.g. people on 'welfare', immigrants, immoral people).

Some challenges in contesting far right-wing movements (and why we should)

There are numerous challenges for activists working to challenge or contest radical/right-wing movement activities and messages. For one thing, as Mudde (2010) notes, many core ideas held by these groups are widespread in European and US populations, though to a lesser degree than in extreme movements. For another, the socio-political issues right-wing groups mobilize around, such as immigration, are complex and real and have direct or perceived effects on target recruits and potential sympathizers. Third, as we have seen, right-wing groups have made savvy use of the Internet, social media and slick media messaging to mainstream their views, recruit youth and new members, and radicalize them. For those who overtly reject violence and neo-Nazi symbols, their discourse, aesthetic and tactics often mimic those of progressive or mainstream groups. In Madrid, for example, there is a long history of progressive squatted social centres, which hold explicit anti-racism, anti-sexism and open community values. Yet, in recent years, a fascist squatter collective called *Hogar Social Madrid* has been growing in the city with several squatted buildings. Like progressive squats, it presents itself as a space to benefit the community and mimics some 'squatter' narratives about the right to housing and welfare but advocates a nativist anti-immigrant definition of community and a fascist neo-Nazi ideology. Right-wing movements find fertile ground to exploit legitimate grievances in deprived areas and groups – with scholars noting the decaying buildings, lack of services and poor environments as playing a role in ethnic violence by right-wing movements in Western Europe (Selmini, 2016; Braun, 2011). At the same time, their agendas can serve very well the purposes of political and economic elites in some cases, as we have seen with the Tea Party in the US, and these elites have access to (and in some cases ownership of) influential media outlets and forums, and substantial organizational resources, including funding not only for movements but for the think tanks and other influential bodies that support them. As Westermeyer (2016) and Parkin *et al.* (2015) show, right-wing movements like the Tea Party very effectively frame discursive narratives that mobilize supporters not only from the top down but from the grassroots. Contesting right-wing movements becomes even more difficult when their discourses and ideologies become institutionalized.

Mudde (2011) has argued that the political effects of most radical right-wing parties in Europe have been limited for two reasons: they tend to be the junior partner in the government and 'they are controlled by a resilient judicial apparatus that protects the fundamentals of liberal democracy' (2011: 14). He recognizes, however, that the indirect political effects are less easy to disentangle or measure. He argues too that these parties are not on the whole anti-democratic. I think his assessment is overly sanguine and rests on a procedural understanding of democracy that fails to consider the extent to which robust democracies depend on democratic values and not simply guarantees for democratic mechanisms. Radical right-wing parties use democratic mechanisms to gain power and then seek to undermine and restrict democratic rights and freedoms, especially for 'out' groups, restricting the guarantee of universal human rights that should underlie democracy. Kincaid's (2016) discussion of the role of the Christian Right movement in pushing the Republican Party in Texas further to the right shows the impact right-wing movements can have on right-wing political parties, even those that are not defined as radical right - wing. Radical right-wing movements prepare the terrain for radical right-wing parties.

Consider the relation between the English Defence League and UKIP in the UK, which increasingly resembles the racist British National Front (Dearden, 2018) and whose recruitment of racist 'Tommy Robinson' was celebrated by UKIP's leader Batten as giving the party access to 'a million Facebook followers' (Dearden, 2018). UKIP members can then make their way into the Conservative Party (e.g. Agriculture Minister George Eustice, who stood for UKIP in 1999). Far-right, pro-violence CasaPound in Italy has a close alliance to Liga Nord (Selmini, 2016), whose leader is currently (2018) Matteo Salvini, Deputy Prime Minister of Italy and Minister of the Interior, where he oversees immigration, elections and domestic security. The party was the second largest partner in government after the 2018 elections and has dominated media coverage as well as promoting a far-right racist and anti-immigrant agenda. The leader of recently voted far-right party Vox in Spain, Santiago Abascal, is a judge committed to rolling back legislation protecting women from gender violence. Other European radical right parties also seek to decriminalize hate.

The institutionalization of the radical right poses real threats to democracy and human rights. In the US state of Ohio, radical conservative legislators have proposed a bill (565) that would extend the definition of a person in the criminal code to include the 'unborn human', which would leave people who perform or undergo an abortion vulnerable to severe criminal penalties (the death penalty exists in Ohio), with no exception for pregnancies resulting from rape, incest or when the mother's life is at risk. In Greece, the radical violent right-wing party Golden Dawn, which was founded in 1980 and was a fringe organization until after the global financial crash in 2009, after which it gained parliamentary representation but also has members being tried for belonging to an extreme right-wing militia. Golden Dawn has been responsible for extreme violence, and in 2013–2014 the majority of its MPs, including its leader, were imprisoned (Vasilopoulou and Halikiopoulou, 2015) (the trial was ongoing at the time of writing). Its ideology is openly fascist and national socialist (Nazism) (ibid).

The online media ecology presents another challenge for activists hoping to contest right-wing narratives: a major study of social media sharing patterns conducted by scholars at Harvard and MIT shows that political polarization is more common among conservatives than liberals (Benkler *et al.*, 2018). This means that US conservatives are much more likely to draw their information and share it only from polarized outlets such as Breitbart, which became 'the center of a distinct right-wing media ecosystem, surrounded by Fox News, the Daily Caller, the Gateway Pundit, the Washington Examiner, Infowars, Conservative Treehouse, and Truthfeed'. The effects of this asymmetrical sharing are disturbing. Although the most shared stories are more accurately defined as misleading than entirely fake, during the election the right-wing media system became 'an internally coherent, relatively insulated knowledge community, reinforcing the shared worldview of readers' creating an environment where 'the President can tell supporters about events in Sweden that never happened, or a presidential advisor can reference a non-existent "Bowling Green massacre"'. What is more, the 'Breitbart-led right-wing media ecosystem altered the broader media agenda' (Benkler *et al.*, 2018).

The results of this study suggest that, in the US at least, the media ecology poses two challenges for progressive activists: the fact that right-wing people will be less permeable to alternative messages (because they restrict their sources more) and the fact they are effectively influencing mainstream media agendas, an arena it is already very difficult for progressive social movement activists to influence, although 'liberal' journalists still outnumber conservative ones in mainstream media outlets (see Chapter 5). In addition, progressive social media sites that hope to reach a broad public and allow for comments and interaction have to contend with right-wing trolling, hate speech or conspiracy theories. As an exasperated progressive Irish activist on Facebook put it, 'The speed at which those public protest pages have degenerated into pure hate is alarming. Finding it a bit difficult to manage, not just task-wise but also emotionally.' They also can't compete with the funding: Open Democracy (2019) reported that far-right US groups have poured over 50 million dollars of 'dark money' into Europe to support far right-wing media, movements and politicians.

Why does this matter? Social movements are key political actors that challenge the status quo, channel grievances, put the spotlight on key issues, generate new discourses or work to spread existent ones and, in some cases, seek institutional power through supporting or becoming political parties with institutional power and representation. While some far-right movements, notably radical libertarians in the US, have strong antipathy to government, and many are sharply critical of political elites, others have close ties to political parties, either far-right parties or conservative parties like the Republican Party with radical right-wing factions that can be extremely influential. This matters because the way issues are framed discursively has implications for how policy and laws are written and implemented.

For example, when the *Defend Europe* vessel that sought to impede the search-and-rescue attempts of migrants and refugees in the Mediterranean largely failed, some media accounts (understandably) celebrated their setbacks and failures. But the narrative of *Defend Europe* (amplified and celebrated by radical right websites and sympathetically covered by media outlet Breitbart in the US) was that search-and-rescue efforts were engaged in 'illegal human trafficking'. Neo-Nazi website Daily Stormer celebrated the fact that Defend Europe's efforts would have 'a massive impact' on the 'media narrative' that would acknowledge that 'NGOs are engaged in a criminal human trafficking racket that is being funded by the state and private Jews' (quoted in Mulhall, 2017a, 2017b). At first sight, such discursive twisting of the facts seems ludicrous – who in their right mind could actually think that humanitarian activists saving people from drowning in the Mediterranean, whatever their visa status, were perpetrating an act of human trafficking? But consider this: in 2017, journalist and activist Helena Maleno, who devotes her energy to humanitarian aid by alerting the Spanish Maritime Safety and Rescue Society services of lives at risk in the Mediterranean, was accused by the Spanish Police (who reported her to the Moroccan authorities) of fostering human trafficking (Peregil, 2018). In another case, when faced with the human drama of the mass exodus of Syrian refugees to Europe in which many were drowning in the Mediterranean, three Spanish firefighters joined the NGO Proem Aid to assist in search-and-rescue efforts off the coast of Greece. Rather than thanking them for their help, Greek authorities arrested them and accused them of human trafficking of immigrants, asking for a 10-year jail sentence (Rodríguez, 2018). While Maleno and the three firefighters were ultimately absolved, their respective cases caused extreme emotional distress and sent a warning to others who might be motivated to assist refugees in need. In 2019, the arrest in Italy of German sea captain Carola Rakete for rescuing migrants made headlines. The Italian judge ultimately dismissed the case on humanitarian grounds. But such a view is by no means widespread in judicial arenas. In the UK, 15 activists, known as the Stansted 15, carried out a direct action (involving cutting a hole in the perimeter fence, locking themselves around the wheel of the airplane, and erecting a tripod and chaining themselves around the wing) at Stansted airport to prevent the deportation of several people on a flight bound for Nigeria. Although their defence argued that they were acting lawfully by preventing greater harm, the judge ruled this defence inadmissible. Their protest 'expressly challenged the detention and deportation practices of the Home Office' and as a result of it they were found guilty of 'endangerment at an aerodrome, under legislation brought in to combat international terrorism' (Cammiss *et al.*, 2018).

Whatever one's views on the protest tactic used, the use of terrorism legislation to condemn activists for a non-violent humanitarian action sends a powerful and chilling message. All 15 were found guilty and faced a maximum penalty of life imprisonment. (They ultimately received suspended sentences or community orders.) Note that the action was altruistic, it held no personal benefit, only high risk (including to their own personal safety), for the activists involved. Terrorism legislation has frequently been used to stifle protest in both democratic and authoritarian contexts. Cammiss *et al.* (2018) note that the potential consequences of the trial have grave potential consequences for freedom of assembly and expression in the UK.

As right-wing discourses become mainstreamed, they also find their way into the criminal code directly. In Spain, for example, the reform of the penal code not only restricted the right to protest and freedom of expression; the law also criminalizes solidarity: activists, concerned citizens and NGOs working on migrant rights and issues who help people who are not in the country legally or who do not have their documents in order can be found guilty of a crime unless they can prove it was for humanitarian reasons. However, as with much of the language in the reforms, what counts as 'humanitarian' is not specified and is left to the discretion of the judge. The penalty is between 6 months and 2 years of prison. For migrants seeking to regularize their legal status, the costs of helping a fellow migrant are even higher; because the act is classified as a crime, it puts their own status at risk and can be a cause for deportation (Sos Racismo, 2015). The law allows for arbitrary identification by state authorities (something illegal in the case of Spanish citizens), giving rise to what groups like SOS Racism have called 'racist roundups' where people who look like they might be undocumented are stopped and searched. In France, Amnesty International also highlights that although solidarity *per se* is not a crime according to the penal code, existing laws are used to criminalize those engaged in humanitarian/solidarity action for people who do not have regularized documents (which, by definition, people seeking asylum or refugee status do not), in part because (as in Spain) the language of the exceptions and the conditions under which they are applicable under law are open to wide interpretation. This is why activists protest against the so-called *délit de solidarité* (or crime of solidarity).

In this way, we can see how a hostile environment for foreigners combines with the increased criminalization of protest and solidarity, which has a chilling effect on democracy and ultimately makes fighting the radical right, and the policies and narratives they promote, all the more difficult.

Yet it is possible. Activists like Hope not Hate maintained pressure against the *Defend Europe* Campaign, alerting the media and providing counter-spin to the narratives of the Identitarians who were hoping to see people drown in the Mediterranean rather than come to Europe. In Crete, teachers and activists in Heraklion organized to drive Golden Dawn off the island. Golden Dawn had set up a base on the island, seeking to recruit young people by taking them for coffee and talking about Greek history. When two Pakistani workers were stabbed, islanders began to organize against the organization. Although Golden Dawn is a political party that has won parliamentary seats, it was created and remains a grassroots movement, and local support is key to its success (Vasilopoulou and Halikiopoulou, 2015). To fight Golden Dawn's influence in Crete, anti-fascist activists first tried to monitor the group and call neighbourhood assemblies, but they did not get as much support as they needed (Bateman, 2018). People felt greater alarm after a high-profile murder of an anti-fascist rapper allegedly on the orders of Golden Dawn shocked the country and shook people out of their complacency. The anti-fascist activists in Crete also began to work locally, going door to door to discuss the dangers of fascism and to remind islanders about what had happened in the past and how history could be repeated. Meanwhile, teachers organized against the 'clever and sneaky' way Golden Dawn was radicalizing school children, by designing an anti-fascist curriculum and teaching Greek history in a less nationalistic way, also including multicultural celebrations of the migrant groups living on the island. They organized in the Cretan League of Anti-Fascist Teachers and held an anti-fascist festival that brought together 56 schools (Bateman, 2018). The teachers openly challenged Golden Dawn's ideas in the classroom, asking their students whether they really believed that their immigrant school friends were inferior to them as Golden Dawn claimed and espousing democratic ideals (ibid.).

Other more militant activists decided to fight fire with fire, raiding Golden Dawn offices one night and destroying everything. While not everyone was in agreement with this tactic, it seems to have had an effect, as Golden Dawn left the island shortly thereafter (ibid).

Conclusion

What is at stake as a result of the increasing strength and influence of right-wing groups? Nobel Memorial Prize winner Paul Krugman writes that:

'In recent decades a number of nominally democratic nations have become de facto authoritarian, one-party states. Yet none of them have had classic military coups, with tanks in the street.

What we've seen instead are coups of a subtler form: takeovers or intimidation of the news media, rigged elections that disenfranchise opposing voters, new rules of the game that give the ruling party overwhelming control even if it loses the popular vote, corrupted courts. The classic example is Hungary, where *Fidesz*, the white nationalist governing party, has effectively taken over the bulk of the media; destroyed the independence of the judiciary; rigged voting to enfranchise supporters and disenfranchise opponents; gerrymandered electoral districts in its favor; and altered the rules so that a minority in the popular vote translates into a supermajority in the legislature'.

Krugman argues that, though less obvious and extreme, similar processes are happening in the US: 'Elected Republicans don't just increasingly share the values of white nationalist parties like Fidesz or Poland's Law and Justice; they also share those parties' contempt for democracy. The G.O.P. is an authoritarian party in waiting.' Radical right political parties and candidates don't just emerge from thin air; in all the cases mentioned in this chapter (and many more not covered here), these parties are supported by grassroots social movements.

Taken as a whole, right-wing movements simultaneously occupy a space between widely held assumptions that underpin social institutions (including religions, political institutions, legal institutions, media and publicity and cultural institutions), such as racism and sexism, and an outsider status that places them in a stigmatized category when they make racism and sexism explicit and practice physical violence directly (as opposed to indirect 'symbolic' violence resulting from deeply entrenched racism and sexism). For contemporary 'radical' or 'extreme' movements, much of their activity is oriented precisely toward moving out of the stigmatized category by mainstreaming their discourse and appealing to the latent vague sentiments and human propensity to othering that is most easily channelled when grievances or perceived grievances are salient. And this mainstreaming tactic seems to be working as the right-wing agenda gains ground across a number of democracies.

It is important to continue to fight extreme right-wing groups as well as any ideology that seeks to justify inequality and deteriorate democratic values and rights. But it is also clear that until politicians begin to take the well-being of their citizens seriously and create living conditions that do not leave deprived people vulnerable to the desire to blame other disadvantaged people for their situations, the far right will continue to mobilize effectively to the detriment of democracy and all who support it. Austerity politics and the dismantling of the welfare state cannot be directly blamed for the rise of the far right but certainly play a role in fostering the conditions in which it can thrive. Unfortunately, even in prosperous times, there are those who subscribe to and benefit from racist, misogynistic and ultranationalist ideals as well as a desire to impose their strict moralism and fundamentalism on others. Therefore, democracy is never a finished project or an end point but a constant process of struggle and conflict in which increasingly cultural politics become the vehicle through which interests are promoted. Supporters of democracy will therefore need to continue to work for and reimagine a society that is organized around the common good and a politics that supports all forms of life. A world in which the quality of democratic societies is measured not only by adherence to certain procedural mechanisms, such as voting, but by the degree to which fundamental principles of human rights and equality are promoted and protected and how well the most vulnerable members of society are cared for and supported. In this process, social movements will continue to play a key role in the socio-economic and cultural political struggles that characterize our modern world.

7 MOVEMENTS AFTER THE CRASH: A GLOBAL WAVE?

In 2008, the collapse of the Lehman Brothers Bank triggered a global financial crisis that was felt through financial markets around the world. In Iceland, the nation's three main banks collapsed, triggering a political and economic crisis in which much of the island nation's population took to the streets in what became known as the Saucepan Revolution. This response was the first mass response to the crisis by citizens who were angry at the lack of political oversight of the financial sector and the mishandling of the nation's finances. In December 2010, another unexpected mass uprising was born – this time eventually managing to garner much greater media attention. In Tunisia, a 26-year-old street vendor, Mohamed Bouazizi, immolated himself on 17 December[1] in protest against the terrible socio-economic situations and police corruption rampant in Tunisia, reportedly as an act of desperation after police had repeatedly hassled him for bribes and confiscated his scales and wares (Ryan, 2011a). This iconic event is said to have sparked the Tunisian Revolution, in which President Ben Ali was ousted from power by mass mobilization (Ryan, 2011b). Soon, a number of countries in the Middle East and North Africa (MENA) region were seeing popular uprisings against authoritarian regimes, demanding 'bread, freedom and human dignity' in what would become known as the 'Arab Spring'. Then, in Spain in 2011, another highly visible event – the occupation of Madrid's central square by protesters demanding 'Real Democracy Now!' on 15 May – made headlines around the world. In September 2011, it was the USA's turn, with the birth of the Occupy Wall Street (OWS) movement, in which activists occupied New York City's Zuccotti Park and proclaimed themselves to be the 99 per cent who demanded a deep reform of the financial sector and the political class that operated in the interests of the world's wealthy 1 per cent. Observers linked these protests together and called them a 'global wave of protest'. In this chapter, I will describe and analyse some of the central mobilizations – Iceland, the Arab Spring in Tunisia and Egypt, 15-M/*Indignados* in Spain and OWS in New York – highlighting some of the key topics of debate around each of these protests, including the role of information and communications technologies (ICTs). Then, I will raise a series of questions: To what extent can we understand these protest events to be part of a global wave? In what ways are they connected to each other; that is, what is their *transnational* dimension in terms of ideational and practical diffusion? In what ways are they responding to a common set of concerns and reacting to a common global political economic context?

The second question refers back to the discussion of the global justice movement (GJM) in Chapter 3: is this a fundamentally new series of protests or is it better seen as a continuation of the central demands, claims and practices of the GJM? Finally, I will provide a tentative idea of the challenges and significance of these movements at the time of writing (June 2013) – tentative because these events continue to unfold in a dynamic and changing environment.

First, however, I will briefly discuss the political-economic context of the crisis against which these protests unfold.

Global financial crisis, 2007/08

Explaining the complexities of the global financial crisis lies outside the scope of this book. For my purposes here, however, some central facts can be determined. The financial crisis was triggered as a result of the indiscriminate proliferation of subprime mortgage lending in the US – encouraged, in part, by the low Federal Reserve rates from 2001 to 2005, which created an unsustainable housing bubble. The crisis became global because US investment banks had been bundling home loans from the US housing market into complex mortgage-backed securities and selling them to banks and other investors around the world as high-yield but low-risk investments.

When the housing bubble 'popped', many banks in the US and elsewhere were saddled with huge losses. Some banks collapsed; others were bailed out by the government. The situation shifted rapidly from excessive credit to a credit freeze, where troubled banks stopped lending to each other and to consumers. The crisis was ultimately caused by deregulation of the financial sector (a political process fuelled by a belief in neoliberalism), essentially amounting to a failure to monitor and regulate banks adequately, which enabled them largely to 'self-regulate', encouraging ever riskier and less sound lending practices. Essentially, banks were lending money to borrowers who had little chance of paying off the loans, but then passing on the loans to US investment banks that bundled them into securities and sold them worldwide. The 'cheap money' provided by the Federal Reserve Bank's low interest rates, coupled with corporate marketing strategies, also encouraged consumers to 'buy now and pay later' – despite not having sufficient income to pay later – encouraged by a generalized widespread failure of banks and lenders to assess credit risk properly (Orlowski, 2008).

The US was not the only country following a policy to increase domestic consumption based on credit, and the Anglo-American financial crisis was followed by a sovereign-debt crisis in the Eurozone, exacerbated by the European Monetary Union's low interest rates and suppression of national bond risks, which led some countries to take on huge public debt. The high globalization of the financial sector and the pegging of national currencies to others (or joining a monetary union) means that individual nations lose some capacity to determine national economic policies, which leads to declining citizen trust in national political elites' capacity to solve problems. The financial crisis led to a generalized loss of trust in the financial sector and in the political classes, and it caused increased economic inequality, higher unemployment, widespread feelings of economic insecurity and pessimism for the future.

The roots of the financial crisis are political (Helleiner, 2011). The political response in the US and Europe was to bail out banks at a huge cost to taxpayers and the imposition of harsh – and some would argue, punitive – austerity measures by international financial institutions including the International Monetary Fund (IMF). In Europe, the political response was led by the European Commission, in which Germany had the leading voice as the most powerful political actor. The crisis happened in the context of increased social inequality and precarious labour conditions for many workers. This, in turn, triggered mass protest in a number of countries, from right-wing, ultra-nationalist and xenophobic actors and also from more progressive actors calling for political reforms, an increase in democracy and an end to persistent social inequality. The effects of the crisis provide a context for the emerging protests but do not tell the whole story of cross-country variation in protest by any means. Iceland, Spain and Greece, for example, were extremely hard hit and witnessed mass mobilizations, but Ireland was also one of the worst affected and has so far seen relatively little mobilization, despite some very large protests by Irish standards. Nevertheless, the crisis was of key importance in shaping protests in Europe and North America, and, as I will show, the demands articulated by these movements were strongly linked to its causes and consequences. The link in the case of the Arab Spring is less direct.

Before we delve into the dynamics of these mobilizations, it is worthwhile remembering the human cost of austerity measures. In a major comparative study of the health impacts of austerity programmes across the world, Stuckler and Basu (2013) estimate that, in Europe and the US, there has been an increase in depression (about 1 million) and suicides (some 10,000 more) since the introduction of austerity measures after the crisis. In Greece, where the Troika have imposed radical austerity cuts in exchange for an economic bailout, HIV rates have increased by 200 per cent. Their most crucial finding is not that financial crises cause unemployment, foreclosure and debts which lead to negative health outcomes but, rather, that the way governments respond radically affects public and economic health outcomes. When governments enact austerity cuts, they slow the economic cycles further, and the social and economic costs are much higher than the 'savings' generated from the cuts. On the other hand, when governments intervene with stimulus packages early on, not only do they help build the economic cycle over time, but they also avert health crises and increase the welfare of citizens. Work such as that of Stuckler and Basu shows that challenging austerity is much more than simply trying to maintain individual gains in a bad situation; it is about overturning the flawed logic of a system that is not working to meet people's needs. The environment is another potential victim of austerity measures. Lekakis and Kousis (2013) show how austerity measures imposed by the Troika on Greece could lead to natural resource depletion, environmental decay and, consequently, national wealth reduction over time.

Iceland's Saucepan Revolution: Start of a global wave of protest?

Iceland was the first nation to feel the full and devastating impact of the crisis. In the period before the crisis, Iceland had privatized three national banks, together comprising 85 per cent of its financial system. These banks engaged in the same risky practices as had the US: they had grown enormously on easy international credit and, by 2007, had accrued liability amounting to more than ten times Iceland's gross domestic product (GDP): stock market and housing bubbles grew rapidly. Despite early warnings from economists, neither the politicians nor the institutions charged with overseeing Iceland's financial stability reacted (Matthiasson, 2008). When the crisis caused the stock exchange to crash, the three banks went bankrupt in two weeks and the state was unable to bail out the banks. Investors and the state suffered huge losses and the Icelandic króna tumbled on the currency markets (over 95 per cent against the US dollar). The Icelandic state was at risk of bankruptcy and turned to the IMF for help, the first developed country to request IMF intervention in 30 years. Emergency laws were passed protecting the savings of Icelandic citizens, but many investors in the UK and The Netherlands were not protected and lost their savings (about 400,000 in the UK alone, greater than the entire population of Iceland) in amounts over Iceland's entire GDP, causing their governments to demand compensation from Iceland. Inflation and unemployment skyrocketed and cuts in welfare were swift (Matthiasson, 2008; Zoega, 2009).

Iceland not only was the first real casualty of the crisis but also was where the world witnessed the first mass protests in response to it, centred upon a set of demands that would find a strong echo in later protests around the world. This response was surprising in its speed and nature, given the relatively weak social movement activity in the period preceding the crisis. Unlike many of the countries that would later have mass protests (such as Spain, Greece and the USA), Iceland did not witness any significant mobilization in the GJM (discussed in Chapter 3), although some participants in the protests had been politically active in the wave of 1968 (Júlíusson and Helgason, 2013). The emergence of anti-capitalist and anti-neoliberal claims closely related to those of the GJM was therefore unexpected. In a context of confusion, uncertainty and stunned horror, by 11 October 2008, less than two weeks after the 29 September public announcement of the severity of the situation, a protest was organized in Austurvöllur, Rejkyavik's central plaza, in front of the parliament at 3 p.m. Over the next four months, activists met almost every Saturday with a clear set of demands: the government should resign, Central Bank directors should resign, parliamentary elections should be held, a new constitution should be drafted with participatory methods, politicians and bankers responsible for mishandling the nation's finances should be held accountable for their actions, electoral reform to a 'one person, one vote' system and Icelanders should be able to decide whether or not to assume the debt responsibilities of the IMF bailout in public referenda. Citizen meetings were organized every Monday evening. Leading the protests were young cyber and punk anarchists, neo-Marxists, gay and environmental activists, and members of the cultural intelligentsia. Anarchists would organize their own well-attended preparatory meetings, and Black Bloc activists became a staple presence (Júlíusson and Helgason, 2013).

After a brief Christmas hiatus, protests resumed in January, gaining in intensity and momentum: at the 15 January protest, activists called for a mass protest on the opening of parliament on 20 January, suggesting people bring pots and pans to make enough noise to be heard across the nation through the television news coverage. Thousands of protesters showed up, banging pots and pans, some lobbing eggs at politicians, and stayed even after police charged and attacked them with pepper spray (Reuters, 2009; Júlíusson and Helgason, 2013).

The protests were very successful, if measured by their explicit demands: the government resigned, a new constitution was drafted using participatory methods and Icelanders voted 'No' to the assumption of the debt from the bailout in two referenda (held on 6 March 2010 and 10 April 2011). The prime minister in power at the time of the crisis was taken to court, as were a number of bankers.

Júlíusson and Helgason (2013: 201) highlight the impact of the mobilizations beyond the immediate political gains:

> The protest movement had indeed succeeded, in just four months, in establishing a new and effective tradition of protest and democratic activism by the common people. It had also intervened in the political process in a way that exposed the alienation of the political elite and the media from the lives of ordinary people.

Iceland: Precursor or anomaly?

Iceland's mass response to the crisis foreshadowed some central themes echoed in later movements across Europe and the US as well as foreshadowing the occupation of the central parliamentary plaza as a symbolic site of protest in which ordinary citizens demand to be heard in the democratic process, also central to the Arab Spring in Egypt.

Three shared masterframes connecting Iceland and the global wave

In terms of central frames, a number stand out. The first is the recognition that *the financial crisis has political roots* and is the result of specific political decisions based on ideology (a belief in neoliberal capitalism). This stands as an important counter-narrative to a dominant neoliberal ideology that posits that markets regulate themselves and are best left to their own devices. Indeed, when Iceland's politicians were held accountable for their role in creating the crisis, they took refuge in the discourse that they were simply victims of global financial forces over which they had no control (Matthiasson,

2008; Freeman, 2009; BBC, 2010). This leads to the second major frame, which is that *financial and political actors are accountable to ordinary citizens and should pay for the consequences of their actions. A recognition of a lack of sufficient citizen oversight of the political class* led to demands for significant democratic reforms which took a number of specific forms: the drafting of a new constitution using participatory methods of citizen input into its elaboration; a move from a system whereby country-dwellers had significantly more power per vote (because their votes were weighted) than urban dwellers to a system of one person, one vote; and the use of referenda to determine the way forward for Iceland's economy in terms of its assumption of debt repayment obligations. In general, these reforms – and, of course, the powerful symbolism of occupying the parliamentary square (citizens simultaneously reclaiming public space and the seat of power) – stem from the claim/frame that *ordinary citizens should have a voice in political decisions and play an active role in the democratic process* (beyond simply voting). The emphasis on promoting greater democracy linked to a critique of restricting rampant neoliberal capitalism and its effects on ordinary people is a key master frame that resonates throughout the protests in Europe and the US.

Actors and networks

From the perspective of activist networks and mass participation, Iceland also has some features that are similar to movements in Spain, Greece and the US. A heterogeneous mix of progressive/leftist actors fuelled the initial protests, but participation broadened quickly beyond this nucleus to encompass wide sectors of civil society and all age groups and classes. The national 'moral shock' and the depth of the crisis undoubtedly facilitated the ability of Icelanders to transcend divisive identities and generate a strong collective identity around the protests and their main demands. Radical youth participation played a key role in the mobilizations (although the leadership role of youth in other countries, such as Spain, was much greater, as was the youth impetus behind the original protests, not the case in Iceland), and ICTs and alternative media were used to foment awareness, raise consciousness and activate social networks. As with Tunisia in the Arab Spring, the protests called for the opening of a new constitutional process. Although modifications or the upholding of existing constitutions formed a central part of the claims of protesters in Spain and Greece, for example, there was not a call for entirely new constitutional processes.

Iceland as anomaly

In other ways, Iceland was an anomaly. First, it was largely ignored by international media, despite the great political transformation of the mobilizations and the devastating impact of the crisis on Iceland's economy and society. Second, it was far more successful than other protests in Europe and the US in having its central demands met – Icelandic politicians were eventually much more responsive to the will of the people as expressed on the streets and squares. Third, despite becoming an important influence on activists elsewhere (notably Spain), the movement itself was largely home-grown and self-referential; it did not adopt frames or tactical repertoires from elsewhere. This is likely due to the fact that it was the first mass protest response to the crisis and to the fact that there was very little previous activist activity in Iceland prior to the crisis. Unlike in other countries like Greece, the US, Italy or Spain, in Iceland there were no GJM networks to reactivate in the context of the crisis. The lack of transnational coverage of the protest and its largely self-referential nature as the first protest mean that Iceland is often ignored in the narrative of the 'global wave of protest', yet it exemplifies many of the central features, claims and practices of subsequent mobilizations against the crisis.

The Arab Spring

'Arab Spring' is a term given to a series of revolutions, uprisings, mass mobilizations, protests and riots in the Arab World that began in December 2010. Arab Spring protests also centred on claims for democracy and against social inequality, and as with the protests in Europe, they emerged in a context of widespread socio-economic insecurity, precarious labour, high unemployment and increasing social inequality. Given the influence and inspiration of Tunisian and Egyptian revolutions on movements against the crisis elsewhere, including the European wave of anti-austerity protests and OWS, it is tempting to fit these into a global wave of crisis-related protests. Yet, the trigger events and the contexts of these protests were radically different in many ways from those in Europe. However flawed, unresponsive or corrupt the democratic systems in Europe might be, the routinized levels of repression and corruption (e.g. from police) and the authoritarian nature of the state in countries such as Tunisia and Egypt, the two countries I will discuss here, make the political and mobilizing context very different. Poverty levels there are also higher, although youth unemployment rates in Tunisia, for example, are similar to those in Spain and Greece. In addition, key political actors (once the protests were under way, although not initially leading the protests) include religious political organizations such as the Muslim Brotherhood in Egypt, whereas there was no significant politico-religious dimension to the protests in Europe. If we look at other countries in the region that also witnessed mass protests during this period (e.g. Syria, Yemen, Libya, Bahrain), the differences between national contexts becomes more striking, with outcomes shaped strongly by regime types and historical legacies of colonialism. Some places, such as Morocco and Jordan, saw the introduction or promise of constitutional reforms – but not significant *democratic* reforms in political or socio-economic terms – as a response to the protests, yet the reforms still leave the overwhelming power in the hands of the King.

In Tunisia and Egypt, it is questionable that the global crisis acted as a trigger event (as it clearly did in Iceland, Greece, Spain and the US) or that protests were directly responding to the global crisis, although it may have had an impact because of the dramatic increase in food and energy prices in the second half of 2012, which some claim as an important factor in the level of support for protests since this directly affected many people in North Africa living very near the poverty line (Joffé, 2011). But Bush (2010), for example, shows that the food riots that spread across the MENA in 2007–08 (and were brutally repressed in many cases) were actually as much about injustice, inequality and political repression as about food prices *per se*. Instead, the socio-economic polarization in both countries predates the post-2008 crisis and is, instead, more strongly correlated with the neoliberal reforms carried out in both countries since the late 1990s (Ayeb, 2011; Teti and Gervasio, 2011). Also, the latest cycles of labour movement/protests also predate 2008, although in Egypt middle-class unions (e.g. teachers) became increasingly involved as economic reforms hit their purchasing power. Key to the protests in both countries were deep-rooted structural problems that predate the protests and which the population was very well aware of (police corruption, police brutality and elite enrichment at the expense of the people) (Ayeb, 2011; Teti and Gervasio, 2011). It is not true that these protests, however unexpected, sprung from nowhere; as El-Ghobashy (2011) and Abdelrahman (2011) show in the case of Egypt, and as Ayeb (2011) argues in the case of Tunisia, people had already been protesting about these issues over the course of the previous decade. They had not managed, however, to build sufficient support and cross-sectoral alliances to overcome state repression and media blackouts to overthrow their authoritarian regimes. At the same time, Islamist organizations such as the Muslim Brotherhood actively undermined a unified opposition front. Although the precise confluence of factors that come together to produce revolutionary processes is a source of scholarly debate and cannot be resolved here, I will present some of the main events and dynamics in the Tunisian and Egyptian revolutions, whose revolutionary processes caused a remarkable 'demonstration effect', spreading across the pan-Arab world (Owen, 2012), and then consider the question of the role of social media in fuelling the protests.

Tunisia

The Tunisian revolution was kick-started by the self-immolation of Tunisian street vendor Mohamed Bouazizi on 17 December 2010, an act whose repercussions spread from his home city of Sidi Bouzid to the Tunisian capital and beyond. He was not the first Tunisian to self-immolate, nor were the protests in Sidi Bouzid the first in Tunisia (Ryan, 2011a). The difference was that coverage of them had not managed to transcend the Tunisian media blackout. In contrast, videos posted by relatives of a protest led by Bouazizi's mother managed to circumvent all the state's strategies for suppression, including electricity and Internet blackouts and a sustained government Internet phishing operation intended to root out and suppress dissidents, some of whom were arrested (Ryan, 2011b).

While the initial protests were spontaneous, they quickly became organized with the immediate engagement and backing of the local chapter of the Tunisian General Labour Union (UGTT), despite the fact that the national leadership of the union was closely aligned to the ruling class (Ryan, 2011b).

Popular participation was fuelled by anger at terrible socio-economic conditions and political corruption. When protesters in nearby towns were killed, the protests spread and gained more momentum. While Ben Ali's regime cracked down on protesters, he also tried to calm things down by visiting Mohamed Bouazizi in hospital. The photograph, presumably intended to portray him as a caring leader, instead probably enraged people further (Ryan, 2011a) amid widespread rumours that he had already died. President Ben Ali's regime was a brutal dictatorship that operated with a firmly entrenched economic mafia and a highly modernized and repressive security system (Ayeb, 2011). The economic mafia operated as a corrupt patronage system that demanded bribes for even basic services such as water or sewage but that appeased the middle classes with increases in income, access to loans and credit, and consumption which rose quickly over the previous two decades (Ayeb, 2011). Anti-terrorist laws enacted after 9/11 were used as a pretext to allow security forces to engage in systematic torture with impunity, presumably in order to protect citizens from Islamic fundamentalism and terrorism. Ayeb (2011: 469) argues that, unlike citizens of Egypt or Morocco, Tunisians had very little public space available to express opposition; censorship of books, the Internet and oppositional politics limited exchange of information yet also fostered a 'challenging spirit and will to defy the bans'. Young Tunisians became experts in circumventing government censorship, and their IT skills became crucial during the uprising. Ayeb (2011: 472) argues that systematic exclusion from social and economic benefits of marginalized people in the south and south-eastern regions of the country – many of them with educational qualifications – coupled with intolerable increases in unemployment and the cost of living, were aggravated by the 'humiliating and provocative behaviour by local authorities'. This meant that these large segments of the population strongly identified with Bouazizi's demand for dignity, recognition and socio-economic justice. Once the revolts were under way, they spread from the southern and south-eastern regions to the north and from the marginalized neighbourhoods of the major cities to the rest of the population who joined in the chanting of such slogans as 'We may live by only eating bread and drinking water, but never more with Ben Ali'. Ayeb (2011) stresses that, despite the spontaneous nature of the original street protests, it is important to recognize the long build-up of workers' struggles, political actions for basic rights to health-care, and other forms of oppositional politics that claimed many lives since 2008. He highlights the support of local leadership in the UGTT in providing young demonstrators with 'practical skills and knowledge, networks and material support, such as rooms for meetings, speakers, etc.' (Ayeb, 2011: 474).

These local forms of organizational support were crucial in a context of little initial international support for the uprising. Despite celebrating the revolution after the fact, the US and the European Union (EU) did not express support for the uprising and had actively backed Ben Ali's regime, despite the fact that it was a notorious security state. Instead, EU and US agencies funded government 'NGOs' and invested in businesses that strengthened the state and increased its clientilistic reach (Aliboni, 2011; Gervasio and Teti, 2014). But if the international geopolitical context was not favourable, the people mobilizing in Tunisia did have the support of social movements and NGOs acting transnationally, as in the example of Anonymous' #OpTunisia discussed in Chapter 5.

On 14 January 2011, the Army forced Ben Ali to depart the country, leaving his Prime Minister Mohammed Ghannouchi in charge. The protests continued, demanding a real transition of power; on 27 February, Ghannouchi resigned and, on 3 March, the president of the transitional government announced a constitutional assembly for 24 June 2011. According to a UN report, more than 300 people died in the Tunisian uprising (Allagui and Kuebler, 2011).

Egypt

If the Tunisian revolution was unexpected, that in Egypt was even more so. Despite high levels of inequality, high youth unemployment rates and high food prices, and routinized police abuse and corruption, President Mubarak's regime was considered the 'quintessential case of durable authoritarianism' (El-Ghobashy, 2011: 1). Although the regime was authoritarian, Egyptians had many more opportunities for political expression than did their counterparts in Tunisia, a factor some consider important in containing opposition by means of a safety valve mechanism that allowed people to 'blow off steam' (Gervasio and Teti, 2014). An oppositional political culture and numerous labour, street politics and associational protests had taken place over the preceding decades, despite strong repression (Abdelrahman, 2011; El-Ghobashy, 2011). One such organization was the youth-based April 6th movement, whose name pays homage to the thousands of Egyptians who supported the worker's strike in Mahalla in 2008. The April 6th movement used Facebook and social networks to call for the initial mass mobilization of 25 January 2011, the protest known as the 'Friday of rage' on 28 January 2011 and the 'March of millions' on 1 February 2011. The April 6th movement was joined by independent trade unions and small liberal parties in lending initial support to the protests (Teti and Gervasio, 2011) as well as by numerous actors previously involved in the small and short-lived, but influential, Egyptian GJM, which later went on to become active in numerous NGOs and civic associations (Abdelrahman, 2011). On 25 January 2011, mass protests took place in Cairo, where protesters converged in and around Tahrir Square, Alexandria, Suez and Ismaliyya, growing over the next days and resulting in several dozen deaths and violent confrontations with police, with the violence of police and protesters' reactions increasing as the army appeared to block the protesters (Shenker, 2011). Only on 27 January did the Muslim Brotherhood, whose youth had been involved from the beginning, change their initial position and declare explicit support for the uprising. Mohamed El-Baradei, a Nobel Peace Prize winner (2005), also returned to Egypt to lend his support. The April 6th movement put out another call for protest on 28 January, and the Internet and mobile phone services were cut off throughout most of the country. El-Baradei was arrested, and in Suez thousands of protesters took over the police stations to free arrested demonstrators.

Various members of the Muslim Brotherhood were arrested and President Hosni Mubarak appeared publically to promise economic and political reforms and to create a new government – but refused to resign. The protests intensified and the ruling party headquarters were set on fire. On 31 January, the army refused to act against the demonstrators in Tahrir Square, shifting the balance of power significantly. Tahrir became even more packed by 1 February, and by 2 February incidents were registered by supporters of Mubarak against protesters in Tahrir. The April 6th movement issued Mubarak an ultimatum for 4 February, but he refused to step down. Despite another public appearance on 10 February promising reforms, the protesters were relentless in their demands for his resignation, to which he finally acceded on 11 February. The military junta, the Supreme Council of the Armed Forces, assumed control of the government after dissolving both houses of parliament.

El-Ghobashy (2011) argues that three arguments are invoked to explain how this most durable of authoritarian regimes fell in such a short time: technology (the power of social media and the transmission of radical information and texts by radical, tech-savvy activists), Tunisia (the demonstration effect) and tribulation (the deep-seated economic and political grievances of Egyptians). El-Ghobashy (2011: 2) agrees that all of these factors played a role but that the street politics that 'pitted the people against the police all over the country' and did not let up for days shifted the balance of power between the state and the people, a people who, she argues, were by then well versed in street politics and protest. Recall from Chapter 5 the protests following the murder of Khaled Said in Alexandria in June 2010 and the role of the Facebook page created by Google executive Wael Ghoneim and others in channelling outrage against police brutality. El-Ghobashy also highlights the importance of protests against the blatantly rigged national legislative elections in November–December 2010, uniting opposition members and outraging the public who took to the streets all over the country (see also Teti and Gervasio, 2011). El-Ghobashy (2011: 3) argues that the diffusion of protests during 25–27 January 2011 'shattered both the mental and the material divisions between Egypt's three protest sectors, forcing the regime to confront them simultaneously'.

The Egyptian case highlights some key points of similarity between the protests discussed here, where the successful protests manage to move beyond a core set of actors to encompass broad participation of society across multiple cleavages, including class, religious and political identities. The central demands for freedom, dignity and justice also reflect the aspirations of protesters who rose up across the Arab world.

Egypt, as Tunisia, was successful in ousting its leader but has been less successful in replacing that leader with a more democratic alternative. Whereas in Tunisia there was a more fundamental leadership change, in Egypt elements of the old regime and a retrenchment of military power have meant that the constitutional reform process has been less than inspiring or satisfying for many participants, if not an outright betrayal of the revolutionary demands of millions of people. As is often the case, those who assume power after revolutionary mobilization are not necessarily those who took to the streets, and in both Egypt and Tunisia there is a complex array of actors vying to impose their vision on the political process. In both cases, Islamist parties and organizations have assumed important roles, despite not having taken leadership roles initially (Joffé, 2011). These organizations are the best-organized political forces (Teti and Gervasio, 2011) and have strong links to the population through long-standing social and charitable organizations. They also have a high degree of legitimacy, not only because their values are shared by large numbers of the population but also because they suffered repression under previous regimes (Owen, 2012). However, their values and their vision of society are not shared by all demonstrators in the uprisings, and the reconciliation of diverse political visions will be a complex challenge in the post-revolutionary processes.

In Egypt, the Muslim Brotherhood government, far from improving civil liberties, has restricted the right to protest (ironically, given how they came to power, but unsurprisingly, given their orientation), has pursued a violent and systematic repression of protesters (Abaza, 2013) and is continuing to implement the neoliberal economic agenda set in place by the ousted president's son, betraying in both cases the demands of most of the demonstrators on the streets (Sayed, 2013). Egyptian women have been excluded from political institutions and have been subject to sexualized violence for political participation both during and after the uprising. While demonstrators created a sexual harassment-free zone in Tahrir Square, there were wide reports and documentation of sexual violence against women by gangs of men and by military police forces not only during the uprising but also on the anniversaries of the events (Mikdashi, 2012; Pratt, 2013). The Supreme Council of Armed Forces (which assumed rule after Mubarak resigned) forced women demonstrators to undergo 'virginity tests', a practice condemned by human rights organizations (Pratt, 2013). Egyptian women today are being pressured to conform to the Muslim Brotherhood's and military leaders' definition of 'authentic femininity', which is tied to nationalist symbolism that they view as incompatible with women's political participation. Women are therefore delegitimized as protesters, attacked to terrorize them out of the public sphere and blamed for the violence they experience (Pratt, 2013). Charges of immorality were brought against women (and men) by all the regimes being contested in the demonstrations of the Arab Spring (e.g. Yemen, Bahrain) as a means of discrediting their political demands (Mikdashi, 2012).

Egyptian women are contesting these representations of their rights and roles in myriad ways and from a diversity of political and ideological perspectives but face a difficult and challenging legal and political climate. In a study of 11 female political bloggers in Egypt, Galán (2012) traces their frustration and resignation prior to the uprisings to a sense of hope after the protests around Khaled Said's murder and the Tunisian uprising and through the Egyptian revolts back to a sense of disappointment and frustration in the post-revolutionary transitional period.

In Tunisia, the situation for women is better, with moderate Islamist party Ennahda ruling in a coalition government, initially assuring women that they would not lose their rights under the new constitution. The party assured the public that they would not backtrack on rights, promising freedom of religion, freedom to wear their choice of clothes, 'even bikinis', not introducing polygamy and not banning alcohol. The Ennahda party also introduced gender parity in its electoral lists with the principle of alternating male and female candidates on the lists, the first such gender parity ruling in the Arab world (Al Jazeera, 2011). Yet, the constitutional process has been severely criticized by protesters in Tunisia. In August 2012, protesters again took to the streets in Tunis to protest against the use of the word 'complementarity' to refer to women's status in relation to men as opposed to 'equality'. Protesters carried signs that read 'Rise up women for your rights to be enshrined in the constitution' and 'Ghannouchi clear off, Tunisian women are strong'. Initially, the majority party (Ennahda) was pushing for a purely parliamentary system, but opposition members pushed for more sharing of the executive powers between the prime minister (currently the leader of Ennahda), Rachid Gannouchi, and the president (currently Marcef Marzouki from the secular centre-left Congress for the Republic Party). This new configuration seems set to be the model that will be used to form the new political system. Concerns remain over vague language in the draft constitution over human rights, religion and gender equality (*Daily Star*, 2013).

Local, national and transnational dimensions of the Arab Spring

The same period (2010–12) witnessed numerous revolts, protests and mass mobilizations across the Arab world, with very different outcomes, from violent crackdowns (e.g. Bahrain) to extended civil war (e.g. Libya, Syria). This highlights the importance of the transnational dimension of mobilization dynamics, in terms of both international intervention in the resistance processes, whether by military or diplomatic means, and transnational social movement diffusion processes (discussed in Chapter 2), which undoubtedly stimulated people in connected countries to take to the streets. The range of outcomes across countries also highlights the continued crucial importance of the nation-state context (regime type, socio-economic indictors, levels of internal cohesion and integration) in shaping the dynamics of protest and their outcomes. Although states used (and, in the case of Egypt, continue to use) the spectre of 'foreign hands' (the notion that protest is fuelled by Western intervention) in repression against participants (ironically, given the extent to which these regimes benefited from Western funding and support that helped maintain their autocratic grip on the population, and enrich political and economic elites in the process), crucial to these protests is the *home-grown* nature of the mobilizations. This home-grown dimension centred on notions of national solidarity, pride and collective identity, which were key to the consolidation of a protest identity that encompassed wide sectors of society and transcended the divisions of class, political and religious identities. At the same time, as each process was very oriented towards national regimes, the contagion between mobilization processes in the region clearly reflected a shared Arab identity that transcended national borders. The contagion or demonstration effect between vastly disparate and geographically distant countries has been partly explained by a pan-Arab identity fuelled by shared history and by 'many webs of Arab interconnectedness, including travel, regular meetings of officials and professionals at all levels, and the activities of major radio and television networks, including, most recently, the Internet' (Owen, 2012: 373). Post-colonial experiences in many Arab countries led to the creation of presidential regimes that emphasized centralized power, strong leadership and state security forces as a means of maintaining sovereign independence but that also served to repress internal dissent. Owen (2012: 374) argues that these major presidential regimes became increasingly similar in their exercise of political and economic power, where the main task of all state institutions was to maintain presidential power, supported by a circle of cronies whose wealth stemmed from state-protected monopolies, technocrats and advisors who put a democratic gloss on the system by holding periodic elections and managed the economy to appease the middle classes (see also Gervasio and Teti, 2014). Similar experiences of political corruption and repression and economic suffering, coupled with a strong pan-Arab collective identity forged not only by shared history and experiences but also by the 'War on Terror' with its attendant indiscriminate demonizing of all Muslims and Arabs (and the conflation of the two), meant that people across the Arab world identified with and responded to protest events happening far from their borders. Similar slogans were heard across the region with dignity, freedom and justice being central themes. Political demands and economic and social justice demands were inextricably linked and, in this, the Arab Spring shared a key feature with the other protests discussed here.

One important mechanism of transnational diffusion is the media, including mainstream coverage (e.g. Al-Jazeera), alternative media (e.g. political blogs), social media (e.g. Twitter and Facebook) and literature and cinema. Mass media accounts and some scholars have made so much of the importance of social media in fuelling the Arab Spring that these claims merit greater attention.

Arab Spring: A Twitter revolution?

The role of social media in the Arab Spring has stimulated a plethora of scholarly articles. In Chapter 5, I showed the myriad ways ICTs facilitate mobilization at local, national and transnational levels. It is therefore unsurprising to find arguments recognizing the role of political bloggers, the impact of Facebook pages like 'We are all Khaled Said' and the intervention of Anonymous and other hacktivists to help Tunisians and Egyptians to circumvent state censorship as key factors in the mobilizations. At the same time, Internet penetration rates are about 35–39 per cent in Egypt and Tunisia (Internet World Stats, 2012), and the state did succeed in maintaining blackouts for at least part of the time during peak days of mobilization, making some question the extent to which social media, and ICTs more generally, were the determining 'fuel' for mobilization factors as many have claimed. Why mainstream media actors were so keen to press for the role of ICTs in Arab Spring mobilizations as opposed to other factors is an open question. It is clear that ICTs facilitate mobilization in many different ways and the Arab Spring provides a wonderful case study. The interesting question, however, is not *whether* ICTs played a decisive role in the Arab Spring, but *how*.

As I discussed in Chapter 5, ICT media form part of a complex media environment in which different forms of media interact and flow throughout social networks. In Tunisia, for example, one of the key ways that political content circulated was from alternative activist- or citizen-produced digital content to mainstream media and from there to people with no access to the Internet (Allagui and Kuebler, 2011). Howard (2010) rejects arguments that low Internet penetration rates mean digital technologies will not have great impact in Arab countries. He argues that political and social content is transmitted by means of the Internet within friend and family networks as opposed to high numbers of individuals accessing content directly. Media networks are embedded in social networks, and social networks put people on the streets.

Key roles of new media in the Arab Spring

There are a number of key roles ICTs or new media played in the Arab Spring, centred on two processes: the facilitation of the generation of political opposition cultures prior to the uprisings and as a tool to foment mobilization as events unfolded.

Role of cyberactivists and political bloggers: Generating oppositional political cultures

Numerous studies highlight the importance of cyberactivism in Egypt and Tunisia in generating oppositional cultures, which can be seen as paving the way for the Arab Spring mobilizations (Fahmi, 2009; Khamis and Vaughn, 2011; Galán, 2012). One key aspect of this is political blogging, which Fahmi (2009) shows was important in Cairo in reclaiming political space before the uprising and highlights the relationship between online and offline activism around the right to the city and the right to freedom of political expression. In a context of repression, urban political bloggers engaged in a mix of cyberactivism and street protest, including protest art installations in contested public spaces such as Tahrir Square, graffiti, boycott campaigns and new strategies for the articulation of popular democracy and pluralist cultural identities. Their grassroots activism opened up a 'new public sphere' in which dissenting political voices could be heard. Bloggers also provided practical advice and useful guidance for mobilization. An Egyptian ex-police officer named Omar Afifi wrote a book advising Egyptians on how to avoid police brutality and later sought political asylum in the US, from whence he continued to provide instructional videos on peaceful protest by means of YouTube videos, Facebook and Twitter (Eltantawy and Wiest, 2011).

Other bloggers provided guidance on avoiding police surveillance, setting up barricades and other practical advice. Egyptian bloggers posted images and videos from Tunisia to inspire Egyptians to protest; celebrities and prominent figures used blogs, Facebook and Twitter to show support for protesters and to encourage people to join (Eltantawy and Wiest, 2011).

Role of tech-savvy youth: Generating cultures of resistance

This category clearly overlaps with the category above. Many youths in Tunisia and Egypt generated grassroots cultures of resistance to the regimes, popularizing or creating chants, videos, jokes and caricatures that satirized and demystified authority, producing counter-narratives to challenge an official story that delegitimized dissent (Mabrouk, 2011). They have used their IT skills to circumvent censorship, in conjunction with activists around the world, but have also been subject to imprisonment and other forms of repression (Allagui and Kuebler, 2011). In this way, they have defied 'commonsense' narratives about depoliticized Arab youth who use the Internet for social networking only and not for political transformation (Mabrouk, 2011). Solidarity between activists in neighbouring countries is another transnational dimension of cyberactivism in the Arab Spring, with Tunisian activists helping Egyptian activists obtain access to information during the blackouts in Egypt as one example. The Internet has also been used as a forum for the transmission of offline forms of cultural resistance, such as the case of Lhaqed in Morocco, a young rapper whose lyrics against the restrictions on freedom and the power of the monarch landed him in jail but inspired many people to demonstrate in Morocco's 20 February movement and to press for his release from jail.[2]

Role of ICTs in enabling citizens and journalists to produce and disseminate political and practical content

Khamis and Vaughn (2011) argue that civic engagement and citizen journalism 'tilted the balance' in the Egyptian revolution. They highlight the role of new media in a vibrant communication environment in generating an oppositional protest culture and the interaction between different types of media in shaping the mobilizations.

During the mobilizations, people used Twitter and other social media to alert people to tear gas, blockades, free food and other important events and their locations. In Egypt, once the blackout began on 28 January, people shared instructions for how to bypass the blackout using proxies and dial-up connections, used phones for 'speak to tweet' software (where phone messages from lines in Egypt to an international number were automatically converted to tweets) or called people outside Egypt to tweet or post for them (Castells, 2011a; Eltantawy and Wiest, 2011). Telecomix, a hacker group, created an automated Google search engine to locate all the possible fax machine numbers in Egypt to provide people with information about all the communication possibilities that were still available to them. Italian anarchists provided the April 6th movement with advice on how to use ghost servers to confuse monitoring systems and continue to share information (Khamis and Vaughn, 2011). In fact, the media blackout brought more people onto the streets; unable to call, check the Internet or TV, they went to the squares to see what was happening.

But Eltantawy and Wiest (2011) highlight the real costs of the blackout that demonstrators were unable to overcome, such as the inability to call for ambulances to save the lives of injured demonstrators. They also highlight the many non-Internet based forms of communication – such as placards with slogans, graffiti, messages written in stones or plastic teacups, and leaflets, many of which were then transmitted through mass media to the rest of the world. Some activists published a manual on how to communicate using any medium and distributed it by hand to demonstrators on the streets (Castells, 2011a).

Role of digital media interaction with more mainstream or mass media

Mass media (e.g. Al-Jazeera, France-24, Al-Hiwar, BBC, *Guardian*) were also crucial in transmitting content produced by journalists, political bloggers and demonstrators, and making this digital content available on both television and Internet-based platforms. Activists and journalists used Twitter to provide minute-by-minute coverage of the protests and to tweet links to video coverage of the demonstrations. Once the government banned journalists from Tahrir Square in Egypt, for example, citizens took over the journalistic role, continuing to provide coverage and reaching international audiences through various mass media outlets. Allagui and Kuebler (2011) argue that ICTs play a crucial role in enabling citizens and citizen journalists to carry out a 'watchdog' function for ensuring democratic process after the revolutionary uprisings. However, Gervasio and Teti (2014) question the extent to which ICTs enable this citizen watchdog function, pointing instead to the role of human rights NGOs and unions in exercising democratic oversight.

Clearly, during the Arab Spring ICTs facilitated and shaped mobilization. ICTs were used to generate oppositional cultures before periods of mobilization by connecting people in user networks and acting as a conduit for the production and transmission of political content and myriad forms of cultural resistance within user networks and from user networks to the wider social networks in which Internet users were embedded. At the same time, ICTs served as a tool to facilitate communication during the mobilizations themselves, to publicize the calls for action, such as the April 6th movement's Facebook pages, to provide citizen coverage of events and to keep demonstrators abreast of unfolding events and changing conditions. The use of ICTs by activists, demonstrators and the public took place in a wider media system (or media ecologies) in which ICT-facilitated media interacted with mainstream media and other non-digital media platforms such as radio, newspapers and television. The local, national and transnational spheres interacted to connect people and networks with information and powerful images that reached a global audience.

As powerful as the effects of ICT-enabled media were in the Arab Spring, there is no reason to believe they were any *more* important than in other mass mobilization processes where people have access to ICT tools and resources. In a globalized world where ICTs now form an integral part of social and political communication for many people, they will continue to form a crucial part of the toolkits activists creatively use to mobilize. At the same time, they will be as integral a part of the resources used by states and counter-movements to repress, delegitimize and challenge them. All of the ICT-related features claimed as extraordinary or noteworthy by scholarly accounts of the Arab Spring – for example, its capacity to enable activists to network, share information, call for protest, provide evidence of government brutality and repression, provide counter-information, circumvent media blackouts, project messages to a wider audience, forge links among local, national and transnational or global spheres of action, create forums for free speech, provide space for virtual assemblies and enable citizen journalism – have already been discussed in Chapter 5 in the context of other social movements. It is worth remembering that ICTs play a crucial role but do not cause mobilizations, although they do shape their dynamics. As Castells (2011b) wrote in relation to Tunisia, 'obviously communication technologies did not give birth to the insurgency. The rebellion was born from the poverty and exclusion that afflict much of the population, from a fake democracy, from the censorship of information, from the arrests and torture of thousands of people, from the transformation of an entire country into the private fiefdom of the Ben Ali and Trabelsi families with the support of the United States, Europe and the Arab dictatorships.'

Castells also stresses that, without these technologies, the demonstrations would not have been characterized by spontaneity, lack of leaders and the high presence of students and professionals with the support of opposition politicians and labour unions. Castells is highlighting a crucial aspect of the Arab Spring and, indeed, of all the protests discussed in this 'global wave': the leadership role of non-institutional actors and the truly grassroots nature of the mobilizations. If the emphasis on spontaneity and leaderlessness of many narratives tends to downplay the role of social movement and civic association networks in providing an organizational infrastructure to the preparation and development of the protests, it is also important to remember that political parties and major trade unions were not at the forefront of these mobilizations and that they did not lead the way. Castells also highlights an even more fundamental point: ICTs do not cause revolutions; deep-seated structural problems, mass grievances and people willing and able to act collectively do.

There is a complex relationship between online and offline activism and the hybrid space between. Although there are forms of cyberactivism that only take place online, ultimately cyberactivism is intended to produce *effects* in the non-virtual world, that is, on the streets and in people's daily offline lives. As Howard and Hussain (2011: 48) write, '[people] were not inspired by Facebook; they were inspired by the real tragedies *documented* on Facebook'. The Arab Spring provides a rich example of the powerful potential of ICTs for mobilization, both in paving the way by developing a virtual oppositional political sphere and in calling for, coordinating and disseminating information about action. Ultimately, however, it was on the streets that the outcomes of these uprisings were decided, some leading to new regimes, some brutally repressed and some still under way.

15-M and Spanish *Indignados*: From radical autonomy to encompassing movement

The Spanish *Indignados* (or Indignant/Outraged) were not the first of the European anti-austerity mobilizations; mass protests had already taken place in Iceland, Greece, Portugal and Italy before the first groups of activists decided to call for a protest in the run-up to Spain's regional election in May 2011. Yet, the Spanish protests are notable for their strength, longevity and the extent to which they inspired activists elsewhere, including OWS. They are also remarkable because they managed to spread beyond the initial core of mostly young demonstrators to encompass wide sectors of Spanish civil society and enjoyed very high levels of public support. The crisis hit Spain very hard, with the bursting of Spain's real estate bubble (the IMF estimates an almost 20 per cent slump in housing prices in 2012), the crash of the lending market and recession. Youth unemployment has been a long-term problem in Spain but the crisis drove youth unemployment rates up to around 50 per cent and, by 2013, the unemployment rate stood at 27 per cent (INE, 2013). 'Austerity' cuts have been steep, with education, public health and other key services having budgets slashed, while failing banks were bailed out with public money (but not nationalized). In 2013, the Popular Party announced budget cuts of 39 billion euros while budgeting 38.6 billion euros for interest payments (Torres López, 2013). In 2012, they asked the IMF for a 100 billion euro bailout (Pérez and Doncel, 2012).

The immediate lead-up to the 15-M mobilizations was a call put out by a number of collectives under the shared name of 'Real Democracy Now!'. Despite seeming to come out of nowhere, they were the result of a coming together of a number of networks and campaigns in Spain that had been mobilizing against university reforms (many forming part of the Bologna process), labour and social precariousness, lack of affordable housing, and campaigns related to freedom of Internet, among other issues (Flesher Fominaya, 2015a, 2015c, 2017, 2020). Different but overlapping groups of activists participated in these different campaigns, many with roots in the GJM (see Chapter 3), university student movements and various autonomous networks active in and around Madrid's squatted social centre scene.

Figure 7.1

15-M demonstrators hug near the Puerta del Sol, Madrid, Spain

Copyright: Eduardo Romanos

One of the key actors behind the 15-M call to protest was the university-based youth activist group *Juventud sin Futuro* (JSF, Youth without Future). As with the April 6th youth movement in Egypt, JSF had been active prior to 15-M around issues of youth unemployment, youth labour and social precariousness (see Chapter 4), university reform and lack of affordable housing. They have been a key mover behind 15-M and have carried out a continuous coherent series of campaigns that has not let up since the beginning of the movement to the present. JSF started off as a group of university students from three of Madrid's public universities (Universidad Complutense, Universidad Carlos III de Madrid, and Universidad Autónoma de Madrid) who organized first around anti-Bolonia[4] university reforms and then began to participate in a range of protests around pension cuts and labour reforms, including the general strike of 29 September 2010. They wanted to show that youth are concerned about these issues and were keen to reach out beyond the university to a broader youth identity based around shared concerns about youth conditions and their future (JSF, 2011a, 2011b).

When the major trade unions signed a social pact with the government instead of calling for another general strike, the disappointment together with the inspiration from the movements with high youth participation and often explicit youth issues in Iceland, France, Portugal, Italy, Greece and the UK, and later the impetus of Tunisia and Egypt, inspired them to try to organize some protests themselves. They decided to organize under the slogan *Sin Casa, Sin Curro, Sin Pension, Sin Miedo* (No house, No job, No pension, No fear) as a way of summarizing their main concerns and to express their right to protest. JSF has always been very autonomous in orientation, with a central critique being that political parties and major trade unions do not represent them or their interests, symbolized by the often-chanted autonomous slogan 'They do not represent us'. They highlight the courage of the 50,000 British youths who demonstrated in front of the Conservative Party headquarters in London on 10 November 2010, 'While the labour unions refused to call for protest' (JSF, 2011a, 2011b: 16). JSF also links clearly the idea of the university as a site of critical thinking and resistance, as symbolized by the 'book block' tactic used by university protesters from Italy to the UK, who fabricated shields made in the form of books, symbolizing the idea of books (critical thinking) as weapons. All in a context of 'austerity': government cuts to education, dismantling of the welfare state and multimillion bank bailouts. They therefore called for a youth protest in Madrid under the name 'Youth Without Future' on 7 April 2011, which was attended by several thousand youths, organized around a shared identity as political subjects who were particularly affected by the crisis and holding the political class responsible for imposing the costs of the crisis on them. One slogan read 'Your Plunder,[5] Our Crisis' (Su Botín, Nuestra Crisis). Unusually for Madrid, they did not organize this in coalition with other social movement groups but, instead, used social media and social networks to appeal directly to youth. JSF cast youth issues as a social problem and social issues as a youth problem. The April 7th protest was the immediate precursor to 15-M and formed a jumping off point for the creation of the Real Democracy Now (DRY) platform (DRY, 2013), which called for the original protest in Madrid on 15 May 2011.

The JSF shows the importance of youth activism in the birth of 15-M, but JSF was influenced by other important precursor movements, some of which they had also participated in as representing issues of central concern to them. One key movement was the Movement for the Right to Housing, which began in 2003 and encompasses collectives such as *V de Vivienda* ('H for Housing' and a play on 'V for Vendetta') and the Platform for those Affected by Mortgages (PAH).[6] Initially, a platform that encompassed unions and political parties, by 2006 it had changed its composition and was mobilizing under the slogan of 'no acronyms, no flags' in reference to the desire to have no parties or unions 'advertising' at their protests (Haro and Sampedro, 2011), in keeping with autonomous principles. The PAH is currently one of the most active platforms against austerity measures in Spain, and JSF has collaborated closely with the PAH in support of their campaign for the reform of the mortgage law, which in Spain does not allow mortgage holders to cancel their debt upon repossession of their homes by the lender but, instead, holds them liable for the remainder of the debt. This law then plunges homeowners facing the loss of their homes into homelessness and

crippling debt. The PAH's main activities centre on a popular initiative pro-
posal to change the law on mortgages as well as providing information and
support for those facing evictions and mortgage payment problems. In contemporary Spain, where rates of suicide due to the loss of a home (with
widely publicized suicides by former homeowners throwing themselves off
their balconies as the bailiffs enter the premises to evict them) and rates of
repossession due to bankruptcy are skyrocketing, mortgage 'justice' is a key
social issue in the context of austerity cuts. Activists and supporters of the
PAH find a very receptive audience in the Spanish public for their claims
that current mortgage laws are unjust and inhumane and have adopted a
direct action tactic of the '*escrache*' or public shaming of politicians who fail
to support the proposed reform (Flesher Fominaya and Montañes Jiménez,
2014). The *escrache* tactic is controversial because it involves going to the
politicians' homes to protest rather than confining protest to the public
arena.

Also crucial were the 'cyberactivist' campaigns (in which Anonymous
were also active; see Chapter 5) against the Sinde Law that restricted Internet
freedom, regulating webpages and intellectual property rights. These campaigns were fuelled by the Free Culture movements very active in Spain prior
to 15-M. The campaign became *Nolesvotes* (or 'Don't vote for them'), a call
to boycott political parties who supported the Sinde Law, and evolved further to boycott all parties involved in corruption cases. These mobilizations
combined three important elements of the 15-M movement: high youth
involvement, the use of Internet activism to support street mobilizations and
the increasing focus on political corruption as a central mobilizing theme.
The strong overlap in activists in the initial 15-M and the *Nolesvotes* campaign is demonstrated by the high overlap in the Twitter hashtags used in
both movements (#nolesvotes and #spanishrevolution, the latter being one
of the most used and followed hashtags in 15-M) (Monterde, 2013;
Monterde and Postill, 2014). Also involved in the DRY platform were long-
standing groups active in the GJM such as Ecologistas en Acción (Ecologists
in Action) and ATTAC Spain.

On 15 May 2011, thousands of activists protested in the Puerta del Sol,
Madrid's central plaza. The original slogans on the posters calling for the
protest provide a good indication of the central demands and concerns of the
protesters and the frames they used to make their critique. A series of posters
declaring 'Take the Streets (*Toma la Calle*) 15.05.11' (echoing the 'Reclaim
the Streets' slogan of the British anti-roads movement, which in turn was
active in the GJM) offered citizens diverse reasons to join the protest, each
poster offering one of the reasons found in Box. 7.1. The main banner at the
front of the march read 'REAL DEMOCRACY NOW! We are not merchandise in the hands of politicians and bankers!', and protesters carried
myriad hand-painted signs reading such slogans as 'We are not anti-system,
the system is anti (against) us!', 'There is not enough bread for so much *chorizo*!' (*chorizo* is Spanish for 'sausage' and slang for 'thief'), and 'System error
404: Democracy Not Found'.[7]

Box 7.1 Real Democracy Now! 15-M call for protest poster slogans

TAKE THE STREETS

- Because while you pay taxes, the super wealthy avoid taxes in off-shore tax shelters

- Because you won't get a pension unless you have worked continuously for 35 years

- Because the minimum wage for a congressman is €3.996 per month

- Because almost 50 per cent of Spanish youth are unemployed

- Because we are not merchandise in the hands of politicians and bankers

- Because while your social rights (benefits) are being cut, they are giving banks public subsidies

- Because our politicians govern for the markets and not for the citizens

- Because our current electoral law benefits the major parties who have over 700 lawsuits for corruption

- [Because] when you don't have a job, your parents have no pension, your mortgage goes up, they take your house and you still owe the banks

- Because Spain's five largest banks posted €14 billion profit in 2010

- Because now corporate profits are an excuse for layoffs

Note: Translated by author from the Spanish originals, which can be viewed on http://www.democraciarealya.es/promocion/material-oficial/.

After the initial 15-M mass protest, a small group of about 40 activists decided to stay overnight and occupy the Puerta del Sol (Madrid's central plaza), partly in support of those protesters arrested during the demonstration and partly out of a desire to do more, becoming *Acampada Sol* (Sol Camp) (Romanos, 2013). As the discussion of the roots of 15-M shows, activists who decided to take the square and remain in the square were bringing with them a set of practices and principles developed over time in Madrid's autonomous social movement networks, including a strong commitment to *asamblearismo*, the name given to a deliberative and participatory political practice predicated on the sovereignty of the assembly as the primary deliberative and decision-making forum for collective action. This tradition has strong roots in Madrid's social movement scene and is consistent with the autonomous principles discussed in Chapter 3: a rejection of

Figure 7.2

15-M General Assembly, Puerta del Sol, Madrid

Copyright: Eduardo Romanos

representative democracy and majority rule and a prefigurative attempt to practise politics based on a participatory model; horizontal (non-hierarchical) structures; decision-making through consensus or common minimum agreements; a forum of an assembly (usually open); and rarely with permanent delegations of responsibility (Flesher Fominaya, 2005, 2007a, 2010b). A large number of the original activists in 15-M and those that organized the assemblies once the camp was under way and after the camps dissolved were related to Madrid's *Okupa* or squatted social centre scene (Martínez and García, 2011).

Over the next weeks, activists were joined by citizens young and old, many of them new to politics, to participate in a popular social experiment in deliberative politics following a consensus-based assembly format. Using a combination of face-to-face and online politics, participants contributed to a discussion about what the movement's demands should be. The protest rapidly spread to Barcelona and some 50 other Spanish cities. By 20 May, the *Acampada Sol* assembly had collated and distilled a wide-ranging set of demands for a preliminary 'open and collaborative' manifesto (Acampada Sol, 2011a), centred on the following themes:

- Political reform with an emphasis on eliminating the privileges of the political class and changing electoral law which favours the large parties

- Reducing unemployment
- The right to housing
- The right to high-quality public services, including health-care, education and public transportation
- Regulation of banks and financial institutions, nationalization of the banks that have been bailed out with public funds
- Fiscal reform, eliminating tax benefits for corporations and the super-wealthy
- Citizen freedom and right to political participation, including the abolition of the Sinde Law; mandatory public referenda on EU directives imposed on nation-state members; separation of powers between the legislative, judicial and executive branches of the state
- Decrease in military spending, defining the movement in pacifist terms.

There were also diverse items calling for a closing of nuclear installations, renewable energy, a separation of church and state, and a reference to the Movement for the Recovery of Historical Memory, which seeks to set right some of the outstanding injustices and legacies of the Franco dictatorship and help families locate their relatives' (killed in the Spanish Civil War and afterwards) remains.

This list highlights two things. The first is the centrality of demands for democratic reforms of a corrupt political class which are seen as inextricably linked to the critique of global capitalism, as in the case of Iceland, and the *responsibility* of the political classes in creating and mismanaging the crisis. Many of the demands are actually in respect of the Spanish Constitution – which guarantees the right to decent housing, for example. Article 128 of the Constitution, which reads 'all the nation's wealth in its different forms and whoever owns it is subordinated to the general interest', is explicitly referenced. The second is the presence of a wide-ranging set of long-term social movement demands of the many collectives in Madrid who were present in the 15-M movement from its inception, including environmentalists, anti-war activists and others involved in the GJM and subsequent movements. This is clearly distinct from the Icelandic case, where the movement was directly born out of the crisis, rather than reflecting a combination of firmly established actors with their own primary agendas that converge with a broader anti-austerity agenda. Despite the presence of already established collectives, 15-M was, for the most part, able to transcend internal differences to blend together in a broad collective identity around 15-M. Interestingly, in Italy, despite having a very strong initial university student impetus similar to that in Spain, the movement was unable to coalesce around a shared *Indignados* identity. Zamponi (2012) suggests that it was because established social movement actors were not willing to give up their particular agendas and identities, developed over the course of anti-austerity mobilizations, to merge into a shared political project.

Figure 7.3

A L'Oréal billboard is 'jammed' in Madrid. The Elvive shampoo brand has been altered to read 'The Revolution lives', and L'Oréal has become 'Real' Democracy, after losing the 'L' and the 'O'. Another sign reads 'The struggle is in the streets, not in the ballot boxes'

Copyright: Eduardo Romanos

After a few weeks, on 12 June 2011, in a move consistent with the move-ments' roots in local collectives, the Camp made a deliberate decision to leave the square rather than continue to resist repression, and return to the neighbourhoods to continue working in weekly local assemblies, organized around different themes (such as economy, general strike, short-term actions, coordination, education, feminism, migration and mobility).[8] (The theme-organized 'working group' is also a classic form of both autonomous and Institutional Left politics in Spain.) Although mass participation has declined, dozens of assemblies continued, and continue, to be organized every week. Perhaps even more striking than the assemblies – impressive as this level of civic participation is – is the way in which 15-M has spread to encompass and inspire a wide range of sectors of Spanish civil society to protest against austerity cuts. A series of 'colour tides' movements emerged, with different colours representing sectors such as health-care workers (white), education workers (green) and public library workers (yellow) as well as the *iaioflautas*, a movement of pensioners who engage in direct actions, including occupation of banks and public administration buildings (Cerrillo Vidal, 2013). One smaller '*marea*' has a transnational dimension yet is strongly rooted in the nation-state in terms of identity and this is the Maroon Tide (*Marea Granate*), named for the colour of the Spanish pass-port, which is made up of young 'financial exiles' linked to JSF and 15-M (Bollero, 2013). Under the slogan 'We are not leaving, we are being thrown out' (*No nos vamos, nos echan*), they protest what they consider to be their forced exile from Spain due to the lack of opportunities for youth caused by austerity cuts to student scholarships, social welfare cuts and high youth unemployment. The *Marea Granate* has small groups across Europe and Latin America and mobilizes on the 'global days of action' such as 'People United against the Troika' (the European Commission, International Monetary Fund and European Central Bank) on 1 June 2013.

15-M activists have engaged in a wide range of tactics and initiatives, including organizing solidarity economies (such as bartering systems); assis-tance for those affected by the crisis (such as people losing their homes); the creation of counter-information (such as 15-M wikipages listing all the poli-ticians in any party charged with corruption); direct actions (such as the *escraches* or politician shaming); and very active use of ICT platforms (such as Twitter, blogs, webpages and other forms of social media as well as live-streaming assemblies and the creation of digital archives of the movement). They have also used crowd-source funding to hire a lawyer to bring charges for fraud against Rodrigo Rato, former head of the IMF and President of Bankia, one of the banks bailed out by the state that also owned a high num-ber of mortgages over which citizens were evicted for being unable to pay (Democracy Now!, 2012).

15-M activists actively sought to reach a global audience through their global outreach teams using humour and creative forms of ICT-enabled communication to do so (Romanos, 2013). The original 15-M protest was followed by a number of other mass mobilizations, including a 19-J (19 June) 2011 anti-Euro pact protest that brought hundreds of thousands to the streets of Spain's major cities and a Global Day of Action in which many

Figure 7.4

The crowd reacts to a police helicopter flying overhead at the 19-J anti-austerity protests in Barcelona, Spain, in 2011

Copyright: Cristina Flesher Fominaya

cities across the world participated on 15 October 2011, 12 May 2012 and 13 October 2012. An estimated 2.2 million people in Spain participated in the movement, with participation increasing from the original May action to October (Castells, 2012).

Despite a strong commitment to non-violence, the evictions and protests were marred by police brutality, with the eviction of the Plaça de Catalunya in Barcelona resulting in 121 injured and one gravely injured (El Diario24, 2011; Europa Press, 2011). Other forms of repression included the cutting-off of water and WIFI near the camps and blocking access to the movement webpages in Madrid's public libraries (García de Blas, 2011).

Unlike the protests in Iceland, 15-M has not managed to have its central demands met. Yet, the 15-M movement has been extremely successful in encompassing and inspiring a vast part of Spanish civil society, as reflected in the many colour tides and in the acts of civil disobedience from certain local police and firefighter unions that have refused to conduct evictions and repression against demonstrators. However, the 15-M movement also faces challenges common to many grassroots movements; namely, how to keep up the mobilization and pressure to bring about real social change. Over time, mobilization has declined. 15-M also faces a classic dilemma for autonomous movements: the problem of co-optation by institutional actors hoping to gain political capital from grassroots protest. In a move all too familiar to observers of the Spanish social movement scene, one minority faction of the original assembly of Real Democracy Now! registered the name as a formal political association (Elola, 2012), violating the sovereignty of the assembly and prompting a series of clarifications from the original DRY spokespeople each time the press publicizes an act ostensibly called for or promoted by the 'DRY Association', especially their intention to form a political party along the lines of the 5-Star Movement in Italy, and establishing formal links with them (Sanz Paratcha, 2013).

The DRY dilemma highlights not only the classic problem of co-optation of grassroots social movements by institutional actors but also the ease with which ICTs enable the falsification and usurpation of webpages, accounts and movement icons and symbols (Chapter 5).

15-M has politicized or re-politicized a whole generation of activists and inspired activists around the world, just as the original 15-M protesters had themselves been inspired by protests in Europe, Latin America and the Arab Spring. One important movement that 15-M directly inspired and influenced was OWS, to which I now turn (For more on the 15-M movement see Flesher Fominaya 2020).

Figure 7.5

Occupy Boston protester holds sign with the now famous '99%' slogan, near Dewey Square encampment.

Copyright: Jeffrey S. Juris

Occupy Wall Street (OWS): US progressives respond to the crisis

OWS, in the US, was a somewhat belated response to the global financial crisis. By 2011, it seemed to many that the far-right Tea Party movement was offering the only vocal criticism of the handling of the crisis and, apart from criticizing the bailouts, their proposals, which revolve around minimizing the role of the state in safeguarding citizen welfare – such as reduction of government spending, reduction of taxes, elimination of health-care benefits and not using stimulus measures to assist in refinancing home mortgages – were clearly not in line with the spirit of the protesters in places such as Tahrir Square and the Puerta del Sol. Although there had been protests in the US around issues related to the crisis and its effects before OWS, there had not been a mass mobilization from progressives with a clear and cohesive identity. The most significant OWS precursor protest in the US with clear linkages to protest events elsewhere was the Walkerville encampment in Wisconsin, set up by public workers against Governor Walker's proposed bill that would strip them of collective bargaining rights (Altman, 2011). People from all over the world, including Egyptian activists, sent the protesters pizzas and messages of solidarity (Shiner, 2011). These protests then inspired the Bloombergville encampment in New York City against Mayor Bloomberg's austerity proposals (Castells, 2012). The Bloombergville encampment participants, together with New Yorkers Against Budget Cuts, would later become involved in the preparation for what was to become the OWS movement.

Just as 15-M did in Spain, OWS in 2011 had clear transnational inspiration, from the magazine *Adbusters*[9] that first proposed an occupation of Wall Street that read 'Are you ready for a Tahrir Moment?', to the direct participation of Spanish, Greek, Egyptian and other international activists in the OWS preparatory meetings (Kroll, 2011; Lawrence, 2012; Romanos, 2016). These preparatory meetings and the influence of Spanish autonomous activists inspired by 15-M were crucial in giving shape to OWS – in terms of both the establishment of a General Assembly that operated on a participatory consensus model and the framing of the movement as all-encompassing – in what would become the 'We are the 99%' slogan (Kroll, 2011; Lawrence, 2012; Romanos, 2016). But ideas and practices cannot be imported wholesale from elsewhere; they need to resonate and connect with established political cultures. The US has a long and rich tradition in deliberative and participatory movements (Epstein, 1991; Poletta, 2002), including the recent US experience of the GJM, which itself has been nourished and influenced by a flow of activists inspired by horizontal movements elsewhere, such as Argentina. Spanish and Greek activists expressed disappointment with the first General Assembly held on 2 August 2011 in Bowling Green Park, feeling it was too similar to an 'ordinary' rally, with speakers talking at people instead of truly exemplifying the spirit of the all-inclusive general assemblies in the 15- M and *Indignados* movements (Kroll, 2011). They were not alone in their feelings and, together with other US and international activists, committed to the idea of a consensus-based participatory assembly and shaped the establishment of a NYC General Assembly, which met on Saturdays in Tompkins Square Park.

On 17 September, the day *Adbusters* had called for the occupation of Wall Street, a few thousand people occupied Zuccotti Park near Wall Street and set up a tent city. As in 15-M, many of the OWS participants had experience with horizontal-style social movement practices in the context of the GJM (Juris, 2012) and other social movements practising consensus-style deliberative practices. They became active in the facilitation of the Working Groups and the General Assembly that organized the day-to-day workings of the OWS occupation (Costanza-Chock, 2012). The initial encampment was largely ignored by mainstream mass media (Castells, 2012). Yet, OWS (as with the protests in Tunisia, Egypt and Spain) managed to bypass the mainstream media and connect directly with a national and global public. In this, too, expertise gained from previous activist experience played a key role, as media activists drew on experience gained from Indymedia (see Chapter 5) and other citizen and activist media collectives (Costanza-Chock, 2012). OWS participants used a range of low-tech offline media production techniques combined with high-tech online tools and platforms to communicate with participants and to reach a global audience (Costanza-Chock, 2012). This combined with regular protest marches, the novelty of the three-month occupation, the creativity and humour of the protesters' slogans and actions, and the documented police repression (widely circulated on social networking sites) managed to generate significant sustained mass media attention. Live video streaming attracted up to 80,000 viewers per day from around the world (Costanza-Chock, 2012).

Long before the occupation of Zuccotti Park, Anonymous pledged its support for the occupation of Wall Street[11] and, later, when the movement faced police repression, took actions such as publishing the personal information of a police officer caught on video pepper spraying a peaceful protester. In a video threatening the NYPD, they refer to 'what happened to the police force in Egypt when they disregarded human rights'.

The OWS NY protests were nowhere near as large as those in Spain or Greece and did not manage to garner such high levels of public support (about 28 per cent, according to an NBC poll cited in Castells (2012) as opposed to about 76 per cent in Spain).[12] According to participants, it also suffered from some classic problems associated with consensus-based decision-making – such as fatigue caused by endless meetings and too much talk and too little action for some participants' taste (Gitlin, 2012). The fetishization of consensus as an end in itself as opposed to a means to an end was a criticism levelled not only at OWS but also in 15-M.

Despite adopting the General Assembly model used in Spain's 15-M, and even referring to a produced guide by 15-M for managing assemblies, OWS was in many ways quite different. One difference was that OWS accepted financial support from donations (some $300,000 remaining after the eviction), leading to debates about to what use the money should be put. Autonomous activists in Spain, in contrast, favour a more Do-It-Yourself approach and are generally very sceptical about financial contributions that are not specifically earmarked *beforehand* for a particular use. Another key difference was an emphasis on occupation for occupation's sake. Hammond

Figure 7.6

Occupy Wall Street demonstrators hold hand-made signs in Zuccotti Park, New York City.

Copyright: James Jasper

(2013) argues that some activists in Zuccotti were so concerned with remaining in the park they gave little thought to what would happen once the park was actually evicted. Activists in the Puerta del Sol, by contrast, deliberately left the central plaza to return to the neighbourhood assemblies, in a move very much in keeping with Madrid's alternative social movement culture (Flesher Fominaya, 2015a). While OWS also produced important off-shoot groups that continue to be active, and re-energized many existing ones, it was not followed by the dozens of weekly local assemblies with hundreds of participants – as had been the case in Madrid – reflecting differences in associational contexts prior to the occupation.

The Occupation tactic *per se* is by its very nature easily replicated across contexts yet, paradoxically, somewhat limited in its scope for participation. While the creation of a public agora in a central location is potentially inclusive, the long-term occupation of a central urban space is not, in that only people with the means and availability to remain in the square can do so. Despite the best efforts to create a welcoming space for children and people with diverse living situations, people with family responsibilities, or who cannot give up their jobs to occupy, are unable to camp out over long periods of time, even if they can participate in the assemblies.

On the other hand, the creation of Occupy-style encampments provides a public space that brings diverse members of the community together in new ways to discuss and debate important political issues. The use of ICT-enabled media means that the extension of the occupation reaches beyond

Figure 7.7

Occupy Boston participants play music outside their tent.

Copyright: Jeffrey S. Juris

the physical space itself, and this aspect was very actively pursued in Tahrir, in the Puerta del Sol, and in OWS.[13] As the description of Occupy Boston by Juris (2012) shows, occupation of the central squares does not involve just milling around waiting for a general assembly. As with the anti-roads protest camps described in Chapter 4, Occupy encampments are places in which people can not only debate a rich variety of topics and experience but also express themselves in myriad ways, including performances, organize the internal life of the camp and plan for protest marches.

Juris (2012: 265) also describes the heterogeneous nature of participants who had to negotiate tensions not only between historical class and racial divides but also between 'mostly white progressive religious and peace communities, various anarchist and socialist formations, and existing social and economic justice spaces'.

OWS spread rapidly across the US, with a remarkable 462 local 'occupies' with Occupy Boston, Occupy Oakland and the occupations on various University of California campuses drawing attention for their strength, impact and/or levels of police repression. Participating in Occupy encampments, large or small, can have a life-transforming impact on participants and communities. Participants in Occupy Windsor,[14] in Canada – a 'small' Occupy that is just one of hundreds in the global list – spoke of how the occupation of a local park brought together people from all walks of life and forged personal and political bonds that have carried over into other protest campaigns such as 'Idle No More', which brings together Canada's first nation peoples and their supporters to protest against legislative abuses of indigenous treaty rights and for socio-economic and environmental justice. Participants stressed the wrong-headedness of attempting to quantify or measure 'success' or 'failure' for the Occupy movements based on measurable changes in policy or government. Instead, the focus has been the many new connections forged during the encampments, the sense of solidarity and the political revitalization of local communities.[15]

OWS inspired activists not only in the US but also around the world. The two discursive symbols of OWS, 'We are the 99%' and the 'Occupy' label, had a phenomenal global diffusion, being adopted even in movements such as 15-M which predated OWS.

The Arab Spring, European *Indignados* and Occupy: Global wave or global movement?

Protest waves have been of interest to historians, political scientists, international relations scholars and sociologists since at least 1848, when contemporary observers spoke of a 'springtime of peoples'. Palmer's (1964) ground-breaking work on the 'Atlantic revolutions' of the late eighteenth century (USA, France, Haiti, Ireland – 1798) also contributed to scholarship on global waves. Over time, new 'waves' have attracted scholarly interest (e.g. European anti-fascism, de-colonization movements in Asia and Africa 1968, post-soviet transitions 1989–91, Latin America's 'pink tide'). Previous waves lacked the political diversity and geographical scope of current global protests, often being concentrated within a particular international political regime (i.e. Soviet bloc) or geographical area (Europe, Latin America). Classic Marxist and world-systems approaches (e.g. Halperin, 2004) link these waves to changing balances of power between popular forces and states, driven by underlying economic shifts. Others, such as Skocpol (1979), focus on breakdowns in particular international relations regimes, whereas Katsiaficas (1987) focused on the cross-boundary diffusion of the movements, and Castells (2004) highlighted the role of communications tools, as did Linebaugh and Rediker (2001) in relation to the mercantile processes of the early-modern Atlantic. By necessity or choice, many of the studies have relied on historical, secondary or macro data. This has limited their ability to provide a systematic theorization of why such waves should occur at all and what factors explain their particular timing, geographical reach and movement characteristics. Therefore, despite substantial scholarship on global waves of protest, the term itself has not yet been systematically or coherently defined.

Defining global waves and global movements

I consider a global wave of protest to be temporally bound (in that related protests are overlapping or sequential within a period of time), responding to a certain extent to a common macro political-economic context, and with significant levels of transnational diffusion between movements. This allows for a discussion of commonalities across cases while retaining recognition of national specificities and differences. For this wave, for example, this allows for a common discussion of the pro-democracy and anti-austerity protests in Europe and the pro-democracy movements in the Arab Spring while highlighting significant differences in the effect of the global financial crisis and the meaning of democracy between regions.

A global wave of protest, then, is not synonymous with a global movement, which I defined in Chapter 2 as 'those movements that are heterogeneous, diverse and global in scope; who explicitly link their activism to a recognition of the interconnectedness of issues that are a result of globalization processes, and are therefore anti-systemic rather than single issue; and who self-identify as belonging to a global movement that is committed to collective action and protest ultimately to transform the whole world, rather than just parts of it'.

I believe this series of mass mobilizations in many different places around the world is a global wave of protest, although not a global movement in the sense that the GJM was (see Chapter 3), in that it is marked by a roughly contemporaneous series of nationally rooted protest movements with strong transnational diffusion processes, but neither primarily driven by transnational networks of actors or transnational organizational infrastructures nor characterized primarily by a transnationally organized series of protest events. This global wave is also what Tarrow (1998) has called a *cycle of contention*, characterized by a rapid diffusion of collective action, innovation in forms of contention, shared new major frames of meaning, discourse and action, the incorporation of new unorganized actors (people new to protest) with organized actors and increased contention between challengers and authorities. Although I have only discussed in depth the cases of Iceland, Tunisia, Egypt, Spain and OWS, this wave also encompasses a wide range of mobilizations in the Arab world, mass student protests in Chile (Smink, 2011), Mexico (Candón Mena, 2012), Italy (Zamponi, 2012), UK (Halvorsen, 2012), Portugal (Baumgarten, 2013) and Canada (Annis, 2012), mass protests in Greece (Lekakis and Kousis, 2013; Sergi and Vogiatzoglou, 2013) and Brazil, and Occupy movements in Australia (Jackson and Chan, 2012; Humphrys, 2013), Canada, Slovenia, Germany, Belgium, France, Ireland, Israel and many more, some 462 local 'Occupy's in the US (Mother Jones, 2011) and over 80 countries and 1000 cities taking part in the Global Day of Action on 15 October 2011.[16]

Arguments for a global wave

Many key elements are shared across contexts, further strengthening the argument for viewing this as a global wave:

- Shared *master frames*, epitomized by common slogans and symbols such as *Indignados!*, *We are the 99%*, *Occupy everywhere* and *Bread, freedom and human dignity*. At the heart of all the protests is an inextricable *linking* of the notion of ineffective, insufficient or deficient *democracy* and the negative effects of *neoliberal global capitalism*. The financial crisis is explicitly linked to a crisis of democracy.

- *Prefigurative action* (see Chapter 1) is another common element, whether through deliberative and participatory democracy in assemblies such as in the 15-M and Occupy movements; alternative solidarity economies such as bartering and exchange systems and support systems for precarious and vulnerable people suffering the effects of the crisis; or the self-organization of tent cities around shared principles of respect and mutual cooperation from Tahrir Square to OWS.

- The shared use of the *tactic of occupation* of central plazas or emblematic sites in front of or near seats of political and economic power, or in sites where austerity measures are cutting funding such as universities, unites all of these movements. The tactic is powerful, symbolically charged and quickly and easily replicated, with a strong unmediated transgressive and Do-It-Yourself (DIY) ethos that infuses all of these mobilizations. Occupation is much more than just a tactic but also involves creating a new agora which extends beyond the actual physical site. Reclaiming public *space* (as in Take the streets! and Occupy!) and engaging in a politics of space are also central. While neither occupation nor reclaiming the streets is new, such a widespread adoption of these tactics across multiple sites is.

- *Autonomy* as a central organizing principle also characterizes all of these movements, reflecting a shared critique of representative political systems and a commitment to the power of grassroots mobilization and giving voice to ordinary people. Whereas the critique of representative democracy is much more marked in Europe and North America, the mobilizations in the Arab world also demand a voice for the common people. In all cases, the mobilizations were led by non-institutional actors as opposed to established political parties and unions.[17]

- A *shared collective identity* also characterized these movements (and could be seen as an argument for understanding this as a global movement) – this collective identity was explicitly invoked by protesters in one site referring to protesters in another and linking their struggles, from solidarity pizzas from Tahrir Square activists to Wisconsin, to signs held by Spanish activists saying 'We too can be Iceland'.

- The wave was characterized by a *global circulation of information, resources, ideas, practices, tactics and people,* not only through indirect diffusion processes (such as with social and mass media) but also in the direct transnational face-to-face interactions of protesters from one site to the other, as in the case of international activists in the origins of OWS or the training of April 6th movement activists in Egypt by members of Serbian-based Otpor! (Foran, 2014).

Explaining the emergence of the global wave

Four key explanations have been given to explain the global wave, all of which I believe should be seen as factors operating synergistically rather than as competing explanations: the global financial crisis as definitive contextual factor, the development of oppositional political cultures of resistance, specific transnational diffusion processes and the creative use of ICTs and other forms of media.

The global financial crisis as definitive contextual factor

Crisis does not *cause* mass protest (if it did, we would have seen it earlier and in all places affected by the crisis, and we would not have seen it in places such as Australia where the crisis has yet to 'hit' (Humphrys, 2013). Yet, some of these protests *were* a direct response to the crisis and the protester demands were directly linked to both the crisis and the austerity measures imposed in the name of the crisis. In other cases, the connection is less direct. As has been discussed in relation to Tunisia and Egypt, while increases in food prices and other economic impacts of the global downturn may have exacerbated conditions for many people and increased their proclivity to protest, the demands, dynamic and nature of the protests are clearly tied to long-standing structural and political problems. Foran (2014) argues that these recent mobilizations need to be understood in the context of the increasing awareness of the 'glaring contradictions of neoliberal capitalist globalization'.

The development of oppositional political cultures of resistance

As the discussion in this chapter shows, the emergence of mass mobilizations is not possible without the development of oppositional political cultures of resistance and the historical legacies of previous movements. These oppositional political cultures develop what Foran (2014) calls 'threads of resistance' that are woven together – in particular, (rare) historical moments that manage to bring diverse oppositional cultures together around a shared goal. In all of the contexts of sustained mass mobilization discussed in this chapter, diverse movements were able to first *transcend* their particular differences (identitarian, ideological, issue-focus) to coalesce around a common goal and then *encompass* broad, previously non-active sectors of civil society within a shared identification with the movement and its main goals and frames.

Specific transnational diffusion processes

While these processes took place within specific local and national contexts, the movements grew, gained legitimacy and spread through specific transnational diffusion processes, including indirect (e.g. accessing information through the Internet or television) and direct (e.g. direct interaction between activist networks) mechanisms of diffusion. The political science term 'demonstration effect', which refers to the effect observing events elsewhere has on behaviour, is particularly apropos when describing contagion effects between mass demonstrations. In describing the global wave of protests in 1968, Katsiaficas (1987), drawing on Marcuse's notion of *political eros*, speaks of the 'eros effect', whereby, at certain points in time, universal, as opposed to individualistic, interests become generalized and shared across vast distances, and actions in one place around these universal goals (such as peace, social justice, liberty) inspire and influence others to act for the same goals.[18]

The creative use of ICTs and other forms of media

All of these mobilization and diffusion processes were facilitated, enabled and shaped by the creative use of ICTs and other forms of media by activists and participants. The combination of online and offline activism generated an autonomous hybrid space for mass public contestation, and the speed of transmission and the scope of the protests cannot be understood without recognizing the role of ICTs.

The mobilizations in this global wave shared many commonalities across contexts, were explicitly and demonstrably linked by specific transnational processes and reached a global audience. Yet, the local and national contexts – including regime type, structural conditions, protest cultures and levels of repression – all shaped the dynamics and outcomes of the protests in very particular ways. Even the shared emphasis on autonomy, for example, was understood and embodied in different ways across contexts (e.g. Spain and OWS) rather than being a self-contained and homogeneous organizing principle. These protests were clearly rooted in a politics of *place*, and symbols such as national flags were significant emblems of the importance of national historical legacies and the reclaiming of the nation-state (Sergi and Vogiatzoglou, 2013), as were cultural symbols with deep roots in the national movement histories, such as the singing of 'We shall overcome' in OWS.

Global wave of anti-austerity and pro-democracy movements: A continuation from the GJM or a new wave?

Many observers have noted the similarity between the two key critiques of the GJM (democracy and global capitalism) and the claims of the global wave of anti-austerity and pro-democracy movements (Della Porta, 2012; Shihade *et al.*, 2012). This raises the question of whether the current wave is a continuation or revival of this previous wave or whether it represents something qualitatively different. It is clear that there is continuity of actors, social movements, activist networks, master frames and participatory repertoires of deliberation from the GJM to the current wave (see e.g. Abdelrahman, 2011; Romanos, 2013; Flesher Fominaya, 2017).

Long-established political opposition cultures are being remobilized but now in a very different context of global financial crisis. This context has shifted the receptivity of the public towards the anti-neoliberal capitalist critique and the calls for greater democracy and socio-economic justice, particularly in those contexts where people are feeling strong effects of the crisis. There are also some clear qualitative differences between the GJM and the current wave of protests. The most striking, in my view, is that the state has once again resumed centre stage. This aspect of this wave of protest manifests itself in a number of ways, discursively, tactically, spatially and in the repertoires of action. The GJM activists' dominant critique of global capitalism and lack of responsiveness of economic and political elites to the will and needs of the people was almost always pitched to abstract financial process (global capitalism) and/or transnational or supranational actors (e.g. World

Trade Organization, IMF). During the period of the GJM, the social theories of cosmopolitanism and globalization and the dominant movement narratives both stressed the transnational and global dimensions of power, stressed the limits of national sovereignty and, therefore, underplayed or ignored the role of national elites in active implementation of the neoliberal capitalist agenda. It is not that supranational actors are ignored in this wave; there are still protests organized against the European Central Bank, the IMF and the EU Commission, which are singled out and blamed for imposing austerity measures. What is different now is the way in which protesters are explicitly making visible the *overlap* between the economic and political classes and the role of national political classes in fomenting these global or supranational processes. If the master narratives of the GJM often bypassed the state as less important, if not downright irrelevant, now activists are *reclaiming* state democracy. They are making visible the neoliberal state, which Harvey (2011: 7) defines as one that 'facilitates conditions for profitable capital accumulation on the part of both domestic and foreign capital'.

Perhaps the clearest example of this is the reaction of Icelandic demonstrators to the attempt by the directors of the Icelandic Central Bank to absolve themselves of responsibility for the national crisis, invoking global financial capitalist processes over which they had no control. Icelanders refused to accept their excuses – instead, bringing charges against them for their role in destroying the economy. Whoever is right in that debate, clearly the dominant narrative across protests in this wave is that national politicians are directly implicated in the crisis and in implementing harsh anti-austerity measures that pass the bill to ordinary citizens for corporate welfare extended to the banks and other financial institutions. The bringing of charges against former IMF head and Bankia president Rodrigo Rato is another example of this. This master narrative, which establishes an explicit link between nation-state actors and global financial processes, therefore represents a significant departure from the GJM.

While the GJM's most visible encounters were transnationally organized counter-summit protests focused on transnational or multilateral actors, in this wave the nation-state and, more precisely, the centres of state and economic power, be they parliament squares or Wall Street in the US, are the focus and locus of protest. Space, and its occupation, has become a crucial element of symbolic and tactical importance. If reclaiming the streets was crucial in the GJM, reclaiming the squares and symbolic centres of democracy has been of key importance in this wave. The decision to occupy public space for a long period of time in order to engage actively with the public also represents a departure from the most common models of protest which, in the GJM, tended to be organized more within 'movement' spaces (such as squatted social centres, in Europe) and then mobilized for a short term in the streets. The reclaiming of the state, or what I have called the 'democratic turn' (Flesher Fominaya, 2015a), also represents a key departure for autonomous activists, at least in Europe, where the corruption of the state was regarded as a reason to refuse engagement with it for the most part, to reject it outright as illegitimate rather than demand its reform. At the same time, the autonomous desire to engage in unmediated politics, however, has found new expression in the widespread adoption of social media as a mobilizing tool. Activists in Spain, for example, deliberately embraced the use of social media for its unmediated nature (Romanos, 2016); that is, whereas alternative radical media is still channelled through particular social movement collectives, social media flows through networks with the direct intervention of individuals, eliminating moderators and middle-men.

The state of crisis has also encouraged the development of strong cultures of solidarity and creative alternative economies as a direct means of engaging with the needs of people who are suffering. In Spain, for example, in the *corralas* movement, political squatting and needs-based squatting have come together in new ways, with occupations of empty buildings by families in need being organized collectively along the lines of squatted social centres and with a clear political agenda: demands for social housing for the most needy as a basic right (Cenizo, 2013). In Malaga, a sign outside the occupied building reads: 'We don't open the door to the police. This is our home. This is our right.'

In Cantabria, Spain, firefighters have engaged in civil disobedience, refusing to participate in the eviction of those losing their homes (EFE, 2013). In Catalonia, Spain, they have faced riot police demonstrating in opposition to the cuts and in Pamplona, another Spanish city, firefighters donated one day of their pay to the assembly of unemployed workers and the local food bank. Riot police in Madrid sabotaged 97 of their own vans to prevent the riot police from being called out during protests by civil servants in 2012 (Barroso, 2012).

Finally, the biggest change from the GJM has been the levels of public support for these mobilizations. However media-worthy and impressive the GJM protests, they never managed to win the support of such high numbers of the public, nor did they encompass such wide sectors of civil society.

Conclusion

Challenges and outcomes of the 'global wave'

Where now for this global wave? In June 2013, when I first wrote this chapter, protesters in Taksim Square, Istanbul, Turkey, calling their campaign 'Occupy Gezi Park' (Saka, 2013), were being routed by riot police, with two dead, several blinded and hundreds injured (*Hürriyet Daily News*, 2013; Roar Collective, 2013). In Hong Kong, China, an Occupy movement for universal suffrage continued to grow despite arrests and repression (Tatlow, 2013). On 4 June 2013, tens of thousands of people defied the authorities and participated in a candlelight vigil under the pouring rain in Hong Kong's Victoria Park to commemorate the military's massacre of pro-democracy activists and students at Tiananmen Square in Beijing in 1989. In Istanbul, what began as a peaceful 'occupy' protest against a park (Gezi Park) being destroyed to make way for a shopping mall in a central square with a few hundred people in tents with their families, swelled to hundreds of thousands of people joining in as police brutality transformed the protest into a much wider rejection of authoritarian government (Farro and Demirhisar, 2014).

Tens of thousands of demonstrators of all ages banged on pots and pans (as in Iceland) and faced water cannon, tanks, pepper spray and barricades. Residents placed supplies for the protesters on their windowsills, and people created a 'wall of needs' where food and water were left for those who needed them. One striking image of the demonstrations shows a woman dressed in traditional Turkish garb wearing an 'Anonymous' mask.

The political outcomes of these mobilizations vary greatly from one context to another and range from changes in policy or governments to changes in the parameters of public debate and the politicization of a new generation of activists. As with the retrenchment of authoritarian power in Egypt, where protests continued in the face of brutal and systematic repression, not all gains are long-lived. On 30 June 2013, tens of thousands of protesters again took to the Tahrir Square, and in other cities across Egypt, demanding that President Morsi call early elections, and with protesters chanting for him to resign. Morsi was ousted in a military coup and ultimately replaced by President el-Sisi, a former general who has instituted a brutal regime greatly curtailing human rights in Egypt. The result if anything was worse than what Egyptians had *before* Tahrir's revolt against Mubarak, or under Morsi, a crushing disillusionment for the protesters and so many who gave their lives for greater democracy and justice in Egypt. Iceland too has been through several political turns: the centre-right parties widely blamed for Iceland's economic meltdown in 2008 were again voted into government in the 2013 elections. As we saw in Chapter 6, one unintended (for progressive activists at least) response to the global wave has been the resurgence and retrenchment of fascist, authoritarian and anti-democratic movements and the rise of far-right political parties.

Whatever the precise (narrowly defined) political outcomes in the short and long term, the biographical outcomes, the political cultural outcomes and the effects on communities that have come together in new ways are potentially great and longer-lasting. The intense feeling of shared emotions during collective action is a well-documented phenomenon and has implications for future political activism as well as for a newfound sense of community. The experiencing of collective emotions through collective action (anger, outrage and indignation but also hope, joy and solidarity) have now been experienced by masses of people and have, if nothing else, awakened a sense of possibility in many of them. Perhaps the clearest, yet intangible, outcome of this wave of mobilizations is the politicization of civil society, a widespread participation and engagement with politics from a diverse cross-section of society in a newly created agora.

In one way, the mass participation in these protests around the world is the fulfilment of the aspirations of many actors in the GJM who hoped to counter the seemingly unshakeable belief that global neoliberal capitalism was the only ideology around which to organize modern life. That ideology, it seems, is now being questioned by masses of people around the world who demand a new logic based on human needs rather than corporate profit. The message to 'put people first' and to deepen democracy runs clearly through all the protests here and in all likelihood will be a master frame that will be present in some of those that are yet to come. What alternatives or changes people will be able to create in addition to the particular gains made in many areas is an open question. Participants in these movements who have already concluded their occupations face the same questions always faced by activists once a particular episode of mobilization is over: how to keep going after the square has been evicted, after some of the movements' demands have been met, after repression has enacted too high a cost to keep a presence in the streets, after the last protester has gone home? One answer is through the revitalization of myriad political projects at the local and national level, which has clearly happened in some cases. Another is to build a truly 'global' movement along the lines of the GJM and, indeed, a number of initiatives have been attempted.

As in the GJM, activists in these movements have been criticized for being too vague in their demands or for having too many demands or having the wrong demands, all of which are seen as diminishing the potential effectiveness of the movements. In response, some activists have highlighted the *prefigurative* nature of the movement, arguing that the process is the message or that the movement is its own demand. But if it is true that 'freedom is an endless meeting' (as the saying from the 1960s US movement Students for a Democratic Society goes), it is also true that many people do not have the time or desire to commit to 'endless meetings' and look for other options. In this vein, some have pressed for a more institutionalized channelling of the movements' energy, even into movement-based political parties, such as the Syriza Party in Greece, the Pirate Party in Iceland or the Green Parties before them (still active in many countries). For many, however, the desire to remain encompassing and inclusive means remaining resolutely non-partisan, whereas a widely shared belief in autonomy makes any form of institutionalization unpalatable. Political parties such as the 5-Stelle (5-Star) movement party in Italy have seen, in the twin crises of the economy and democracy, a political opportunity to make the electoral leap into parliament and like Podemos in Spain, have successfully converted that opportunity into parliamentary representation. Detractors feel this is simply opportunism, in line with the co-optation so frequently experienced by social movements; supporters feel it is an opportunity to reform the political system from the inside. As I discussed in Chapter 3 in the context of the GJM, these tensions and cleavages are long-standing and are unlikely to be resolved any time soon. In the meantime, activists all around the world from Chile to Lebanon, from Hong Kong to Iraq, continue to fight for socio-economic justice and greater democracy, suggesting that the movement wave described in this chapter is still going strong.

CONCLUSION

One goal of this book has been to expand our understanding of social movements' importance and 'success' beyond the narrowly defined arena of the political. Earlier scholarly definitions of social movement success have been too focused on policy outcomes and state or institutional responses to social movement demands and actors (Amenta *et al.*, 2019; Guigni, 2008). While the state is an important target for many social movements, policy or legal changes are not necessarily the best indicators of social movement impact or of social change more broadly (one only has to remember the old joke that any country with the word 'Democratic' in its name is guaranteed not to be). Despite a 'cultural turn' in social movement studies, practices of cultural resistance and change are often marginalized in favour of more overtly political aspects of mobilization (Amenta *et al.*, 2019, Van Dyke and Taylor, 2019). While political gains are often short-lived (e.g. one government or leader is forced to resign only to be re-elected a short while later; a law is changed only to be reinstated), cultural changes are often much slower to show effects but more durable once achieved (i.e. the increasing status of women in many parts of the world, despite important backlashes, set-backs and sexist movements). However, not all social movements develop in a linear progression: I have heard many activists despair over having to raise the same issues (such as women's equality) that they raised 30 years ago. Rights hard won through centuries of grassroots struggle can be eroded or reversed by changes in government or Supreme Court decisions. Democracy, it would appear, is not a fixed state but needs to be defended and continually nourished, and in this social movements can play a key role.

We are living in turbulent times, and the threats to democracy are great and coming from several directions. These include many that have been discussed in this book, including the rise of authoritarian tendencies in states and movements; the increase in criminalization of protest and restriction of democratic freedoms even in democratic states; the interference in elections by 'hackers' and trolls (as in the 2016 US election, see Chapter 5); the manipulation of political opinions on social media platforms (e.g. the Cambridge Analytica scandal in the BREXIT campaign); the proliferation of 'fake' news and the ease with which lies and misinformation spread across the media ecosphere; the troubling threats to internet freedoms, data injustice, data extraction and commodification; politically motivated denial of service by corporations which opens the door to extra-legal public-private partnerships to censor whistle-blower media outlets (as in the case of WikiLeaks, discussed in Chapter 5); or the criminalization of solidarity and humanitarian action (see Chapter 6).

Rapid changes in technological advances, shifts in geopolitical configurations, alarming rates of environmental degradation and habitat loss, climate change, global increasing social inequalities and labour precariousness, changes in migration flows, new patterns of cultural production, integration and resistance, all fuelled by neoliberal economic globalization, have created new areas of contestation and provided new challenges and opportunities for social movements.

In such a scenario, it can seem that there is little point in engaging in protest or collective action, that the costs are too high, the risks and challenges too great. Despite all these challenges, the commitment to democracy as a value and a system remains very strong among citizens of the world. Social movements are key players in these turbulent times, as either actors who fuel the crisis of democracy by advocating for greater division and hatred of others, such as radical right-wing movements, or actors who shake up the political establishment by demanding greater or 'real' democracy as with so many of the movements of the squares following the global crash. Social movement actors have risen to all the challenges above and many more besides: activists continue to challenge the rise of the radical right, the continued encroachment on privacy, the commodification of data, the criminalization of protest. Media activists create websites and Twitter accounts to flag fake news, hackers and whistle-blowers uncover political corruption and injustices, pro-migrant activists rescue migrants drowning in the Mediterranean, feminists denounce gender-based violence and engage in pedagogical work to shift bias in its media reporting, anti-austerity activists make sure citizens understand what is happening with bailouts and austerity measures, schoolchildren skip school to lead the charge against government inaction on climate change, Black Lives Matter activists put systemic racial injustices on the political agenda, women in India join hands for hundreds of miles across the country to demand gender equality and an end to sexist violence. The list is endless. In all of these instances, effective and sustained collective action and mobilization require commitment, hard work and the ability to keep going despite many challenges and defeats. Given the sorry state of the world in so many important ways, asking whether social movements make any difference is a valid question. As I discussed in Chapter 1, it is hard to clearly measure social movements, impact on policy, politics, society, economics or culture or to trace a direct line of influence from a specific movement to specific impact. But what I hope to have shown in this book is that regardless of our ability to 'measure' their impact neatly, social movements matter and are a *sine qua non* for democracy. I want to illustrate this further by returning to the example of Spain's anti-austerity and pro-democracy movement to show the wide range of effects a movement can have.

Central to the 15-M movement's visions and demands was the need to transform really existing democracy into what activists called 'real democracy'. In part, 15-M activists were making clear policy demands. Governments, through policy, determine groups that are worthy and unworthy beneficiaries of action on their behalf (Meyer, 2003). Those deemed unworthy are neglected through inaction or become the targets of punitive or paternalistic action. Social movements challenge these classifications, expanding (or restricting) the range of worthy beneficiaries of state attention. They define and attempt to legitimate groups often excluded from consideration such as the marginalized or dispossessed. In the face of mass evictions and foreclosures following the global financial crash, for example, anti-austerity and housing activists associated with the 15-M movement demanded social housing for people who had lost their homes because of foreclosure, framing them as victims of the crisis who deserve state attention. Social movements play a role in the policy arena by agenda setting and framing social problems. Although they did not manage to significantly change housing policy or social provision directly in the short term, they did manage to shift public opinion and pressure to keep housing at the top of the political agenda. When a former housing activist was elected mayor of Barcelona, a victory that would not have been possible without the support and impact of the 15-M movement (Font and García Espín, 2019; Faus, 2016), her government took proactive measures against the housing crisis at the municipal level. Yet, as I discussed in Chapter 1, the impact of movements on policy and politics is often mediated rather than direct, partly through shifts in public opinion that put pressure on governments (whether governments *respond* to that pressure, or do so in line with movement demands, is a different matter and many contextual factors affect outcomes; see Amenta *et al.*, 2019).

Policies are important, of course, but I want now to offer some examples of why a purely instrumental approach to evaluating social movements, and a focus on 'success' understood in these terms, runs the risk of missing their full significance. 15-M activists who took to the squares of Spain to demand 'real democracy now!' and to protest against austerity cuts were indeed entering into a direct dispute with the state, and engaging in civil disobedience to do it, but not only to demand specific policy changes or concessions. If that had been the sole motivator, it is doubtful that the movement would have continued to maintain its pressure on the government, since they achieved very little (or nothing) in the way of explicit demands or being taken seriously as a political challenger in the short term. Instead, participants in the movement challenged not only specific austerity policies but the underlying logic of those policies, a logic that, through its justification of the need to dismantle welfare state provisions and prioritize private over public interests, reinforced a competitive model of existence constructed around winners and losers and insiders and outsiders. Such a logic shapes each individual's relation not only to the state but to each other and to themselves; that is, it shapes notions of citizenship and belonging, social relations, and personal identity.

15-M activists sought to redefine the underlying social values of austerity politics: in the face of competition, they advocated solidarity, and when told the public had to fund private bank rescues, they demanded that people's welfare should be the most important political priority. For activists in the movement then, it wasn't a question of debating issues such as whether or not immigrants should or should not be able to access public health-care or social services, or whether this or that social service should be cut, but rather to question what sort of society we want to live in and what priorities or values should guide the way that society is organized. But they did this in a way that reclaimed democratic institutions and rights – such as highlighting the rights to decent housing established in the Spanish Constitution – as well as calling for change.

Arguably the greatest impact of anti-austerity resistance in the public sphere has been the challenge to hegemonic narratives that justified the crisis, austerity policies and the neoliberal order. In Spain, these counter-hegemonic narratives have been mobilized through many forms of mediated and embodied contestation. Spain's 15-M initial slogan was 'We are not merchandise in the hands of politicians and bankers. Real Democracy Now!' With this slogan, the 15-M movement opposed the market fundamentalism or neoliberal capitalist logic that justified austerity policies and the bailouts with a demand for a democracy that put government and policy at the service of citizens' needs.

One of the crucial features of the 15-M movement's discourse was the framing of a collective identity (a 'we') that was elastic, ambiguous, open and inclusive, constituted around notions of 'we the people' and ordinary citizens (Errejón, 2015; Flesher Fominaya, 2015a; Tejerina and Perugorría, 2012). In addition, the movement played a crucial role in defining the 'them' against which they mobilized, political and economic elites that abused their power for self-interest and against the direct interest of the people and, adding insult to injury, passing on the cost of their 'crisis/swindle' to hardworking people. The movement's counter-hegemonic (or 'anti-systemic' if we adopt the terminology used by political elites) discourse unleashed a public struggle over the meaning of 'legitimate democracy' (Flesher Fominaya, 2015b).

Social movements create and disseminate new repertoires of action, new 'cultural codes' as Melucci (1986) put it. In the camps of the squares, participants experimented with prefigurative politics, modelling participatory and deliberative forms of democratic dialogue, debate and decision-making. Feminists introduced the use of the universal plural feminine (as opposed to the universal masculine plural), which became widespread in social movement milieux. The shared experience of the camp politicized many newcomers to activism and political engagement, forged new alliances between participants and led to the creation of new groups and civic and political projects that emerged and lasted beyond the mobilization in the plazas. This contributed to the creation of 'critical communities' where the new ideas cultivated in movement spaces influence and spread through academia and intellectual and cultural production (Van Dyke and Taylor, 2019). The aftermath of 15-M in Spain included the creation of new cooperative critical news outlets and strengthening of existing ones, transforming the mass media landscape significantly (Flesher Fominaya and Gillan, 2017). This is an example of how social movements can have powerful cultural consequences even when they fail to reach their goals (Van Dyke and Taylor, 2019). On a personal or biographical level, shared experiences in emotionally charged mobilization processes can have long-lasting effects (Fernández-Savater and Flesher Fominaya, 2017; Passy and Monsch, 2019). In a process common to many movements (Van Dyke and Taylor, 2019), 15-M also produced new collective identities and a 15-M 'way of doing politics' (Flesher Fominaya, 2019).

Another way social movements have an influence on the world is by inspiring and influencing social movements elsewhere, even if they are not 'successful'. Prior to planning the protest and setting up the Madrid Acampada Sol camp, for example, 15-M organizers were deeply influenced and inspired by the mass movements of Egypt (particularly Tahrir Square in Cairo), Iceland and WikiLeaks (Flesher Fominaya, 2020). 15-M in turn influenced Occupy Wall Street and many other movements around the world (Romanos, 2016; Roos and Oikonomakis, 2014).

National social movements also can inspire increased protests within their own country. Prior to 15-M, but following the global crisis in 2008, the number of authorized or reported protests in Spain doubled to 8,760, climbed to 18,568 in 2009, increased further to 21,941 in 2010, dropped slightly to 21,297 in 2011 and then had a radical increase post 15-M to 44,233 in 2012. In 2013, the number of authorized protests dipped very slightly to 43,170, but the number of unauthorized protests rose from 294 in 2012 to 1,682 in 2013 (Flesher Fominaya, 2020). The impact of 15-M, however, extends far beyond the number of people who participated in 15-M-related demonstrations (three times more), assemblies or other activities (eight times more). As Sampedro and Lobera (2014: 65) show, between seven and eight of every ten Spaniards agreed with protester demands, a remarkable degree of consensus ranging 'from 81% at the outset, to 68% a few days before the first anniversary' (2014: 65).

Koopmans (2004) and Tarrow (1998) argue that repression and institutionalization are two common outcomes of waves of protest that also contribute to 'contraction' or a decrease in mobilization (along with other factors, such as protest fatigue). In Spain, the strong challenge to the legitimacy of 'democracy as usual' is revealed in the two most visible and unintended consequences of the mobilizations: the legal reforms enacted in the wake of the protests to restrict the right to protest and the institutionalization of the movements in the form of new hybrid parties, such as Podemos and the municipal movements for change which emerged from 15-M. Spain's reform of the penal code and the Law for the Protection of Citizen Security, known as the 'Gag Law' (Ley Mordaza), was a clear response to anti-austerity and pro-democracy protest. The clear causal link between the high levels of citizen mobilization and the new legal restrictions has been made by International Organizations, including the UN Human Rights Office of the High Commissioner (2015). One such tactic is the increasing use of fines to punish and dissuade peaceful protest (from 100 to 600,000 euros depending on the infraction) and, in a 2013 report, the Commissioner for Human Rights for the Council of Europe (2013: 18) considered this to constitute a violation of freedom of expression and association, as the possibility of incurring steep, disproportionate fines is intended to dissuade protest and silence the voices of critical citizens. Given the key role of the Internet and digital media in disseminating counter-hegemonic narratives and in facilitating the organization of protest, unsurprisingly Internet freedoms are also being curtailed and online expression is being criminalized (Reporteros sin Fronteras, 2016). In this regard, ironically, this pro-democracy movement can be said to have had a detrimental effect on democratic freedoms, at least in the short term, highlighting the fact that social movements can have unintended consequences.

The 15-M movement has also reconfigured the political landscape in that it has led to the creation of new parties such as Podemos and new 'progressive' municipal platforms (Antentas, 2016; Font and García Espin, 2019; Flesher Fominaya, 2020). Although the creation of new political parties has long been an outcome of social movements (Amenta *et al.*, 2019: 452), in this case it was less expected since the movement was deeply rooted in 'horizontal' autonomous traditions and initially strongly rejected and resisted institutional politics. Despite this, the new hybrid movement parties that emerged from the movement did later manage to introduce some policies such as the increase in the national minimum wage or environmental and housing policies at the municipal levels in Madrid and Barcelona, which were in line with other 15-M demands. Movements have multiple and sometimes conflicting demands and contain within them people with conflicting and changing points of view about collective identities, strategy, acceptable alliances or outcomes, among other debates. Some 15-M activists remain sceptical of any political party's ability to change politics or even represent a new form of political party, but many others shifted the arena of their political activity to the electoral sphere, seeing it as a more effective way of making change and supporting these new 'movement parties' (Flesher Fominaya, 2020). Regardless of their view, the new parties would not have managed to overcome the high barriers to entry in the electoral arena without the existence of the movement itself. Yet the impact of the 15-M movement on democracy goes beyond these concrete political outcomes. As Ada Colau, the mayor of Barcelona put it (in Corcuera, 2014):

> There is an awareness that goes beyond the sphere of social movements, an awareness of citizens in general who have become conscious of the fact that delegating politics to the politicians leads to the confusion between private and public interests, to the revolving doors, to widespread corruption. We should never again delegate politics, democracy is not made on its own, it isn't an end point as we have been told [...], it is a starting point, a permanent gerund, otherwise there is no democracy.[1]

As the (admittedly unusually significant) example of 15-M shows, social movements can have widespread consequences across space and time and their significance can extend far beyond what we have the capacity to measure precisely. They are the essence of the possibility for democratic renewal, which cannot be delegated to professional politicians and to the realm of

---

1   Translated from Spanish original by the author,

institutional politics alone but which needs to be continually nourished by collective citizen engagement. This is not to say social movements are the only relevant actors in the process of democratic regeneration by any means, and some movements are actively *anti-democratic*, but historically they have played an important role in democratizing processes (Tilly and Wood, 2015), and they continue to do so today.

In 2015, after giving a talk on the wave of anti-austerity protests, I was asked whether I did not think that there would be a day when the political system changed to such an extent that social movements would no longer be necessary. The person posing the question likely was thinking about the rise of the movement parties that had emerged from 15-M in Spain and the resurgence of Syriza in Greece. My answer was an unequivocal 'no'. All societies experience social conflict: be it class or power struggles; material conflicts; or conflicts over cultural orientations, or over what Touraine (1988) calls 'historicity', or society's capacity to act upon itself and transform itself. How a given society transforms itself is the result of decisions over ethical, social and economic investments, and these decisions are at the heart of contemporary social conflicts. Social movements are a key expression of these struggles.

In this book, I have primarily discussed contemporary progressive social movements from the 1960s to the present. In regard to progressive grassroots movements during this period, the words of Alain Touraine (1988: 18) come to mind:

> As our capacity to act upon ourselves increases notably because of science and technology, a greater number of us, as well as a larger part of ourselves, are drawn into public life ... Social actors no longer can speak in the name of history, but only in their own names, as determinate subjects ... we no longer demand to direct the course of things; we simply claim our freedom, the right to be ourselves without being crushed by the apparatuses of power, violence and propaganda.

While it is always possible to find exceptions to any generalization, it seems to me that these words sum up the essence of the spirit of masses of people who have taken to the streets from the countercultural movements of the 1960s to the pro-democracy movements of the contemporary global wave. The rise of autonomous movements from the 1960s to the present also reflects this spirit, and the opposition of autonomous social movements, to which I have paid particular attention here, to more institutionalized forms of political organizations continues to represent a central cleavage in the global social movement landscape. At the same time, periods of crisis spur the creation of new alliances, as differences are (sometimes temporarily) put aside in an attempt to find creative solutions to social problems, and the emergence of hybrid movement parties reflects attempts to bridge these differences. In the years since I published the first edition of this book, radical right-wing, fascist and authoritarian movements have grown and continue to flourish and thankfully the long-standing resistance to paying attention to these movements in social movement scholarship is diminishing. Paying attention to right-wing, fundamentalist and conservative movements, as I have done here, is necessary because they are extremely important political actors whose arguments find significant resonance among the public, and they shape contemporary society in crucial ways.

While social movements, like the rest of society, are caught in a dynamic, changing environment, history, culture and identity prove to be surprisingly durable and resilient influences on social movement communities. In the study of social movements, the search for the 'new' and the attention to the 'global' need to be balanced with a recognition of the importance historical legacies, cultural practices and identities have to social movements, and the ways in which these are often experienced by activists in locally and nationally rooted ways, despite often having a wider commitment to global issues and movement networks. What I have tried to show in this book is that thinking about social movements and globalization should not be limited to thinking about global movements or transnational social movements. Some scholars of social movements are frustrated by the continued academic attention to the nation-state in a context in which the importance of the nation-state is arguably waning. I believe that, as much of the discussion in this book shows, in many cases national contexts continue to provide the most immediate and relevant point of reference for movement actors – from legal restrictions or opportunities for protest, levels of repression, national political cultures that facilitate or constrain mobilization, national alliance structures between political parties, trade unions and grassroots movements, and much more. Indeed, this has been an important characteristic of the recent European wave of anti-austerity and pro-democracy movements (Flesher Fominaya, 2017). Social movement actors are strategic and, as the many cases in this book show, shift from levels of action as convenient, necessary and possible – at times targeting the nation-state and national audiences, at other times appealing to an international community of actors, a supranational legal authority, international conventions or declarations (such as the United Nations Universal Declaration of Human Rights), a global audience or a transnational network of NGOs or social movements. At times, what begins as a local act of resistance becomes the trigger for a national or global response as actors creatively use the resources available to them to translate local acts into powerful and even iconic symbols. Through the use of specific case studies throughout the book, I have also tried to highlight the uneven effects of globalization processes globally. Too often, globalization processes are discussed as if they were felt everywhere in the same way, yet this is not the case – there are still great disparities in resources, rights and access to technology, for example, and the effects of globalization processes are experienced to greater or lesser degrees across nations, gender differences, class lines and other differences. While gay marriage is legal in 26 countries or in some of their jurisdictions, in other countries homosexuality carries the death penalty (Iran, Mauritania, Saudi Arabia, Sudan and Yemen plus some parts of Nigeria and Somalia), and homosexual activity is illegal in some 70 countries around the world. In South Africa, lesbians live in fear of 'corrective' rape and murder – 31 such murders were reported between 2000 and 2011 and many more rapes, an estimated 10 a week in Cape Town alone, according to a local charity (Fihlani, 2011). While global human rights discourse is invoked to bring pressure to bear on the latter nations, and transnational advocacy and social movement networks mobilize around these issues, the continuing disparity in lesbian, gay, bisexual and transgender rights provides a compelling reminder of the persistent differences in national contexts – differences that affect the ways in which social movements mobilize around issues and the strategies they pursue as they navigate among local, national, transnational and global levels of action.

Finally, in this book, I have provided a thorough grounding in social movement theory but have also deliberately drawn on a broad range of social theory to make sense of the social movements under discussion. My concern has been to draw on the richest and most appropriate theoretical approach for the movement or issue under discussion rather than to simply build on a self-contained field of 'social movement studies'. Recent work from fields such as geography, media, and communication studies has provided rich insights that build on more established sociological and political science contributions to the study of social movements, whereas contemporary social theory and social movements have informed each other since the classic social theorists first attempted to make sense of modernity. Social movement studies can only benefit from encouraging cross-disciplinary dialogues to continue to explore the fascinating world of social movements in our globalized world.

BIBLIOGRAPHY

Abaza, M. (2013) 'The violence of Egypt's counter-revolution', *Global Dialogue*, 3. Available: http://www.isa-sociology.org/global-dialogue/2013/04/the-violence-of-egypt%E2%80%99s-counter-revolution/.

Abdelrahman, M. (2011) 'The transnational and the local Egyptian activists and trans-national protest networks', *British Journal of Middle Eastern Studies*, 38(3): 407–24.

Abramsky, K. (ed) (2001) *Restructuring and Resistance* (UK Amnesty International).

Acampada Sol (2011a) *Propuestas aprobadas en la Asamblea de hoy día 20 de mayo de 2011 en Acampada Sol*, 20 May 2013. Available: http://madrid.tomalaplaza.net/2011/05/20/propuestas-20-mayo/.

Acampada Sol (2011b) *Guía rápida para la dinamización de asambleas populares*, 3 May. Available: http://madrid.tomalaplaza.net/2011/05/31/guia-rapida-para-la-dinamizacion-de-asambleas-populares/.

Acme Collective (1999) 'N30 Black Bloc Communiqué', *Urban*, 75. Available: http://www.urban75.com/action/seattle9.html.

Adamovsky, E. (2004) 'Another forum is possible', in E. Yuen, D. Burton-Rose and G. N. Katsiaficas (eds), *Confronting Capitalism* (New York: Soft Skull Press).

Al Jazeera [Online] (2011) 'Tunisian gender-parity "revolution" hailed', 21 April. Available: http://www.aljazeera.com/news/africa/2011/04/2011421161714335465.html.

Aliboni, R. (2011) 'The international dimension of the Arab Spring', *International Spectator: Italian Journal of International Affairs*, 46(4): 5–9.

Allagui, I. and Kuebler, J. (2011) 'The Arab Spring and the role of the ICTs', *International Journal of Communication*, 5: 1435–42.

Altman, A. (2011) 'Public workers protest in Wisconsin', *Time Swampland* [Online], 16 February. Available: http://swampland.time.com/2011/02/16/public-workers-protest-in-wisconsin/.

Amenta, E., Andrews, K. and Caren, N. (2019) 'The political institutions, processes, and outcomes movements seek to influence', in D. Snow, S. Soule, H. Kriesi and H. McCammon (eds), *The Wiley Blackwell Companion to Social Movements*, 2nd ed. (Oxford: Wiley).

Amenta, E., Dunleavy, K. and Bernstein, M. (1994) 'Stolen thunder? Huey Long's "share our wealth," political mediation, and the second new deal', *American Sociological Review*, 59: 678–702.

Anarchist N30 Black Bloc (1999) Anarchist N30 Black Bloc Communiqué. Available: http://www.urban75.com/Action/seattle9.html.

Anderson, P. (2000) 'Renewals', *New Left Review*, 1: 5–25.

Annis, R. (2012) 'Quebec: students mobilise against draconian law aimed at breaking four-month strike', *Links International Journal of Socialist Renewal*, 19 May.

Anonymous (2001) *On Fire* (London: One-Off Press).

Anonymous (2003) 'Europrecariat call for Mayday 2003'. Available: http://www.chain-workers.org/chainw/mayday003/autonomo_hispano.htm.

Anonymous (2004) 'Call for autonomous spaces during the ESF'. Available: http://www.wombles.org.

Anonymous (2008) 'Youtube message to Scientology', 21 January. Available: http://www.youtube.com/watch?v=jcbkv9yiliq.

Ansell AE. (2001) 'The color of America's culture wars', in A. Ansell (ed), *Unraveling the Right: The New Conservatism in American Thought and Politics*, (Boulder, CO: Westview), pp. 173–91.

Antentas, J. M. 2016 'Spain: From the Indignados rebellion to regime crisis (2011–2016)', *Labor History*: 1–27.

Appadurai, A. (1996) *Modernity at Large* (Minneapolis: University of Minnesota Press).

Aro, J. (2016) "The cyberspace war: Propaganda and trolling as warfare tools", *European View* 15(1). Springer Berlin Heidelberg: 121–32. https://doi.org/10.1007/s12290-016-0395-5.

Arribas, A. (2012) 'Sobre la precariedad y sus fugas', *Interface*, 4(2): 197–229.

Askanius, T. and Gustafsson, N. (2010) 'Mainstreaming the alternative', *Interface*, 2(2): 23–41.

Atkinson, D. (2010) *Alternative Media and Politics of Resistance* (New York: Peter Lang).

Autonome a.f.r.i.c.a gruppe, Luther Blissett and Sonja Bruenzels (1998) list serv message. Available: http://www.nettime.org/Lists-Archives/nettime-l-9809/msg00044.html.

Autonome a.f.r.i.k.a gruppe (1997) 'All or none? Multiple names, imaginary persons, collective myths', EIPCP multilingual webjournal. Available: http://www.republicart.net/disc/artsabotage/afrikagruppe02_en.pdf.

Autonome a.f.r.i.k.a gruppe (2002) 'Communication guerrilla'. Available: http://subsol.c3.hu/subsol_2/contributors3/afrikatext2.html.

Ávila, R., Harrison, S. and Richter, A. (2017) *Women, Whistleblowing, WikiLeaks: A Conversation* (New York: OR Books).

Ayeb, H. (2011) 'Social and political geography of the Tunisian revolution', *Review of African Political Economy*, 38(129): 467–79.

Ayers, M. D. (1999) 'From the streets to the Internet: the cyber-diffusion of contention', *Annals of the American Academy of Political and Social Science*, 566: 132–43.

Ayers, M. D. (2003) 'Comparing collective identity in online and offline feminist activists', in M. McCaughey and M. D. Ayers (eds), *Cyberactivism* (New York: Routledge).

Ayres, J. (2004) 'Framing collective action against neoliberalism', *Journal of World-Systems Research*, 10(1): 11–34.

Bagdikian, B. H. (2000) *The Media Monopoly* (Boston: Beacon Press).

Baker, M. (2013) 'Translation as an alternative space for political action', *Social Movement Studies*, 12 (1): 23–47.

Baker, M. and Blaagaard, B. B. (eds) (2016) *Citizen Media and Public Spaces* (London: Routledge).

Ball, J. (2018) 'What on earth is going on with WikiLeaks, Trump and Russia?' 28 November, 2018. Available: https://www.newstatesman.com/politics/media/2018/11/what-earth-going-wikileaks-trump-and-russia.

Barkawi, T. and Laffey, M. (1999) 'The imperial peace', *European Journal of International Relations*, 5(4): 403–34.

Barroso, C. (2012) 'Sabotaje a 97 furgones policiales antes de la manifestación de funcionarios', *El País*, 19 July. Available: http://ccaa.elpais.com/ccaa/2012/07/19/madrid/1342683022_123677.html.

Bateman, J. (2018) 'Their ideas had no place here: How Crete kicked out Golden Dawn', *The Guardian*, 3 December. Available: https://www.theguardian.com/cities/2018/dec/03/their-ideas-had-no-place-here-how-crete-kicked-out-golden-dawn.

Baumgarten, B. (2013) 'Geração à Rasca and beyond', *Current Sociology*, July, 61(4): 457–73.

BBC (2010) 'Icelandic authorities "negligent" over banking collapse', *BBC*, 12 April. http://news.bbc.co.uk/1/hi/business/8616113.stm.

BBC Online (2011) '"SlutWalk" marches sparked by Toronto officer's remarks', *BBC*, 8 May. Available: http://www.bbc.co.uk/news/world-us-canada-13320785.

BBC Online (2012) '1989: Massacre in Tiananmen Square', On this day, *BBC*, 4 June. Available: http://news.bbc.co.uk/onthisday/hi/dates/stories/june/4/newsid_2496000/2496277.stm.

Beck, U. (1992) *Risk Society: Towards a New Modernity* (London: Sage).

Bell, M. (2016) 'Meet the Identitarians, Europe's New Right', *PRI*, 19 December. Available: https://eu.usatoday.com/story/news/world/2016/12/20/meet-identitarians-europes-new-right/95649618/.

Beller, E. and Hout, M. (2006) 'Intergenerational social mobility', *The Future of Children*, 16: 19–36.

Benford, R. and Snow, D. (2000) 'Framing Processes and Social Movements: An overview and assesment', *Annual Review of Sociology*, 26: 611–639.

Benkler, Y. (2011) 'A free irresponsible press: Wikileaks and the battle over the soul of the networked fourth estate', *Harvard Civil Rights-Civil Liberties Law Review*, 46: 311–397.

Benkler, Y. (2006) *The Wealth of Networks: How Social Production Transforms Markets and Freedom* (New Haven: Yale University Press).

Benkler, Y., Faris, R., Roberts, H. and Zuckerman, E. (2018) 'Study: Breitbart-led right-wing media ecosystem altered broader media agenda' *Columbia Journalism Review*. Available: https://www.cjr.org/analysis/breitbart-media-trump-harvard-study.php.

Bjørgo, T. (1997) *Racist and Right-Wing Violence in Scandinavia: Patterns, Perpetrators and Responses* (Tano Aschehoug).

Blee, K. M. (2013) *Inside Organized Racism : Women in the Hate Movement* (University of California Press).

Blee, K. M. and Creasap, K. (2010) 'Conservative and Right-Wing Movements', *Annual Review of Sociology*, 36(1). *Annual Reviews*: 269–86. https://doi.org/10.1146/annurev.soc.012809.102602.

Blood, D. J. and Phillips P. C. (1995) 'Recession headline news, consumer sentiment, and the state of the economy', *International Journal of Public Opinion Research*, 7: 2–22.

Blumer, H. (1951) 'Social movements', in A. McClung (ed), *Principles of Sociology*, 2nd ed. (New York: Barnes and Noble).

Blumer, H. (1971) 'Social problems as collective behavior', *Social Problems*, 18: 298–306.

Böhm, S. (2013) 'Open-access initiatives to benefit the academy', *Times Higher Education*, 30 May [Online]. Available: http://www.timeshighereducation.co.uk/comment/opinion/open-access-initiatives-to-benefit-the-academy/2004174.article.

Bollero, D. (2013) 'Los emigrantes españoles alumbran la Marea Granate', *El Público*, 1 June. Available: http://www.publico.es/internacional/456410/los-emigrantes-espanoles-alumbran-la-marea-granate.

Breines, W. (1980) 'Community and organization', *Social Problems*, 27: 419–29.

Buckley, W. (2006) 'On the right', *National Review Online*, 13 March.

Buechler, S. M. 2000. *Social Movements in Advanced Capitalism: The Political Economy and Cultural Construction of Social Activism* (Oxford: Oxford University Press).

Burgess, J. E. and Green, J. B. (2009) *YouTube: Digital Media and Society* (Cambridge: Polity Press).

Bush, R. (2010) 'Food riots', *Journal of Agrarian Change*, 10: 119–29.

Caiani, M, della Porta, D. and Wagemann, C. (2012) *Mobilizing on the Extreme Right: Germany, Italy, and the United States* (Oxford: Oxford University Press).

Caiani, M. (2017) 'Radical Right-Wing Movements: Who, when, how and why?' *Sociopedia.Isa*: 1–15. https://doi.org/10.1177/205684601761.

Caiani, M. and Císař, O. (2019) *Radical Right Movement Parties in Europe* (London: Routledge).

Calhoun, C. (1993) "New Social Movements' of the early nineteenth century', *Social Science History*, 17(3): 385–427.

Callahan, M. (2004) 'Zapatismo and global struggle', in E. Yuen, D. Burton-Rose and G. Katsiaficas (eds), *Confronting Capitalism* (New York: Soft Skull Press).

Cammaerts, B. (2007) 'Jamming the political', *Continuum*, 21(1): 71–90.

Cammaerts, B. (2012) 'Protest logics and the mediation opportunity structure', *European Journal of Communication*, 27: 117–34.

Cammaerts, B. and Carpentier, N. (2009) 'Blogging the 2003 Iraq War', *Observatorio*, 3: 1–23.

Cammiss, S., Doherty, B. and Hayes, G. (2018) 'The use of anti-terror laws to convict the Stansted 15 will chill public dissent', *New Statesman*, 10 December. Available: https://www.newstatesman.com/2018/12/use-anti-terror-laws-convict-stansted-15-will-chill-public-dissent.

Campani, G. (2016) 'Neo-fascism from the twentieth century to the third millennium: The case of Italy', in G. Lazaridis, G. Campani and A. Benveniste (eds), *The Rise of the Far Right in Europe* (London: Palgrave).

Candón Mena, J. (2012) 'Movimientos por la democratización de la comunicación', *Razón y Palabra*, 82.

Caren, N., Jowers, K. and Gaby, S. (2012) 'A Social Movement Online Community: Stormfront and the White Nationalist Movement', *Research in Social Movements, Conflict and Change*, 33(January): 163–93.

Carter, E. (2005) *The Extreme Right in Western Europe: Success or Failure?* (Manchester: Manchester University Press).

Carty, V. (2002) 'Technology and counter-hegemonic movements', *Social Movement Studies*, 1(2): 129–46.

Castells, M. (2004) *The Information Age: Economy, Society and Culture*, 3 vols (Cambridge, MA: Blackwell).

Castells, M. (2009) *Communication Power* (Oxford: Oxford University Press).

Castells, M. (2011a) 'Revolución en Egipto', *La Vanguardia*, 2 February.

Castells, M. (2011b) 'Internazionale Italian', *I gelsomini tunisini viaggiano in rete*, 4 February.

Castells, M. (2012) *Networks of Outrage and Hope* (Cambridge: Polity Press).

Castells, M., Qiu, J. L., Fernandez-Ardevol, M. and Sey, A. (2006) *Mobile Communication and Society: A Global Perspective* (Cambridge, MA: MIT Press).

Cenizo, N. (2018) 'Benahavís: el pueblo donde los ricos indignados votan a Vox', *Eldiario.es*, 4 December. Available: https://www.eldiario.es/andalucia/Benahavis-ricos-indignados-votan-Vox_0_842716818.html.

Cenizo, N. (2013) 'El fenómeno de las corralas se extiende a Málaga', *El Diario.es.*, 30 May. Available: http://www.eldiario.es/andalucia/fenomeno-corralas-extiende-Malaga_0_137536591.html.

Cerrillo Vidal, J. (2013) 'From general strike to social strike', *Interface*, 5(2).

Chainworkers Crew (2001) 'Reportage Mayday Parade'. Available: http://www.chainworkers.org/MAYDAY/index.html.

Chainworkers Crew (Undated) *Serpica Naro*. Available: http://www.chainworkers.org/SERPICANARO/index.html.

Chatterton, P. (2010) 'So what does it mean to be anti-capitalist?', *Urban Studies*, 47: 1205–24.

Chesters, G. and Welsh, I. (2011) *Social Movements: The Key Concepts* (London: Routledge).

Chomsky, N. and Herman, E. S. (2010) *Manufacturing Consent* (New York: Random House).

CNN Politics [Online] (2017) Video: Trump's day by day response to the events in Charlottesville, 13 August. Available: https://edition.cnn.com/2017/08/13/us/charlottesville-white-nationalist-rally-car-crash/index.html.

Cockburn, A. and St. Clair, J. (2000) *Five Days That Shook the World* (London: Verso Books).

Coleman, E. G. (2013) *Coding Freedom: The Ethics and Aesthetics of Hacking* (Princeton: Princeton University Press).

Coleman, E. G. (2015) *Hacker, Hoaxer, Whistleblower, Spy: The Many Faces of Anonymous.* (London: Verso Books).

Coleman, G. (2011) 'Anonymous: *Politics in the Age of Secrecy and Transparency*, The new everyday'. Available: http://mediacommons.futureofthebook.org/tne/cluster/politics-age-secrecy-and-transparency.

Coleman, G. (2012a) 'Anonymous', in C. Wiedermann, N. Rossiter and S. Zehle (eds), *Depletion Design* (Institute of Network Cultures).

Coleman, G. (2012b) 'Our weirdness is free', *Canopy*. Available: http://canopycanopycanopy.com/15/our_weirdness_is_free.

Coleman, L. M. , Bassi, S. A. (2011) "Deconstructing militant manhood: Masculinities in the disciplining of (anti-) globalisation politics", *International Feminist Journal of Politics*, 13(2): 224–44.

Collins, T. (2004) 'A protestography', in E. Yuen, D. Burton-Rose and G. Katsiaficas (eds), *Confronting Capitalism* (New York: Soft Skull Press).

Conway, J. (2011a) 'Cosmopolitan or Colonial? The World Social Forum as 'contact zone", *Third World Quarterly*, 32(2): 217–36.

Conway, J. (2011b) 'Analysing hegemonic masculinities in the antiglobalization movement(s)', *International Feminist Journal of Politics*, 13(2): 225–30.

Conway, Janet M. (2013) *Edges of Global Justice: The World Social Forum and Its Others* (London: Routledge).

Corcuera, Laura (2014) 'Delegar la política nos ha llevado al desastre generalizado', *Diagonal*, 2 December. https://www.diagonalperiodico.net/global/24924-delegar-la-politica-nos-ha-llevado-al-desastre-generalizado.html.

Costanza-Chock, S. (2012) 'Mic Check! Media cultures and the Occupy Movement', *Social Movement Studies*, 1(3): 375–85.

Cottle, S. (2008) 'Reporting demonstrations', *Media, Culture and Society*, 30(6): 853–72.

Cowburn, Ashely (2018) 'Theresa May's 'hostile environment' policy seen as 'almost reminiscent of Nazi Germany', says former civil service chief', *The Independent* [Online], 19 April. Available: https://www.independent.co.uk/news/uk/politics/theresa-may-uk-immigration-nazi-germany-home-office-civil-service-lord-kerslake-a8311701.html.

Cox, L. and Flesher Fominaya, C. (2009) 'Movement knowledge', *Interface*, 1: 1–20.

Crossley, N. (2002) *Making Sense of Social Movements* (Buckingham: Open University Press).

Cumbers, A., Routledge, P. and Nativel, C. (2008) 'The entangled geographies of global justice networks', *Progress in Human Geography*, 32(2): 183–201.

Cuninghame, P. G. (2007) 'A laughter that will bury you all', *International Review of Social History*, 52: 153–68.

Dahlberg, L. (2001) 'The internet and democratic discourse: Exploring the prospects of online deliberative forums extending the public sphere', *Information, Communication & Society*, 4: 615–33.

Dahlberg, L. (2005) 'The corporate colonization of online attention and the marginalization of critical communication?', *Journal of Communication Inquiry*, 29: 1–21.

Dahlberg, L. (2007) 'The Internet, deliberative democracy, and power', *Media and Cultural Politics*, 3: 47–64.

Daily Star (2013) 'Tunisia constitution talks make progress', Lebanon, 4 May. Available: http://www.dailystar.com.lb/News/Middle-East/2013/May-04/215966-tunisia-constitution-talks-make-progress.ashx#ixzz2U6vRIyhN.

Dalton, R. (1996) *Citizen Politics* (Chatham, NJ: Chatham House Publishers).

Danaher, K. and Burbach, R. (eds) (2000) *Globalize This!* (Monroe, ME: Common Courage Press).

Daphi, P. (2019) 'The global justice movement in Europe', in Flesher Fominaya and Feenstra (eds), *The Routledge Handbook of Contemporary European Social Movements* (London: Routledge).

Darnovsky, M., Epstein, B. L. and Flacks, R. (eds) (1995) *Cultural Politics and Social Movements* (Philadelphia: Temple University Press).

Davies, C. (2007) 'Humour and protest', *International Review of Social History*, 52: 291–305.

De Angelis, M. (2000) 'Globalization, new internationalism and the Zapatistas', *Capital & Class*, Spring, 24(1): 9–35.

De Angelis, M. (2001) 'From movement to society', *The Commoner*, 2.

De Jong, W., Shaw, M. and Stammer, S. N. (eds) (2005) *Global Activism Global Media* (London: Pluto Press).

De Sousa Santos, Boaventura (2016) *Epistemologies of the South: Justice against Epistemicide* (London: Routledge).

De Witte, H. (2006) 'Extreme right-wing activism in the Flemish part of Belgium', in B. Klandermans and N. Meyer (eds), *Extreme Right Activists in Europe: Through the Magnifying Glass.* (London: Routledge).

Dearden, L. (2018) 'Far-right groups across Europe 'using Islamist techniques' to recruit followers, report says', 9 December. Available: http://www.independent.co.uk/news/world/europe/far-right-groups-europe-afd-tommy-robinson-generation-identity-recruitment-islam-a8674136.html.

Dearden, Lizzie (2017) 'Far right extremists targeting the UK as they 2weaponose internet culture" to spread hatred around the world,' *The Independent*, 23 October Available:

https://www.independent.co.uk/news/uk/home-news/far-right-uk-identitarian-movement-alt-right-defend-europe-isd-research-nazis-national-action-a8013331.html.

Della Porta, D. (1999) 'Protest, protesters, and protest policing', in M. Giugni, D. McAdam and C. Tilly (eds) *How Social Movements Matter* (Minneapolis: University of Minnesota Press).

Della Porta, D. (2005a) 'Making the polis', *Mobilization*, 10: 73–94.

Della Porta, D. (2005b) 'Multiple belongings, tolerant identities, and the construction of "another politics"', in D. Della Porta and S. Tarrow (eds), *Transnational Protest and Global Activism* (Lanham, MD: Rowman & Littlefield).

Della Porta, D. (2007) *The Global Justice Movement* (Boulder, CO: Paradigm).

Della Porta, D. (2012) 'Mobilizing against the crisis', *Interface: A Journal For and About Social Movements*, event analysis, 4(1): 274–7.

Della Porta, D. (2013) *Can Democracy be Saved?* (Cambridge: Polity Press).

Della Porta, D. and Reiter, H. (1998) *Policing Protest* (Minneapolis: University of Minnesota Press).

Della Porta, D. and Diani, M. (2009) *Social Movements : An Introduction.* (Oxford: Blackwell Publisher).

Della Porta, D., Peterson, A. and Reiter, H. (eds) (2006) *The Policing of Transnational Protest* (London: Ashgate).

Dell Paorta, Donatella (2013) *Clandestine Political Violence.* (Cambridge: Cambridge University Press).

Della Porta, D. (2015) *Social Movements in Times of Austerity: Bringing Capitalism Back into Protest Analysis.* (Cambridge: Polity).

Denny, C. (2003) 'Nestle U-turn on Ethiopia debt', *The Guardian*, 24 January.

Desalambre (2018) '10 bulos sobre inmigración que han circulado durante la campaña de las elecciones andaluzas', *Eldiario.es*, 4 December. Available: https://www.eldiario.es/desalambre/inmigracion-circulado-campana-elecciones-andaluzas_0_842716844.html.

Diani, M. (1992) 'The concept of social movement', *Sociological Review*, 40: 1–25.

Diani, M. (1995) *Green Networks* (Edinburgh: Edinburgh University Press).

Diani, M. (2015) *The Cement of Civil Society* (Cambridge: Cambridge University Press).

Diani, M. and Lodi, G. (1988) 'Three in one: Currents in the Milan Ecology Movement', in B. Klandermans, H. Kriesi and S. Tarrow (eds), *From Structure to Action: Comparing Social Movement Research* (London: JAI Press).

Diani, M. and McAdam, D. (2003) *Social Movements and Networks : Relational Approaches to Collective Action* (Oxford: Oxford University Press).

Doerr, N. (2007) 'Is "another" public sphere actually possible? The case of "women without" in the European Social Forum process as a critical test for deliberative democracy', *Journal of International Women's Studies*, 8(3): 71–87.

Doerr, N. (2009) 'Language and democracy 'in movement': Multilingualism and the case of the European Social Forum process', *Social Movement*.

Doerr, N. (2010) 'Exploring cosmopolitan and critical Europeanist discourses in the ESF process as a transnational public space', in S. Teumne (ed), *The Transnational Condition: Protest Dynamics in an Entangled Europe* (New York: Berghahn).

Doerr, N. (2011) 'The disciplining of dissent and the role of empathetic listeners in deliberative publics: A ritual perspective', *Globalizations*, 8(4): 519–34. https://doi.org/10.1080/14747731.2011.585859.

Douglas, C. (2008) 'Barricades and boulevards', *Interstices*, 8.

Downing, J. (2001) *Radical Media* (Thousand Oaks, CA: Sage).

Downing, J. (2008) 'Social movement theories and alternative media', *Communication, Culture and Critique*, 1: 40–50.

Doyle, K. (undated) *Tlatelolco Massacre* (Washington, DC: National Security Archive Electronic Briefing Books).

Drache, D. (2008) *Defiant Publics* (Cambridge: Polity Press).

DRY (Democracia Real Ya!) (2013) 'Manifiesto'. Available: http://www.democracia-realya.es/manifiesto-comun/.

Duncombe, S. (2002) *Cultural Resistance Reader* (New York: Verso).

Durham, M. (2000) *The Christian Right : The Far Right and the Boundaries of American Conservatism.* (Manchester: Manchester University Press).

DW (2017) 'Identitarian Movement- Germany's New Right Hipsters', 23 June. Available: https://www.dw.com/en/identitarian-movement-germanys-new-right-hipsters/a-39383124.

Edwards, Gemma (2004) 'Habermas and social movements: What's 'new'?', *The Sociological Review*, 52(1_suppl): 113–30. https://doi.org/10.1111/j.1467-954X.2004.00476.x.

Edwards, G. (2014) *Social Movements and Protest* (Cambridge: Cambridge University Press).

EFE (2013) 'Bomberos de La Coruña se niegan a desahuciar a una anciana de 85 años', *ABC*, 19 February. Available: http://www.abc.es/local-galicia/20130218/abci-bombe-ros-anciana-desahucio-galicia-201302181858.html.

Einwohner, R. L. (2002) 'Bringing the outsiders in', *Mobilization*, 7: 253–68.

El Diario24 (2011) 'Hay un manifestante en grave estado por la represión policial en Barcelona'. Available: http://m.eldiario24.com/nota.php?id=222713.

El-Ghobashy, M. (2011) 'The praxis of the Egyptian Revolution', *The Middle East Research and Information Project (MERIP)*, 41: 2–13.

Elola, J. (2012) 'Democracia Real YA, la organización que impulsó el 15-M, se parte en dos', *El País*, 23 April Available: http://politica.elpais.com/politica/2012/04/23/actualidad/1335212093_805436.html.

Eltantawy, N. and Wiest, J. (2011) 'Social media in the Egyptian revolution', *International Journal of Communication*, 5: 1207–24.

Entman, R. (1993) 'Framing', *Journal of Communication*, 43: 51–8.

Epstein, B. (1991) *Political Protest and Cultural Revolution* (Berkeley: University of California Press).

Epstein, B. (2001) 'What happened to the Women's Movement?', *Monthly Review Press*, 53: 1–13.

Errejón Galván, Íñigo (2015) 'We the People El 15-M: ¿Un Populismo Indignado?' *ACME: An International Journal for Critical Geographies*, 14(1): 124–56. https://ojs.unbc.ca/index.php/acme/article/view/1144.

Eschle, C. (2005) '"Skeleton Women": Feminism and the antiglobalization movement', *Signs: Journal of Women in Culture and Society*, 30(3): 1741–69.

Eschle, C. (2018) 'Troubling stories of the end of occupy: Feminist narratives of betrayal at occupy Glasgow', *Social Movement Studies*, 17(5): 524–540.

Eschle, Catherine, and Maiguashca, Bice (2010) *Making Feminist Sense of the Global Justice Movement* (Lanham: Rowman & Littlefield Publishers).

Eubanks, V. (2018) *Automating Inequality: How High-Tech Tools Profile, Police, and Punish the Poor* (London: St. Martin's Press).

Europa Press (2011) '15-M. La cifra de heridos en plaza Catalunya se eleva a 121', *Europa Press*, 27 May. Available: http://www.europapress.es/sociedad/sucesos-00649/noticia-15-cifra-heridos-plaza-catalunya-eleva-121-20110527153221.html.

Evans, P. (2000) 'Fighting marginalization with transnational networks', *Contemporary Sociology*, 29: 230–41.

Eyerman, R. and Jamison, A. (1991) *Social Movements* (London: Polity Press).

Fahmi, W. S. (2009) 'Bloggers' street movement and the right to the city', *Environment and Urbanization*, 21: 89–107.

Farro, A. L. and Demirhisar, D. (2014) 'The Gezi Park movement: A Turkish experience of the twenty-first-century collective movements', *International Review of Sociology*, 24(1): 176–89.

Faus, P. (2016) Alacaldesa (Ada for Mayor) (Spain: Nanouk Films).

Federici, S. and Caffentzis, G. (2004) 'Genoa and the anti-globalization movement', in E. Yuen, D. Burton-Rose and G. Katsiaficas (eds), *Confronting Capitalism* (New York: Soft Skull Press).

Fenton, N. (2008) 'Mediating hope', *International Journal of Cultural Studies*, 11: 230–48.

Fernández Durán, R. (2005) 'Interview in Madrid', conducted by David Garcia and Cristina Flesher Fominaya for the radio programme *Sin Cuartel*.

Fernández-Savater, Amador and Flesher Fominaya, Cristina (2017) 'Life after the squares: Reflections on the consequences of the Occupy movements', *Social Movement Studies*, 16(1): 119–51. https://doi.org/10.1080/14742837.2016.1244478.

Fihlani, P. (2011) 'South Africa's lesbians fear "corrective rape"', *BBC*, 30 June. Available: http://www.bbc.co.uk/news/world-africa-13908662.

Fillieule, O. and Sommier, I. (2013) 'The emergence and development of the no global movement in France', in C. Flesher Fominaya and L. Cox (eds), *Understanding European Movements* (London: Routledge).

Firat, B. Ö. and Kuryel, A. (eds) (2011) *Cultural Activism* (Amsterdam: Rodopi Bv Editions).

Firer-Blaess, Sylvain (2016) *The Collective Identity of Anonymous : Web of Meanings in a Digitally Enabled Movement*. PhD dissertartion. Uppsala: Acta Universitatis Upsaliensis: Uppsala Studies in Media and Communication 12. Available: http://www.diva-portal.org/smash/record.jsf?pid=diva2%3A926671&dswid=5513; accessed 12/05/2017.

Flesher Fominaya, C. (2005) *The Logic of Autonomy* (Berkeley: University of California) (Published as Cristina Flesher Eguiarte).

Flesher Fominaya, C. (2007a) 'Autonomous movement and the Institutional Left', *South European Society and Politics*, 12: 335–8.

Flesher Fominaya, C. (2007b) 'The role of humour in the process of collective identity formation in autonomous social movement groups in contemporary Madrid', *International Review of Social History*, 52: 243–58.

Flesher Fominaya, C. (2010a) 'Collective identity in social movements: Central concepts and debates', *Sociology Compass*, 4(6): 393–404.

Flesher Fominaya, C. (2010b) 'Creating cohesion from diversity: The challenge of collective identity formation in the global justice movement', *Sociological Inquiry*, 80(3): 377–404.

Flesher Fominaya, C. (2011) 'The Madrid bombings and popular protest', *Contemporary Social Science*, 6: 289–307.

Flesher Fominaya, C. (2013) 'Movement culture continuity', in C. Flesher Fominaya and L. Cox (eds), *Understanding European Movements* (London: Routledge).

Flesher Fominaya, C. (2014) 'Movement culture as habit(us)', in B. Baumgarten, P. Daphi and P. Ullrich (eds), *Conceptualizing Culture in Social Movement Research* (London: Palgrave).

Flesher Fominaya, C. (2015a) 'Debunking spontaneity: Spain's 15-M/Indignados as autonomous movement', *Social Movement Studies*, 14(2): 142–63.

Flesher Fominaya, C. (2015b) 'Autonomous social movements and the paradox of anti-identitarian collective identity', in A. McGarry and J. Jasper (eds), *The Identity Dilemma* (Philadelphia: Temple University Press).

Flesher Fominaya, C. (2015c) 'Redefining the crisis/redefining democracy: Mobilising for the right to housing in Spain's PAH movement', *South European Society and Politics*, 20(4): 465–85.

Flesher Fominaya, C. (2016) 'Unintended consequences: The negative impact of e-mail use on participation and collective identity in two "horizontal" social movement groups', *European Political Science Review*, 8(1): 95–122.

Flesher Fominaya, C. (2017) 'European anti-austerity and pro-democracy protests in the wake of the global financial crisis', *Social Movement Studies*, 16(1): 1–20.

Flesher Fominaya, C. (2019) 'Collective identity in social movements: Assessing the limits of a theoretical framework' in D. Snow, S. Soule, H. Kriesi and H. McCammon (eds), *The Wiley Blackwell Companion to Social Movements*, 2nd ed. (Oxford: Wiley), pp. 429–45.

Flesher Fominaya, C. (2020) *Democracy Reloaded: Inside Spain's Political Laboratory from 15-M to Podemos* (Oxford: Oxford University Press).

Flesher Fominaya, C. and Cox, L. (eds) (2013) *Understanding European Movements* (London: Routledge).

Flesher Fominaya, C. and Montañes Jiménez, A. (2014) 'Transnational diffusion across time: The adoption of the Argentinian dirty war "escrache" in the context of Spain's housing crisis', in D. Della Porta and A. Mattoni (eds), *Spreading Protests: Social Movements in Times of Crisis* (Colchester, UK: ECPR Press).

Flesher Fominaya, C. and Wood, L. (2011) 'Repression and social movements', *Interface*, 3: 1–11.

Flesher Fominaya, C. and Gillan, K. (2017) 'Navigating the technology-media-movements complex', *Social Movement Studies*, 16(4): 383–402.

Font J and García Espín, P (2019) 'From Indignad@s to Mayors? Participatory dilemmas in Spanish municipal Movements', in C. Flesher Fominaya and R. Feenstra (eds), *Routledge Handbook of Contemporary European Social Movements: Protest in Troubled Times* (London: Routledge), pp. 387–401.

Foran, J. (2014) 'Global affinities: The new cultures of resistance behind the Arab Spring', in M. Kamrava (ed), *The Evolving Ruling Bargain in the Middle East* (New York: Columbia University Press).

Forbes (2012) 'The world's most powerful people in the world', *Forbes*.

Forchtner, B. and Tominc, A. (2017) 'Kalashnikov and cooking-spoon: Neo-Nazism, veganism and a lifestyle cooking show on YouTube', *Food, Culture & Society*, 20(3). Routledge: 415–41.

Frank, T. (2004) *What's the Matter with Kansas* (New York: Metropolitan Books).

Fraser, N. (1993) 'Rethinking the public sphere', in C. J. Calhoun (ed), *Habermas and the Public Sphere* (Cambridge, MA: MIT Press).

Freeman, C. (2009) 'Former Iceland bank governor David Oddsson defends role in meltdown', *Daily Telegraph*, 27 April. Available: http://www.telegraph.co.uk/finance/newsbysector/banksandfinance/5231082/Former-Iceland-bank-governor-David-Oddsson-defends-role-in-meltdown.html.

Freeman, J. (1973) 'The tyranny of structurelessness', in A. Koedt, E. Zevine and A. Rapone (eds), *Radical Feminism* (New York: Quadrangle).

Freud, S. (1945) *Group Psychology and the Analysis of Ego.* (London: Hogarth).

Froehling, O. (1997) 'The cyberspace "war of ink and Internet" in Chiapas, Mexico', *Geographical Review*, 87: 291–307.

Gaber, I. and Willson, A. W. (2005) 'Dying for diamonds', in W. D. Jong, M. Shaw and N. Stammers (eds), *Global Activism, Global Media* (London: Pluto Press).

Galán, S. (2012) 'Today I have seen angels in shape of humans', *Journal of International Women's Studies*, 13: 17–30.

Gamson, W. (1990) *The Strategy of Social Protest* (Homewood, IL: Dorsey Press).

Gamson, W. (1992) *Talking Politics* (Cambridge: Cambridge University Press).

Gamson, W. and Wolfsfeld, G. (1993) 'Movement and media as interacting systems', *Annals of the American Academy of Political and Social Science*, 578: 104–25.

Ganesh, S. and Stohl, C. (2010) 'Qualifying engagement', *Communication Monographs*, 77: 51–74.

García de Blas, E. (2011) 'Veto a las webs del 15-M en las bibliotecas municipales', *El País*, 10 August. Available: http://elpais.com/diario/2011/08/10/madrid/1312975457_850215.html.

Garofoli, J. (2016) 'UC Davis pepper-spray officer awarded $38,000', *SFGATE*. Available: https://www.sfgate.com/politics/joegarofoli/article/UC-Davis-pepper-spray-officer-awarded-38-000-4920773.php.

Garrett, R. K. (2006) 'Protest in an information society', *Information, Communication and Society*, 9: 202–24.

Gayle, Damien and Thalassites, John (2017) 'Protesters begin effort to disrupt Britain's biggest arms fair in East London', *The Guardian*, September 4, 2017.

Gelb, J. and Hart. V (1999) 'Feminist politics in a hostile environment', in M. Giugni, D. McAdam and C. Tilly (eds), *How Social Movements Matter* (Minneapolis: University of Minnesota Press).

Gerlach, Luther (2001) 'Networks and netwars: The future of terror, crime, and militancy', in John Arquilla and David Ronfeldt (eds), *Networks and Netware: The Future of Terror, Crime and Militancy* (Santa Monica: Rand), p. 375.

Gerlach, L. P. and Hine, V. H. (1970) *People, Power, Change: Movements of Social Transformation* (Indianapolis: Bobbs-Merrill).

Gervasio, G. and Teti, A. (2014). 'When informal powers surface', in L. Anceschi, G. Gervasio and A. Teti (eds), *Informal Power in the Greater Middle East* (London: Routledge).

Giddens, A. (2011) *Runaway World* (London: Profile Books).

Gillan, K., Pickerill, J. and Webster, F. (2008) *Anti-war Activism* (Basingstoke: Palgrave Macmillan).

Gillham, P. and Edwards, B. (2003) 'Global justice protestors respond to the September 11th terrorist attacks', in J. L. Monday (ed), *Beyond September 11th: An Account of Post-Disaster Research* (University of Colorado Public Entity Risk Institute), pp. 483–520.

Gitlin, T. (2003 [1980]) *The Whole World is Watching* (Berkeley: University of California Press).

Gitlin, T. (2012) *Occupy Nation* (New York: HarperCollins Publishers).

Giugni, M. (2008) 'Political, biographical, and cultural consequences of social movements', *Sociology Compass*, 2: 1582–600.

Giugni, M. and Grasso, M. (2019) 'Nothing is lost, nothing is created, everything "Is Transformed": From Labor Movements to Anti-Austerity Protests', in Flesher Fominaya and Feenstra (eds), *The Routledge Handbook of Contemporary European Social Movements* (London: Routledge).

Goldstone, J. A. (1980) 'The weakness of organization: A new look at Gamson's the strategy of social protest', *American Journal of Sociology*, 85(5): 1017–42.

Goodwin, J. and Jasper, J. (1999) 'Caught in a winding, snarling vine: The structural bias of political process theory', *Sociological Forum*, 14(1). Springer: 27–54.

Goodwin, J. and Jasper, J. (2015) *The Social Movements Reader : Cases and Concepts*, 3rd ed. (Malden, MA: Wiley-Blackwell).

Goodwin, J. and Jasper, J. (2009) *The Social Movements Reader* (Oxford: Blackwell).

Goodwin, J., Jasper, J. M. and Polletta, F. (eds) (2009) *Passionate Politics: Emotions and Social Movements* (University of Chicago Press).

Gramsci, A. (1971 [1929–35]) *Selections from Prison Notebooks* (London: Lawrence & Wishart).

Granovetter, M. (1973) 'The strength of weak ties', *American Journal of Sociology*, 78(6): 1366–74.

Grupo Autónomo a.f.r.i.k.a., Blisset, L. and Brunzels, S. (2000) *Manual de Guerrilla de la Comunicación* (Barcelona: Virus).

Gurr, T. (2010) *Why Men Rebel* (Boulder: Paradigm Publishers).

Guzman Bouvard, M. (1994) *Revolutionizing Motherhood* (Oxford: Rowman & Little).

Habermas, J. (1981) 'New social movements', *Telos*, 49: 33–7.

Habermas, J. (1987) *The Theory of Communicative Action Volume II* (Cambridge: Polity).

Habermas, J. (1988) *Legitimation Crisis* (Cambridge: Polity).

Hagopian A, Flaxman AD, Takaro TK, Esa Al Shatari SA, Rajaratnam J, Becker S, et al. (2013) 'Mortality in Iraq associated with the 2003–2011 war and occupation: Findings from a National Cluster Sample Survey by the University Collaborative Iraq Mortality Study', *PLoS Medicine*, 10(10): e1001533.

Haiven, M. (2007) 'Privatized resistance', *Review of Education, Pedagogy, and Cultural Studies*, 29: 85–110.

Hall, S. (1993 [1973]) *Encoding and Decoding in the Television Discourse* (Birmingham: University of Birmingham).

Halperin, S. (2004) *War and Social Change in Modern Europe* (Cambridge: Cambridge University Press).

Halvorsen, S. (2012) 'Beyond the network?', *Social Movements Studies*, 11: 427–33.

Hammond, J. L. (2013) 'The significance of space in Occupy Wall Street', Conference on *Reclaiming Democracy and Social Justice*, University of Windsor, 18 May.

Harding, L. and Collyns, D. (2018) 'Manafort held secret talks with Assange in Ecuadorian embassy, sources say', *The Guardian*, 27 November 2018. Available: https://www.theguardian.com/us-news/2018/nov/27/manafort-held-secret-talks-with-assange-in-ecuadorian-embassy.

Hardisty, J. (2000) *Mobilizing Resentment: Conservative Resurgence from the John Birch Society to the Promise Keepers* (Boston: Beacon Press).

Hardisty, J. (ed) (2001) *Kitchen Table Backlash: The Antifeminist Women's Movement* (Boulder, CO: Westview).

Hardt, M. and Negri, A. (2001) 'What the protesters in Genoa want', in Anonymous (ed), *On Fire* (London: One-Off Press).

Haro Barba, C. and Sampedro Blanco, V. (2011) 'The new social movements in Spain', *6th ECPR General Conference*, Reikjavik.

Harrington, D. E. (1989) 'Economic news on television', *Public Opinion Quarterly*, 53: 17–40.

Harvey, D. (2011) *A Brief History of Neoliberalism* (Oxford: Oxford University Press).

Hausmann, R., Tyson, L. D. and Zahidi, S. (2011) 'Global gender gap report', *World Economic Forum*.

Hayden, T. (2012) 'Participatory democracy', *The Nation*, 16 April. Available: http://www.thenation.com/article/167079/participatory-democracy-port-huron-statement-occupy-wall-street.

Heath M. (2003) 'Soft-boiled masculinity: Renegotiating gender and racial ideologies in the Promise Keepers movement', *Gender and Society*. 17: 423–44.

Heim, J. (2017) 'Recounting a day of rage, hate, violence and death', *Washington Post* [online], 14 August. Available: https://www.washingtonpost.com/graphics/2017/local/charlottesville-timeline/?utm_term=.b3dc453e8901

Heitmeyer, W. (2003) 'Right-wing extremist violence', in W. Heitmeyer and J. Hagan (eds), *International Handbook of Violence Research* (Dordrecht: Springer Netherlands), pp. 399–436.

Helleiner, E. (2011) 'Understanding the 2007–2008 global financial crisis', *Annual Review of Political Science*, 14: 67–87.

Hermanns, H. (2008) 'Mobile democracy', *Politics*, 28: 74–82.

Hill, C. (1972) *The World Turned Upside Down* (New York: Viking Press).

Hintz, A. (2015) 'Social media censorship, privatized regulation and new restrictions to protest and dissent', in L. Dencik and O. Leistert (eds), *Critical Perspectives on Social Media and Protest: Between Control and Emancipation* (London: Rowman & Littlefield).

Hochschild, J. L. (1996) *Facing up to the American Dream* (Princeton, NJ: Princeton University Press).

Hodkinson, S. (2002) *Another European Social Forum Is Necessary* (London: Red Pepper).

Howard, P. N. (2010) *The Digital Origins of Dictatorship and Democracy: Information Technology and Political Islam* (Oxford: Oxford University Press).

Howard, P. N. and Hussain, M. M. (2011) 'The role of digital media', *Journal of Democracy*, 22: 35–48.

Howley, K. (2005) *Community Media* (Cambridge: Cambridge University Press).

Humphrys, E. (2007) 'With their Bodies on the line', Paper presented at *Queer Space: Centres and Peripheries*, University of Technology Sydney.

Hucal, S. (2018) 'Right-wing protests fueled by anti-immigrant sentiment continue in Germany', *ABC News* [online], 2 September. Available: https://abcnews.go.com/International/wing-protests-fueled-anti-immigrant-sentiment-continue-germany/story?id=57545743.

Humphrys, E. (2013) 'Global justice organising in Australia', *Globalizations*, 10: 369–82.

Ibrahim, Y. (2011) 'Political distinction in the British anti-capitalist movement', *Sociology*, 45(2): 318–34.

Ignazi, P. (1992) 'The silent counter-revolution', *European Journal of Political Research*, 22(1): 3–34.

IMC London (2012) 'Time to move on: IMC London signing off', *Indymedia London*, 13 October. Available: http://london.indymedia.org/articles/13128.

Indymedia Documentation Project (2007) Available: http://docs.indymedia.org/.

Indymedia (2007) 'Indymedia's frequently asked questions (FAQ)', Indymedia NYC.

INE (Instituto Nacional De Estadística) (2013) Encuesta de Población Activa, 1º Trimestre.

Inglehart, R. (1997) *Modernization and Postmodernization : Cultural, Economic, and Political Change in 43 Societies* (Princeton: Princeton University Press).

Internet World Stats (2012) *Internet Usage Statistics for Africa*. Available: http://www.internetworldstats.com/stats1.htm.

Irvine, J. M. (2000) 'Doing it with words: Discourse and the sex education culture wars', *Critical Inquiry*, 27(1): 58–76.

Jackson, R. (2009) 'Knowledge, power and politics in the study of political terrorism', in R. Jackson, M. Smyth and J. Gunning (eds), *Critical Terrorism Studies* (London: Routledge).

Jackson, S. and Chan, P. (2012) 'Understanding occupy in Australia', *Journal of Australian Political Economy*, 69: 1–24.

Jacobs, Ben, Siddiqui, Sabrina and Bixby, Scott (2016) 'You can do Anything': Trump brags on tape about using fame to get women', *The Guardian*, October 8: 2016.

James, H. and Albanese, M. (2011) 'Goodbye to "globalization"', *Rightways*, 6 February. Available: http://rightways.wordpress.com/2011/02/06/goodbye-to-%E2%80%9Cgl obalization%E2%80%9D/.

Jasper, J. (2008) *The Art of Moral Protest: Culture, Biography, and Creativity in Social Movements*. (Chicago: University of Chicago Press).

Jasper, J. (2010) 'Social movement theory Today: toward a theory of action?', *Sociology Compass*, 4(11): 965–76.

Joffé, G. (2011) 'The Arab Spring in North Africa', *Journal of North African Studies*, 16: 507–32.

Jordan, J. (1998) 'The art of necessity', in G. McKay (ed), *DiY Culture, Party and Protest in Nineties Britain* (London: Verso).

Jordan, T. (2002). *Activism! Direct Action, Hacktivism and the Future of Society* (London: Reaktion).

Jordan, T. (2015) *Information Politics: Liberation and Exploitation in the Digital Society* (London: Pluto Press).

JSF (Juventud Sin Futuro) (2011a) *Juventud sin futuro* (Barcelona: Icaria Editorial).

JSF (Juventud Sin Futuro) (2011b) 'Manifiesto'. Available: http://juventudsinfuturo.net/manifiesto-jsf/.

Júlíusson, A. and Helgason, M. (2013) 'The roots of the saucepan revolution in Iceland', in C. Flesher Fominaya and L. Cox (eds), *Understanding European Movements* (London: Routledge).

Juris, J. S. (2008) *Networking Futures*. Durham, NC: Duke University Press.

Juris, J. S. (2012) 'Reflections on # Occupy everywhere', *American Ethnologist*, 39: 259–79.

Juris, J. S., Caruso, G., Couture, S. and Mosca, L. (2013) 'The cultural politics of free software and technology within the social forum process', in J. S. Juris and A. Khasnabish (eds), *Insurgent Encounters: Transnational Activism, Ethnography, and the Political* (Durham, NC: Duke University Press), pp. 342–65.

Kapoor, D. (2005) 'NGO partnerships and the taming of the grassroots in rural India', *Development in Practice*, 15: 210–15.

Katsiaficas, G. (1987) *The Imagination of the New Left* (Boston, MA: South End Press).

Katsiaficas, G. (1997) *The Subversion of Politics* (New Jersey: Humanities Press International).

Katsiaficas, G. (2004) 'Seattle was not the beginning', in E. Yuen, D. Burton-Rose and G. Katsiaficas (eds), *Confronting Capitalism* (New York: Soft Skull Press).

Keane, J. (2009) *The Life and Death of Democracy* (New York: Simon and Schuster).

Keane, J. and Mier, P. (1989) 'Preface', in A. Melucci (ed), *Nomads of The Present* (Philadelphia: Temple University Press).

Keck, M. and Sikkink, K. (1998) *Activists beyond Borders* (Ithaca: Cornell University Press).

Kennedy, D. (2018) 'Lying like there's no tomorrow: It's Trump's Strategy', *WGBH*, 18 October. Available: https://www.wgbh.org/news/commentary/2018/10/18/lying-like-there-is-no-tomorrow-its-trumps-strategy.

Kessler, G., Rizzo, S. and Kelly, M. (2018) 'Fact Checker. President Trump has made 4,229 false or misleading claims in 558 days', *Washington Post* [Online 1 August (updated 18 October). Available: https://www.washingtonpost.com/news/fact-checker/wp/2018/08/01/president-trump-has-made-4229-false-or-misleading-claims-in-558-days/?utm_term=.2cf4057775da.

Khamis, S. and Vaughn, K. (2011) 'Cyberactivism in the Egyptian revolution', *Arab Media and Society*, 13.

Kincaid, J. D. (2016) 'The rational basis of irrational politics', *Politics & Society*, 44(4): 525–50.

Kingsnorth, P. (2003) *One No, Many Yeses* (London: Free Press).

Kirkpatrick, G. (2011) *Technology and Social Power* (Basingstoke: Palgrave Macmillan).

Klandermans, B. and Oegema, D. (1987) 'Potentials, networks, motivations, and barriers: Steps towards participation in social movements', *American Sociological Review*, 52(4): 519–31. http://www.jstor.org/stable/2095297.

Klatch, R. E. (1999) *A Generation Divided : The New Left, the New Right, and the 1960s* (Berkeley: University of California Press).

Klein, N. (1999) *No Logo* (New York: Picador).

Kobie, N. (2019) "The complicated truth about China's social credit system", *Wired*, 21 January, Available: https://www.wired.co.uk/article/china-social-credit-system-explained.

Koopmans, R. (2004) 'Protest in time and space: The evolution of waves of contention', in D. A. Snow, S. A. Soule and H. Kriesi (eds), *The Blackwell Companion to Social Movements* (London: John Wiley & Sons, pp. 19–46).

Koopmans, R., Statham, P., Giugni, M. and Passy, F. (2005) 'The extreme right: Ethnic competition or political space?', in R. Koopmans (ed), *Contested Citizenship: Immigration and Cultural Diversity in Europe* (Minneapolis: University of Minnesota Press).

Kriesi, H., Grande, E., Lachat, R., Dolezal, M., Bornschier, S. and Frey, T. (2008) *West European Politics in the Age of Globalization* (Cambridge: Cambridge University Press).

Kroll, A. (2011) 'How Occupy Wall Street really got started', *MotherJones*, 17 October. Available: http://www.motherjones.com/politics/2011/10/occupy-wall-street-international-origins.

Krugman, P. (2018) 'The G.O.P goes full authoritarian', *New York Times*, December 10. Available: https://www.nytimes.com/2018/12/10/opinion/trump-gop-authoritarian-states-power-grab.html.

Kuzio, T. (2006) 'Civil society, youth and societal mobilization in democratic revolutions', *Communist and Post-Communist Studies*, 39: 365–86.

Lakoff, G. (2014) *The All New Don't Think of an Elephant! : Know Your Values and Frame the Debate* (White River Junction: Chelsea Green Publishing).

Lakoff, G. (2018) 'Midterms and Metaphors Radio Interview', FrameLab SoundCloud. https://soundcloud.com/user-253479697.

Lawrence, J. (2012) 'El papel del movimiento 15-M en los orígenes de Occupy Wall Street', *Interferencias (El.Diario.es)*, 14 May. Available: http://www.eldiario.es/interferencias/15-M-Occupy_Wall_Street_6_132346774.html.

Lazaridis, G., Campani, G. and Benveniste, A. (2016) *The Rise of the Far Right in Europe* (London: Palgrave).

Le Bon, G. (1995) *The Crowd: A Study of the Popular Mind* (New York: Routledge).

Lee, M. and Currier, C. (2018) 'In Leaked chats, Wikileaks discusses preference for GOP over Clinton...', *The Intercept*, 14 February. Available: https://theintercept.com/2018/02/14/julian-assange-wikileaks-election-clinton-trump/.

Leeds Mayday Group (2001) 'Anti-capitalist movements', *The Commoner*, 16 January. Available: http://www.commoner.org.uk/01-4groundzero.htm.

Leistert, O. (2015) 'The revolution will not be liked: On the systemic constraints of corporate social media platforms for protests', in L. Dencik and O. Leistert (eds), *Critical Perspectives on Social Media and Protest: Between Control and Emancipation* (London: Rowman & Littlefield).

Lekakis, J. N. and Kousis, M. (2013) 'Economic crisis, troika, and the environment in Greece', *South European Society and Politics*, 18: 1–27.

Lessig, L. (1999) *Code and Other Laws of Cyberspace* (New York: Basic Books).

Levy, Stephen (1984) *Hackers: Heroes of the Computer Revolution* (New York: Delta Trade Paperbacks).

Lievrouw, Leah (2011) *Alternative and Activist New Media: Digital Media and Society* (New York: Polity).

Linebaugh, P. and Rediker, M. (2001) *The Many-Headed Hydra* (Boston: Beacon Press).

Livni E. and Timmons, H. (2018) 'The bitter reality for journalists covering a President who lies and then lies some more' *Quartz*, 4 November. Available: https://qz.com/1448460/the-bitter-reality-for-journalists-covering-a-president-who-lies-and-lies-and-lies-some-more/.

Mabrouk, M. (2011) 'A revolution for dignity and freedom', *Journal of North African Studies*, 16: 625–35.

Mac Sheoin, T. (2013) 'Framing the movement, framing the protests', *Interface*, 5: 272–365.

MacFarquhar, L. (2013) 'Requiem for a dream', *New Yorker*, 11 March. Available: http://www.newyorker.com/reporting/2013/03/11/130311fa_fact_macfarquhar?currentPage=3.

Maeckelbergh, M. (2009) *The Will of the Many: How the Alterglobalisation Movement Is Changing the Face of Democracy* (London: Pluto Press).

Maeckelbergh, M. (2012) 'Horizontal democracy now', *Interface*, 4: 207–34.

Maiba, H. (2005) 'Grassroots transnational social movement activism', *Sociological Focus*, 38: 41–63.

Malets, O. and Zajak, S. (2014) 'Moving culture: Transnational social movement organizations as translators in a diffusion cycle', in B. Baumgarten, P. Daphi and P. Ullrich (eds), *Conceptualizing Culture in Social Movement Research* (London: Palgrave).

Mamatas, N. (2004) 'Fascists for Che', in E. Yuen, D. Burton-Rose and G. N. Katsiaficas (eds), *Confronting Capitalism* (Brooklyn, NY: Soft Skull Press).

Mandela, N. (2000) 'Freedom award speech', 22 November, *Nelson Mandela Center of Memory*. Available: http://db.nelsonmandela.org/speeches/pub_view.asp?pg=item&ItemID=NMS919&txtstr=22%20November.

Manion, M. and Goodrum, A. (2000) 'Terrorism or civil disobedience: Toward a hacktivist ethic', *Computers and Society*, 30(2): 14–19.

Margolis, M. and Resnick, D. (2000) *Politics as Usual* (Thousand Oaks, CA: Sage).

Martin, G. (2015) *Understanding Social Movements* (London: Routledge).

Martínez, M. A. and García, Á. (2011) 'Ocupar las plazas, liberar los edificios', *ACME: An International E-Journal for Critical Geographies*.

Marx, K. and Engels, F. (1970 [1845]) *The German Ideology, Vol. 1* (New York: International Publishers Co.).

Marx, K., Engels, F. and Hobsbawm, E. J. (1998[1848]) *The Communist Manifesto : A Modern Edition* (London: Verso).

Matthiasson, T. (2008) 'Spinning out of control', *Nordic Journal of Political Economy*, 34: 1–19.

Mattoni, A. (2012) *Media Practices and Protest Politics* (Burlington: Ashgate).

Mattoni, A., Berdnikovs, A., Ardizzoni, M. and Cox, L. (2010) 'Voices of dissent', *Interface*, 2: 1–22.

Mattoni, A. and Doerr, N. (2007) 'Images within the precarity movement in Italy', *Feminist Review*, 87: 130–5.

Mattoni, A. and Doerr, N. (2014) 'Public spaces and alternative media practices in Europe', in K. Fahlenbrach, E. Sivertsen and R. Werenskjold (eds), *The Revolution will not be Televised?* (New York: Berghahn).

McAdam, D. (1982) *Political Process and the Development of Black Insurgency, 1930–1970* (Chicago: University of Chicago Press).

McAdam, D. (1986) 'Recruitment to high-risk activism: The case of freedom summer', *American Journal of Sociology*, 92(1): 64–90. https://doi.org/10.1086/228463.

McAdam, D. (1988) *Freedom Summer* (Oxford, UK: Oxford University Press).

McAdam, D. (1995) '"Initiator" and "spin-off" movements: Diffusion processes in protest cycles', in M. Traugott (ed), *Repertoires and Cycles of Collective Action* (Durham, NC: Duke University Press), pp. 217–39.

McAdam, D. (1999) 'The biographical impact of activism', in M. Giugni, D. McAdam and C. Tilly (eds), *How Social Movements Matter* (Minneapolis: University of Minnesota Press).

McAdam, D. (2013) 'Cognitive liberation', in *The Wiley-Blackwell Encyclopedia of Social and Political Movements* (Oxford, UK: Blackwell Publishing Ltd).

McAdam, D. and Rucht, D. (1993). The cross-national diffusion of movement ideas. *The Annals of the American Academy of Political and Social Science*, 528(1), 56–74.

McCarthy, J. and Zald, M. (1973) *The Trend of Social Movements in America: Professionalization and Resource Mobilization* (Morristown, NJ: General Learning Press).

McCarthy, J. D. and Zald, M. N. (1977) 'Resource mobilization and social movements', *American Journal of Sociology*, 82: 1212–41.

McCarthy, J. D., Smith, J. and Zald, M. (1996) 'Accessing media, electoral and government agendas', in D. McAdam, J. D. McCarthy and M. Zald (eds), *Comparative Perspectives on Social Movements* (Cambridge: Cambridge University Press).

McCaughey, M. and Ayers, M. (eds) (2003) *Cyberactivism* (New York: Routledge).

McKay, G. (1996) *Senseless Acts of Beauty* (London: Verso).

McKay, G. (1998) 'DiY culture: notes towards an intro', in G. McKay (ed), *DiY Culture, Party and Protest in Nineties Britain* (London: Verso).

McVeigh, R. (1999) 'Structural incentives for conservative mobilization: Power devaluation and the rise of the Ku Klux Klan, 1915–1925', *Social Forces*, 77: 1461–1496.

McVeigh, R. (2001) 'Power devaluation, the Ku Klux Klan, and the Democratic National Convention of 1924', *Sociological Forum*, 16(1). Kluwer Academic Publishers-Plenum Publishers: 1–30.

Meadowcroft, J. and Morrow, E. (2017) 'Violence, self-worth, solidarity and stigma: How a dissident, far-right group solves the collective action problem', *Political Studies*, 65(2): 373–90.

Meikle, G. (2008) 'Whacking Bush: tactical media as play', in M. Boler (ed), *Digital Media and Democracy: Tactics in Hard Times* (Cambridge: MIT Press), pp. 367–82.

Melucci, A. (1980) 'The new social movements: A theoretical approach', *Social Science Information*, 19(2): 199–226.

Melucci, A. (1988) 'Getting involved: Identity and mobilization in social movements', *International Social Movement Research*, 1: 329–48.

Melucci, A. (1989a) *Nomads of the Present* (Philadelphia: Temple University Press).

Melucci, A. (1989b) 'The symbolic challenge of contemporary movements', *Social Research*, 52: 781–816.

Melucci, A. (1991) 'New perspectives on social movements', in J. Keane and P. Mier (eds), *Alberto Melucci. Nomads of the Present: Social Movements and Individual Needs in Contemporary Society* (London: Hutchinson Radius).

Melucci, A. (1994) 'A strange kind of newness: What's 'new' in new social movements?', in Enrique Laraña, Hank Johnston and Joseph R. Gusfield (eds), *New Social Movements: From Ideology to Identity* (Philadelphia, PA: Temple University Press), pp. 103–30.

Melucci, A. (1995a) 'The global planet and the internal planet', in M. Darnovsky, B. Epstein and R. Flacks (eds), *Cultural Politics and Social Movements* (Philadelphia: Temple University Press).

Melucci, A. (1995b) 'The process of collective identity', in H. Johnston and B. Klandermans (eds), *Social Movements and Culture* (Minneapolis: University of Minnesota Press).

Melucci, A. (1996) *Challenging Codes: Collective Action in the Information Age* (Cambridge: Cambridge University Press).

Menn, Joseph (2019) *Cult of the Dead Cow* (New York: Public Affairs).

Mepschen, P., Duyvendak, J. W. and Tonkens, E. H. (2010) 'Sexual politics, orientalism and multicultural citizenship in the Netherlands', *Sociology*, 44: 962–79.

Meyer J. W., Boli, J., Thomas, G. N. and Ramirez, F. O. (1997) 'World society and the nation state', *American Journal of Sociology*, 103(1): 144–81.

Meyer, D. (1999) 'How the Cold War was really won', in M. Giugni, D. M. Adam and C. Tilly (eds), *How Social Movements Matter* (Minneapolis: Minnesota University Press).

Meyer, D. (2003) Social Movements and Public Policy: Eggs, Chicken, and Theory, *UC Irvine Working Paper*. Permalink: https://escholarship.org/uc/item/2m62b74d.

Mayer, J. (2017a) *Dark Money, The Hidden History of Billionaires behind the Rise of the Radical Right* (New York: Doubleday).

Mayer, J. (2017b) 'Can Time Inc. Survive the Kochs?' *The New Yorker*, 28 November. Available: https://www.newyorker.com/sections/news/can-time-inc-survive-the-kochs.

Mikdashi, M. (2012) 'The uprisings will be gendered', *Jadaliyya Reports*, 28 February. Available: http://www.jadaliyya.com/pages/index/4506/the-uprisings-will-be-gendered.

Milan, S. (2012) 'Guardians of the Internet?', *Inter-Asia Roundtable on Cyberactivism Research*, Asia Research Institute, National University of Singapore.

Milanovic, B. (2005) *Worlds Apart* (Princeton: Princeton University Press).

Milanovic, B. (2012) *Global Income Inequality by the Numbers*, Policy Research Working Paper Series (World Bank).

Milligan, T. (2013) *Civil Disobedience* (London: Bloomsbury).

Mirowski, P. (2009) 'Defining neoliberalism', in P. Mirowski and D. Plehwe (eds), *The Road from Mont Pèlerin* (Cambridge, MA: Harvard University Press).

Monforte P. (2019) 'From 'Fortress Europe' to 'Refugees Welcome': Social movements and the political imaginary on European borders,' in C. Flesher Fominaya and R. Feenstra (eds), *The Routledge Handbook of Contemporary European Social Movements* (London: Routledge).

Monterde, A. and Postill, J. (2014) 'Mobile ensembles: The uses of mobile phones for social protest by Spain's indignados', in G. Goggin and L. Hjorth (eds), *Routledge Companion to Mobile Media* (London: Routledge).

Monterde, J. (2013) '15M: El potencial de la tecnopolítica', *El diario.es.*, 13 May.

Morena, E. (2013) 'Constructing a new collective identity for the alterglobalisation movement', in C. Flesher Fominaya and L. Cox (eds), *Understanding European Movements* (London: Routledge).

Morozov, E. (2012) *The Net Delusion: The Dark Side of Internet Freedom* (London: Public Affairs Store).

Morris, A. D. (1984) *The Origins of the Civil Rights Movement : Black Communities Organizing for Change* (New York: Free Press).

Morris, C. (2011) 'Danish men labeled "terrorist" for funding FLP and FARC', *Prisma*, 3 July. Available: http://www.theprisma.co.uk/2011/07/03/danish-men-labeled-%E2%80%98terrorist%E2%80%99-for-funding-flp-and-farc/.

Mosca, L. (2007) 'A double-faced medium? The challenges and opportunities of the Internet for social movements', *European University Institute Working Papers*, Report no. EUI MWP, 2007/23. Available: http://hdl.handle.net/1814/7358. ISSN: 1830-1541.

Mosca, L. and Della Porta, D. (2009) 'Unconventional politics online', in D. Della Porta (ed), *Democracy in Social Movements* (Basingstoke: Palgrave Macmillan).

Mother Jones News Team (2011) 'Map: Occupy Wall Street, a global movement', *Mother Jones*, 4 October. Available: http://www.motherjones.com/politics/2011/10/occupy-wall-street-protest-map.

Motta, S. (2011) 'Notes towards pre-figurative epistemologies', in S. C. Motta and A. G. Nilsen (eds), *Social Movements in the Global South* (New York: Palgrave Macmillan).

Motta, S. and Nilsen, A. (eds) (2011) *Social Movements in the Global South* (New York: Palgrave Macmillan).

Mozur, P. (2018) "Inside China's Dystopian Dreams: A.I., Shame and Lots of Cameras", *New York Times*, 8 July. Available: https://www.nytimes.com/2018/07/08/business/china-surveillance-technology.html.

Mudde, C. (2007) *Populist Radical Right Parties in Europe* (Cambridge: Cambridge University Press).

Mudde, C. (2010) 'The populist radical right: A pathological normalcy', *West European Politics*, 33(6). Routledge: 1167–86.

Mudde, C. (2011) 'Radical right parties in Europe: What, who, why?', *Participation*, 35(1).

Mudde, C. and Rovira Kaltwasser, C. (2013) 'Exclusionary vs. inclusionary populism: Comparing contemporary Europe and Latin America', *Government and Opposition*, 48(2): 147–74.

Mulhall, J. (2017a) 'HNH explains... The Identitarian Movement and the Alt-Right', *Hope Not Hate*, 31 October. Available: https://www.hopenothate.org.uk/2017/10/31/explained-identitarian-movement-alt-right/.

Mulhall, J. (2017b) 'Failed defend Europe Mission comes to an end', *Hope Not Hate*, 17 August. Available: https://www.hopenothate.org.uk/2017/08/17/failed-defend-europe-mission-comes-end/.

Murphy, G. H. and Pfaff, S. (2005) 'Thinking locally, acting globally?', *Political Power and Social Theory*, 17: 151–76.

Myers, D. J. (1994) 'Communication technology and social movements', *Social Science Computer Review*, 12: 250–60.

Myers, D. J. (2001) 'Social activism through computer networks', in O. V. Burton (ed), *Computing in the Social Science and Humanities* (Urbana: University of Illinois Press).

Navarro, M. (2001) 'The personal is political', in S. Eckstein and M. Merino (eds), *Power and Popular Protest* (Berkeley: University of California Press).

Noakes, J. and Gillham, P. F. (2007) 'Police and protester innovation since Seattle', *Mobilization*, 12: 335–40.

Nodo50.org. (2004) 'Manifiesto de la plataforma "No a la Constitución Europea"', October. Available: http://www.nodo50.org/noconstitucion/.

Norris, P. (2001) *Digital Divide* (Cambridge: Cambridge University Press).

Norton, Q. (2012) '2011: The year Anonymous took on cops, dictators and existential dread', *Wired Magazine*, 11 January.

Notes from Nowhere (ed) (2003) *We Are Everywhere* (London: Verso).

O'Neil, C. (2017) *Weapons of Math Destruction: How Big Data Increases Inequality and Threatens Democracy* (New York: Penguin Random House).

Oberschall, A. (1973) *Social Conflict and Social Movements.* (New York: Pearson).

October 15th (2011) 'October 15th united for #globalchange'. Available: http://15october.net/.

OECD (2019) Income inequality (indicator). https://doi.org/10.1787/459aa7f1-en (Accessed on 11 July 2019)

Offe, C. (1997) 'Microaspects of democratic theory', in A. Hadenious (ed), *Democracy's Victory and Crisis* (New York: Cambridge University Press).

Olesen, T. (2005) *International Zapatism* (London: Zed Books).

Olesen, T. (2007) 'The funny side of globalization', *International Review of Social History*, 52: 21–34.

Olesen, T. (2013) 'We are all Khaled Said', *Research in Social Movements, Conflicts and Change*, 35: 2–26.

Oliver, P. E. and Maney, G. M. (2000) 'Political processes and local newspaper coverage of protest events', *American Journal of Sociology*, 106: 463–505.

Olson, M. (1965) *The Logic of Collective Action.* (Cambridge, MA: Harvard University Press).

Open Democracy (2019) 'Revealed: Trump linked US fundamentalists pour millions of 'dark money' into Europe, boosting the far right?'. Available: https://www.opendemocracy.net/en/5050/revealed-trump-linked-us-christian-fundamentalists-pour-millions-of-dark-money-into-europe-boosting-the-far-right/?utm_ source=newsletter&utm_campaign=wcf.

Opp, K-D. (2009) *Theories of Political Protest and Social Movements* (London: Routledge).

Orlowski, L. (2008) 'Stages of the 2007/2008 global financial crisis', *Economics E-Journal*, 43.

Osterweil, M. (2013) 'The Italian Anomaly', in C. Flesher Fominaya and L. Cox (eds), *Understanding European Movements: New Social Movements, Global Justice Struggles, Anti-Austerity Protests* (London: Routledge).

Owen, R. (2012) 'The Arab "demonstration" effect and the revival of Arab unity in the Arab Spring', *Contemporary Arab Affairs*, 5: 372–81.

Owens, L., Katzeff, A., Lorenzi, E. and Baptiste, C. (2013) 'At home on the road', in C. Flesher Fominaya and L. Cox (eds), *Understanding European Movements* (London: Routledge).

PAH Madrid (2012) 'Manifiesto'. Available: http://afectadosporlahipotecamadrid.net/ manifiesto.

Palmer, R. (1964) *The Age of the Democratic Revolution* (Princeton: Princeton University Press).

Parkin, W. S., Freilich, J. D. and Chermak, S. M. (2015) 'Tea Party mobilization and power devaluation', *Sociological Spectrum*, 35(4). Routledge: 329–48.

Pascual, M. (2019) ¿Quién vigila que los algoritmos no sean racistas o sexistas? *El País*, 17 March, Available: https://retina.elpais.com/retina/2019/03/14/tenden-cias/1552564034_268678.html.

Passy, F. and Monsch, G. A. (2014) 'Do social networks really matter in contentious politics?', *Social Movement Studies*, 13(1): 22–47.

Passy, F. and Monsch, G.A. (2019) 'Biographical consequences of social movements', in D. Snow, S. Soule, H. Kriesi and H. McCammon (eds), *The Wiley Blackwell Companion to Social Movements*, 2nd ed. (Oxford: Wiley).

Penny, L. (2011) 'Rise of the digital natives', *Nation*, 31 October.

Peregil, F. (2018) 'La justicia marroquí vuelve a citar a la activista española Helena Maleno el 31 de enero', *El País*, 10 January. Available: https://elpais.com/politica/2018/01/10/ actualidad/1515573025_526798.html.

Peréz, C. and Doncel, L. (2012) 'España pide un rescate de hasta 100.000 millones para la banca', *El País*, 10 June. Available: http://economia.elpais.com/econo-mia/2012/06/09/actualidad/1339230670_176850.html.

Petras, J. (2002) 'Porto Alegre 2002', *Monthly Review*, 1: 15–30.

Pew Reesearch Center (2017) 'The Future of Free Speech, Trolls, Anonymity, and Fake News Online', 29 March. Available: http://www.elon.edu/docs/e-web/imagining/ surveys/2016_survey/Pew%20and%20Elon%20University%20Trolls%20Fake%20 News%20Report%20Future%20of%20Internet%203.29.17.pdf.

Pichardo, N. A. (1997) 'New social movements: A critical review', *Annual Review of Sociology*, 23(1): 411–30.

Pickard, V. W. (2006) 'United yet autonomous', *Media, Culture and Society*, 28: 315–36.

Pickerill, J. (2004) 'Rethinking political participation: Experiments in Internet activ-ism in Australia and Britain', in R. Gibson, A. Roemmele and S. Ward, *Electronic Democracy: Mobilisation, Organisation and Participation via New ICTs* (Routledge: London), pp. 170–93.

Pilkington, E. (2017) 'Donald Trump Jr communicated with WikiLeaks during final stages of election', *The Guardian*, 14 November 2017. Available: https://www.

theguardian.com/us-news/2017/nov/13/donald-trump-jr-communicated-with-wikileaks-during-final-stages-of-election.

Piven, F. F. and Cloward, R. (2012 [1977]) *Poor People's Movements* (New York: Vintage).

Piven, F. F. and Cloward, R. (1991) 'Collective protest: A critique of resource mobilization theory', *International Journal of Politics Culture and Society*, (4): 435–58.

Pizzorno, A. (1978) 'Political science and collective identity in industrial conflict', in C. Crouch and A. Pizzorno (eds), *The Resurgence of Class Conflict in Europe Since 1968* (New York: Holmes and Meier).

Platon, S. and Deuze, M. (2003) 'Indymedia journalism', *Journalism*, 4: 336–55.

Plehwe, D. (2009) 'Introduction', in P. Mirowski and D. Plehwe (eds), *The Road from Mont Pèlerin* (Cambridge, MA: Harvard University Press).

Poitras, L. (2016) "Risk" Showtime/ DogWoof Productions.

Polletta, F. (2002) *Freedom is an Endless Meeting* (Chicago: University of Chicago Press).

Polletta, F. and Jasper, J. (2001) 'Collective identity and social movements', *Annual Review of Sociology*, 27(1): 283–305.

Pratt, N. (2013) 'Egyptian women: between revolution, counter-revolution, orientalism, and "authenticity"', *Jadaliyya Reports*, 6 May. Available: http://www.jadaliyya.com/pages/index/11559/egyptian-women_between-revolution-counter-revoluti.

Prowe, D. (2004) 'The fascist phantom and anti-immigrant violence', in: E. Weitz and A. Fenner (eds), *Fascism and Neofascism* (New York: Palgrave Macmillan).

Rawls, J. (1971) *A Theory of Justice*, (Cambridge: Harvard University Press).

Reimel, Erin and Arneson, Krystin. 2017. 'Here's the powerful story behind the pussyhats at the women's march'. *Glamour.* https://www.glamour.com/story/the-story-behind-the-pussyhats-at-the-womens-march.

Renzi, A. (2008) 'The space of tactical media', in M. Boler (ed), *Digital Media and Democracy* (Cambridge: MIT Press).

Reporteros sin Fronteras (2016) 'Un año de la 'Ley Mordaza': los periodistas afectados hacen balance' [Journalists without borders: One year after the Gag Law, journalists take stock of its effects]. Available: http://periodismohumano.com/sociedad/libertad-y-justicia/un-ano-de-la-ley-mordaza-los-periodistas-afectados-hacen-balance.html.

Reuters (2009) 'Iceland protesters demand government step down', *Reuters*, 20 January. Available: http://www.reuters.com/article/2009/01/20/iceland-protests-idUSLK69268520090120.

Rheingold, H. (1993) *The Virtual Community* (Boston: Addison Wesley).

Ridgeway, C. L. (2011) *Framed by Gender* (Oxford: Oxford University Press).

Rivat, E. (2013) 'The continuity of transnational protest', in C. Flesher Fominaya and L. Cox (eds), *Understanding European Movements* (London: Routledge).

Roar Collective (2013) 'The day the people of Turkey rose up – in pictures', 2 June. Available: http://roarmag.org/2013/06/the-day-the-people-of-turkey-rose-up-in- pictures/.

Robertson, R. (1992) *Globalization Social Theory and Global Culture* (London: Sage).

Robinson, W. I. (1996) *Promoting Polyarchy* (Cambridge: Cambridge University Press).

Robinson, W. I. (2004) *A Theory of Global Capitalism* (Baltimore: Johns Hopkins University Press).

Rodriguez, C. (2018) 'Absuelto los tres bomberos sevillanos juzgados en Lesbos por tráfico de inmigrantes', *El Mundo*, 7 May. Available: https://www.elmundo.es/andalucia/2018/05/07/5aeff288ca4741b3448b458d.html.

Roggeband, C. (2007) 'Translators and transformers: International inspiration and exchange in social movements', *Social Movement Studies*, 6(3): 245–59.

Romanos, E. (2013) 'Collective learning processes within social movements: Some insights into the Spanish 15M/Indignados movement', in C. Flesher Fominaya and L. Cox (eds), *Understanding European Movements* (London: Routledge).

Romanos, E. (2016) 'Immigrants as brokers: Dialogical siffusion from Spanish *Indignados* to occupy Wall Street', *Social Movement Studies*, 15(3): 247–62.

Ronson, J. (2013) 'Security alert: Notes from the frontline of the war in cyberspace', *Guardian*, 4 May. Available: http://www.guardian.co.uk/technology/2013/may/04/security-alert-war-in-cyberspace.

Roos, J. E. and Oikonomakis, L. (2014) 'They don't represent us!: The global resonance of the real democracy movement from the Indignados to occupy', in D. della Porta and A. Mattoni. (eds), *Spreading Protest. Social Movements in Times of Crisis* (Colchester: ECPR Press).

Routledge, P. (2004) 'Convergence of commons', *The Commoner*, 8. Available: http://www.polkagris.nu/wiki/images/08routledge.pdf.

Rowell, A. (1996) *Green Backlash* (London: Routledge).

Rucht, D. (1999) 'The impact of environmental movements in western society', in M. Giugni, D. McAdam, and C. Tilly (eds), *How Social Movements Matter* (Minneapolis: University of Minnesota Press).

Rucht, D. (2005) 'The quadruple "A"', in W. Van de Bonk, B. D. Loader, P. G. Nixxon and D. Rucht (eds), *Cyber Protest* (London: Routledge).

Rupar, A. (2018) 'CNN sues White House for using doctored video to bar Jim Acosta', *Vox*, 13 November. Available: https://www.vox.com/policy-and-politics/2018/11/13/18091546/cnn-sues-white-house-jim-acosta-doctored-video.

Ryan, C. (1991) *Prime Time Activism* (Boston: South End Press).

Ryan, C., Carragee, K. M. and Meinhofer, W. (2001) 'Theory into practice', *Journal of Broadcasting and Electronic Media*, 45: 175–82.

Ryan, Y. (2011a) 'The tragic life of a street vendor', *Al Jazeera*, 20 January. Available: http://www.aljazeera.com/indepth/features/2011/01/201111684242518839.html.

Ryan, Y. (2011b) 'How Tunisia's revolution began', *Al Jazeera*, 20 January. Available: http://www.aljazeera.com/indepth/features/2011/01/2011126121815985483.html.

Sádaba, Igor (2019) 'Technopolitical frameworks', in Flesher Fominaya and Feenstra (eds), *The Routledge Handbook of Contemporary European Social Movements* (London: Routledge).

Sainz, J. (2014) 'Spain's XNet corruption fighters expose graft', *AP News*, 12 December 2014. Available: https://www.apnews.com/a67563e720d84d86943974e6e7befac2.

Saka, E. (2013) 'Turkey's genuine occupy movement: Happening right now in Gezi Park, Taksim, Istanbul', *Social Network Unionism*, 30 May. Available: http://snuproject.wordpress.com/2013/05/30/turkeys-genuine-occupy-movement-happening-right-now-in-gezi-parki-taksim-istanbul-direngeziparkierkan-saka/.

Salter, L. (2006) 'Democracy and online news', *Scan Journal of Media, Arts and Culture*, 4: 336–55.

Sampedro, Víctor and Lobera, Josep (2014) 'The Spanish 15-M movement: A consensual dissent?', *Journal of Spanish Cultural Studies*, no. ahead-of-print: 1–20.

Sandlin, J. A. and Milam, J. L. (2008) 'Mixing pop (culture) and politics', *Curriculum Inquiry*, 38: 323–50.

Sanz Paratcha, D. (2013) 'Democracia Real Ya niega proyectar un partido político', *Periódico Diagonal*, 27 May. Available: https://www.diagonalperiodico.net/movimientos/democracia-real-ya-niega-proyectar-partido-politico.html.

Sassen, S. (2004) 'Local actors in global politics', *Current Sociology*, 52: 649–70.

Saunders, C. (2007) 'Using social network analysis to explore social movements. A relational approach', *Social Movement Studies*, 6(3): 227–43.

Saunders C. (2008) 'The stop climate chaos coalition', *Third World Quarterly*, 29(8): 1509–26.

Saunders, Clare (2013) *Environmental Networks and Social Movement Theory* (Bloomsbury Publishing).

Sayed, A. (2013) 'The brothers, the revolution, and the right to protest', *Jadaliyya Reports*, 4 May. Available: http://www.jadaliyya.com/pages/index/11707/the-brothers-the-revolution-and-the-right-to-prote.

Schnews (2001) *Monopolise Resistance?* (Brighton: Schnews).

Seidman, G. (2001) 'Guerrillas in their midst', *Mobilization*, 6: 111–27.

Seiler, C. (2000) 'The commodification of rebellion', in M. Gottdiener (ed), *New Forms of Consumption: Consumers, Culture, and Commodification* (Oxford: Rowman & Littlefield).

Selmini, Rossella (2016) 'Ethnic conflicts and riots in Italy: The case of Rome, 2014', *European Journal of Criminology*, 13(5): 626–38. https://doi.org/10.1177/1477370816636903.

Seoane, J. and Taddei, E. (2002) 'From Seattle to Porto Alegre: The anti-neoliberal globalization movement', *Current Sociology*, 50: 99–122.

Sergi, V. and Vogiatzoglou, M. (2013) 'Think globally, act locally? Symbolic memory and global repertories in the Tunisian uprising and the Greek anti-austerity mobilizations', in C. Flesher Fominaya and L. Cox (eds), *Understanding European Movements* (London: Routledge).

Sharma, A. (2012) 'Mega dams: Campaigning against the plans of the Indian government', *Open Democracy*, 20 January. Available: http://www.opendemocracy.net/openindia/tanmoy-sharma/mega-dams-campaigning-against-plans-of-indian-government.

Shenker, J. (2011) 'Tahrir Square protesters killed by live ammunition, say doctors', *The Guardian UK online*, 24 November. Available: http://www.guardian.co.uk/world/2011/nov/24/tahrir-square-protesters-killed-ammunition.

Shihade, M., Flesher Fominaya, C. and Cox, L. (2012) 'The season of revolution', *Interface*, 4: 1–16.

Shiner, M. (2011) 'From Cairo to Madison, some pizza', *Politico*, 2 February. Available: http://www.politico.com/news/stories/0211/49888.html.

Shirky, C. (2009) *Here Comes Everybody: How Change Happens When People Come Together* (London: Penguin UK).

Simpson, P. A. (2016) 'Mobilizing meanings: Translocal identities of the far right web', *German Politics and Society*, 34(4). Berghahn Journals: 34–53.

Sitrin (2011) 'Fuelling the flames of dignity', in S. Mott and A. Nilsen (eds), *Social Movements in the Global South* (London: Palgrave Macmillan), pp. 250–274.

Sklair, L. (1997) 'Social movements for global capitalism', *Review of International Political Economy*, 4: 514–38.

Skocpol, T. (1979) *States and Social Revolutions* (Cambridge: Cambridge University Press).

Skocpol, T. and Williamson, V. (2016) *The Tea Party and the Remaking of Republican Conservatism* (Oxford: Oxford University Press).

SlutWalk Toronto (2011) 'Mission statement "why"'. Available: http://www.slutwalk-toronto.com/

Smink, V. (2011) 'Las razones de las protestas estudiantiles en Chile', *BBC Mundo*, 10 August. Available: http://www.bbc.co.uk/mundo/noticias/2011/08/110809_chile_estudiantes_2_vs.shtml.

Smith, J. (2001) 'Globalizing resistance', *Mobilization*, 6: 1–19.

Smith, J., McCarthy, J. D., McPhail, C. and Augustyn, B. (2001) 'From protest to agenda building', *Social Forces*, 79: 1397–423.

Smith J. and Patterson J. (2019) 'Global climate justice activism: "The New Protagonists" and their projects for a just transition', in R. Frey, P. Gellert and H. Dahms (eds), *Ecologically Unequal Exchange* (London: Palgrave Macmillan).

Snow, D. (2001) 'Collective identity and expressive forms', University of California, Irvine eScholarship Repository. http://repositories.cdlib.org/csd/01-07.

Snow, D. A., Rochford, E., Worden, S. and Benford, R. (1986) 'Frame alignment processes, micromobilization, and movement participation', *American Sociological Review*, 51(4): 464–81.

Snow, D. and Benford, R. (1988) 'Ideology, frame resonance and participant mobilization', *International Social Movement Research*, 1: 197–219.

Sommer, B. (2008) 'Anti-capitalism in the name of ethno-nationalism: Ideological shifts on the German extreme right', *Patterns of Prejudice*, 42(3): 305–16.

SOS Racismo (2015) 'SOS Racismo Madrid Participa En Acto Contra La Ley Mordaza Organizado Por No Somos Delito', *Sosracismomadrid.Es*. 2015. http://www.sosracismomadrid.es/web/blog/2015/02/04/sos-racismo-madrid-participa-en-acto-contra-la-ley-mordaza-organizado-por-no-somos-delito/.

Speed, S., Hernández Castillo, R. and Stephen, L. (2006). *Dissident Women: Gender and Cultural Politics in Chiapas* (Austin: University of Texas Press).

St Clair, J. (2004) 'Seattle diary', in E. Yuen, D. Burton-Rose and G. N. Katsiaficas (eds), *Confronting Capitalism* (Brooklyn, NY: Soft Skull Press).

Staggenborg, S. (1988) 'The consequences of professionalization and formalization in the pro-choice movement', *American Sociological Review*, 53: 585–605.

Stalder, F. (2010) 'Digital commons', in K. Hart, J. L. Laville and A. D. Cattani (eds), *The Human Economy* (Cambridge: Polity Press).

Starhawk (1999) 'How we really shut down the WTO', *Peacework Magazine*, February. Available: http://www.starhawk.org/activism/activism-writings/shutdownWTO.html.

Stark, R. and Bainbridge, W. S. (1980) 'Networks of faith: Interpersonal bonds and recruitment to cults and sects', *American Journal of Sociology*, 85(6): 1376–1395.

Starr, A. (2000) *Naming the Enemy: Anti-corporate Movements Confront Globalization* (London: Zed Books).

Starr, M. (2004) 'Reading *The Economist* on globalisation', *Global Society*, 18: 373–95.

Stiglitz, J. (2000) 'The Insider – what I learned at the world economic crisis', *New Republic*, 17 April: 56. Available: http://sandovalhernandezj.people.cofc.edu/index_files/egl_20.pdf.

Stoycheff and Nisbet (2016) 'Is Internet Freedom a tool for democracy or authroitarianism?', *The Conversation*. Available: https://theconversation.com/is-internet-freedom-a-tool-for-democracy-or-authoritarianism-61956.

Strang, D. and Meyer, J. W. (1993) 'Institutional conditions for diffusion', *Theory and society*, 22(4): 487–511.

Stuckler, D. and Basu, S. (2013) *The Body Economic* (London: Allen Lane).

Style, S. (2004) 'People's global action', in E. Yuen, E. Burton-Rose and G. Katsiaficas (eds), *Confronting Capitalism* (Brooklyn: Soft Skull Press).

Sullivan, S., Spicer, A. and Bohm, S. (2010) *Becoming Global (Un)civil Society* (London, UK, Working Paper, LSE Non-Governmental Public Action Programme).

Szasz, A. (1995) *EcoPopulism* (Minneapolis: University of Minnesota Press).

Tarrow, S. (1998) *Power in Movement* (Cambridge: Cambridge University Press).

t'Hart, M. (2007) 'Humour and social protest', *International Review of Social History*, 52(S15): 1–20.

Tarrow, S. (1989) *Struggle, Politics, and Reform: Collective Action, Social Movements and Cycles of Protest* (Ithaca, NY: Center for International Studies, Cornell University).

Tarrow, S. (1993) 'Cycles of collective action: Between moments of madness and the repertoire of contention', *Social Science History*, 17(2): 281–307.

Tarrow, S. (2001) *Beyond Globalization*, Global Solidarity Dialogue, Cornell. Available: http://www.antenna.nl/~waterman/tarrow.html.

Tarrow, S. (2005a) *The New Transnational Activism* (Cambridge: Cambridge University Press).

Tarrow, S. (2005b) 'Rooted cosmopolitans and transnational activists', prepared for a special issue of *Rassegna Italiana di Sociologia*. Available: http://government.arts.cornell.edu/assets/faculty/docs/tarrow/rooted_cosmopolitans.pdf.

Tarrow, S. (2011) *Power in Movement: Social Movements and Contentious Politics* (Cambridge: Cambridge University Press).

Tarrow, S. (2013) *The Language of Contention: Revolutions in Words, 1688–2012* (Cambridge: Cambridge University Press).

Tatlow, D. K. (2013) '"Occupy" Hong Kong, for universal suffrage', *International Herald Tribune*, 4 April. Available: http://rendezvous.blogs.nytimes.com/2013/04/04/occupy-hong-kong-for-universal-suffrage/.

Taylor, R. (2002) 'Interpreting global civil society', *Voluntas: International Journal of Voluntary and Nonprofit Organizations*, 13(4), December.

Taylor, V. (1989) 'Social movement continuity: The women's movement in abeyance', *American Sociological Review*, 54(5): 761–75.

Taylor, V. and Whittier, N. (1992) 'Collective identity in social movement communities: Lesbian feminist mobilization', in C. M. Mueller and A. D. Morris (eds), *Frontiers in Social Movement Theory* (New Haven: Yale University Press).

Tejerina, B. and Perugorría, I. (2012) 'Continuities and discontinuities in recent social mobilizations. From new social movements to the alter-global mobilizations and the 15M', *From Social to Political*: 93–111.

Teti, A. and Gervasio, G. (2011) 'The unbearable lightness of authoritarianism: lessons from the Arab uprisings', *Mediterranean Politics*, 16(2): 321–7.

Teti, A. and Gervasio, G. (2012) 'After Mubarak, before transition: the challenges for Egypt's democratic opposition', *Interface: A Journal For and About Social Movements*, May, 4(1): 102–12.

Thayer, M. (2000) 'Travelling feminisms', in M. Buroway (ed), *Global Ethnography* (Berkeley: University of California Press).

The Economist (2018) 'How identitarian politics is changing Europe' , 28 May. Available: https://www.economist.com/europe/2018/03/28/how-identitarian-politics-is-changing-europe.

Tilly, C. (1978a) *From Mobilization to Revolution* (New York:McGraw-Hill).

Tilly, C. (1978b) 'The routinization of protest in nineteenth century France', *CRSO Working* Paper, University of Michigan.

Tilly, C. (1983) 'Speaking your mind without elections, surveys, or social movements', *The Public Opinion Quarterly*, 47(4): 461–78.

Tilly, C. (2003) *The Politics of Collective Violence* (Cambridge: Cambridge University Press).

Tilly, C. (2008) *Contentious Performances* (Cambridge: Cambridge University Press).

Tilly, C. and Tarrow, S. (2006) *Contentious Politics* (Oxford: Oxford University Press).

Tilly, C. and Wood, L. (2012) *Social Movements 1768–2012* (Boulder, CO: Paradigm Publishers).

Tilly, Charles and Wood, Lesley (2015) *Social Movements 1768-2012*, 2nd ed. (London: Routledge).

Tilly, C., McAdam, D. and Tarrow, S. (2001) *Dynamics of Contention* (Cambridge: Cambridge University Press).

Topping, A. (2011) '"SlutWalking" phenomenon comes to UK with demonstrations in four cities', *Guardian*, 9 May. Available: http://www.guardian.co.uk/world/2011/may/09/slutwalking-phenomenon-comes-to-uk.

Torres López, J. (2013) 'El gran engaño', *El País*, 14 February. Available: http://ccaa.elpais.com/ccaa/2013/02/14/andalucia/1360863012_421809.html.

Touraine, A. (1981) *The Voice and the Eye: An Analysis of Social Movements* (Cambridge: Cambridge University Press).

Touraine, A. (1988) *The Return of the Actor* (Minneapolis: University of Minnesota Press).

Touraine, A. (1997) *What is Democracy?* (Boulder, CO: Westview Press).

Treanor, P. (2004) 'Who controls the European Social Forum?', *Indymedia*, 20 December. Available: http://web.inter.nl.net/users/Paul.Treanor/esf.html.

Tucker, K. H. (1991) 'How new are the new social movements?', *Theory, Culture & Society*, 8(2): 75–98.

Tufekci, Z. (2015) 'Algorithmic harms beyond Facebook and Google: Emergent challenges of computational agency. *Colorado Technology Law Journal*, 13: 203–17.

Union General De Trabajadores (2012) 'Lo que no sabías sobre la precariedad laboral', *UGT Juventud*. Available: http://www.ugt.es/juventud/lo_que_no_sabias_juventud_UGT.pdf.

United Nations (2012) 'Secretary General's Report on Violence against Women'. Available: http://www.un.org/en/events/endviolenceday/2012/sgmessage.shtml.

UNDP-United Nations Development Programme (2012) 'Gender Inequality Index'. Available: http://hdr.undp.org/en/statistics/gii/.

United Nations Women Watch (2009) 'Women, gender equality and climate change'. Available: http://www.un.org/womenwatch.

United States Census Bureau (2010a) 'Table F-4. Gini ratios of families by race and Hispanic origin of householder, 1947 to 2009'. Available: http://www.census.gov/hhes/www/income/data/historical/families/index.html.

United States Census Bureau (2010b) 'Gini ratios of families by race and Hispanic origin of householder, 1947 to 2009' (Table F-4). Available: http://www.census.gov/hhes/www/income/data/historical/inequality/.

Van de Donk, W., Loader, B., Nixon, P. and Rucht, D. (2004) *Cyberprotest* (London: Routledge).

Van Dyke, N. and Soule, S. (2002) 'Structural social change and the mobilizing effect of threat: Explaining levels of patriot and militia organizing in the United States', *Social Problems*, 49(4): 497–520.

Van Dyke, N. and Taylor, V. (2019) "The cultural outcomes of social movements" in D. Snow, S. Soule, H. Kriesi and H. McCammon (eds), *The Wiley Blackwell Companion to Social Movements*, 2nd ed. (Oxford: Wiley).

Vasilopoulou, S, and D Halikiopoulou. 2015. *The Golden Dawn's "Nationalist Solution": Explaining the Rise of the Far Right in Greece. The Golden Dawn's "Nationalist Solution"* London: Palgrave Macmillan. https://doi.org/10.1057/9781137535917.0006.

Verhulst, J. and Walgrave, S. (2010) 'Politics, public opinion, and the media', in S. Walgrave and D. Rucht (eds), *The World Says No to War* (Minnesota: University of Minnesota Press).

Vidal, J. (1997) *McLibel: Burger culture on trial* (New York: New Press).

Villarreal, T. and Gil, G. (2001) 'Radical Internet use', in J. Downing (ed.), *Radical Media* (Thousand Oaks: CA: Sage).

Virchow, F. (2015) 'The 'Identitarian Movement'. What kind of identity? Is it really a movement?', in P. Simpson and H. Druxes (eds), *Digital Media Strategies of the Far Right in Europe and the United States* (Lanham et al.: Lexington Books).

Wagemann C (2005) 'Right-wing extremism in Germany', in D. Della Porta and C. Wagemann (eds), *Patterns of Radicalization in Political Activism: Research Design* (Florence: Veto Project Report).

Wainwright, H. (1994) *Arguments for a New Left* (Oxford: Blackwell Publishers).

Walgrave, S. and Rucht, D. (2010) *The World Says No to War* (Minneapolis: University of Minnesota Press).

Wallerstein, I. (2011) 'Structural crisis in the world system', *Monthly Review*, 62(10).

Walton, J. and Seddon, D. (1994) *Free Markets and Food Riots* (Oxford: Blackwell).

Wekker, G. (2009) '"Van homo nostalgie en betere tijden". Multiculturaliteit en postkolonialiteit', Amsterdam, George Mosse Lecture.

Weller, C., Scott, R. and Hersch, A. (2001) *The Unremarkable Record of Liberalized Trade* (Washington, DC: Briefing paper, Economic Policy Institute).

Westermeyer, W. H. (2016) 'Local Tea Party groups and the vibrancy of the movement', *PoLAR: Political and Legal Anthropology Review*, 39(S1): 121–38. https://doi.org/10.1111/plar.12175

Whitehead, L. (2009) 'Losing "the force"?', *Democratization*, 16: 215–42.

Whitney, J. (2003) 'Infernal noise', in Notes from Nowhere (ed.), *We Are Everywhere* (London: Verso).

Whittier, N. (1995) *Feminist Generations: The Persistence of the Radical Women's Movement* (Philadelphia: Temple University Press).

Wilkes, R., Corrigall-Brown, C. and Myers, D. J. (2010) 'Packaging protest', *Canadian Review of Sociology/Revue canadienne de sociologie*, 47: 327–57.

Women's March (2017) *Manifesto*. Available at: https://womensmarch.com/.

Wong, K. (2004) 'Shutting us out', in E. Yuen, E. Burton-Rose and G. N. Katsiaficas (eds), *Confronting Capitalism* (Brooklyn: Soft Skull Press).

Wood, L. (2007) 'Breaking the wave', *Mobilization*, 12: 377–88.

Wood, L. (2010) 'Horizontalist youth camps and the Bolivarian Revolution', *Journal of World System Research*, 16: 48–62.

World Economic Forum (2011) 'Global gender gap report'. Available: http://www.weforum.org/issues/global-gender-gap.

Wright, S. (2004) 'Informing, communicating and ICTs in contemporary anti-capitalist movements', in W. Van de Donk, B. D. Loader, P. G. Nixon and D. Rucht (eds), *Cyberprotest* (London: Routledge).

Yo Mango (2011) 'YoMango, la otra cara del deseo'. Available: http://yomango.net/en/2011/10/yomango-la-otra-cara-del-deseo/.

Yo Mango Team (2012) 'YoMango porque tú lo vales'. Available: http://yomango.net/2012/02/yomango-porque-tu-lo-vales/.

Zamponi, L. (2012) 'Why don't Italians occupy?', *Social Movement Studies*, 11: 416–26.

Zibechi, R. (2008) *Territorios en resistencia: Cartografía política de las periferias urbanas latinoamericanas* (Buenos Aires: lavaca editora)

Zikode, S. (2005) 'The third force', *Abahlali baseMjondolo*. Available: http://www.abahlali.org/node/17.

Zoega, G. (2009) 'Iceland faces the music', in A. Felton and C. Reinhart (eds), *The First Global Financial Crisis of the 21st Century* (London: CEPR).

INDEX

Printed in the USA
CPSIA information can be obtained
at www.ICGtesting.com
LVHW010255031023
759978LV00010B/389